EARLY
VISUAL
LEARNING

EARLY
VISUAL
LEARNING

EDITED BY

SHREE K. NAYAR
Columbia University

AND

TOMASO POGGIO
Massachusetts Institute of Technology

New York   Oxford
Oxford University Press
1996

Oxford University Press

Oxford   New York
Athens   Auckland   Bangkok   Bombay
Calcutta   Cape Town   Dar es Salaam   Delhi
Florence   Hong Kong   Istanbul   Karachi
Kuala Lumpur   Madras   Madrid
Mexico City   Nairobi   Paris   Singapore
Taipei   Tokyo   Toronto

and associated companies in

Berlin   Ibadan

Published by Oxford University Press, Inc.
198 Madison Avenue, New York, New York 10016

Library of Congress Cataloging-in-Publication Data
Early visual learning / edited by Shree K. Nayar and Tomaso Poggio.
    p.   cm.
Includes bibliographical references and index.
ISBN 0-19-509522-7
1. Computer vision.   2. Visual perception.   3. Algorithms.
4. Optical pattern recognition.   I. Nayar, Shree K.   II. Poggio, Tomaso.
TA1634.E37   1996
006.3'7—dc20   95-48209

Cover photo courtesy of Charles E. Manley, Columbia University,
Center for Biomedical Communications

Typesetting by Danilo Florissi, Columbia University,
Department of Computer Science

9 8 7 6 5 4 3 2 1

Printed in the United States of America
on acid-free paper

Contents

CONTRIBUTORS

- **Ruzena Bajcsy.** 3401 Walnut Street, Suite 301C, University of Pennsylvania, Philadelphia, PA 19104, USA. *bajcsy@central.cis.upenn.edu.*

- **David Beymer.** Artificial Intelligence Laboratory, Massachusetts Institute of Technology, 545 Technology Square, Cambridge, MA 02139, USA. *beymer@ai.mit.edu.*

- **Bir Bhanu.** College of Engineering, University of California, Riverside, CA 92521, USA. *bhanu@engr.ucr.edu.*

- **Emanuela Bricolo.** Department of Brain and Cognitive Sciences, Massachusetts Institute of Technology, E25-201, Cambridge, MA 02139, USA. *emanuela@it-cortex.ai.mit.edu.*

- **Michael C. Burl.** Electrical Engineering, M/S 116-81, California Institute of Technology, Pasadena, CA 91125, USA. *burl@systems.caltech.edu.*

- **Usama M. Fayyad.** Machine Learning Systems Group, M/S 525-3660, Jet Propulsion Laboratory, California Institute of Technology, Pasadena, CA 91109, USA. *fayyad@aig.jpl.nasa.gov.*

- **Hayit Greenspan.** Electrical Engineering Department 116-81, California Institute of Technology, Pasadena, CA 91125, USA. *hayit@micro.caltech.edu.*

- **Sungkee Lee.** Department of Computer Science, Kyungpook National University, Taegu, South Korea. *sklee@bh.kyungpook.ac.kr.*

- **Nikos Logothetis.** Division of Neuroscience, Baylor College of Medicine, One Baylor Plaza, Houston, TX 77030, USA. *nikos@bcmvision.bcm.tmc.edu.*

- **David G. Lowe.** Department of Computer Science, University of British Columbia, 201–2366 Main Mall, Vancouver, BC V6K 2M9, Canada. *lowe@cs.ubc.ca.*

- **Baback Moghaddam.** The Media Laboratory, Massachusetts Institute of Technology, Room E15–384a, 20 Ames St., Cambridge, MA 02139, USA. *baback@media.mit.edu.*

- **Hiroshi Murase.** 3-1, Morinosato Wakamiya, Atsugi-shi, Kanagawa 243-01, Japan. *murase@siva.ntt.jp.*

- **Shree K. Nayar.** Department of Computer Science, Columbia University, New York, NY 10027, USA. *nayar@cs.columbia.edu.*

- **Randal C. Nelson.** Department of Computer Science, University of Rochester, Rochester, NY 14620, USA. *nelson@cs.rochester.edu.*

- **Sameer A. Nene.** Department of Computer Science, Columbia University, New York, NY 10027, USA. *sameer@cs.columbia.edu.*

- **Jon Pauls.** Division of Neuroscience, Baylor College of Medicine, One Baylor Plaza, Houston, TX 77030, USA. *jpauls@bcmvision.bcm.tmc.edu.*

- **Alex Pentland.** The Media Laboratory, Massachusetts Institute of Technology, Room E15–387, 20 Ames St., Cambridge, MA 02139, USA. *sandy@media.mit.edu.*

- **Pietro Perona.** Electrical Engineering, M/S 116-81, California Institute of Technology, Pasadena, CA 91125, USA. *burl@caltech.edu.*

- **Tomaso Poggio.** Artificial Intelligence Laboratory, Massachusetts Institute of Technology, 545 Technology Square, Cambridge, MA 02139, USA. *poggio@ai.mit.edu.*

- **Dean Pomerleau.** The Robotics Institute, Carnegie Mellon University, Pittsburgh, PA 15213, USA. *pomerleau@cs.cmu.edu.*

- **Arthur R. Pope.** GE Corporate Research & Development, P.O. Box 8, Schenectady, NY 12301, USA. *pope@crd.ge.com.*

- **Michele Rucci.** 10640 John Jay Hopkins Drive, The Neurosciences Institute, San Diego, CA 92121, USA. *rucci@nsi.edu.*

- **Marcos Salganicoff.** Applied Science and Engineering Laboratories, A.I. duPont Institute, University of Delaware, 1600 Rockland Road, Wilmington, DE 19803, USA. *salganic@asel.udel.edu.*

- **Padhraic J. Smyth.** Machine Learning Systems Group, M/S 525-3660, Jet Propulsion Laboratory, California Institute of Technology, Pasadena, CA 91109, USA. *pjs@aig.jpl.nasa.gov.*

- **John J. Weng.** Department of Computer Science, A714 Wells Hall, Michigan State University, East Lansing, MI 48824, USA. *weng@cs.msu.edu.*

- **Xing Wu.** College of Engineering, University of California, Riverside, CA 92521, USA. *xingwu@constitution.ucr.edu.*

EARLY
VISUAL
LEARNING

1   EARLY VISUAL LEARNING

Shree K. Nayar
Columbia University

Tomaso Poggio
Massachusetts Institute of Technology

1.   INTELLIGENCE AND LEARNING

Cast as the balance between internal representation and external regularities, learning has long been a central issue in the understanding of intelligence. It may be argued however that until recently its indispensable role had not been entirely embraced in computer science. Indeed, the definition of intelligence that is frequently invoked in the field of artificial intelligence does not quite provide learning its deserved stature. For many years, the Turing test has served as an operational definition of intelligence, using which, most investigators in artificial intelligence have either directly or implicitly measured their goals and achievements: If a computer behaves in a way indistinguishable from a human, then it can be called intelligent, even if this "intelligence" has been painstakingly programmed by a highly skilled individual.

Consistent with Turing's implicit definition, intelligence was perceived thirty years ago as mainly reasoning, problem solving, theorem proving, or game playing (chess, for instance). In contrast, today, we understand intelligent lower animals better and comprehend the complexities of the tasks that our senses routinely solve. We have also realized through experience how intractable the problem of producing software can prove, and how much of it would be needed to replicate even the simplest aspects of intelligence. In light of these submissions, it may be argued that a somewhat altered definition of intelligence may be more suited to our present notions of the underlying problems. It seems to us that such a modified Turing test should emphasize the development and learning of perceptual, motor, and language competence. In particular, many would agree that a system should be declared intelligent only if it is capable of first acquiring and then exhibiting motor, perceptual, and language skills. This revised Turing test expresses, in an explicit manner, the central role of learning in the art and science of replicating intelligence.

That the brain is not hard-wired but rather can be modified by experience is one of the most remarkable features of the nervous system [7]. At the systems level, the view of how neurons of the cerebral cortex mediate perception and action is presently undergoing a radical paradigm shift. Rather than being fixed in configuration, the functional anatomy of the cortex appears to display activity-dependent plasticity on a time-scale sufficiently short to play a role in most perceptual and motor tasks. Even simple brain functions, such as the definition of visual acuity, appear to involve a short-term learning phase and hence seem to depend upon experience. Computational methods have supported these findings and have provided models in which perceptual tasks are learned by simple experiential modifications of networks of cells. Thus, activity-dependent and task-dependent plasticity presents itself as a plausible explanation to how networks of neurons accomplish perception and action.

As a result of these findings, in both computer science and neuroscience, learning has in recent years advanced to the forefront of research. From this revolution – exemplified by the area of neural networks and connectionism [6] – has emerged an intriguing trend. What we would call low-level learning appears to produce more interesting results than one would have anticipated just a few years ago. In other words, "simple" learning techniques based on statistics, pattern recognition, neural networks, and function approximation – all of which are intimately related to one another – have demonstrated their utility in a number of real problems and in a broad spectrum of applications [4] [5] [6].

2.   LEARNING AND VISION

The above arguments in favor of learning are directly applicable to the field of computational vision. The emphasis in machine vision has been the development of recovery methods and algorithms that seek to extract from images information that is pertinent to the task at hand. The trend has been to allow the vision practitioner to input all of his or her expert knowledge of the application into the system in the form of models, constraints, or parameters. This procedure may suffice in the case of small vision systems that are configured for highly structured tasks. However, versatility and scalability are desirable attributes in most vision systems. From this viewpoint, the manual input (hard-wiring) of models, constraints, and parameters has proven itself impractical. The only solution, therefore, is to incorporate learning capabilities within the vision system that allow it to both learn to see, as well as, learn by seeing.

Does this argument imply that a vision system that learns can thrive without the use of models and constraints? Quite the contrary. In most instances, the process of learning in the absence of physical and geometrical constraints turns out to be hopelessly underconstrained. Those models and constraints that are powerful in their generality, can serve as important foundations and guides during the process of learning. It is the less powerful ones with narrow scope that we desire the vision system to automatically acquire. For instance, in the context of object recognition, the perspective projection model of image formation would serve as a general *a priori* constraint that may be hard-wired into the system. In contrast, the geometry of a particular object can be viewed as specific knowledge that the system must be capable of learning without assistance.

As stated earlier, the learning capabilities of neurons in the brain are becoming increasingly well-understood. Does it suffice then to use a connectionist architecture to solve all vision problems? In some instances, the answer is in the affirmative. However, we must acknowledge the fact that in many settings machine intelligence is not merely the enterprise of replicating human intelligence. Real-world applications, more often than not, demand machines to be far more quantitative than any known biological system. This calls for the creation and implementation of learning techniques and architectures that are complementary to biologically motivated ones.

Machine learning stands as an active research field all by itself [9] [8]. Over the years, this discipline has put forth a variety of methodologies, including inductive learning, connectionist learning, case-based learning, and genetic algorithms, to name a few. Is it not possible to view these results as a complete bag of tricks and simply cast visual learning as the art of selecting the appropriate machine learning technique for any given vision task? In some cases, such a strategy would work. However, visual perception brings with it its unique set of constraints and problems. For instance, the simultaneous occurrence of two objects in vision is not analogous to that of two voices in speech. The former could manifest the non-linear phenomenon of occlusion while the latter results in simple superposition. It may well be the case that the complexities inherent to visual perception require the creation of novel learning techniques. What a system needs to learn, and how the system learns it, has everything to do with the intrinsic properties of the data available to the system.

3. THE BOOK AT A GLANCE

This book focuses on visual learning techniques that are applied more or less directly to the signals provided by vision sensors. Hence, the use of the term "early" in the title of book; it is meant to reflect the stage of visual processing at which learning is invoked and does not connote learning in an infantile system, biological or artificial. Each chapter of the book presents recent results within this domain of signal-based visual learning. Each result is novel in either the underlying theory, the problem formulation, or the application that it seeks to solve. The chapters are designed to serve as technical overviews with extensive references to related work. It is hoped that this format will enable a novice to get quickly familiarized with the main issues in low-level visual learning, while providing an expert pointers to technical details. Additional reading material on the topic can be found in other recent proceedings and reports [3] [1] [2].

We begin with a chapter that brings to light recent psychophysical and electrophysiological results on the internal representation of three-dimensional objects. Pauls, Bricolo and Logothetis present a series of experimental data, obtained from macaque monkeys, that provide compelling evidence that the brain adopts a viewer-centered rather than an object-centered approach to visual representation. Single neuronal units in the inferior temporal cortex are found to exhibit high specificity, in that, they respond to particular views of three-dimensional objects. The response functions of these neurons are analyzed and shown to have unimodal bell-shaped structures. The authors argue that a small set of such neurons, each tuned to a different view of the same object, may together constitute a network that achieves view-invariant recognition via generalization. The authors report detailed experiments on the invariance of recognition to object position, scale, and orientation.

The type of network that Pauls *et al.* posit is the topic of the second chapter by Poggio and Beymer. They formulate the learning-from-example problem as one of multivariate function approximation from sparse data. The authors provide an overview of regularization networks and establish ties between such networks and classical techniques in pattern recognition as well as a number of popular neural network architectures. The notion of virtual examples is introduced as a means of solving the frequently encountered problem of insufficient training data. The authors apply their techniques to image analysis in vision and image synthesis in graphics, with particular emphasis on the pertinent problem of face recognition. Regularization networks are used to estimate parameters such as pose, expression, and face identity. The authors conclude with recent results on the detection of objects in cluttered scenes.

In the next chapter, a probabilistic framework for visual learning of objects is described by Pope and Lowe. The authors model three-dimensional objects as probability distributions that capture variations in visual appearance in image space. These distributions are organized at two levels. Large appearance variations are handled by partitioning the training data into clusters that correspond to different views. Within each cluster, smaller variations are represented as distributions that describe the presence (or absence) of features, their positions, and their physical attributes. The features used thus far include intensity edges, lines, junctions, parallel segments, and convex regions. Recognition is based on the relative positions and attributes of features in a novel image. Matching with a stored object database is done using the concept of probabilistic alignment.

The subsequent chapter by Moghaddam and Pentland also addresses the use of a probabilistic framework for unsupervised learning of objects. Principal component analysis is used to first reduce the dimensionality of the training image set. The result is a low-dimensional eigenspace that is tuned to the objects of interest. Within the eigenspace, individual classes of objects form clusters that in an unsupervised setting need to be automatically identified. Two types of density estimates are proposed for modeling the clusters. One assumes a multivariate unimodal Gaussian model while the other is a mixture-of-Gaussians model for multimodal distributions. The authors present algorithms for automatically deriving the above structures from training data. The proposed scheme of probabilistic visual modeling is applied to the problems of face recognition, face coding, and gesture recognition.

Nayar, Murase, and Nene present the parametric eigenspace as a continuous representation of visual appearance. Given a vision task, its parameter space is coarsely sampled to obtain the training image set. Principal component analysis is used to achieve dimension reduction and the training images are projected to the resulting eigenspace to obtain a cluster of discrete points. The authors argue that, given the structured nature of our visual world, the clusters often lie on smooth continuous manifolds in eigenspace. These appearance manifolds are constructed from the discrete eigenspace projections by interpolation. Given a novel input projection, recognition and parameter estimation are done using efficient search algorithms that determine the closest appearance manifold point. The authors demonstrate the utility of parametric appearance manifolds in real-time applications, such as, object recognition and visual servoing.

The next chapter by Pomerleau describes the application of classical neural networks to the problem of vision-based autonomous navigation. The chapter stresses on the importance of careful design and implementation in visual learning. The significance of preprocessing of visual data to extract pertinent features while removing less-informative ones is described. It is shown how transformations can be applied to a single image to generate shifted and rotated ones, consistent with perspective projection, that can serve as additional training data. The author describes the implementation of "on-the-fly" learning where the network learns the mapping between steering direction and visual input while a human drives the vehicle. The autonomous navigation system has been demonstrated to function in a variety of settings, including, single-lane paved and unpaved roads, multi-lane and unlined roads, and obstacle ridden roads, at speeds up to 55 miles an hour.

The next contribution by Weng brings together a collection of existing tools such as dimension reduction using principal component analysis, hierarchical feature grouping, space partitioning trees, bayesian decision theory, and search techniques, into a single architecture for visual learning. The author argues that to attain the level of generality required to deal with arbitrary scenes, a system must be capable of self-organizing itself based on the visual information it encounters. The proposed system uses coarse-to-fine attention selection and a multi-level network to facilitate simultaneous recognition and segmentation. In the early levels of the network, the visual input is classified into rough categories that are grouped together and refined in subsequent levels. Experimental results are reported on the application of the proposed architecture to the problems of object recognition, motion understanding, and autonomous navigation.

Nelson explores the complexity of visual learning. It is argued that among the known techniques of computational learning, the only one that can effectively assemble the large amounts of information that comes with a typical vision problem is the construction of an indexed memory. While backpropagation, simulated annealing, reinforcement learning, and genetic algorithms are N^2 in complexity, a locally optimized indexed memory can be constructed in $N \log N$. For object recognition, the author advocates an associative memory organization coupled with the use of robust semi-invariant features that can be computed from images. To demonstrate these ideas, the author presents a memory-based recognition system for polyhedral objects.

In their chapter, Fayyad, Smyth, Burl, and Perona remind us of the importance of scalability in visual learning. While the previous chapters have explored either specific domains or small sets of training data, this one addresses the role of learning in the context of very large image databases (ones that typically include terabytes of information) that are common in the areas of astronomy, remote sensing, and medicine. The authors illustrate the need for efficient image processing, data classification, and data management. Techniques are implemented for varying focus-of-attention and extracting principal features for dimension reduction. A variety of decision tree based learning algorithms are employed for automatic rule-extraction and classifier construction. The applications discussed include the classification of volcanoes in 30,000 SAR images of Venus gathered by the spacecraft Magellan. As a future application, the authors hope to detect galaxies and stellar objects from enormous amounts of image data.

Whereas the above chapters are concerned with the problems of recognition and navigation, the one by Bhanu, Wu, and Lee addresses the problem of image segmentation. Existing segmentation algorithms rely on an expert to use his or her instincts to tune the parameters of the algorithm until a reasonable segmentation is obtained. For instance, in the case of outdoor scenes, current segmentation techniques would need to be continuously tuned based on environmental conditions, the properties of the imaging devices used, and the time of day. The authors describe an adaptive segmentation system that uses a feedback loop consisting of a machine learning subsystem, a typical image segmentation algorithm, and a performance evaluation component. The learning subsystem is based on genetic adaptation and uses a combination of a classical genetic algorithm and hill climbing. Segmentation results for outdoor color imagery are presented.

Greenspan addresses the problem of learning and recognizing image textures. Gabor wavelet decomposition is used to represent textures in frequency and orientation space and extract a small number of pertinent features. A few different non-parametric supervised learning schemes are used to learn the visual properties of the textures. For classification, k-nearest neighbor and multi-layered perceptron based algorithms have been implemented. The recognition process is shown to be rotation-invariant due to the orientation sensitive representation used. The author reports experiments on the robustness of classification in the case of structured and unstructured textures, the scalability of the developed system, and the use of texture recognition for image segmentation.

Departing from mainstream vision problems, the final chapter by Salganicoff,

Rucci, and Bajcsy addresses the problem of learning based control of a robot manipulator that relies on both visual and tactile information. The two sensory inputs are found to be consistent in a way that permits them to share information with one another. For instance, a particular visual event can lead to a sequence of tactile events and vice versa. This interplay allows one form of stimulus to corroborate as well as complement the other. The authors use a neural network to enable the manipulator to shift its gaze direction and foveate based on visual and tactile stimuli. In addition, an active learning approach is proposed for automatically generating object grasping strategies based on range scanner and tactile sensor inputs.

Needless to say, the chapters of this book by no means serve as a complete survey of low-level visual learning. It only embodies a coarse sampling of some of the representative paradigms that have emerged in recent years. Furthermore, of equal importance are learning issues related to higher levels of visual representation and perception. This is the topic of a companion book edited by K. Ikeuchi and M. Veloso that summarizes recent results on symbolic methods for visual learning. It is hoped that the two books together will provide a useful overview of the present state of visual learning and aid in the investigation of this relatively unexplored area of vision research.

REFERENCES

[1] Y. Aloimonos, R. S. Michalski, and A. Rosenfeld, "Machine Vision and Learning: Research Issues and Directions," *Report on the NSF/ARPA Workshop on Machine Vision and Learning*, Harpers Ferry, WV, Oct. 1992.

[2] B. Bhanu and T. Poggio, Editors, Special section on "Learning in Computer Vision," *IEEE Trans. on Pattern Analysis and Machine Intelligence*, Vol. 16, No. 9, Sept. 1994.

[3] K. Bowyer and L. Hall, Editors, *Proc. of AAAI Fall Symposium on Machine Learning in Computer Vision: What, Why, and How?*, Raleigh, NC, Oct. 1993.

[4] R. O. Duda and P. E. Hart, *Pattern Classification and Scene Analysis*, Wiley, NY, 1973.

[5] K. Fukunaga, *Introduction to Statistical Pattern Recognition*, Second edition, Academic Press, San Diego, CA, 1990.

[6] S. Haykin, *Neural Networks: A Comprehensive Foundation*, Maxwell Macmillan International, NY, 1994.

[7] E. R. Kandel, J. H. Schwartz, and T. J. Jessell, Editors, *Principles of Neural Science*, Third edition, Appleton & Lange, Norwalk, CN, 1991.

[8] P. Langley, *Elements of Machine Learning,* Morgan Kaufmann Publishers, San Fransisco, CA, 1996.

[9] R. S. Michalski, J. G. Carbonell, and T. M. Mitchell, Editors, *Machine Learning: An Artificial Intelligence Approach,* Vols. 1 & 2, Morgan Kaufmann, San Fransisco, CA, 1986.

VIEW INVARIANT REPRESENTATIONS IN MONKEY TEMPORAL CORTEX: POSITION, SCALE, AND ROTATIONAL INVARIANCE

Jon Pauls
Baylor College of Medicine

Emanuela Bricolo
Massachusetts Institute of Technology

Nikos Logothetis
Baylor College of Medicine

ABSTRACT

In characterizing the representation used by the brain for encoding three-dimensional objects, one of the first issues that needs to be addressed is whether the frame of reference used is object-centered or viewer-centered. In combined psychophysical-electrophysiological experiments, monkeys were tested for their ability to generalize recognition for views generated by rotating objects around any arbitrary axis while the activity of single units in inferior temporal cortex was recorded. Recognition at the subordinate level was found to become increasingly difficult as the stimulus was rotated away from a familiar attitude. This provides evidence in favor of memorial representations that are viewer-centered in the primate. Single-unit recordings in the inferotemporal cortex (IT) revealed a small population of neurons with remarkable selectivity for individual views of objects that the monkey had learned to recognize. Plotting the response of such neurons as a function of rotation angle resulted in systematic view-tuning curves for rotations in depth. For some of the tested objects, different neurons were found to be tuned to different views of the same object. These results are also in agreement with a recognition model that accomplishes view-invariant performance by interpolating between a limited number of stored views.

9

1. THE PROBLEM OF OBJECT RECOGNITION

The ability to recognize objects is a remarkable accomplishment for biological systems. Familiar objects can be readily recognized based on their shape, color, or texture. Even when partially occluded, an object's identity can be deduced based on contextual information. Furthermore, visually similar members of object classes can become easily discriminable through repeated exposure, as when a geologist learns to recognize rock formations or a botanist learns to discriminate species of plants.

In striking contrast, recognition has proved to be very difficult to achieve in artificial systems. This is partly because we know very little about what constitutes an object. The shape of an object, or its "characteristic regions", cannot always be determined by a predictable combination of visual primitives. Any given $2D$ image can be parsed into an arbitrary set of objects, each of which can be recursively decomposed into smaller objects or components, but none of which is clearly labeled as belonging to one object or another. There is nothing special about objects, or their components, at least not in the way they are represented at the input level of the visual system. Even so, most theories of object recognition posit that the visual system stores a representation of an object and that recognition occurs when the stored representation is matched to its corresponding sensory representation generated from the viewed object. This assumption, then, raises two obvious questions: what are these representations and how is matching achieved? Are objects represented explicitly in the visual cortex, say, by the activation of a set of selective neurons on the top of a visual processing hierarchy, or are they implicitly represented by the activity of large populations of cells, each of which might have little selectivity for any of the complex features of an object? Furthermore, are the stored representations object-centered, three-dimensional descriptions of the objects, or are they viewer-centered descriptions corresponding to two-dimensional perspective views?

In attempting to determine a possible reference system for object representation it is useful to consider first the different taxonomic levels of abstraction at which object recognition can occur. Objects are usually recognized first at the *basic level* [58]. This level refers to the initial classification of individual visual entities, such as a piano or a horse. When detailed distinctions between objects of the same category are required, for instance, when discriminating different horse breeds, recognition is said to occur at the *subordinate* level. Subordinate categories share a great number of object attributes with other subordinate categories, and have to a large extent similar shape [58, 57, 29]. Recognition above the basic level is said to be on the *superordinate* level and involves distinguishing between more general categories such as mammals and avians. Atypical exemplars of basic-level categories can be occasionally classified faster at the subordinate than at the basic level [29]. For example, the image of a penguin is more likely to be identified as a penguin before it is determined to be a bird. Since the notion of "basic level" was defined for entire categories based on the degree of inclusiveness of perceptual and functional attributes [58], the term "entry point level" was coined by Jolicoeur and colleagues [29] to denote the abstraction level at which stored information can be fastest accessed, regardless of what the taxonomic level may be. Most of these classifications are closely related to propositional representations and their linguistic meaning. Interestingly, clinical studies indicate that recognition at different categorization levels may involve different neural circuitry. Damage of the visual pathways at different sites can disturb recognition for very circumscribed fields of knowledge that reflect the boundaries of conceptual-lexical categories, such as those described above [10, 66]. Patients with bilateral lesions in ventral occipital and temporal association cortices fail to recognize the identity of a face or another unique, individual object of a category, while they may preserve their ability to recognize facial expressions or basic level objects. Other patients may experience a disproportionate difficulty in recognizing natural objects, which tend to exhibit greater shape similarity, whereas they can readily recognize a variety of man-made items, such as tools or trucks [12, 11]. Objects at different taxonomic levels may, therefore, differ in the neural representation of their attributes and the reference frame used for their description.

Representations may vary for different recognition tasks as well, requiring in one case only a general classification, and in another, the identification of a specific object. Object-centered representations imply the existence of a complete three-dimensional description of an object [67], or a structural description of the image specifying the relationships among viewpoint-invariant volumetric primitives [36, 1]. When tested against human behavior, the verification of the predicted performance of object-centered representations appears to depend on the object classification level. While humans can recognize familiar objects or objects at the "entry point level" in a viewpoint-independent fashion [1], they fail to do so at the subordinate level, where fine, shape-based discriminations are required for identifying an individual entity [52, 53, 62, 63, 7, 15, 35]. Viewer-centered representations, on the other hand, can explain human recognition performance at any taxonomic level, but they have been often considered implausible because of the amount of memory required to store all views that a $3D$ object can generate when viewed from different distances and orientations. Recent theoretical work, however, has indicated that a viewer-centered representation system may accomplish viewpoint invariance by relying on a small number of $2D$ views. For example, it has been shown that under conditions of orthographic projection all possible views of an object can be expressed simply as the linear combination of as few as three distinct $2D$ views, given that the same features remain visible in all three views [68]. The model of linear combinations of views, however, relies only on geometrical features, and fails to predict human behavior for subordinate level recognition [52, 53, 35].

An alternative to the linear-combination-of-views model is a model based on nonlinear interpolation among stored orthographic or perspective views. Indeed, it has been shown that a simple network, which synthesizes an approximation to a multivariate function representing the object can achieve viewpoint-invariance by interpolating between a small number of stored views [48] corresponding to an object's training views. The approximation technique, known by the name of Generalized Radial Basis Functions (GRBFs), is mathematically equivalent to a multilayer network [49]. A special case of such a network is that of the Radial Basis Functions (RBFs), which can be conceived of as "hidden-layer" units, the activity of which is a radial function of the disparity between a novel view and a template stored in the unit's memory. Such an interpolation-based network makes psychophysical predictions [47] that have been supported by work in both humans [52, 53] and monkeys [35]. It also predicts that learning a novel object from example-views may rely on the formation of new, bell-shaped receptive fields tuned to the trained views. The combined activity of such units could then be one possible mechanism for achieving view-independent recognition.

The long-term goal of our research is to study the neural representation of visual objects using combined psychophysical and electrophysiological experiments in behaving monkeys. To this end, we first examined how nonhuman primates achieve viewpoint invariance for previously unfamiliar objects. Monkeys can clearly recognize faces and facial expressions, as well as a variety of other objects in their natural environment. Moreover, they do so despite differences in the retinal projections of objects seen at different orientations, sizes and positions. Is their performance in acquiring viewpoint invariance, however, consistent with a viewer-centered representation of objects? If so, is view invariance achieved by interpolating between a small number of views learned and stored through frequent exposure?

2.   OBJECT RECOGNITION IN THE NONHUMAN PRIMATE: PSYCHOPHYSICS

In order to address these questions several experiments were carried out which examined whether the performance of monkeys is view-invariant or it is a function of the disparity between a novel view and a view that the animal learned to recognize in short training sessions. The monkeys were trained to recognize novel objects presented from one view, and subsequently tested for their ability to generalize recognition to views generated by mathematically rotating the objects around arbitrary axes. The stimuli, examples of which are shown in the top row of Figure 1, were similar to those used by Edelman and Bülthoff (1992) [15] in human psychophysical experiments. Other stimuli used included a variety of other $2D$ or $3D$ patterns, including simple geometric solids, commonplace objects, faces, and scenes (Fig. 1, bottom row). All of the target objects were generated mathematically and rendered using a visualization system (see methods, see also Logothetis et al. [35] for details).

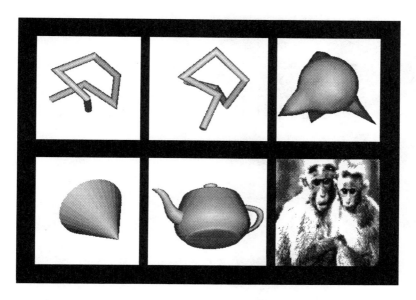

Figure 1: *Examples of stimuli used in the psychophysical and electrophysiological experiments.*

2.1. TASK DESCRIPTION AND DATA COLLECTION

Three monkeys (*macaca mulatta*) were trained extensively to perform a generalized-match-to-sample recognition task irrespective of the position, size, or orientation of the objects. In the early stages of teaching the monkeys to perform the task, the training view was the only target view presented during testing and the animals were required to recognize this view among a large set of very dissimilar distractors. Over the course of the training, both the similarity of the distractors to the targets and the rotational extents of the object that had to be remembered were gradually increased, such that in the final stage of training the distractor objects were generated by adding different degrees of positional or orientation noise to the target objects (compare the two wires shown in Figure 1) and the monkeys learned to recognize a given object from any viewpoint in the range of ±90°. A criterion of 95% correct for several objects was required to proceed with psychophysical data collection. The training procedure and data collection paradigms are described in detail by Logothetis et al. [35, 33].

Data were collected in observation periods, an example of which is shown in Figure 2. Each observation period was divided into a *learning phase* and a *testing phase*. During the learning phase the target was inspected for 2 to 4 seconds from one or two viewpoints, called the *training views*. In order to provide the subject with adequate 3D structural information, the target was presented as a motion sequence of 10 adjacent, Gouraud-shaded views, 2° apart, centered around the zero view. This yields a vivid and accurate perception of 3D structure via the kinetic depth effect (motion parallax) [4, 56]. The learning phase was followed

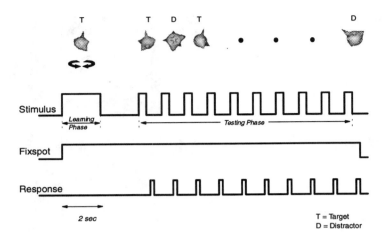

Figure 2: *An observation period in the recognition task.*

by a short fixation period after which the *testing phase* began. The testing phase consisted of up to 10 trials. The beginning of a trial was indicated by a low-pitched tone, immediately followed by the presentation of the test stimulus, a shaded, static view of either the *target* or a *distractor*. Two levers were attached to the front panel of the chair, and reinforcement was contingent upon pressing the right lever each time the target was presented, and the left lever upon presentation of a distractor. The end of an observation period was signalled by an increased juice reward and a green flash which filled the screen.

2.2. VIEWPOINT-DEPENDENT RECOGNITION PERFORMANCE

The first set of behavioral experiments was designed to test the ability of the monkeys to generalize recognition to novel target views. The animals were first trained to recognize the zero view of the target object when presented among 60 distractors of the same object class. This "familiarization" phase was the only period in which the monkey was given feedback, receiving a reward only for correct performance. No feedback was given during testing and data collection. Training was considered complete when the monkey's hit rate for the target view was consistently above 95%, the false alarm rate remained below 10%, and the dispersion coefficient of reaction times was minimized. Following familiarization, the animals were tested on their ability to discriminate target views evenly distributed around one axis of rotation. This is a typical "old-new" recognition memory task which tests the subject's ability to remember stimuli to which it has been exposed by presenting those stimuli intermixed with other objects never before encountered. The subject is required to state whether a stimulus is familiar (old, target), or unfamiliar (new, distractor). The probability of the subject reporting *familiar* when presented with a target determines the *hit rate*, while the probability of reporting *familiar* when presented with a distractor determines the *false alarm rate.* Figure 3 illustrates the view-dependent performance, in terms of hit rate and false alarm rate, observed in the subordinate level task.

Figure 3a shows the performance of one of the monkeys for rotations around the vertical axis. Thirty target views and 60 distractor objects were used in this experiment. On the abscissa of the graph is plotted the rotation angle and on the ordinate the experimental hit rate. The small squares show performance for each tested view for 240 presentations. The solid line was obtained by a distance weighted least squares (DWLS) smoothing of the data using the McLain algorithm [37]. The small insets show examples of the tested views. The monkey could identify correctly the views of the target around the zero view, while its performance dropped below chance levels for rotations greater than about 30° in either direction away from the learned view. Performance below chance level is probably the result of the large number of distractors used in a session, which limited learning of the distractors *per se.* Therefore an object that was not perceived as a target view was readily classified as a distractor.

Figure 3b shows the false alarm rate, that is, the percentage of time that a distractor object was reported as a view of the target. The abscissa shows the distractor number, and the squares the false alarm rate for 20 presentations of each distractor. Figure 3c gives a more complete description of the animal's ability to generalize recognition to novel views of the object, showing the results of testing for rotations around the vertical, horizontal, and two oblique axes, (±45°), situated in the XY plane. The X and Y axes on the bottom face of the plot show the rotations in depth, and the Z axis the experimental hit rate.

The observed view dependency was not specific to non-opaque structures lacking extended surface. Spheroidal, amoeba-like objects with characteristic protrusions and concavities were also tested in the context of a subordinate level recognition task. Thirty-six views of a target amoeba and 120 distractors were used in any given session. As illustrated in Figure 4a the monkey was able to generalize only for a limited number of novel views, correctly identifying the views of the target around the zero view, while its performance dropped below chance levels for disparities larger than 30° for leftward rotations, and 90° for rightward rotations. The false alarm rates for each of the distractors are shown in Figure 4b, and the results of testing recognition performance around each of the above-mentioned four axes is shown in Figure 4c. The conventions for the figure are indentical to those described for Figure 3.

In some experiments the same object was used for more than 15 sessions. The monkeys' ability to generalize improved in the first couple sessions yielding recognition performance like that illustrated in Figures 3a and 4a. No further improvement was observed for objects experienced from only one view.

A strong viewpoint-dependence in the recognition of novel objects was first demonstrated in humans by Rock and his collaborators [53, 52]. They examined the ability of subjects to recognize three-dimensional, smoothly-curved wire-like objects experienced from one viewpoint, when presented from a novel viewpoint.

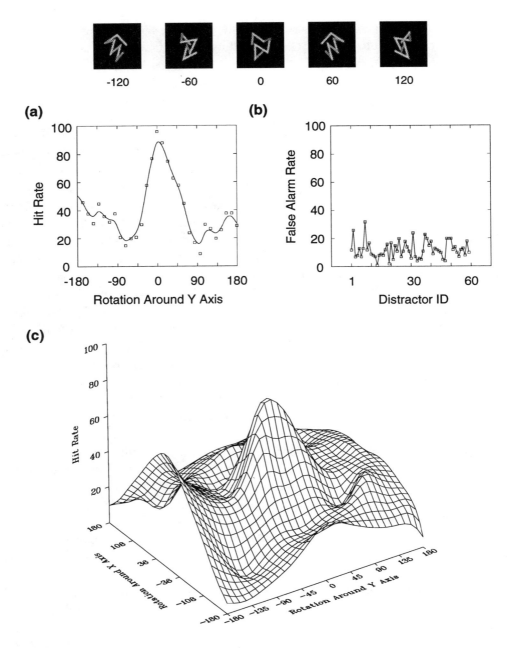

Figure 3: *Recognition performance for a wire-like object (adapted from [35]). The monkey was trained on the 0° view of the object (see inset labelled "0"), and subsequently tested using other views of the target object or distractors. (a) View-dependent performance (in terms of Hit Rate, on the ordinate) for rotation of the target around the vertical (Y) axis, and (b) performance (in terms of False Alarm Rate) for 60 distractor wire objects. (c) View-dependent performance for rotation around the Y-axis, X-axis, and two axes, 45° away from X and Y, situated in the XY plane.*

Three-dimensional, wire objects were presented in one quadrant of the visual field, *e.g.* the upper right, and the subjects' recognition performance was subsequently tested when the object was presented in another quadrant. Viewpoint changes in their experiments were the result of changes in the position of a real, three-dimensional object. Rock et al. found that humans are unable to recognize views corresponding to object-rotations as small as 30 to 40 degrees around a given axis. This result was obtained even though their stimuli provided the subject with full 3D information. Furthermore, subsequent investigations showed that subjects could not even imagine what a wire-like object looks like when rotated, despite instructions for visualizing the object from another viewpoint [54]. A study by Farah et al. [16] compared recognition for contour-defined (wire) stimuli, identical to those used by Rock, and surface-defined stimuli generated by filling in the wire contours. They, too, found a strong view dependence in the behavior of their subjects, with performance for contour-defined objects falling off more quickly than that for surface-defined objects. Similar results were obtained in experiments by Edelman and Bülthoff (1992) with computer-rendered, wire-like objects presented stereoscopically or as flat images [7, 15].

2.3. INVARIANT PERFORMANCE FOR REFLECTIONS

For some objects the monkeys showed the typical view-dependent performance described above, however, they could also recognize the target from views resulting from approximately 180° rotations of the training view. This type of behavior is evident in Figure 5. The abscissa of the graph shows rotation angle around the horizontal axis and the ordinate the true hit rate. The insets are views of the target object. As can be seen in the figure, performance drops for views farther than 30° but it resumes as the unfamiliar views of the target approach the 180° view of the target. This behavior was specific to those wire-like objects for which the zero and 180° views appeared as mirror-symmetrical images of each other, due to accidental minimal self-occlusion (see insets). In this respect, the improvement in performance parallels the reflectional invariance observed in human psychophysical experiments [2].

Reflectional invariance may also partly explain the observation that information about bilateral symmetry simplifies the task of 3D recognition by reducing the number of views required to achieve object constancy [70]. Not surprisingly, performance around the 180° view of the object did not improve for any of the opaque, spheroidal objects used in these experiments.

2.4. INTERPOLATION OF RECOGNITION BETWEEN VIEWS

In order to further investigate the nature of object representation, the ability of the monkeys to generalize recognition to novel views was examined after training the animals with two views of the target separated by either 75°, 120°, or 160°. The animals were initially trained to identify two views of an object among 60 distractor objects and received feedback as to the correctness of each response.

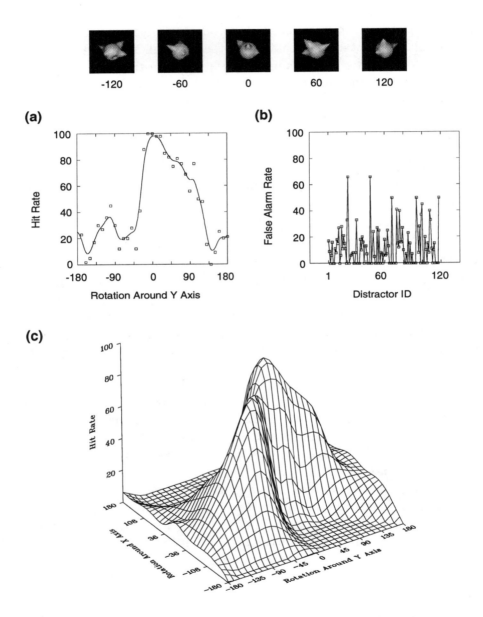

Figure 4: *Recognition performance for an amoeba-like object (adapted from [35]).*
Conventions are the same as in Figure 3.

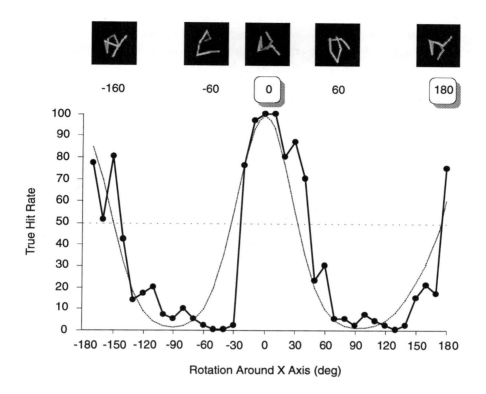

Figure 5: *Invariant recognition performance for "pseudo-mirror-symmetric" object views. The solid, black circles represent the animal's performance, in terms of True Hit Rate (on the ordinate), for rotation of the target around the horizontal axis. The thin, solid curve is a fit of the data using two Gaussian curves. Chance performance is 50%.*

Usually a total of 500-600 presentations were required to achieve the criterion of 95% correct. During testing, both training views were presented successively in the training phase beginning each observation period, after which the observation period proceeded as usual.

Interpolation was found to be complete for training with views 75° apart. That is the monkeys were able to perform at or above 95% correct for all views between the two training views. Error rate increased when the training views were 120° apart, and for a disparity of 160° the monkeys were unable to interpolate recognition. Figure 6 shows the results of an experiment in which the monkey had been familiarized with the 0 and 120 degree views of the object. The conventions of the figure are identical to those for Figure 5. In this experiment each of the 36 tested target views was presented 30 times. The gray data points indicate the monkeys performance after the initial training with two views, 120° apart. As can be seen, the performance of the animal remains above 60% for almost all views between and around the trained views. The interpolation between views shown here is not merely the sum of two view-dependent performance curves centered on the learned views, because performance for the views between the samples was at least two times better than that expected from the conjunction of two such performance curves [33]. Note the somewhat increased hit rate for views around the $-120°$ view. The thin, gray curve is a fit of the data using two gaussians.

The experiment with two views, $120°$ apart, was repeated after briefly training the monkey to recognize the $60°$ view of the object. During the second training period, as with training in the first experiment, feedback was given with respect to the correctness of responses for the $60°$ view of the target only. No other target views were presented during this brief "familiarization period". The black, filled circles in Figure 6 show the performance of the monkey after training with the $60°$ view. The animal's recognition performance has now improved to better than 90% for nearly all views between the two training views. Note also the improved performance around the "pseudo-mirror-symmetric" $(-120°)$ view of the recently learned $60°$ view.

2.5. Viewpoint-invariant recognition

Performance was found to be viewpoint-invariant when the animals were trained with multiple views of a wire-like or an amoeba-like object. In most cases, explicit training on as few as three views spaced $120°$ apart was sufficient to achieve complete recognition around one axis of rotation. Likewise, viewpoint-invariant performance was also achieved for a number of common-type objects when the animals were tested for basic-level classifications. It should be noted that the term "basic-level" is used here to denote that the targets were largely different in shape from the distractors. For example, testing the teapot, shown in Figure 1, against distractors selected from the wire-like or amoeba-like object classes would qualify, by our criterion, as a basic-level task. Since the animals were already trained to perform the task, independent of the object type used as a target, no familiarization with the object's zero-view preceded data collection in the basic-level experiments. Yet, the animals generalized recognition for all tested novel views (see Logothetis et al. [35]).

2.6. Generalization fields and a model of recognition

The behavioral data presented above indicate that training with one single view results in a bell-shaped generalization field for both the wire and amoeba objects. This seems to be consistent with the idea that view-based approximation modules synthesized during training may indeed be one of several algorithms the primate visual system uses for object recognition. These results, while hard to reconcile with the predictions of models of recognition based on object-centered representations, are, in fact, predicted by models based on a viewer-centered representation. Poggio and Edelman described a regularization network capable of performing

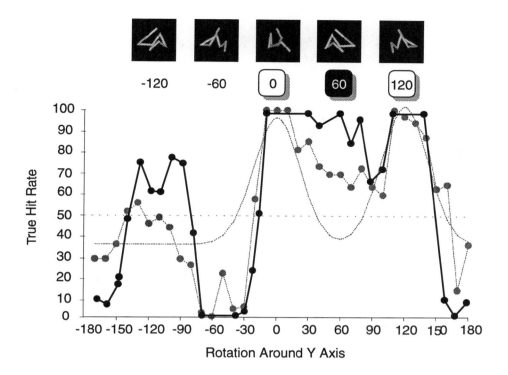

Figure 6: *Interpolation of recognition to novel views. The gray, filled circles indicate the monkey's performance, in terms of True Hit Rate (on the ordinate), after familiarization with two views of the target at $0°$ and $120°$. The black, filled circles show the monkey's performance after brief training with the $60°$ view. The thin, gray curve is a fit of the performance after the training with two views using two Gaussian curves. Chance performance is 50%.*

view-independent recognition of three-dimensional wire-like objects, after initial training with a limited set of $2D$ views of an object [48].

Figure 7 illustrates an example of such a network and its output activity. A $2D$ view (Fig. 7a) can be represented as a vector of some visible feature points on the object. In the case of wire objects, these features could be the x, y coordinates of the vertices, the orientation, corners, size, length, texture and color of the segments, or any other characteristic feature. In the example of Figure 7b the input vector consists of seven segment orientations. For simplicity we assume as many basis functions as the views in the training set. Each basis unit, U_i, in the "hidden-layer" calculates the distance $\|V - T_i\|$ of the input vector V from its center T_i, *i.e.* its learned or "preferred" view, and it subsequently computes the function $exp(-\|V - T_i\|)$ of this distance. The value of this function is regarded as the activity of the unit and it peaks when the input is the trained view itself. The activity of the network is conceived of as the weighted, linear sum of each unit's output. In the present simulations we assume that each unit's output is

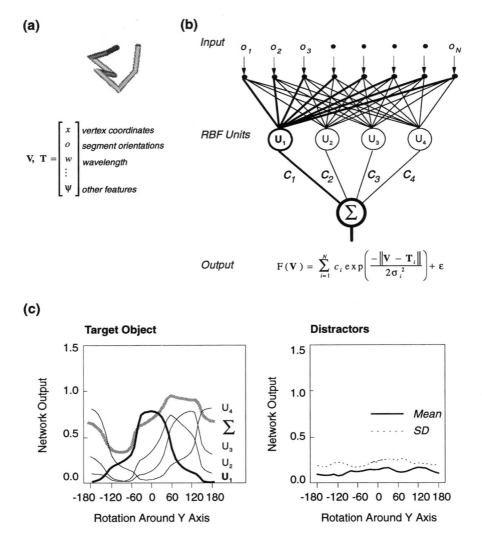

Figure 7: *Regularization network capable of performing view-invariant object recognition (adapted from [35]). (a) The input to the network is a vector of features representing an object. (b) In this case the input (o_1 to o_N) to the network is segment orientation, and each RBF unit (U_1 to U_4) is trained on one segment configuration corresponding to an object view. The network's output is the sum of the units' activities given a particular input. (c) The left panel shows the activity of each RBF unit (black curves), after training on a particular view ($0°$, $60°$, $120°$, $180°$ for U_1 through U_4 respectively), when tested with 36 target views around the Y-axis, and the network's output (gray curve) under the same test conditions. The network's activity for 36 distractors undergoing the same rotation is shown in the right panel. The thick lines in (b) and the thick curve in the left panel in (c) represent the activity of RBF unit U_1 that was trained on the $0°$ view of the target.*

superimposed on Gaussian noise, $N(\mathbf{V}, \sigma_u^2)$, the sigma σ_u^2 of which was estimated from single-unit data in the inferotemporal cortex of the macaque monkey [34]. The plots in Figure 7c show the output of each RBF unit (black curves), as well as the network's output (thick, gray curve), when presented with views generated by rotations around the vertical axis. Units $\mathbf{U}_1$ through $\mathbf{U}_4$ are centered on the 0, 60, 120, and 180 degree views of the object respectively. The abscissa of the left plot shows the rotation angle and the ordinate the units' outputs normalized to the response at the center of each of the units. Note the bell-shaped response of each unit as the target object is rotated away from its familiar attitude. The output of each unit can be highly asymmetric around the center since the independent variable in the plots (rotation angle) is different from the argument of the exponential function. The thick, gray line in the left plot of Figure 7c illustrates the network's output, under "zero" noise conditions, when the input is any of the 36 tested target views. The right plot shows its mean activity for any of the 36 views of each of the 60 distractors. The thick, black lines in Figures 7b and c show the representation and the activity of the same network when trained with only the zero view, simulating the actual psychophysical experiments described above.

Poggio and Edelman (1990) found that 80-100 views of an object for the entire viewing sphere was sufficient for the network to achieve view-invariant recognition. This predicts a generalization field of about 30° for any given rotation axis, which is in agreement with human psychophysical work [7, 15, 52, 53], and with the data discussed here. The generalization performance of monkeys was compared to that of the network by applying a signal detection theoretic [20] approach to the collection of recognition data after training with a single view. (For a more detailed comparison between network and monkey performance refer to Logothetis et al. [35]). Unlike schemes based on the linear combination of $2D$ views [68], the nonlinear interpolation model predicts recognition of novel views beyond the above measured generalization field to occur only for those views situated between the templates. This, too, is consistent with the psychophysical results in humans [7, 15] and monkeys.

2.7. SUMMARY OF PSYCHOPHYSICAL RESULTS

The results of the above psychophysical experiments, as well as those from other labs, suggest recognition at the subordinate level depends on the retinal projection of the object at the time of encounter. Even when complete information about the structure of the object was available, both humans and nonhuman primates were unable to generalize recognition to views farther than 45° from the zero view. The ability of subjects to interpolate between two distant views, and the ability of nonhuman primates to achieve view-invariant performance after learning only a few views, argues that a memory based, viewer-centered recognition system is not an implausible mechanism for object-constancy. Both theoretical work and the results of the experiments described here suggest that only a small number of object views need to be stored to achieve the perceptual invariance that biological visual systems exhibit in everyday life. If a memory-based, view-centered recognition system is used, what information about an object is represented in the memory? What "form" does this information take? Is there a basis set of features represented in a "neural feature space" which is used to construct objects? Are individual views actually represented as single entities?

3.   Object recognition in the nonhuman primate: physiology

3.1.   Inferotemporal cortex and object recognition

The Inferior Temporal Cortex (IT) of monkeys trained to recognize novel $3D$ objects is an obvious brain area to investigate the existence of cells selective for novel objects. A great deal of evidence suggests that IT (roughly coextensive with area TE and TEO [71]; see also the light gray region in Figure 8a), is essential for object vision. Patients undergoing unilateral anterior temporal lobectomy for the relief of focal epilepsy exhibit specific visuoperceptual deficits [39, 40, 41, 30, 32], and significant impairment in remembering complex visual patterns [41, 30, 40, 64]. Similarly, lesions to area TEO and to area TE yield disruptions of pattern perception and recognition [28, 21], while leaving thresholds for low-level visual tasks unaffected. Electrophysiological research has provided further evidence regarding the role of IT cortex in object recognition. Charles Gross and his colleagues were the first to obtain visually evoked responses in this area using both macro and microelectrodes in anesthetized and unanesthetized monkeys [69, 26, 18, 22]. It was found that IT neurons have large, ipsilateral, contralateral, or bilateral receptive fields, that almost always include the fovea, and are generally selective for stimulus attributes, such as size, shape, color, orientation, or direction of movement [22, 25]. A large number of investigations confirmed and extended these initial findings. As it stands, we know that IT neurons respond only to visual stimuli, which can be bars or spots of light, simple geometrical entities, or complex patterns [26, 25, 14, 13]. Selectivity has been also reported for material properties of objects such as texture or color [13, 38, 31]. IT neurons also respond in a selective manner to the shape of various natural or man-made objects [13], parametric shape descriptors [60], or two-dimensional functions that can be made to synthesize any visual pattern to a required degree of accuracy [50]. Pattern tuned neurons maintain their selectivity even when the stimuli are defined by visual cues such as motion or texture differences [59], rather than luminance or color contrast. The shape selectivity of IT neurons is also maintained over changes in stimulus position and size [24]. Although such changes usually alter the absolute firing rate of the neurons [60], the relative preference for a particular stimulus is maintained; to this extent IT neurons exhibit size and position invariance.

In general neurons responsive to similar features seem to be organized in columns that span most of the IT cortical layers [61, 19, 17]. Neurons recorded on the same electrode tend to have similar stimulus selectivity and are more likely to show functional interactions than those recorded on different electrodes spaced farther apart [19].

Perhaps the most striking class of highly selective cells in IT are those responding to the sight of faces [6, 45, 27, 72]. They are usually found deep in the lower bank and fundus of the superior temporal sulcus (STS), and in the polysensory area located dorsal to IT cortex in the fundus and upper bank of STS [13, 45]. Most face selective neurons are two to ten times more sensitive to faces than to other complex patterns, simple geometrical stimuli, or real $3D$ objects [44, 45], responding selectively to face-views [13, 46], features, or subsets of features [43, 73, 73], and maintaining their selectivity over changes in stimulus position [65]. A detailed investigation of these cells by Perrett et al. revealed a total of five cell types each of which was found to be maximally responsive to one view of the head [46]. Recent studies have shown that such selectivity appears early in the visual system of monkeys. Rodman et al. found cells in the IT cortex of infant monkeys (as young as 5 weeks old) that exhibited responses selective for shape, faces, geometrical patterns, and color [55]. So it seems that at least some of the neurons that are selective for highly complex patterns are available to the recognition system even at the earliest developmental stages of the visual system. Is such view-selectivity specific to faces? Could one expect to find neurons in this area that are tuned to views (or parts thereof) of *nonsensical* objects, that the monkey has learned to recognize? If so, what might be the role of such neurons in the representation of objects and the acquisition of view-invariant recognition?

3.2. RESPONSES OF *IT* NEURONS TO ROTATION IN DEPTH OF NOVEL $3D$ OBJECTS

These questions were addressed in a series of experiments examining the activity of neurons in the inferotemporal cortex while a monkey performed either a simple fixation task or the behavioral task described above. Figure 8 shows the recording sites as estimated from the stereotaxic coordinates. The black region in both the whole brain and the section indicates the estimated position of most of the cells recorded. Data were collected from over 1000 isolated neurons in two macaque monkeys. The large majority of these neurons could be driven visually. Isolated units (see appendix) were tested with a variety of simple or complex $2D$ patterns, as well as $3D$ objects and faces, while the animal was involved in a fixation task. The activity of the cells that responded to either the wire or the amoeboid objects was further examined while the animal performed the recognition task.

A number of units (61) were found that showed a remarkable selectivity for individual views of wire objects that the monkey had learned to recognize. An example of a highly selective neuron is shown in Figure 9a. The responses of this cell were studied for 30 different views of a wire-like object that the monkey was trained to recognize. The monkey's performance was above 95% for all the views of this object. The cell was highly selective for views located around 0° while its activity decreased considerably with rotations much beyond a 12° deviation

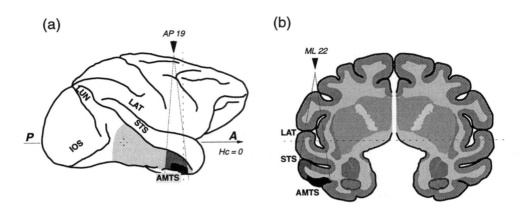

Figure 8: *Anatomical location of Inferior Temporal cortex in the Macaque monkey. (a) lateral view, whole brain; (b) Frontal section at 19mm anterior to Horsley-Clarke zero. The dotted vertical line in (a) indicates the anterior-posterior location of the section in (b). The center and extents of the recording chamber, indicated by the arrow heads and off-vertical dashed lines in (a) and (b), is at AP = 19mm and ML = 22mm.*

from the preferred view. Individual wire segments with the same orientation as the segments of the preferred view did not elicit any response when presented in the same location of the receptive field. Figure 9b shows the responses of the same cell for the six best wire-like distractor objects, none of which elicited any response from the neuron.

A second example of a view-tuned neuron is shown in Figure 9c. This cell responded best for the -24° view with its activity falling off considerably for a 24° deviation from the preferred view in either direction. Figure 9d shows the response of the cell to six distractor objects which vary in their similarity to the target. Initially, the monkey was trained to recognize the zero view of this object, and was tested using 30 views spaced 12° apart around the y-axis. However, at the time of collection of these data the animal's recognition performance for this object was above 95% for all views. It is important to note that no selective responses were ever encountered for views that the animal systematically failed to recognize.

As mentioned above, neurons selective for object views or specific patterns are not uncommon in the inferotemporal cortex. Desimone et al. [13] reported cells that were sensitive to the orientation of the head in depth. They reported cells that responded maximally to one view of a face, and that rotation of the head away from the preferred view resulted in a decrease in their activity, reaching half-maximum within 30 to 40 degrees. These results are in close agreement with the data from view-selective neurons discussed here. Neurons that responded selectively to wire-like objects had a mean generalization field width of about $28°$ (N = 41 cells), as revealed by a gaussian fitted to the response profile, while the mean width for cells selective for amoeboid objects was about $29°$ (N = 20 cells). It should be noted here that cells were considered to be selective if they responded significantly more to target views within two standard deviations of the preferred view, than for any of the distractors.

In addition to the cells selective for a single view, a small percentage of the view-selective cells (5 of the 61) responded strongly for a particular view and its *pseudo-mirror-symmetrical* view. An example of such a neuron is shown in Figure 10. This cell was most responsive for a set of views around $120°$, however, it also gave a large response for a set of views around the $-60°$ view of the target. Neither of the neuron's preferred views represent the view which the monkey was shown in the training period. The monkey's performance for this object was 100% for almost all the tested views. The high performance was the result of having given feedback to the animal for multiple views of the object.

A small percentage of cells (about 1%) responded to wire-like objects presented from any viewpoint, thereby showing view-invariant response characteristics. The activity of such neurons did vary somewhat with rotation, however, the response for any given target view was more than twice that for any distractor across all cells showing this behavior (see [33]).

For five objects that had been used extensively throughout the course of training and testing multiple neurons were found to be tuned to different views of the same object. Figure 11 shows the activity of two units, recorded from one hemisphere in one animal, that responded selectively to different views of the same wire object. The distance between the peaks of the two tuning curves shown is about $90°$. The animal had been exposed repeatedly to this object, and its psychophysical performance was above 95% for all tested views. Across all five objects, the distance between the peaks of the tuning curves of the individual neurons averaged about 60 degrees.

Many other cells showed a nonselective tuning that was likewise independent of the animal's behavioral performance, arguing that the activity of these neurons is not simply the manifestation of arousal, attention, or a sensation of familiarity, but rather relates to the object's characteristic features or views. To date, 6% of the analyzed cells showed view-selective responses similar to those illustrated in Figure 9. In their majority, the rest of the neurons were visually active when plotted with other simple or complex stimuli, including faces. A small percentage of neurons, although frequently firing with a rate of 5 to 20Hz, could not be driven by any of the stimuli used in these experiments.

3.3. RESPONSES OF *IT* NEURONS TO SCALING AND TRANSLATION OF NOVEL 3D OBJECTS

View-selective neurons were also tested with respect to changes in position or size of the preferred view. The task used to test these transformations was identi-

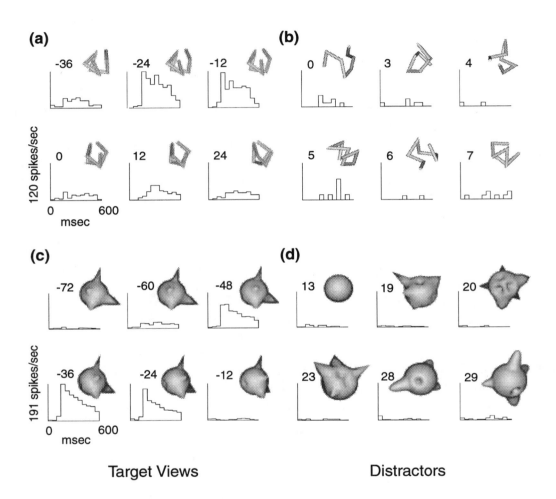

Target Views   **Distractors**

Figure 9: *Activity of two IT neurons, one selective for a wire-like object (a) and the other for an amoeba-like object (c). The abscissa of each histogram is time milliseconds, with 0 indicating the onset of the stimulus. The ordinate is maximum spike rate in Hz. The rotation of the target in both examples is around the Y-axis. (b) and (d) show responses to distractor objects tested at the same time. None of the distractors elicited any response, despite the presence of a number of features common to both the target and the distractors in each of the above examples.*

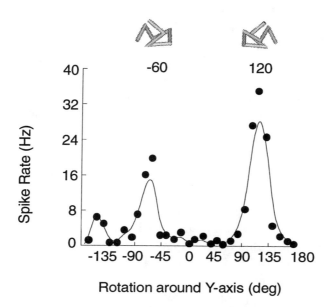

Figure 10: *Response profile of an IT neuron selective for a view of a wire-like object and its 180° rotation.*

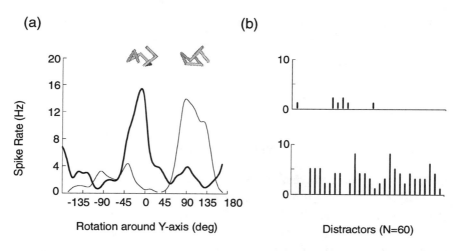

Figure 11: *Response profiles of two IT neurons selective for different views of the same wire-like object (a) and their responses to distractor objects (b). The upper plot in (b) corresponds to the cell depicted by the darker line in (a). The lower plot corresponds to the cell depicted by the lighter line. The ordinate of both plots in (b) is spike rate.*

cal to that described above for all sizes and for small positional displacements. The stimulus sizes used subtended from 1.9 to 5.6 degrees of visual angle. Four eccentric positions were tested all at a distance of 2.25 degrees (the result of a translation of the object's center 2.25 degrees, roughly 1 object radius, from the center of gaze). For larger translations the animal was only required to fixate without performing the recognition task. An example of a view-selective neuron responding invariantly to changes in size but not position is shown in Figure 12. This particular cell was selective for a limited region of the object around $-108°$ (Figure 12a), and responded more that 10 times more for the preferred target view than for the best distractor (Figure 12b).

Figure 12c shows the ratio of the target response to the mean response for the ten best distractors for the sizes tested. Note that all of the distractors were of the default size and were presented foveally. The equality in the height of the bars indicates that the cell maintained both its selecitivity and its mean firing rate for the preferred stimulus over changes in size. The responses of the same cell to translation are plotted in Figure 12d. This particular neuron showed some variance in its response depending on stimulus position, however, in all cases its response for an eccentrically presented target was still at least 2.5 times that for foveally presented distractors. We found seventy-five percent of the view-selective cells tested to be invariant to changes in stimulus size. Responses, however, varied according to the position of the stimulus in the receptive field, with stronger responses usually elicited in the foveal region. Only about thirty-five percent of the cells tested were invariant to changes in stimulus position for the limited range of translation tested. Our data suggest that the responses of IT neurons lie on a continuum composed of cells invariant to either scale, position or both to varying degrees.

3.4. SUMMARY OF ELECTROPHYSIOLOGICAL RESULTS

The results of our electrophysiological experiments indicate that a small population of neurons in inferior temporal cortex exists whose members respond selectively to individual objects tested in this study. The response of some neurons was a function of the object's pose at the time of the recognition encounter, with some of these view-selective neurons responding equally well to the pseudo-mirror-symmetrical view of the preferred view. In comparing the responses of such neurons to psychophysical data collected simultaneously, we found that view-tuning was observed only for those views that the monkey could recognize. A number of neurons were also found that responded to the sight of unfamiliar or distractor objects. Such cells, however, gave non-specific responses to a variety of other patterns presented while the monkey performed a simple fixation task.

(a)

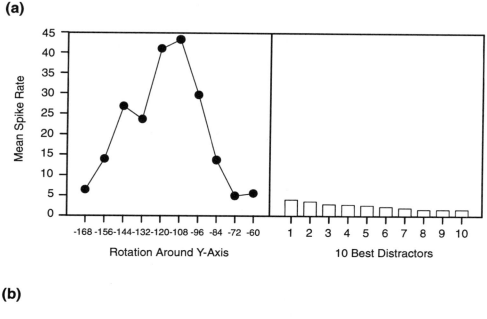

(b)

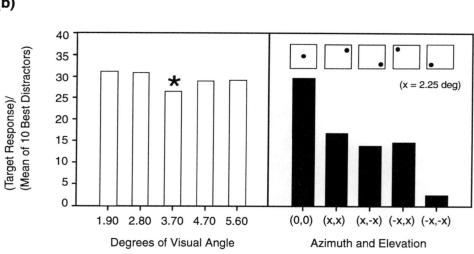

Figure 12: *Responses of a view-selective IT neuron to scaling and translation of the preferred view. (a) The response of this view-selective neuron, shown here as spike rate (on the ordinate) versus rotation angle, was tuned around the $-108°$ view of a particular wire object. (b) Its activity for the ten best distractor wire objects was minimal. In (c) and (d), the $-108°$ view of the target was also used to test the cell's response to changes in size and position. (c) The sizes tested subtended visual angles ranging from 1.9 to 5.6 degrees. The size used to train the animals (indicated by the asterisk) subtended 3.7 degrees. (d) The smallest size $(1.9°)$ was used to test translation out to an eccentricity of 2.25 degrees radially, as indicated by the insets.*

4.   DISCUSSION

The combined usage of psychophysical and electrophysiological techniques allows a
more direct comparison of animal behavior and neuronal responses in a controlled
context. The experiments described above used single-unit recording techniques
to investigate the activity of single cells in the temporal lobe while an animal performed an object recognition task. This approach to studying the representation
of objects in the brain has revealed two commonalities between the behavior and
single-cell responses.

4.1.   INVARIANCE FOR REFLECTIONS

Invariance in performance for "pseudo-mirror-symmetrical" images was observed
in both the psychophysical and physiological data for rotations around all four
axes. At first this might appear surprising since most of the mirror-symmetry
that humans experience is around the vertical axis. In fact, rotations of faces
around the horizontal axis usually have a robust effect on human performance,
while they have no significant effect on the performance of the monkey [5]. Interestingly, some face cells have also been found to respond to views of a face
180° apart, especially the left and right profiles [43]. These cells are presumably
similar to those reported here as responding to the "pseudo-mirror-symmetrical"
views. Reflection invariance has also been shown in the responses of some face
selective IT cells in infant monkeys [55], a finding that suggests that reflectional
invariance may be generated automatically for every learned object, and may be
already present early in an individual's life. Such an invariance may be the cause
of the inability of children to distinguish between mirror-symmetrical letters like
'd' and 'b'. This type of letter confusion was studied intensively in children by
Orton (1928). He observed a delay in the learning of mirror-symmetrical letters
and words in language handicapped children [42] which eventually lead to the
description of a disorder known as *strephosymbolia*. This confusion, observed in
normal children as well, appears to be the rule during development and not the
exception [9]. In fact, children up to 10 years old, which may still have incomplete development of laterality, can remember faces presented upside down almost
as well as they do those presented upright [8], in contrast to adults. Gross and
Bornstein suggest that the confusion of mirror images may be an adaptive mode
of processing visual information and not a real "confusion" [23, 3]. These authors
note that in the natural world there are never any mirror images that would be
useful for an animal to distinguish. Even in the case of bilateral symmetry observed in most animals, the two mirror symmetrical sides are aspects of the same
thing, and it would be more adaptive to treat them as the same.

4.2. VIEW-DEPENDENT PERFORMANCE AND VIEW-SELECTIVITY IN THE TEMPORAL LOBE

The view-dependent performance of both human and nonhuman primates seems to be consistent with the idea that view-based approximation modules synthesized during training may indeed be one of several algorithms the primate visual system uses for object recognition. Training with one single view results in a bell-shaped generalization field for both the wire and the amoeba objects. This suggests that the construction of viewpoint-invariant representations may not be possible for a novel object. The viewpoint-invariant performance typically observed when recognizing familiar objects may eventually be the result of a sufficient number of two-dimensional representations, created for each experienced viewpoint. This position is corroborated by results in humans and monkeys showing that both are capable of interpolating between familiar views, and that training on a limited number of views is sufficient to yield view-invariant recognition performance. The number of viewpoints is likely to depend on the class of an object and may reach a minimum for novel objects that belong to a familiar class, thereby sharing sufficiently similar transformation properties with other class members. Likewise, the context surrounding the learning of an object may have a great deal to do with the information used for its representation. The visual system may use any information available to identify an object, building a representation based on a detailed description of shape or based solely on a characteristic feature, including non-geometrical properties such as color or texture. There is no reason to expect that either humans or monkeys will rely on subordinate shape discriminations when objects can be clearly identified otherwise. However, under subordinate-level conditions it may be information corresponding to a wholistic representation of an entire view that underlies object identification.

The large majority of cells responding selectively for a particular novel object that the monkey had learned to recognize were found to be tuned around one particular view of the object. The generalization fields of such cells were very similar in width to the generalization performance observed in the behavioral data, both in the case of performance for a single view and in cases where performance for the "mirror-reflection" was seen. For a number of objects that the monkeys knew very well, performing above criterion for all views, multiple cells were found that were selective around different views of the same object. In such cases, the average distance between generalization field centers was 60 degrees. Sets of neurons tuned broadly to individual object views may represent the neural substrate of the approximation modules that are predicted by a system relying on nonlinear interpolation [49]. The frequency of encounter of such units may directly reflect the amount of exposure to a particular class of objects and the context in which it occurs.

Interestingly, the frequency of encountering neurons selective to a particular object-type seemed to be related to the animal's familiarity with the object class. In one of the monkeys, the wire-like objects, which were extensively used during the psychophysical experiments, were much more likely to elicit cell responses (71 selective cells) than, for example, spheroidal objects (10 selective cells), which were used to a much lesser extent. The converse was observed in another animal that was extensively trained with the amoeba objects. Thus, it appears that neurons in this area can develop a complex receptive field organization as a result of extensive training in the discrimination and recognition of objects.

5.   CONCLUSION

The main findings of the experimental results discussed here can be summarized as follows. (1) Even when complete information about the structure of an object is available to the subject, recognition at the subordinate level depends on the object's attitude. (2) A memory based, viewer-centered recognition system is not an implausible mechanism for object-constancy. Both theoretical work and the results of the experiments described here suggest that only a small number of object views need to be stored to achieve the perceptual invariance that biological visual systems exhibit in everyday life. (3) A small population of neurons in inferior temporal cortex was found to respond selectively to individual members of several different object-classes. The response of some neurons was a function of the object's view. Some of the view-selective neurons responded equally well to mirror-symmetrical views. (4) For all objects used in the combined psychophysical-electrophysiological experiments, view-tuning was observed only for those views that the monkey could recognize. Several neurons were also found that responded to the sight of unfamiliar or distractor objects. Such cells, however, gave non-specific responses to a variety of other patterns presented while the monkey performed a simple fixation task.

APPENDIX

A.   SURGICAL PROCEDURES

Three juvenile rhesus monkeys (*Macaca mulatta*) weighing 7-9 kg were tested. The animals were cared for in accordance with the National Institutes of Health Guide, and the guidelines of the Animal Protocol Review Committee of the Baylor College of Medicine.

After preliminary training, the animal underwent a aseptic surgery, using isoflurane anesthesia (1.2% - 1.5%), for the placement of the head restraint post and the scleral search eye coil. Throughout the surgical procedure the heart rate, blood pressure and respiration were monitored constantly and recorded every 15 minutes. Body temperature was kept at 37 degrees using a heating pad. Postoperatively, the monkey was administered an opioid analgesic (Buprenorphine hydrochloride 0.02 mg/kg, IM) every 6 hours for one day, and Tylenol (10 mg/kg) and antibiotics (Tribrissen 30 mg/kg) for 3-5 days. At the end of the training period another sterile surgery was performed to implant a chamber for the electrophysiological recordings.

B. Electrophysiological recordings

In the electrophysiological experiments the animal was required to maintain fixation throughout the entire observation period. Eye movements were measured using the scleral search coil technique [51] and digitized at 200Hz.

Recording of single unit activity was done using Platinum-Iridium electrodes of 2-3 Megohms impedance. The electrodes were advanced into the brain through a guide tube mounted into a ball-and-socket positioner. By swivelling the guide tube different sites could be accessed within an approximately 10x10mm cortical region. Action potentials were amplified (Bak Electronics, Model 1A-B), and routed to an audio-monitor (Grass AM-8) and to a time-amplitude window discriminator (Bak Model DIS-1). The output of the window discriminator was used to trigger the real-time clock interface of a PDP11/83 computer.

C. Visual stimuli

The visual objects were presented on a monitor situated 97 cm from the animal. The selection of the vertices of the wire objects within a three-dimensional space was constrained to exclude intersection of the wire-segments and extremely sharp angles between successive segments, and to ensure that the difference in the moment of inertia between different wires remained within a limit of 10%. Once the vertices were selected the wire objects were generated by determining a set of rectangular facets covering the surface of a hypothetical tube of a given radius that joined successive vertices.

The spheroidal objects were created through the generation of a recursively-subdivided triangle mesh approximating a sphere. Protrusions were generated by randomly selecting a point on the sphere's surface and stretching it outward. Smoothness was accomplished by increasing the number of triangles forming the polyhedron that represents one protrusion. Spheroidal stimuli were characterized by the number, sign (negative sign corresponded to dimples), size, density and sigma of the gaussian type protrusions. Similarity was varied by changing these parameters as well as the overall size of the sphere.

The view generated by the selection of the appropriate parameters was arbitrarily named the *zero view* of the object. The viewpoint coordinates of the observer with respect to the object were defined as the longitude and latitude of the eye on an imaginary sphere centered on the object, and right-handed coordinate system was used for the object transformations. Test-views were typically generated by ± 10 to ± 180 degree rotations around the vertical (Y), horizontal (X), or the two oblique ($\pm 45°$) axes lying on the XY plane.

ACKNOWLEDGEMENTS

We would like to thank Dr. David Sheinberg for critical reading of the manuscript. Figures 3, 4, and 7 are copyrighted by Current Science and were reprinted with permission from Current Science Publications. Portions of this text have been parapharsed from other papers by the authors. This research was supported by the McKnight Foundation.

REFERENCES

[1] I. Biederman. Recognition-by-components: A theory of human image under-standing. *Psychol Rev*, 94:115–147, 1987.

[2] I. Biederman and E.E. Cooper. Evidence for complete translational and reflectional invariance in visual object priming. *Perception*, 20:585–595, 1991.

[3] M.H. Bornstein, C.G. Gross, and J.Z. Wolf. Perceptual similarity of mirror images in infancy. *Cognition*, 6:89–116, 1978.

[4] M.L. Braunstein. Motion and texture as sources of slant information. *J Exp Psychol*, 78:247–253, 1968.

[5] C.J. Bruce. Face recognition by monkeys: Absence of an inversion effect. *Neuropsychologia*, 20:515–521, 1982.

[6] C.J. Bruce, R. Desimone, and C.G. Gross. Visual properties of neurons in a polysensory area in superior temporal sulcus of the macaque. *J Neurophysiol*, 46:369–384, 1981.

[7] H.H. Bülthoff and S. Edelman. Psychophysical support for a two-dimensional view interpolation theory of object recognition. *Proc Natl Acad Sci U S A*, 89:60–64, 1992.

[8] S. Carey and R. Diamond. From piecemeal to configuration representation of faces. *Science*, 195:312–313, 1977.

[9] M.C. Corballis and R. McLaren. Winding one's ps and qs: Mental rotation and mirror-image discrimination. *J Exp Psychol [Hum Percept]*, 10:318–327, 1984.

[10] A.R. Damasio. Category-related recognition defects as a clue to the neural substrates of knowledge. *Trends Neurosci*, 13:95–99, 1990.

[11] A.R. Damasio, H. Damasio, D. Tranel, and J. Brandt. Neural regionalization of knowledge access: Preliminary evidence. *Symp Quant Biol*, 55:1039–1047, 1990.

[12] A.R. Damasio, D. Tranel, and H. Damasio. Face agnosia and the neural substrate of memory. *Annu Rev Neurosci*, 13:89–109, 1990.

[13] R. Desimone, T.D. Albright, C.G. Gross, and C.J. Bruce. Stimulus-selective properties of inferior temporal neurons in the macaque. *J Neurosci*, 4:2051–2062, 1984.

[14] R. Desimone and C.G. Gross. Visual areas in the temporal cortex of the macaque. *Brain Res*, 178:363–380, 1979.

[15] S. Edelman and H.H. Bülthoff. Orientation dependence in the recognition of familiar and novel views of 3D objects. *Vision Res*, 32:2385–2400, 1992.

[16] M.J. Farah, R. Rochlin, and K.L. Klein. Orientation invariance and geometric primitives in shape recognition. *Cogn Sci*, 18:325–344, 1994.

[17] I. Fujita, K. Tanaka, M. Ito, and K. Cheng. Columns for visual features of objects in monkey inferotemporal cortex. *Nature*, 360:343–346, 1992.

[18] G.L. Gerstein, C.G. Gross, and M. Weinstein. Inferotemporal evoked potentials during visual discrimination performance by monkeys. *J Comp Physiol Psychol*, 65:526–528, 1968.

[19] P.M. Gochin, E.K. Miller, C.G. Gross, and G.L. Gerstein. Functional interactions among neurons in inferior temporal cortex of the awake macaque. *Exp Brain Res*, 84:505–516, 1991.

[20] D.M. Green and J.A. Swets. *Signal Detection Theory and Psychophysics*. John Wiley and Sons, Inc., New York, 1974.

[21] C.G. Gross. Visual functions of inferotemporal cortex. In R. Jung, editor, *Handbook of Sensory Physiology, Vol.7/3B*, pages 451–482. Springer, Berlin, 1973.

[22] C.G. Gross, D.B. Bender, and C.E. Rocha-Miranda. Visual receptive fields of neurons in inferotemporal cortex of the monkey. *Science*, 166:1303–1306, 1969.

[23] C.G. Gross and M.H. Bornstein. Left and right in science and art. *Leonardo*, 11:29–38, 1978.

[24] C.G. Gross and M. Mishkin. The neural basis of stimulus equivalence across retinal translation. In S. Harnad, R.W. Doty, J. Jaynes, L. Goldstein, and G. Krauthamer, editors, *Lateralization in the Nervous System*, pages 109–122. Academic Press, New York, 1977.

[25] C.G. Gross, C.E. Rocha-Miranda, and D.B. Bender. Visual properties of neurons in inferotemporal cortex of the macaque. *J Neurophysiol*, 35:96–111, 1972.

[26] C.G. Gross, P.H. Schiller, C. Wells, and G.L. Gerstein. Single-unit activity in temporal association cortex of the monkey. *J Neurophysiol*, 30:833–843, 1967.

[27] M.E. Hasselmo, E.T. Rolls, and G.C. Baylis. Object-centered encoding of faces by neurons in the cortex in the superior temporal sulcus of the monkey. *Soc Neurosci Abstr*, 12:1369, 1986.

[28] E. Iwai and M. Mishkin. Further evidence on the locus of the visual area in the temporal lobe of the monkey. *Exp Neurol*, 25:585–594, 1969.

[29] P. Jolicoeur, M.A. Gluck, and S.M. Kosslyn. Pictures and names: Making the connection. *Cogn Psychol*, 16:243–275, 1984.

[30] D. Kimura. Right temporal lobe damage. *Arch Neurol*, 8:264–271, 1963.

[31] H. Komatsu, Y. Ideura, S. Kaji, and S. Yamane. Color selectivity of neurons in the inferior temporal cortex of the awake macaque monkey. *J Neurosci*, 12:408–424, 1992.

[32] H. Lansdell. Effect of temporal lobe ablations on two lateralized deficits. *Physiol Behav*, 3:271–273, 1968.

[33] N.K. Logothetis and J. Pauls. Psychophysical and physiological evidence for viewer-centered representations in the primate. *Cereb Cortex*, 1995.

[34] N.K. Logothetis, J. Pauls, H.H. Bülthoff, and T. Poggio. Responses of inferotemporal (it) neurons to novel wire-objects in monkeys trained in an object recognition task. *Soc Neurosci Abstr*, 19:27, 1993.

[35] N.K. Logothetis, J. Pauls, H.H. Bülthoff, and T. Poggio. View-dependent object recognition by monkeys. *Curr Biol*, 4:401–414, 1994.

[36] D. Marr. *Vision*. W.H. Freeman and Co., New York, 1982.

[37] D.H. McLain. Drawing contours from arbitrary data points. *The Computer Journal*, 17:318–324, 1974.

[38] A. Mikami and K. Kubota. Inferotemporal neuron activities and color discrimination with delay. *Brain Res*, 182:65–78, 1980.

[39] B. Milner. Psychological defects produced by temporal-lobe excision. *Res Publ Assoc Res Nerv Ment Dis*, 36:244–257, 1958.

[40] B. Milner. Visual recognition and recall after right temporal-lobe exicision in man. *Neuropsychologia*, 6:191–209, 1968.

[41] B. Milner. Complementary functional specialization of the human cerebral hemispheres. In R. Levy-Montalcini, editor, *Nerve Cells, Transmitters and Behaviour*, pages 601–625. Pontificiae Academiae Scientiarium Scripta Varia, Vatican City, 1980.

[42] S.T. Orton. Specific reading disability - strephosymbolia. *JAMA*, 90:1095–1099, 1928.

[43] D.I. Perrett, A.J. Mistlin, and A.J. Chitty. Visual neurones responsive to faces. *Trends Neurosci*, 10:358–364, 1989.

[44] D.I. Perrett, E.T. Rolls, and W. Caan. Temporal lobe cells of the monkey with visual responses selective for faces. *Neurosci Lett Suppl*, S3:S358, 1979.

[45] D.I. Perrett, E.T. Rolls, and W. Caan. Visual neurones responsive to faces in the monkey temporal cortex. *Exp Brain Res*, 47:329–342, 1982.

[46] D.I. Perrett, P.A.J. Smith, D.D. Potter, A.J. Mistlin, A.S. Head, A.D. Milner, and M.A. Jeeves. Visual cells in the temporal cortex sensitive to face view and gaze direction. *Proc R Soc Lond [Biol]*, 223:293–317, 1985.

[47] T. Poggio. A theory of how the brain might work. *Cold Spring Harbor Symp Quant Biol*, LV:899–910, 1990.

[48] T. Poggio and S. Edelman. A network that learns to recognize three-dimensional objects. *Nature*, 343:263–266, 1990.

[49] T. Poggio and F. Girosi. Regularization algorithms for learning that are equivalent to multilayer networks. *Science*, 247:978–982, 1990.

[50] B.J. Richmond, L.M. Optican, M. Podell, and H. Spitzer. Temporal encoding of two-dimensional patterns by single units in primate inferior temporal cortex. I. Response characteristics. *J Neurophysiol*, 57:132–146, 1987.

[51] D.A. Robinson. A method of measuring eye movement using a scleral search coil in a magnetic field. *IEEE Trans Biomed Eng*, 101:131–145, 1963.

[52] I. Rock and J. DiVita. A case of viewer-centered object perception. *Cogn Psychol*, 19:280–293, 1987.

[53] I. Rock, J. DiVita, and R. Barbeito. The effect on form perception of change of orientation in the third dimension. *J Exp Psychol*, 7:719–732, 1981.

[54] I. Rock, D. Wheeler, and L. Tudor. Can we imagine how objects look from other viewpoints? *Cogn Psychol*, 21:185–210, 1989.

[55] H.R. Rodman, S.P. Ò Scalaidhe, and C.G. Gross. Response properties of neurons in temporal cortical visual areas of infant monkeys. *J Neurophysiol*, 70:1115–1136, 1993.

[56] B.J. Rogers and M. Graham. Motion parallax as an independant cue for depth perception. *Percept Psychophys*, 8:125–134, 1979.

[57] E. Rosch. Cognitive representations of semantic categories. *J Exp Psychol [Gen]*, 104:192–233, 1975.

[58] E. Rosch, C.B. Mervis, W.D. Gray, D.M. Johnson, and P. Boyes-Braem. Basic objects in natural categories. *Cogn Psychol*, 8:382–439, 1976.

[59] G. Sáry, R. Vogels, and G.A. Orban. Cue-invariant shape selectivity of macaque inferior temporal neurons. *Science*, 260:995–997, 1993.

[60] E.L. Schwartz, R. Desimone, T.D. Albright, and C.G. Gross. Shape recognition and inferior temporal neurons. *Proc Natl Acad Sci U S A*, 80:5776–5778, 1983.

[61] K. Tanaka, H.-A. Saito, Y. Fukada, and M. Moriya. Coding visual images of objects in the inferotemporal cortex of the macaque monkey. *J Neurophysiol*, 66:170–189, 1991.

[62] M. Tarr and S. Pinker. Mental rotation and orientation-dependence in shape recognition. *Cogn Psychol*, 21:233–282, 1989.

[63] M. Tarr and S. Pinker. When does human object recognition use a viewer-centered reference frame? *Psychol Sci*, 1:253–256, 1990.

[64] L. Taylor. Localization of cerebral lesions by psychological testing. *Clin Neurosurg*, 16:269–287, 1969.

[65] M.J. Tovee, E.T. Rolls, and P. Azzopardi. Translation invariance in the responses to faces of single neurons in the temporal visual cortical areas of the alert macaque. *J Neurophysiol*, 72:1049–1061, 1994.

[66] D. Tranel, A.R. Damasio, and H. Damasio. Intact recognition of facial expression, gender, and age in patients with impaired recognition of face identity. *Neurology*, 38:690–696, 1988.

[67] S. Ullman. Aligning pictorial descriptions: an approach to object recognition. *Cognition*, 32:193–254, 1989.

[68] S. Ullman and R. Basri. Recognition by linear combinations of models. *IEEE Trans Pattern Anal Mach Intell*, 13:992–1005, 1991.

[69] H.G. Vaughan and C.G. Gross. Observations on visual evoked responses in unanesthetized monkeys. *Electroencephalogr Clin Neurophysiol*, 21:405–406, 1966.

[70] T. Vetter, T. Poggio, and H.H. Bulthoff. The importance of symmetry and virtual views in three-dimensional object recognition. *Curr Biol*, 4:18–23, 1994.

[71] G. Von Bonin and P. Bailey. *The Neocortex of Macaca Mulatta. 4th edition*. University of Illinois Press, Urbana, 1947.

[72] S. Yamane, S. Kaji, K. Kawano, and T. Hamada. Responses of single neurons in the inferotemopral cortex of the awake monkey performing human face discrimination task. *Neurosci Res*, S5:S114, 1987.

[73] M.P. Young and S. Yamane. An analysis at the population level of the processing of faces in the inferotemporal cortex. In L. Squire, T. Ono, M. Fukuda, and D. Perrett, editors, *Brain Mechanisms of Perception and Memory: From Neuron to Behaviour*, pages 47–71. Oxford University Press, New York, 1992.

3   REGULARIZATION NETWORKS FOR VISUAL LEARNING

Tomaso Poggio and *David Beymer*
Massachusetts Institute of Technology

ABSTRACT

In this chapter, we first review the theoretical background of our approach to supervised learning for image understanding tasks, formulating learning-from-examples as a problem of multivariate function approximation from sparse data. Regularization theory provides a solution in terms of Regularization Networks. We then discuss the generality of the approach and its close relations with other classical techniques and with several Neural Network architectures. We also sketch the key problem for all non-parametric "learning" approaches – the often insufficient size of the training set – and how to overcome it using virtual examples. We then review some of our vision and graphics applications. In particular, we focus on several projects in our group in which we use example-based learning methods for both analyzing and synthesizing images. The basic idea is to label example face images (and for the problem of face detection, "near miss" faces as well) with descriptive parameters for pose, expression, identity, and face vs. non-face. Analysis networks trained using example-based learning techniques perform analysis tasks such as pose and expression estimation and face recognition. In addition to these analysis applications, we show how the example-based technique can also be used to develop synthesis networks as a novel method for computer graphics. At the end we will also describe new techniques for detection of objects of a specific class in cluttered scenes.

1. INTRODUCTION

Learning and vision are two very broad fields of research. In the space of this chapter we will make just a few general observations about supervised learning approaches in vision. Then we will briefly describe some of the applications of learning techniques developed in our group at MIT.

Vision systems that *learn and adapt* represent one of the most important future directions in image understanding research. This reflects an overall trend – to make intelligent systems that do not need to be fully and painfully programmed. It is the only way to develop vision systems that are robust and easy to use in many different tasks. This point of view traces its roots to classical statistical approaches to pattern recognition [11]. There are now, however, extensions of the classical pattern recognition techniques, extensions often called Neural Networks. Neural Networks have provided a new metaphor – learning from examples – that makes statistical techniques more attractive. As a consequence of this new interest in learning, we are witnessing a renaissance of statistics and function approximation techniques and their applications to new domains such as vision.

2. LEARNING FROM EXAMPLES AS MULTIVARIATE FUNCTION APPROXIMATION

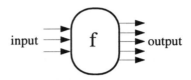

Figure 1: *In the learning-from-examples paradigm, we learn a function f from input-output pairs* $(\mathbf{x}_i, \mathbf{y}_i)$ *called the training set.*

We will concentrate on one aspect of learning: *supervised learning*. Supervised learning – or *learning-from-examples* – refers to systems that are trained, instead of programmed – by a set of examples, that is input-output pairs $(\mathbf{x}_i, \mathbf{y}_i)$ (see Fig. 1). At run-time they will hopefully provide a correct output for a new input not contained in the training set. One way to set the problem of learning-from-examples in a mathematically well-founded framework – and one which is familiar to computer vision – is the following. Supervised learning can be regarded as the regression problem of interpolating or approximating a multivariate function from sparse data (Fig. 2). The data are the examples. Generalization means estimating the value of the function for points in the input space in which data are not available.

Once the ill-posed problem of learning-from-examples has been formulated as a problem of function approximation, an obvious approach to solving it is *regularization*. Regularization imposes a constraint of smoothness on the space of approximating functions by minimizing the cost functional

$$H[f] = \sum_{i=1}^{N}(y_i - f(\mathbf{x}_i))^2 + \lambda\phi[f], \tag{1}$$

where the stabilizer ϕ is typically a measure of smoothness of the solution f. For instance, in the one-dimensional case, using $\phi[f] = \int dx \left(\frac{\partial^2 f(x)}{\partial x^2}\right)^2$ in H provides cubic splines as the solution $f(x)$.

The functional regularization approach can also be regarded from a slightly more general probabilistic and Bayesian perspective. In particular, as Girosi,

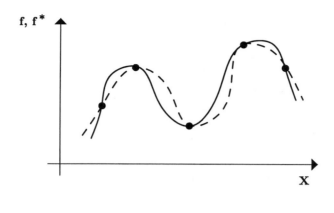

f, f*

X

● = data from the graph of f

——— = function f* that approximates f

— — = function f

Figure 2: *Learning-from-examples as multivariate function approximation or interpolation from sparse data. Generalization means estimating* $f^*(x) \approx f(x)$, $\forall x \in X$ *from the examples* $f^*(x_i) = f(x_i)$, $i = 1, \ldots, N$.

Jones and Poggio ([15], [14]; see also [26],[25], [31]) describe, a Bayesian approach leads to the maximum *a posteriori* (MAP) estimate of

$$P(f|g) \propto P(f)\, P(g|f)\ ,$$

where the set $g = (\mathbf{x}_i, \mathbf{y}_i)_{i=1}^N$ consists of the input-output pairs of training examples. If and only if the noise is additive and Gaussian (thus the model of the noise $P(g|f)$ is Gaussian) and the prior $P(f)$ is a Gaussian distribution of a linear functional of f, then the MAP estimate, that is the f maximizing $P(f|g)$, is equivalent to the f that minimizes equation (1).

2.1. REGULARIZATION IS EQUIVALENT TO FEEDFORWARD NETWORKS: REGULARIZATION NETWORKS

A key result is that under rather general conditions the solution of the regularization formulation of the approximation problem can be expressed as the linear combination of basis functions, centered on the data points and depending on the input $\mathbf{x}$. The form of the basis function G depends on the specific smoothness prior, that is the functional ϕ. More formally, and under some conditions, the f that minimizes

$$H[f] = \sum_{i=1}^{N}(y_i - f(\mathbf{x}_i))^2 + \lambda\phi[f] \qquad (2)$$

has the form

$$f(\mathbf{x}) = \sum_{i=1}^{N} c_i G(\mathbf{x} - \mathbf{x}_i) + p(\mathbf{x}), \tag{3}$$

where G is the basis function associated with ϕ through $\phi[f] = \int \frac{|\tilde{f}(\mathbf{s})|^2}{\tilde{G}(\mathbf{s})} d\mathbf{s}$, the operator ˜ indicates the Fourier transform, and $p(\mathbf{x})$ is a polynomial term that is not needed for positive definite G such as the Gaussian function.

As observed by Poggio and Girosi [26] (and for the special case of Radial Basis Functions by Broomhead and Lowe [7]), the solution provided by equation (3) can always be rewritten as a network with one hidden layer containing as many units as examples in the training set (see Figure 3). We call these networks Regularization Networks (RN). The coefficients c_i that represent the "weights" of the connections to the output are "learned" by minimizing the functional H over the training set (often with $\lambda = 0$, see [15]). The Radial Basis Functions and tensor product splines that we will use in our image analysis and synthesis applications are a special case of RN. The scalar output case described so far can be easily generalized to the multi-output case, that is to the approximation of vector fields, as outlined in the Appendix.

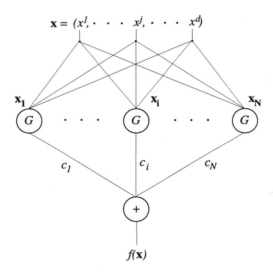

Figure 3: *A Regularization Network. The input vector* **x** *is d-dimensional, there are N hidden units, one for each example* $\mathbf{x}_i$, *and the output is a scalar function* $f(\mathbf{x})$.

2.2. RADIAL BASIS FUNCTIONS

An interesting special case arises for radial ϕ. In this case the basis functions are radial and the network is

$$f(\mathbf{x}) = \sum_{i=1}^{N} c_i G(\|\mathbf{x} - \mathbf{x}_i\|) + p(\mathbf{x}).$$

Allowable G include the Gaussian, the multiquadric, thin-plate splines and others (see [25]). In the Gaussian case, these RBF networks consist of units each tuned to one of the examples with a bell-shaped activation curve. In the limit of very small σ for the variance of the Gaussian basis functions, RBF networks become look-up tables. One may make the following observations:

- each unit computes the distance $\|\mathbf{x} - \mathbf{x}_i\|$ of the input vector $\mathbf{x}$ from its center $\mathbf{x}_i$,

- each unit applies the function G to the distance value, i.e. it computes the function $G(\|\mathbf{x} - \mathbf{x}_i\|)$,

- in the limiting case of G being a very narrow Gaussian, the network becomes a *look-up* table, and

- centers are like *templates*.

"Vanilla" RBF can be generalized to the case in which there are fewer units than data and the centers $\mathbf{x}_i$ are to be found during the learning phase of minimizing the cost over the training set. A weighted norm can also be introduced instead of the Euclidean norm and again the associated matrix can be found during the learning phase. These generalized RBF networks have sometimes been called HyperBF networks [25].

3. THREE OBSERVATIONS

Given this general framework for looking at the problem of learning-from-examples, three observations seem relevant that are described in the following sections.

3.1. REGULARIZATION PROVIDES A GENERAL THEORY

The first point is summarized in Figure 4: *several representations for function approximation and regression in statistics as well as several Neural Network architectures can all be derived from regularization principles with somewhat different prior assumptions on the smoothness of the function space (the stabilizer ϕ).* They are therefore quite similar to each other.

In particular, the radial class of stabilizers is at the root of the techniques on the left branch of the diagram. RBF can be generalized into HyperBF and into some kernel methods and various types of multidimensional splines. A class of priors combining smoothness and additivity [15] is at the root of the middle branch of the diagram. Additive splines of many different forms generalize into ridge regression techniques, such as the representations used in Projection Pursuit Regression [12], hinges [6] and several multilayer perceptron-like networks (with one hidden layer).

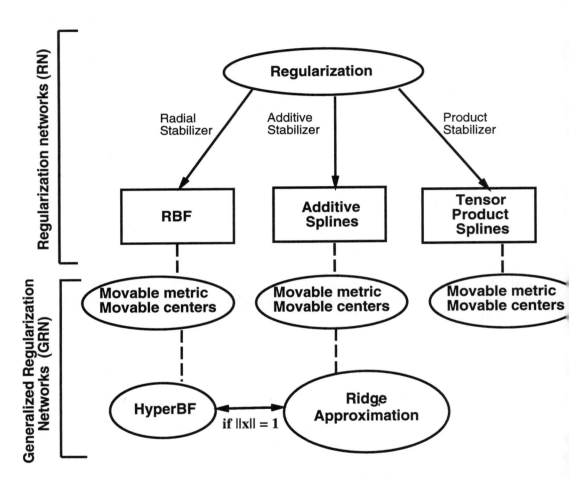

Figure 4: *Several classes of approximation schemes and corresponding network architectures can be derived from regularization with the appropriate choice of smoothness priors and associated stabilizers and basis functions, showing the common Bayesian roots. From Girosi, Jones, and Poggio [14].*

The mathematical results [15] summarized in the table are useful because they provide

1. an understanding of what many different Neural Networks do and what is the function of their hidden units,

2. an approximative "equivalence" of many different schemes for regression, while giving insights into their slightly different underlying (smoothness) assumptions, and

3. a general theory for a broad class of supervised learning architectures.

3.2. THE LEARNING-FROM-EXAMPLES FRAMEWORK ALMOST IMPLIES A VIEW-BASED APPROACH TO OBJECT RECOGNITION

The second general point is that the simplest version of an example-based approach to object recognition – and, as we will see later, to graphics – is equivalent to a view-based approach to recognition. Consider a learning-from-examples network trained to classify different views of a 3D object against views of other distractor objects. Suppose that the network has the form of a Gaussian Radial Basis Function network. Then, as discussed in [19] and [18], each hidden unit is view-tuned to one of the example views, whereas the output can be view invariant but object specific (if a sufficient number of examples and units are available).

This is, of course, a cartoon of an object recognition system, since it assumes isolated objects, a suitable representation for the inputs to the network, and possibly correspondence of features. Different types of simulations with simulated [24] and real "wire-frame" objects [8] show that a view-based scheme of this type can be made to work well, and these computational experiments are supported by similar experiments in psychophysics [10] and physiology [18]. The three systems for face recognition to be described later take the same basic view-based approach and perform satisfactorily.[1]

3.3. PRIOR INFORMATION IS NEEDED TO LEVERAGE THE EXAMPLE SET

The third and last observation has to do with the issue of sample complexity – how many "training examples" are needed for a supervised learning scheme to solve a specific problem.

Niyogi and Girosi [22] have recently proved the following result, which extends to Radial Basis Functions results due to Barron [2] for multilayer perceptrons.

Theorem (Niyogi and Girosi, 1992)

---

[1]One may argue that non-local basis functions do not correspond to a view-based approach. The issue of locality vs. non-locality of the basis functions is a subtle one, however. Girosi, et al. [15] show that even non-local basis functions can be rewritten in terms of local equivalent kernels.

Let $f \in H^{m,1}(R^d)$, where $H^{m,1}(R^d)$ is the space of functions of d variables whose partial derivatives up to order m are integrable, and let $m > d$, with m even.

Let $f_{n,N}$ be a Gaussian basis function network, with n coefficients, n centers and n variances, that has been trained on a set of N data points. Then, with probability $1 - \delta$, the generalization error is bounded by the following inequality:

$$E[(f - f_{n,N})^2] < O\left(\frac{1}{n}\right) + O\left(\left(\frac{nd \ln(nN) - \ln \delta}{N}\right)^{\frac{1}{2}}\right)$$

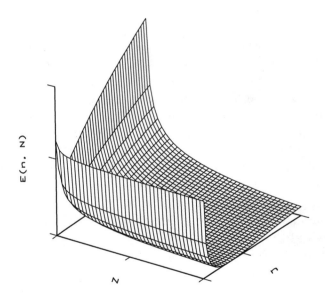

Figure 5: *An illustration of the theorem (from Niyogi and Girosi [22]). The generalization error E depends on the number of examples (N) and the number of parameters (n). For fixed N there is an optimal value of n for which E is minimum.*

The plot of Figure 5 summarizes the main result of the theorem that applies to most of the learning-from-example schemes we are discussing. The figure shows how the generalization error on new data, not used for training, depends on the number of examples N and on the complexity of the network, described here by the number of its free parameters n. One of the several important features of the graph is that for each N there is an optimal n. In many cases, especially when N is not very large, the choice of a good n is often more important in practice than the choice of one regression or classification architecture versus another.

The main point here is however a simpler one. Very often we are forced to work in the region of the plot with very small N. In other words, very often there are not enough training data. We believe that this is one of the most basic limitations of all the nonparametric learning-from-examples schemes discussed here, including most Neural Networks architectures. What can be done? The obvious idea (see [27]) that we have pursued is to exploit *prior information* about the specific problem at hand to generate *virtual examples* and thus expand the size of the training set, that is N. We will come back to specific instances of this approach for face recognition and face detection.

4. LEARNING FOR IMAGE ANALYSIS AND SYNTHESIS: APPLICATION TO FACE IMAGES

We will describe here three specific projects in our group that use the learning-from-examples techniques for approaching problems in computer vision and computer graphics, using human faces as the class of 3D objects.

4.1. EXAMPLE-BASED IMAGE ANALYSIS AND IMAGE SYNTHESIS

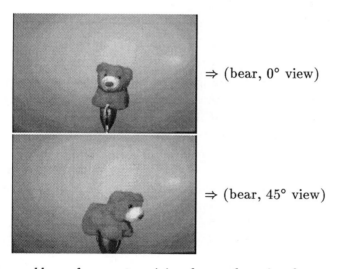

$\Rightarrow$ (bear, 0° view)

$\Rightarrow$ (bear, 45° view)

Figure 6: *The problem of computer vision from a learning-from examples perspective. Given an image, the goal is to recognize the object and to estimate its pose. From Girosi (unpublished).*

In the learning-from-examples approach to the problem of image analysis, a learning module is trained to associate input images to output parameters – such as the classification label for the object in the image and possibly pose and expression parameters associated with it (see Figure 6). After training with a set of images and corresponding parameters, the network is expected to generalize correctly; that is, to classify new views of the same object, recognize another object of the same class, or estimate its pose/expression parameters.

(bear, 0° view) ⇒

(bear, 45° view) ⇒

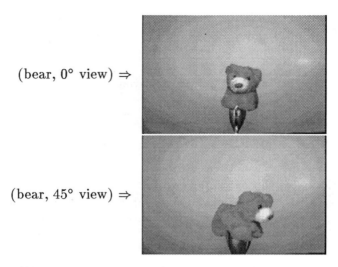

Figure 7: *The problem of computer graphics from a learning-from examples perspective. Given a pose, the goal is to generate the corresponding image. From Girosi (unpublished).*

In the "inverse" problem of computer graphics, a learning-from examples module is used to associate input parameters to output images (see Figure 7). This module synthesizes new images and represents a rather unconventional approach to computer graphics. Traditional 3D computer graphics simulates the physics of the world by building 3D models, transforming them in 3D space, simulating their physical properties and finally rendering them, by simulating geometrical optics. The learning-from-examples paradigm suggests a rather different approach: take several real images of a 3D object – possibly a nonrigid one – and create new images by generalizing from those views, under the control of appropriate pose and expression parameters, assigned by the user during the training phase. Our previous discussion should make clear that this metaphor – of learning-from-examples – is equivalent to performing multidimensional interpolation or approximation, in this case a form of multidimensional morphing.

Clearly these view-based approaches to image analysis and synthesis, which are the traditional domains of computer vision and computer graphics, cannot be seen as substitutes for the more traditional and physically more "correct" approaches. However, the learning-from-examples approach to vision and graphics may represent an effective shortcut to several problems and, furthermore, has a profound appeal in terms of describing what biological visual systems may do.

In the following, we will sketch projects in our group using the learning-from-examples approach for the analysis of face images and for the synthesis of face images. We will also mention how the combination of the two resulting networks may provide a technique potentially useful for videoconferencing or video e-mail systems that aim to achieve very-low bit rates.

4.1.1. THE ANALYSIS NETWORK

Given a set of example images labeled in pose and expression space (Figure 8), an RBF network (see equation (3)) can be trained to estimate the pose-expression parameters of new images of the same person. The input to the network, or our image representation, is a geometrical representation of (x, y) locations of facial features. In [4], we describe facial geometry using pixelwise correspondence with respect to a reference image, here chosen to be the upper left image in Figure 8. Output are in this case two parameters, representing the amount of smile and rotation of the face. The network is constructed using four Gaussian RBF hidden units, one for each of the example images. After "training" with the four examples the network can "generalize" to new images of the same person, estimating the associated rotation and smile parameters. Examples of input images and their estimated parameters are shown ahead in Figure 11, which shows the analysis network as part of a system for low-bandwidth teleconferencing.

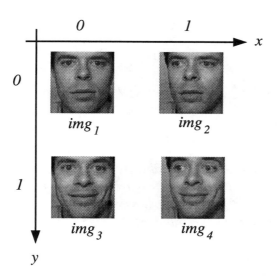

Figure 8: *In our demonstrations of the example-based approach to image analysis and synthesis, the example images, img_1 through img_4, are placed in a 2D rotation-expression parameter space (x, y), here at the corners of the unit square. For analysis, the network learns the mapping from images (inputs) to parameter space (output). For synthesis, we synthesize a network that learns the inverse mapping, that is the mapping from the parameter space to images.*

4.1.2. THE SYNTHESIS NETWORK

In the synthesis case the role of inputs and outputs are exchanged: graphics is indeed the inverse of vision! Figure 9 shows the network used by [4] to synthesize images of faces of a specific person under control of two pose-expression parameters, the same ones used by the analysis network. The basis functions in this Regularization Network were taken to be tensor product linear splines $G(x^1, \ldots, x^d) = |x^1| \cdot \ldots \cdot |x^d|$. Inputs are a two dimensional vector ($d = 2$), representing the amount of smile and rotation of the face. For network output, since our image representation uses pixelwise correspondence with respect to a reference image, the number of outputs, q, is twice the number of pixels in the image (each pixel has an x and y coordinate). The output geometry produced by the network is then "rendered" by applying 2D warping operations to the example image "textures".

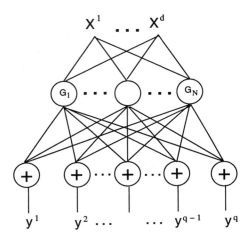

Figure 9: *The network used to synthesize images from pose inputs. It differs from the Regularization Network in Figure 3 simply by having more outputs, q dimensions in this case. Since we use a pixelwise representation for our output images, q is proportional to the number of pixels in the image.*

Figure 10 shows some example images generated by the synthesis network. The four examples used here are the same as for the analysis case and are shown at the four corners of the figure. All the other images are "generalizations" produced by the network after the "learning" phase.

4.1.3. VERY-LOW BANDWIDTH VIDEO E-MAIL

The analysis and the synthesis networks can each be used independently for a variety of applications. The analysis network is not limited to face images and can be regarded as a *trainable man-machine interface* that could perform customizable

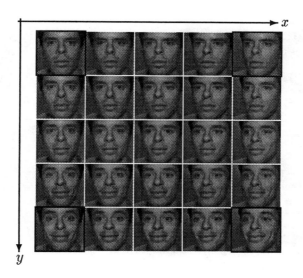

Figure 10: *Multidimensional image synthesis using the example images bordered in black. All other images are generated by the synthesis network. From Beymer, et al. [4].*

gesture recognition and thereby drive a computer interface. The synthesis network is an alternative way to do graphics and animation that extends to real images the approach already demonstrated for line drawings by Poggio and Brunelli [23] and by Librande [17].[2]

A particularly interesting application of the analysis and the synthesis network is very-low bandwidth video e-mail and video-conferencing. Figure 11 shows a demonstration of the basic idea. An analysis network trained on a few views of the specific user analyzes new images during the session in terms of two pose and expression parameters. These two parameters are sent electronically for each frame and used at the receiver site by a synthesis network previously trained on example views of the same user to synthesize appropriate new views. This model-based approach can achieve in principle very high compressions. The example shown in the figure probably needs in the order of 2 bytes per frame at run time, though it is very limited in terms of the range of pose and expressions. A more realistic estimate would consist of around 20 parameters to be estimated and sent, plus a few others defining the image plane transformation for a total of perhaps $20 - 30$ bytes per frame. Of course, the practical feasibility of such a scheme is still unproven, even if it is just a component in more complex compression architecture.

---

[2]Going beyond line drawings, Poggio and Brunelli [23] demonstrated the approach with simple grey-level images, using sparse manual correspondence instead of the automatic, dense correspondence used in Beymer, et al. [4].

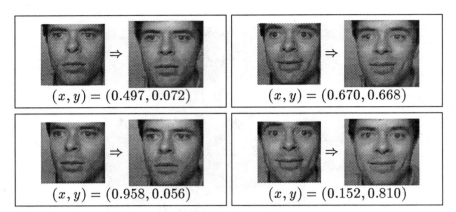

$(x, y) = (0.497, 0.072)$ $(x, y) = (0.670, 0.668)$

$(x, y) = (0.958, 0.056)$ $(x, y) = (0.152, 0.810)$

Figure 11: *In each of the boxed image pairs, the novel input image on the left is fed into an analysis RBF network to estimate rotation x and expression y. These parameters are then fed into the synthesis module of Figure 10 that synthesizes the image shown on the right. This figure can be regarded as a very simple demonstration of very-low bandwidth teleconferencing: only two pose parameters need to be transmitted at run-time for each frame. From Beymer, et al. [4].*

4.2. FACE RECOGNITION

We will now summarize our work over the last 4 years on face recognition, first covering three view-based face recognition systems that rely on several example views per person. We will then discuss on-going work with synthesizing virtual example views to deal with situations in which only one example view (also called model view) per person is available.

4.2.1. THE BRUNELLI-POGGIO FRONTAL FACE RECOGNITION SYSTEM

Following the face recognition work of Baron [1], Brunelli and Poggio [9] use a template-based strategy to recognize frontal views of faces. From an example model view, faces are represented using templates of the eyes, nose, mouth, and entire face. A normalized correlation metric is used to compare the model templates against the input

$$r = \frac{<TI> - <T><I>}{\sigma(T)\sigma(I)},$$

where T is the template, I is the subportion of image being matched against, $<>$ is the mean operator, and $\sigma()$ measures standard deviation. Input images are geometrically registered with the model views by aligning the eyes, which normalizes the input for the effects of translation, scale, and image-plane rotation. The eyes are automatically located in a separate initial step using eye templates. On a data base of 47 people, 4 views per person, the recognition performance is

100% when two views are used as model views and the remaining two views are used for testing. A few different types of image preprocessing were evaluated in terms of recognition performance, and the L_1 norm of the gradient produced the best results.

4.2.2. THE GILBERT-YANG PC-BASED FACE RECOGNITION SYSTEM

Using an algorithm very similar to the Brunelli-Poggio system, Gilbert and Yang [13] developed a fast PC-based face recognition system that uses custom VLSI chips for correlation. Model image templates of the eyes, nose, mouth, and entire face are correlated against a geometrically normalized input, where normalization is done by detecting the eyes in a preliminary step. Eyes are located using grey-level valley and peak detectors which respectively locate the irises and whites of the eye.

The primary innovation is a custom VLSI chip for performing correlations quickly. The correlation chip performs an absolute-difference correlation of a 68×68 template with a 64×64 template, allowing for translational shifts of the latter template from -2 to +2 in both x and y. One correlation takes 0.9 ms, and going through their library of 173 model images takes only 0.3 sec. A PC implementation that uses the chip in a special accelerator board takes only 2 to 3 seconds to go from frame grabbing to recognition. Using a cross-validation approach to test the system on their data base containing 173 images of 34 people, a recognition rate of 93% was obtained in a forced-choice experiment (i.e. system always reports best match).

4.2.3. THE BEYMER POSE-INVARIANT FACE RECOGNITION SYSTEM

In a view-based extension of the Brunelli-Poggio system, Beymer [5] developed a pose-invariant face recognizer that uses 15 views per person, views that cover different out-of-plane rotations (see the 5 different left-right rotations and 3 different up-down rotations in Fig. 12). Similar to the previous two systems, translation, scale, and image-plane rotation are factored out by first detecting eyes and nose features and then using these features to register the input with model views. The feature finder must be person and pose independent, so it uses a simple view-based approach that employs a bank of eyes-nose templates covering a variety of "exemplar" people and poses. To recognize a new input, it is matched against all model views of all people and the best match is reported. The matching step consists of a geometrical registration step driven by the eyes and nose features followed by normalized correlation using eyes, nose, and mouth templates. On a database of 62 people and 10 test views per person, we obtained a recognition rate of 98%. The test images were at a variety of image rotations, both in and out of the image plane. Similar to the Brunelli-Poggio system, image preprocessing with the gradient was found to yield the highest recognition performance.

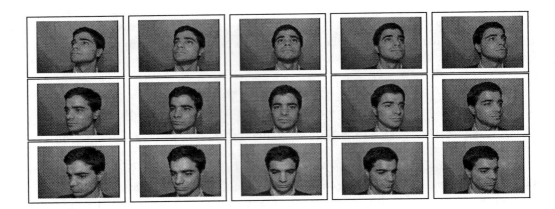

Figure 12: *The pose-invariant, view-based face recognizer uses 15 views to model a person's face. From Beymer [5].*

4.2.4. FACE RECOGNITION WITH VIRTUAL VIEWS

As discussed in Girosi, Jones, and Poggio [15], the key problem for the practical use of learning-from-examples schemes – and for non-parametric techniques in general – is often the insufficient size of the training set. As we mentioned, we have been developing the idea of exploiting prior information about the specific domain to generate additional *virtual* examples. In recent work we have shown how prior knowledge of symmetry properties of the class of 3D objects allows the synthesis of additional examples [27]. Psychophysical evidence in favor of the use of this constraint by biological visual systems was presented in [30]. More generally, we had suggested learning class-specific transformations from examples drawn from objects of the same class in order to synthesize new virtual views of a new object of the same class from a single view [27]. The conjecture is that this may be possible for certain "nice" classes of objects (see [29]). For example, objects that have a similar 3D structure, like faces, may be one instance of a "nice" class.

Figure 13, taken from Beymer and Poggio [3], shows one way to generate virtual views by applying the transformation "learned" from a prototype of the same class. Called *parallel deformation* (see [23]), a 2D deformation measured on the prototype face is mapped onto the novel face. The mapped deformation then drives a 2D warping of the novel face to the virtual view. Figure 14 shows the result of applying this technique to produce several rotated *virtual views* of the same face from a single real image.

The virtual views generated in this way have been used as model views in the pose-invariant recognizer described earlier to achieve recognition rates that are likely to compare well to human performance in the same situation (see [3]).

prototype novel person

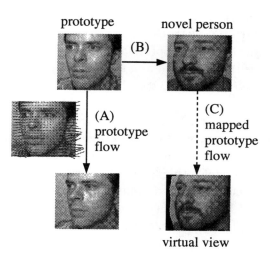

virtual view

Figure 13: *In parallel deformation, (A) a 2D deformation representing a transformation is measured by finding correspondence among prototype images. In this example, the transformation is rotation and optical flow was used to find a dense set of correspondences. Next, in (B), the flow is mapped onto the novel face, and (C) the novel face is 2D warped to a "virtual" view. From Beymer and Poggio [3].*

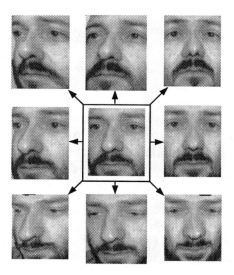

Figure 14: *A real view (center) surrounded by virtual views derived from it using parallel deformation. From Beymer and Poggio [3].*

4.3. EXAMPLE-BASED FACE DETECTION

The last project that we will describe deals with the general problem of object and pattern detection in cluttered pictures. It has been often said that this problem is even more difficult than the problem of isolated object recognition (see for instance Hurlbert and Poggio [16]). As we will see, a key component in the solution to this class of problems is again the use of virtual views to expand very significantly the size of the training set.

Clearly, finding human faces automatically in an image is a difficult yet important first step to a fully automatic face recognition system. It is also a general problem because a successful face detection system can provide valuable insight into how one might approach other similar object and pattern detection problems. We have developed [28] an example-based learning approach for locating vertical frontal views of human faces in complex scenes. The technique models the distribution of human face patterns by means of a few view-based "face" and "non-face" prototype clusters. At each image location, a difference feature vector is computed between the local image pattern and the distribution based model, based on a two-value distance which is identical to the one described later in this book by Moghaddam and Pentland. A trained classifier determines, based on the difference feature vector, whether or not a human face exists at the current image location. We have shown empirically that the prototypes we choose for our distribution-based model and the distance metric we adopt for computing difference feature vectors are both critical for the success of our system.

Figure 15 shows an example of the performance of the system. A key step in the training of the system is the use of virtual examples to expand the training set. From 1000 real face images that are used as positive examples, an additional 3000 virtual positive examples are automatically created.[3]

5. SUMMARY

We reviewed learning-from-examples techniques and their applications to computer vision. The formulation of the learning-from-examples problem as a problem of multivariate function approximation from sparse data leads to the use of regularization techniques. Regularization provides a solution in terms of Regularization Networks. We then discussed the generality of this approach and its close relations with other classical techniques and with many Neural Network architectures. Next, we reviewed some of the vision and graphics applications of these learning-from-examples techniques, demonstrating them on face images. We first showed how networks trained on example (image, pose-expression) input-output pairs from a specific person can be used to estimate the pose and expression of new images of that person. In addition, by reversing the input-output order of the examples, we can train a new network, a synthesis network, that can generate new images of the same person. In our second application, face recognition, we

---

[3]In addition, there are 50,000 negative examples in the training set.

Figure 15: *Some face detection results produced by the Sung-Poggio system. From Sung and Poggio [28].*

described three view-based implementations, the last of which uses many example model views per person to create a pose-invariant recognizer. When only one real model view of each person is available, we use prior knowledge of faces to synthesize new "virtual" views of each person, where prior face knowledge is in the form of 2D example views of prototype faces. Finally, for the problem of detecting faces in cluttered scenes, we present an example-based method that is trained on positive and negative examples of face images.

APPENDIX

A.   NETWORKS FOR LEARNING VECTOR FIELDS AND A KL APPROXIMATION

In this appendix we consider the problem of approximating a vector field from sparse data. We therefore generalize equation (3) by considering the problem of approximating a vector field $\mathbf{y}(\mathbf{x})$ from a set of sparse data, the examples, which are pairs $(\mathbf{x}_i, \mathbf{y}_i)$ for $i = 1, \ldots, N$. We use a Generalized Regularization Network as the approximation scheme, that is, a network with one "hidden" layer and linear output units. Consider the case of N examples, $n \leq N$ centers, input dimensionality d and output dimensionality q. Then the approximation is

$$\mathbf{y}(\mathbf{x}) = \sum_{i=1}^{n} \mathbf{c}_i G(\mathbf{x} - \mathbf{x}_i)$$

with G being the chosen basis function. The equation can be rewritten in matrix notation as

$$\mathbf{y}(\mathbf{x}) = \mathbf{C}\mathbf{g}(\mathbf{x})$$

where $\mathbf{g}$ is the vector with elements $g_i = G(\mathbf{x} - \mathbf{x}_i)$.

Let us define as $\mathbf{G}$ the matrix of the chosen basis function evaluated at the examples, that is, the matrix with elements $G_{i,j} = G(\mathbf{x}_i - \mathbf{x}_j)$. Then the "weights" $\mathbf{c}$ are "learned" from the examples by solving

$$\mathbf{Y} = \mathbf{C}\mathbf{G}$$

where $\mathbf{Y}$ is defined as the matrix in which column l is the example $\mathbf{y}_l$. $\mathbf{C}$ is defined as the matrix in which row m is the vector $\mathbf{c}_m$. This means that $\mathbf{x}$ is a $d \times 1$ matrix, $\mathbf{C}$ is a $q \times n$ matrix, $\mathbf{Y}$ is a $q \times N$ matrix and $\mathbf{G}$ is a $n \times N$ matrix. Then the set of weights C is given by

$$\mathbf{C} = \mathbf{Y}\mathbf{G}^{+}.$$

It follows that the vector field $\mathbf{y}$ is approximated by the network as the linear combination of the example fields $\mathbf{y}_l$, that is

$$\mathbf{y}(\mathbf{x}) = \mathbf{Y}\mathbf{G}^{+}\mathbf{g}(\mathbf{x})$$

which can be rewritten as

$$\mathbf{y}(\mathbf{x}) = \sum_{l=1}^{N} b_l(\mathbf{x})\mathbf{y}_l$$

where the b_l depend on the chosen G, according to

$$\mathbf{b}(\mathbf{x}) = \mathbf{G}^{+}\mathbf{g}(\mathbf{x}).$$

Now consider the equation

$$\mathbf{y}(\mathbf{x}) = \mathbf{C}\mathbf{g}(\mathbf{x}) \tag{4}$$

and its dual

$$\mathbf{y}(\mathbf{x}) = \mathbf{Y}\mathbf{b}(\mathbf{x}). \tag{5}$$

Equation (4) can be regarded as a mapping from $\mathbf{x}$ to $\mathbf{y}$, whereas equation (5) may be regarded as a mapping from the space of the b coefficients into $\mathbf{y}$. The transformation from a point $\mathbf{x}$ in X space to a point b in B space is given by

$$\mathbf{b}(\mathbf{x}) = \mathbf{G}^+\mathbf{g}(\mathbf{x}). \tag{6}$$

Given $\mathbf{x}$, $\mathbf{b}$ is determined by the previous equation: the inverse is not possible in general.

Notice that when $n = N$ each $\mathbf{y}$ is approximated by a linear combination of the N examples: when $n < N$ this is still true.

Consider now the equation

$$\mathbf{y} = \mathbf{Y}\mathbf{b}(\mathbf{x}) = \sum_{l=1}^{N} b_l(\mathbf{x})\mathbf{y}_l \tag{7}$$

and expand each of the columns of $\mathbf{Y}$ – that is each of the examples $\mathbf{y}_i$ – in $Q \leq N$ of the eigenfunctions of $\mathbf{Y}\mathbf{Y}^T$ – which has dimensionality $q \times q$. Thus

$$\mathbf{y}_i = \sum_{m=1}^{Q} d_m^i \mathbf{y}_m' = \mathbf{Y}'\mathbf{d}^i \tag{8}$$

and combining the last two equations yields

$$\mathbf{y} = \sum_{l=1}^{N} b_l(\mathbf{x}) \sum_{m=1}^{Q} d_m^l \mathbf{y}_m' = \mathbf{Y}'\mathbf{b}'(\mathbf{x}) \tag{9}$$

where $\mathbf{Y}'$ is a $q \times Q$ matrix and $\mathbf{b}'(\mathbf{x})$ is a Q dimensional vector of the coefficients of the expansion of the vector $\mathbf{y}$ in the eigenfunctions of $\mathbf{Y}\mathbf{Y}^T$, that is

$$\mathbf{b}'(\mathbf{x}) = \mathbf{Y}'^T\mathbf{y}(\mathbf{x}) \tag{10}$$

where $\mathbf{Y}'$ is the matrix with columns the eigenvectors of $\mathbf{Y}\mathbf{Y}^T$.

Thus each output $\mathbf{y}$ can be approximated by a linear combination of eigenfunctions of the example set $\mathbf{y}_i$. As a consequence, a smaller set of example images may be used in the linear combination technique than the number of examples, provided they are chosen to be the most significant eigenfunctions of the correlation matrix of the example set and they are sufficient to approximate well novel images.

Of course the eigenvectors of $\mathbf{Y}\mathbf{Y}^T$ can be found in terms of the eigenvectors of $\mathbf{Y}^T\mathbf{Y}$ which may have a much lower dimensionality (for instance when the columns of $\mathbf{Y}$ are images).[4]

---

[4]Notice that there is a connection between this formulation and the parametric eigenspace

Acknowledgements

This chapter describes research done within the Center for Biological and Computational Learning in the Department of Brain and Cognitive Sciences, and at the Artificial Intelligence Laboratory. This research is sponsored by grants from the Office of Naval Research under contracts N00014-91-J-1270 and N00014-92-J-1879; by a grant from the National Science Foundation under contract ASC-9217041 (funds provided by this award include funds from DARPA provided under the HPCC program); and by a grant from the National Institutes of Health under contract NIH 2-S07-RR07047. Additional support is provided by the North Atlantic Treaty Organization, ATR Audio and Visual Perception Research Laboratories, Mitsubishi Electric Corporation, Sumitomo Metal Industries, and Siemens AG. Support for the A.I. Laboratory's artificial intelligence research is provided by ONR contract N00014-91-J-4038. D. Beymer is supported by a Howard Hughes Doctoral Fellowship from the Hughes Aircraft Company.

References

[1] R. J. Baron. Mechanisms of human facial recognition. *International Journal of Man Machine Studies*, 15:137–178, 1981.

[2] A. Barron. Approximation and estimation bounds for artificial neural networks. *Machine Learning*, 14:115–133, 1994.

[3] D. Beymer and T. Poggio. Face recognition from one example view. In *Proceedings of the International Conference on Computer Vision*, pages 500–507, Cambridge, MA, June 1995.

[4] D. Beymer, A. Shashua, and T. Poggio. Example based image analysis and synthesis. A.I. Memo No. 1431, Artificial Intelligence Laboratory, Massachusetts Institute of Technology, 1993.

[5] D. J. Beymer. Face recognition under varying pose. In *Proceedings IEEE Conf. on Computer Vision and Pattern Recognition*, pages 756–761, Seattle, WA, 1994.

[6] L. Breiman. Hinging hyperplanes for regression, classification, and function approximation. *IEEE Transaction on Information Theory*, 39(3):999–1013, May 1993.

[7] D. Broomhead and D. Lowe. Multivariable functional interpolation and adaptive networks. *Complex Systems*, 2:321–355, 1988.

representation for visual learning and recognition of Murase and Nayar [21]. In particular, our $b'(x)$ is similar to their parametrized space for pose (Mukherjee and Nayar [20] used eigenfunctions to train a RBF network). A significant difference is the explicit and critical role of pointwise correspondence between images in our approach.

[8] R. Brunelli and T. Poggio. Hyberbf networks for real object recognition. In *Proceedings IJCAI*, Sydney, Australia, 1991.

[9] R. Brunelli and T. Poggio. Face recognition: Features versus templates. *IEEE Transactions on Pattern Analysis and Machine Intelligence*, 15(10):1042–1052, 1993.

[10] H. H. Bülthoff and S. Edelman. Psychophysical support for a 2-D view interpolation theory of object recognition. *Proceedings of the National Academy of Science*, 89:60–64, 1992.

[11] R. O. Duda and P. E. Hart. *Pattern Classification and Scene Analysis*. Wiley, New York, 1973.

[12] J. Friedman and W. Stuetzle. Projection pursuit regression. *Journal of the American Statistical Association*, 76(376):817–823, 1981.

[13] J. Gilbert and W. Yang. A real-time face recognition system using custom VLSI hardware. In *IEEE Workshop on Computer Architectures for Machine Perception*, pages 58–66, New Orleans, LA, December 1993.

[14] F. Girosi, M. Jones, and T. Poggio. Priors, stabilizers and basis functions: From regularization to radial, tensor and additive splines. A.I. Memo No. 1430, Artificial Intelligence Laboratory, Massachusetts Institute of Technology, 1993.

[15] F. Girosi, M. Jones, and T. Poggio. Regularization theory and neural networks architectures. *Neural Computation*, 7:219–269, 1995.

[16] A. Hurlbert and T. Poggio. Do computers need attention? *Nature*, 321:651–652, 1986.

[17] S. Librande. Example-based character drawing. Master's thesis, M.S., Media Arts and Science Section, School of Architecture and Planning, Massachusetts Institute of Technology, Cambridge, MA, September 1992.

[18] N. Logothetis and J. Pauls. Psychophysical and physiological evidence for viewer-centered object representations in the primate. *Cerebral Cortex*, 3:270–288, May/June 1995.

[19] N. Logothetis, J. Pauls, and T. Poggio. Shape Representation in the Inferior Temporal Cortex of Monkeys. *Current Biology*, 5(5):552–563, 1995.

[20] S. Mukherjee and S. K. Nayar. Automatic generation of GRBF networks for visual learning. In *Proceedings of the International Conference on Computer Vision*, pages 794–800, June 1995.

[21] H. Murase and S. K. Nayar. Learning object models from appearance. In *Proceedings AAAI*, pages 836–843, Washington, DC, 1993.

[22] P. Niyogi and F. Girosi. On the relationship between generalization error, hypothesis complexity, and sample complexity for radial basis functions. A.I. Memo 1467, Artificial Intelligence Laboratory, Massachusetts Institute of Technology, 1994.

[23] T. Poggio and R. Brunelli. A novel approach to graphics. A.I. Memo No. 1354, Artificial Intelligence Laboratory, Massachusetts Institute of Technology, 1992.

[24] T. Poggio and S. Edelman. A network that learns to recognize 3D objects. *Nature*, 343:263–266, 1990.

[25] T. Poggio and F. Girosi. Networks for approximation and learning. *Proceedings of the IEEE*, 78(9), September 1990.

[26] T. Poggio and F. Girosi. Regularization algorithms for learning that are equivalent to multilayer networks. *Science*, 247:978–982, 1990.

[27] T. Poggio and T. Vetter. Recognition and structure from one 2D model view: observations on prototypes, object classes and symmetries. A.I. Memo No. 1347, Artificial Intelligence Laboratory, Massachusetts Institute of Technology, 1992.

[28] K.-K. Sung and T. Poggio. Example-based learning for view-based human face detection. In *Proceedings from Image Understanding Workshop*, Monterey, CA, November 1994.

[29] T. Vetter, A. Hurlbert, and T. Poggio. View-based models of 3D object recognition: Invariance to imaging transformations. *Cerebral Cortex*, 5(3):261–269, May/June 1995.

[30] T. Vetter, T. Poggio, and H. Bülthoff. The importance of symmetry and virtual views in three-dimensional object recognition. *Current Biology*, 4(1):18–23, 1994.

[31] G. Wahba. *Splines Models for Observational Data*. Series in Applied Mathematics, Vol. 59, SIAM, Philadelphia, 1990.

4 LEARNING PROBABILISTIC APPEARANCE MODELS FOR OBJECT RECOGNITION

Arthur R. Pope
GE Corporate Research & Development

David G. Lowe
University of British Columbia

ABSTRACT

To recognize an object in an image one must have an internal model of how that object may appear. We describe a method for learning such models from training images. An object is modeled by a probability distribution describing the range of possible variation in the object's appearance. This distribution is organized on two levels. Large variations are handled by partitioning the training images into clusters that correspond to distinctly different views of the object. Within each cluster, smaller variations are represented by distributions that characterize the presence, position, and measurements of various discrete features of appearance. The learning process combines an incremental conceptual clustering algorithm for forming the clusters with a generalization algorithm for consolidating each cluster's training images into a single description. Recognition employs information about feature positions, numeric measurements, and relations in order to constrain and speed match searching. Preliminary experiments have been conducted with a system that implements some aspects of the method; the system can learn to recognize a single characteristic view of an object in the presence of occlusion and clutter.

1. INTRODUCTION

To recognize an object in an image one must have some expectation of how the object may appear. That expectation is based on an internal model of the object's form or appearance. We are investigating how a system might acquire such models directly from intensity images, and then use those models to recognize the objects in other images.

The following scenario illustrates how this recognition learning system would operate. One presents to the system a series of example images that depict a particular object from various viewpoints. From those examples the system develops a model of the object's appearance. This training is repeated for each of the objects the system is to recognize. When given a test image, the system can then identify and rank apparent instances of the known objects in the image.

Few object recognition systems have been designed to acquire their models directly from intensity images. Instead, most systems are simply given models in the form of manually-produced shape descriptions. During recognition, the object's shape description must be combined with a model of the image formation process in order to determine whether the object might have a particular appearance. Successful recognition depends on having good models not only of the objects, but also of the scene illumination, surface reflectance, optical projection, and the sensor. Because modeling image formation has proven difficult, most object recognition systems that follow this approach have been restricted to object models that are relatively simple and coarse.

A system that can learn its models directly from images, on the other hand, may enjoy important advantages:

- The learning system will avoid the problem of having to estimate the actual appearance of an object from some idealized model of its shape. Instead, all of the properties of the object's appearance needed for recognition will be learned directly by observation. Eliminating inaccuracies in appearance estimation should allow recognition to be accomplished more robustly.

- The learning system will acquire new models more conveniently. A new model will be defined not by measuring and encoding its shape, as with traditional object recognition systems, but by merely displaying the object to the system in various poses.

- The learning system could endow a robot with the ability to learn objects as they are encountered for later recognition. This ability would be important in a dynamic, unknown environment.

The difficulty of the recognition learning problem is largely due to the fact that an object's appearance has a large range of variation. It varies with changes in camera position and lighting and, if the object is flexible, with changes in shape. Further variation is due to noise and to differences among individual instances of the same type of object. Accommodating this variation is a central problem in the design of a recognition learning system. The scheme used to describe image content must be stable so that small changes in an appearance induce only small changes in its description. The scheme used to model an object's appearance must describe just what variations are possible. The learning procedure must generalize enough to overcome insignificant variation, but not so much as to confuse dissimilar objects. And the procedure used to identify modeled objects in images must tolerate the likely range of mismatch between model and image.

In investigating the recognition learning problem we have concentrated on one particular version of it: learning to recognize 3-D objects in 2-D intensity images. Objects are recognized solely by the intensity edges they exhibit (although nothing about the approach precludes an extension to other properties, such as color and texture). As for the objects themselves, they may be entirely rigid, possess a small number of articulations, or be somewhat flexible. The system is able to learn to recognize a class of similar objects, accommodating the variation among objects just as it accommodates the variation among images of a single object.

Our method models an object by a probability distribution that describes the range of possible variation in the object's appearance. This probability distribution is organized on two levels. Large variations are handled by partitioning the training images into clusters that correspond to distinctly different views or configurations of the object. Within each cluster, smaller variations are represented by probability distributions characterizing various appearance features. For each feature we represent the probability of detecting that feature in various positions with respect to the overall object, and the probability of the feature having various values of feature-specific, numeric measurements. A rich, partially-redundant, and extensible repertoire of features is used to describe appearance.

The learning method combines an incremental conceptual clustering algorithm for forming the clusters with a generalization algorithm for consolidating each cluster's training images into a single description. Recognition, which involves matching the features of a training image with those of a cluster's description, can employ information about feature positions, numeric measurements, and relations in order to constrain and speed the search for a match. Preliminary experiments have been conducted with a system that implements some aspects of the method; that system can learn to recognize a single view of an object among other occluding and distracting objects.

We have just described the problem being considered, its significance, the source of its difficulty, and the outline of a solution method. The next section begins a detailed description of the method by discussing the representations used for images and models. The process of finding a match between a model and an image is guided by a match quality measure, which is the subject of section 3. This measure supports both the matching procedure described in section 4, and the procedure for learning models described in section 5. Section 6 presents experimental results from a system implemented to test the approach. Section 7 discusses relevant work by others on this and similar problems, and section 8 summarizes the chapter's main ideas. Sections flagged by † contain technical details that can be safely skipped on a first reading. More information may be found in other recent publications [18, 19, 20].

2. Representation schemes

2.1. Image representation

We represent an image in terms of discrete properties called *features*. Each feature has a particular type, a location within the image, and a vector of numeric *attributes* that further characterize it. A feature may, for example, be a segment of intensity edge, a particular arrangement of such segments, or a region of uniform texture or color. Low-level features may be found as responses to feature detectors, such as edge or corner detectors; other, higher-level features may be found by grouping or abstracting the low-level ones. Numerous features of various types describe a typical image.

What attributes a feature has depends on its type. A junction of two circular arcs, for example, may have one attribute for the junction's angle, and another for the ratio of the two arcs' radii. Attributes are expressed so that they are invariant with respect to translation, rotation, and scaling of the feature within the image (using, for example, scale-normalized measures [23]).

The repertoire of feature types must be sufficient to provide a rich description of any relevant image. A degree of redundancy is desirable, for it helps to ensure the completeness of the representation and it contributes stability. Good features are those that can be detected reliably, and are relatively invariant with respect to modest changes in viewpoint or lighting. For efficiency in recognition, it is useful to have some highly-selective features that usually occur only in the presence of certain objects. In recognizing manufactured objects, for example, features denoting various geometric arrangements of intensity edges may serve this role well. Some more commonplace features, such as simple line and curve segments, should supplement the highly-selective ones so that the overall repertoire can still describe a wide variety of objects, at least at a basic level. Of course, distinctions among objects can only be made if the repertoire includes features that express those distinctions.

Apart from these requirements, the recognition learning method is not particular about what features are used or what their attributes are. As any feature is bound to be unreliable in certain situations, the method attempts to compensate for feature shortcomings by learning how reliable various features are for recognizing each object.

The collection of features found in an image is represented by an *image graph*. Graph nodes represent features; directed arcs represent grouping and abstraction relations among them. Formally, an image graph G is denoted by a tuple $\langle F, R \rangle$, where F is a set of image features and R is a relation over elements of F. An image feature $f_k \in F$ is a tuple $\langle t_k, \mathbf{a}_k, \mathbf{b}_k, \mathbf{C}_k \rangle$, where t_k is the feature's type, $\mathbf{a}_k$ is a vector of attributes describing the feature, $\mathbf{b}_k$ is its measured position, and $\mathbf{C}_k$ is a covariance matrix describing the uncertainty in that position. The domain of a feature's attribute vector depends on the feature's type. Section 2.3, below, describes how positions such as $\mathbf{b}_k$ are represented. Finally, an element of R is a tuple $\langle k, l_1, \ldots, l_m \rangle$, indicating that image feature k was found by grouping or abstracting image features l_1 through l_m.

2.2. MODEL REPRESENTATION

An object model is organized on two levels so that it can describe the object's range of appearance both fully and accurately. Significant variations in appearance are handled by subdividing the model into a set of characteristic views, each independent of the others. Smaller variations are handled within each characteristic view by allowing the view to represent a probability distribution over a range of similar image graphs.

Because this explicitly represents how an object appears from various, discrete viewpoints, it is called a *viewer-centered*, or *multiple-view*, representation. To learn a multiple-view model, it is not necessary to recover the object's 3-D structure. Another common approach is the *object-centered* representation, which instead explicitly represents the 3-D geometry of the object. To learn an object-centered model, however, one has to recover the 3-D location of each feature. Recovery is difficult because the viewpoint of each training image is unknown, there is uncertainty in the measurement of each feature's image location, and there may be errors in matching features among images.

In our method, each characteristic view describes a range of possible appearances by defining a joint probability distribution over image graphs. Because the space of image graphs is enormous, however, it is not practical to represent or learn this distribution in its most general form. Instead, the joint distribution is approximated by treating its component features as though they were independent. This approximation allows the joint distribution to be decomposed into a product of marginal distributions, thus greatly simplifying the representation, matching, and learning of models.

One consequence of the simplification is that statistical dependence (association or covariance) among model features cannot be accurately represented within a single characteristic view. An extreme example of such dependence is an object with two subsets of features such that only one subset appears in any one image. Because of the simplification, this object with its strongly covariant features would be poorly represented by a single characteristic view. However, where one characteristic view cannot capture an important statistical dependence, multiple views can. In this example, two characteristic views, each containing one of the two subsets of features, could represent perfectly the statistical dependence among features.

By using a large enough set of characteristic views we can model any object as accurately as we might wish. For the sake of efficiency, however, we would prefer to use relatively few views and let each represent a moderate range of possible appearances. One challenge for our model learning method is to strike an appropriate balance between the number of characteristic views used and the accuracy of those views over their respective ranges. This issue will be revisited when we discuss the model learning procedure in section 5.

A single characteristic view is described by a *model graph*. Like an image graph, a model graph has nodes that represent features and arcs that represent composition and abstraction relations among features. Each node records the information needed to estimate three probabilities:

- *The probability of observing this feature in an image depicting the characteristic view of the object.* The node records the number of times the feature has been identified in training images. A count is also kept of the training images used to learn the overall model graph. The probability is estimated from these two numbers as described in section 3.1.

- *Given that this feature is observed, the probability of it having particular attribute values.* This is characterized by a probability distribution over vectors of attribute values. Little can be assumed about the form of this distribution because it may depend on many factors: the type of feature, how its attributes are measured, possible deformations of the object, and various sources of measurement uncertainty. Thus we use a non-parametric density estimator that makes relatively few assumptions. To support this estimator, which is described in section 3.3, the model graph node records sample attribute vectors acquired from training images.

- *Given that this feature is observed, the probability of it having a particular position.* This is characterized by a probability distribution over feature positions. We approximate this distribution as Gaussian to allow use of an efficient matching procedure based on least-squares estimation. The parameters of the distribution are estimated from sample feature positions acquired from training images.

Formally, a model graph $\bar{G}$ is denoted by a tuple $\langle \bar{F}, \bar{R}, \bar{m} \rangle$, where $\bar{F}$ is a set of model features, $\bar{R}$ is a relation over elements of $\bar{F}$, and $\bar{m}$ is the number of training images used to produce $\bar{G}$. A model feature $f_j \in \bar{F}$ is a tuple $\langle t_j, m_j, A_j, B_j \rangle$, where t_j is the feature's type, m_j is the number of training images in which the feature was observed, and A_j and B_j are sequences of attribute vectors and positions drawn from those training images. Finally, an element of $\bar{R}$ is a tuple $\langle j, l_1, \ldots, l_m \rangle$, indicating that model feature j is a grouping or abstraction of model features l_1 through l_m.

2.3. COORDINATE SYSTEMS

A feature's position is denoted by a location, orientation, and scale, expressed in terms of a 2-D, Cartesian coordinate system. Image features are located in an *image coordinate system* identified with pixel rows and columns. Model features are located in a *model coordinate system* shared by all features within a model graph. The absolute positions of these coordinate systems are not important as they are used only to measure features' relative positions.

Two different schemes are used to describe a feature's position in either coordinate system:

$xy\theta s$ The feature's location is specified by $[x\ y]$, its orientation by θ, and its scale by s.

$xyuv$ The feature's location is specified by $[x\ y]$, and its orientation and scale are represented by the orientation and length of the 2-D vector $[u\ v]$.

We will prefer the $xy\theta s$ scheme for measuring feature positions, and the $xyuv$ scheme for estimating viewpoint in the course of matching a model with an image. They are related by $\theta = tan^{-1}(v/u)$ and $s = \sqrt{u^2 + v^2}$. Where it is not otherwise clear we will indicate schemes using the superscripts $^{xy\theta s}$ and ^{xyuv}.

Part of the task of matching a model with an image is to determine a *viewpoint transformation* that brings the image and model features into close correspondence. In our case, this viewpoint transformation is a 2-D similarity transformation. The $xyuv$ scheme allows such a transformation to be expressed as a linear operation with the advantage that it can then be estimated from a set of feature pairings by solving a system of linear equations.[1]

We take the viewpoint transformation, T, to be from image to model coordinates, and use it to transform the position of an image feature before comparing it with that of a model feature. The result of applying T to the position $\mathbf{b}_k$ is denoted $T(\mathbf{b}_k)$.

A transformation consisting of a rotation by θ_t, a scaling by s_t, and a translation by $[x_t\ y_t]$, in that order, can be expressed in two ways as a matrix operation. We will have occasion to use both. In one case, a matrix $\mathbf{A}_k$ represents the position $\mathbf{b}_k = [x_k\ y_k\ u_k\ v_k]$ being transformed:

$$\mathbf{b}'_k = \begin{bmatrix} x'_k \\ y'_k \\ u'_k \\ v'_k \end{bmatrix} = \begin{bmatrix} 1 & 0 & x_k & -y_k \\ 0 & 1 & y_k & x_k \\ 0 & 0 & u_k & -v_k \\ 0 & 0 & v_k & u_k \end{bmatrix} \begin{bmatrix} x_t \\ y_t \\ u_t \\ v_t \end{bmatrix} = \mathbf{A}_k \mathbf{t}. \tag{1}$$

In the other case, a matrix $\mathbf{A}_t$ represents the rotation and scaling components of the transformation:

$$\mathbf{b}'_k = \begin{bmatrix} x'_k \\ y'_k \\ u'_k \\ v'_k \end{bmatrix} = \begin{bmatrix} u_t & -v_t & 0 & 0 \\ v_t & u_t & 0 & 0 \\ 0 & 0 & u_t & -v_t \\ 0 & 0 & v_t & u_t \end{bmatrix} \begin{bmatrix} x_k \\ y_k \\ u_k \\ v_k \end{bmatrix} + \begin{bmatrix} x_t \\ y_t \\ 0 \\ 0 \end{bmatrix} = \mathbf{A}_t \mathbf{b}_k + \mathbf{x}_t. \tag{2}$$

These linear formulations allow a transformation to be estimated easily from a set of feature pairings. Given a model feature at $\mathbf{b}_j$ and an image feature at

---

[1] Ayache and Faugeras [1], among others, have also used this formulation to express the transformation as a linear operation.

$\mathbf{b}_k$, the transformation aligning the two features can be obtained as the solution to the system of linear equations $\mathbf{b}_j = T(\mathbf{b}_k)$. With additional feature pairings, the problem of estimating the transformation becomes over-constrained; then the solution that is optimal in the least-squares sense can be found by least-squares estimation, as described in section 4.2.

3. MATCH QUALITY MEASURE

Recognition requires finding a consistent set of pairings between some model features and some image features, plus a viewpoint transformation that brings the paired features into close correspondence. Together, the pairings and transformation are called a *match*. The pairings will often be incomplete, with some image features not explained by the model (perhaps there are other objects in the scene) and some model features not found in the image (perhaps due to shadows or occlusion). Nevertheless, the desired match should be a good one that jointly maximizes both the number of features paired and the resemblance between paired features. We use a *match quality measure* to evaluate these qualities.

The match quality measure considers what features are paired, how significant those features are, how similar their attribute values are, and how well their positions correspond. Each factor is evaluated according to past matching experience as recorded by the model. The factors are combined using Bayesian theory to estimate the probability that a particular match represents a true occurrence of the object in the image.

A set of pairings is represented by the tuple $E = \langle e_1, e_2, \ldots \rangle$, where $e_j = k$ if model feature j is paired with image feature k, and $e_j = \perp$ if it is not paired. The hypothesis that the object is present in the image is denoted by H. Match quality is associated with the probability that this hypothesis is correct given a set of pairings and a viewpoint transformation. Bayes theorem allows us to write this probability as:

$$P(H \mid E, T) = \frac{P(E \mid T, H) \, P(T \mid H)}{P(E \wedge T)} P(H). \qquad (3)$$

There is no practical way to represent the high-dimensional, joint probability distributions $P(E \mid T, H)$ and $P(E \wedge T)$ in their most general form. Instead, we approximate them using the feature independence simplification discussed previously in section 2.2. This reduces equation 3 to a product of marginal probability distributions.

$$P(H \mid E, T) \approx \prod_j \frac{P(e_j \mid T, H) \, P(T \mid H)}{P(e_j)} \frac{P(T \mid H)}{P(T)} P(H). \qquad (4)$$

The approximation is a perfect one when two independence properties hold:

(a) $\{e_i\}$ is collectively independent given knowledge of T and H, and

(b) $\{e_i, T\}$ is collectively independent in the absence of any knowledge of H.

In practice we can expect these properties to hold at least somewhat. Given that an object is present at a particular pose, features detected at widely separate locations on the object will be independently affected by occlusion and noise; these features satisfy property (a). And in a random scene cluttered with unknown objects, even nearby features may be largely independent because they could come from any of numerous objects; these features satisfy property (b).

On the other hand, the independence properties fail to the extent that there is redundancy among features. For example, a feature representing a perceptually-significant grouping is not independent of the features it groups; in this case, equation 4 may overstate the significance of pairing these features because it separately counts both the individual features and the feature that groups them. With redundancy uniformly present among all model graphs, however, the resulting bias should have little effect on the outcome of any particular matching problem. Having adopted the hypothesis that this is so, we use equation 4 as the basis for our match quality measure.

The measure is defined using log-probabilities to simplify calculations. Moreover, it is assumed that all positions of a modeled object within an image are equally likely, and thus $P(T \mid H) = P(T)$. With these simplifications the match quality measure becomes

$$g(E, T) = \log P(H) + \sum_j \log P(e_j \mid T, H) - \sum_j \log P(e_j). \qquad (5)$$

$P(H)$ is the prior probability that the object, as modeled, is present in an image; it can be estimated from the proportion of training images that matched the model and were used to create it. Estimates of the conditional and prior probabilities of individual feature pairings, $P(e_j \mid T, H)$ and $P(e_j)$, will be described in the next two sections. We will use the following notation for specific random events within the universe of matching outcomes:

$\tilde{e}_j = k$ model feature j is paired with image feature k

$\tilde{e}_j = \perp$ model feature j is paired with nothing

$\tilde{\mathbf{a}}_j = \mathbf{a}$ model feature j is paired with a feature whose attributes are $\mathbf{a}$

$\tilde{\mathbf{b}}_j = \mathbf{b}$ model feature j is paired with a feature at position $\mathbf{b}$

3.1. CONDITIONAL PROBABILITY OF A FEATURE PAIRING

There are two cases to consider in estimating $P(e_j \mid T, H)$, the conditional probability of a pairing involving model feature j.

1. When j is not paired, this probability is estimated by considering how often j failed to be paired with an image feature during training. We use a Bayesian

estimator with a uniform prior, and the $\bar{m}$ and m_j statistics recorded by the model:

$$\mathrm{P}(\tilde{e}_j = \perp \mid T, H) = 1 - \mathrm{P}(\tilde{e}_j \neq \perp \mid T, H) \approx 1 - \frac{m_j + 1}{\bar{m} + 2}. \tag{6}$$

2. When j is paired with image feature k, this probability is estimated by considering how often j was paired with image features during training, and how the attributes and position of k compare with those of the training features:

$$
\begin{aligned}
\mathrm{P}(\tilde{e}_j = k \mid T, H) &= \mathrm{P}(\tilde{e}_j \neq \perp \wedge \tilde{\mathbf{a}}_j = \mathbf{a}_k \wedge \tilde{\mathbf{b}}_j = T(\mathbf{b}_k) \mid T, H) \\
&\approx \mathrm{P}(\tilde{e}_j \neq \perp \mid T, H)\, \mathrm{P}(\tilde{\mathbf{a}}_j = \mathbf{a}_k \mid \tilde{e}_j \neq \perp, H) \\
&\quad \mathrm{P}(\tilde{\mathbf{b}}_j = T(\mathbf{b}_k) \mid \tilde{e}_j \neq \perp, T, H).
\end{aligned} \tag{7}
$$

$\mathrm{P}(\tilde{e}_j \neq \perp \mid \ldots)$ is estimated as shown in equation 6. $\mathrm{P}(\tilde{\mathbf{a}}_j = \mathbf{a}_k \mid \ldots)$ is estimated using the series of attribute vectors A_j recorded with model feature j, and a non-parametric density estimator described in section 3.3. $\mathrm{P}(\tilde{\mathbf{b}}_j = T(\mathbf{b}_k) \mid \ldots)$, the probability that model feature j is paired with an image feature at position $\mathbf{b}_k$ under viewpoint transformation T, is estimated as described in section 3.4, below.[2]

3.2. PRIOR PROBABILITY OF A FEATURE PAIRING

Estimates of the prior probabilities, $\mathrm{P}(e_j)$, are based on measurements of a large collection of images typical of those in which the object will be sought. This *milieu collection* is used to estimate "background" probability distributions that characterize features found independently of whether any particular object is present. In other words, these distributions describe what can be expected in the absence of any knowledge of H or T. By an analysis similar to that underlying estimates of the conditional probabilities, we obtain estimates for two cases of e_j.

1. The probability of j remaining unpaired regardless of H and T is

$$\mathrm{P}(\tilde{e}_j = \perp) = 1 - \mathrm{P}(\tilde{e}_j \neq \perp).$$

The latter term is estimated from the frequency with which features of j's type, t_j, occur in the milieu collection.

---

[2] For simplicity, our notation does not distinguish between probability mass and probability density. $\mathrm{P}(\tilde{e}_j)$ is a mass because $\tilde{e}_j$ assumes discrete values, whereas $\mathrm{P}(\tilde{\mathbf{a}}_j)$ and $\mathrm{P}(\tilde{\mathbf{b}}_j)$ are densities because $\tilde{\mathbf{a}}_j$ and $\tilde{\mathbf{b}}_j$ are continuous. But since equation 4 divides each conditional probability mass by a prior probability mass, and each conditional probability density by a prior probability density, here we can safely neglect the distinction.

2. The probability of j being paired with k regardless of H and T is

$$
\begin{aligned}
\mathrm{P}(\tilde{e}_j = k) &= \mathrm{P}(\tilde{e}_j \neq \perp \wedge \tilde{\mathbf{a}}_j = \mathbf{a}_k \wedge \tilde{\mathbf{b}}_j = T(\mathbf{b}_k)) \\
&\approx \mathrm{P}(\tilde{e}_j \neq \perp)\, \mathrm{P}(\tilde{\mathbf{a}}_j = \mathbf{a}_k \mid \tilde{e}_j \neq \perp) \\
&\qquad \mathrm{P}(\tilde{\mathbf{b}}_j = T(\mathbf{b}_k) \mid \tilde{e}_j \neq \perp).
\end{aligned}
\tag{8}
$$

$\mathrm{P}(\tilde{\mathbf{a}}_j = \mathbf{a}_k \mid \ldots)$ is estimated using samples of attribute vectors drawn from the milieu collection, and the density estimator described in section 3.3. $\mathrm{P}(\tilde{\mathbf{b}}_j = T(\mathbf{b}_k) \mid \ldots)$ is a constant estimated by assuming a uniform distribution of features throughout a bounded region of model coordinate space.

3.3. PROBABILITY DISTRIBUTION OVER FEATURE ATTRIBUTES †

One component of the match quality measure is the probability that a feature may have a particular attribute vector. To help us estimate this probability, we have samples of attribute vectors that have been acquired by observing the feature in training images. The estimation problem is therefore of the following form: given a sequence of d-dimensional observation vectors $\{\mathbf{x}_i : 1 \leq i \leq n\}$ drawn at random from an unknown distribution, estimate the probability that another vector drawn from that same distribution would have the value $\mathbf{x}$.

This could be solved by assuming that the distribution has some parameterized form (e.g., normal), and then estimating its parameters from the observations $\mathbf{x}_i$. However, the attribute vector distributions could be complex as they depend not only on sensor noise and measurement errors, but also on systematic variations in object shape, lighting, and pose. Hence we use a non-parametric estimation method [28]. In its simplest, form, this method estimates probability density by summing contributions from a series of overlapping kernels. The density at $\mathbf{x}$ is given by

$$
\hat{f}(\mathbf{x}) = \frac{1}{n h^d} \sum_i K\left(\frac{\mathbf{x} - \mathbf{x}_i}{h} \right),
\tag{9}
$$

where h is a constant smoothing factor, and K is a kernel function. We use the Epanechnikov kernel because it has finite support and can be computed quickly. Its definition is

$$
K(\mathbf{x}) = \begin{cases} \frac{1}{2} c_d^{-1}(d+2)(1 - \mathbf{x}^{\mathrm{T}}\mathbf{x}) & \text{if } \mathbf{x}^{\mathrm{T}}\mathbf{x} < 1 \\ 0 & \text{otherwise} \end{cases}
\tag{10}
$$

where c_d is the volume of a d-dimensional sphere of unit radius. The smoothing factor h appearing in equation 9 strikes a balance between the smoothness of the estimated distribution and its fidelity to the observations $\mathbf{x}_i$.

We can adjust h using a locally-adaptive method: with $\hat{f}$ as a first density estimator, we create a second estimator, $\hat{f}_a$, whose smoothing factor varies according to the first estimator's density estimate:

$$
\hat{f}_a(\mathbf{x}) = \frac{1}{n h^d} \sum_i \lambda_i^{-d} K\left(\frac{\mathbf{x} - \mathbf{x}_i}{h \lambda_i} \right),
\tag{11}
$$

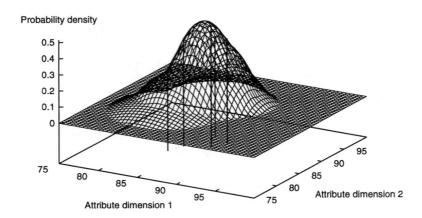

Figure 1: *Example of a locally-adaptive probability density estimate for attribute vectors. The spikes denote the samples from which the density estimate was computed.*

$$\text{where } \lambda_i = \left(\frac{\hat{f}(\mathbf{x}_i)}{\nu}\right)^{-\frac{1}{2}} \text{ and } \nu = \left(\prod_i \hat{f}(\mathbf{x}_i)\right)^{\frac{1}{n}}.$$

The various λ_i incorporate the first density estimates at the points $\mathbf{x}_i$, and ν is a normalizing factor. This adaptive estimator smoothes more in low-density regions than in high-density ones. Thus a sparse outlier is thoroughly smoothed while a central peak is accurately represented in the estimate (see figure 1).

3.4. PROBABILITY DISTRIBUTION OVER FEATURE POSITIONS †

Another component of the match quality measure is the probability that a model feature is paired with an image feature given the positions of the two features and a viewpoint transformation that somewhat aligns them. This position- and transformation-dependent portion of the match quality measure is represented by $\mathrm{P}(\tilde{\mathbf{b}}_j = T(\mathbf{b}_k) \mid \tilde{e}_j \neq \perp, T, H)$ in equation 7. To estimate it, we use the viewpoint transformation to map the image feature's position into model coordinates, where we compare it with the model feature's position (see figure 2). The positions and transformation are characterized by Gaussian probability density functions (pdfs), allowing the comparison to take into account the uncertainty in each.

Image feature k's position is conveniently characterized by a Gaussian pdf in $xy\theta s$ image coordinates. Its mean is the feature's position, $\mathbf{b}_k^{xy\theta s}$, as measured in the image. However, because our system's feature detectors and grouping processes do not supply uncertainty estimates for individual features, we define

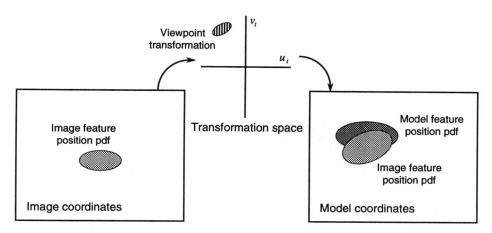

Figure 2: *An image feature's position is transformed from image coordinates (left) to model coordinates (right) according to an estimate of the viewpoint transformation (center). A model feature's position is estimated in model coordinates (right). Uncertainty in the positions and the transformation are characterized by Gaussian distributions. Overlap of the two distributions in model coordinates corresponds to the probability that the two features match given the viewpoint transformation and their respective positions.*

the covariance matrix for this pdf using system parameters:

$$\mathbf{C}_k^{xy\theta s} = \begin{bmatrix} \sigma_l^2 & 0 & 0 & 0 \\ 0 & \sigma_l^2 & 0 & 0 \\ 0 & 0 & (\frac{\sigma_\theta}{s_k})^2 & 0 \\ 0 & 0 & 0 & \sigma_s^2 \end{bmatrix}. \tag{12}$$

The parameters σ_l, σ_θ, and σ_s are our estimates of the standard deviations in measurements of location, orientation, and scale. The orientation variance includes a factor based on the feature scale, s_k, because the orientation of a large feature can usually be measured more accurately than that of a small one.

This Gaussian pdf is then re-expressed in $xyuv$ image coordinates so that the viewpoint transformation can be applied as a linear operation. Unfortunately, a pdf that is Gaussian in $xy\theta s$ coordinates is not necessarily Gaussian in $xyuv$ coordinates. Nevertheless, in this case a good approximating Gaussian can be obtained in $xyuv$ coordinates because the θ and s variances are small. The approximation places the $xyuv$ mean at the same position as the $xy\theta s$ mean, and aligns the Gaussian envelope radially, away from the $[u\,v]$ origin (see figure 3). Its mean and covariance matrix are

$$\mathbf{b}_k^{xyuv} = [x_k \ \ y_k \ \ s_k \cos\theta_k \ \ s_k \sin\theta_k] \tag{13}$$

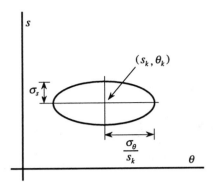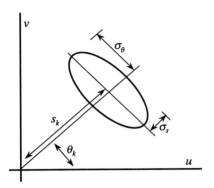

Figure 3: *The Gaussian distribution of an image feature's position in $xy\theta s$ coordinates (left) is approximated by a Gaussian distribution in $xyuv$ coordinates (right), with the parameters of the approximating distribution determined as shown.*

$$\text{and } \mathbf{C}_k^{xyuv} = \mathbf{R} \begin{bmatrix} \sigma_l^2 & 0 & 0 & 0 \\ 0 & \sigma_l^2 & 0 & 0 \\ 0 & 0 & \sigma_s^2 & 0 \\ 0 & 0 & 0 & \sigma_\theta^2 \end{bmatrix} \mathbf{R}^{\mathrm{T}}, \tag{14}$$

$$\text{where } \mathbf{R} = \begin{bmatrix} 1 & 0 & 0 & 0 \\ 0 & 1 & 0 & 0 \\ 0 & 0 & \cos\theta_k & -\sin\theta_k \\ 0 & 0 & \sin\theta_k & \cos\theta_k \end{bmatrix}.$$

The viewpoint transformation is characterized by a Gaussian pdf over $[x_t y_t u_t v_t]$ vectors with mean $\mathbf{t}$ and covariance $\mathbf{C}_t$. (In the course of matching a model with an image, $\mathbf{t}$ and $\mathbf{C}_t$ are estimated as described in section 4.2, below.) We transform the image feature's position from $xyuv$ image coordinates to $xyuv$ model coordinates using the viewpoint transformation. If we would disregard the uncertainty in the transformation estimate, we would obtain a Gaussian pdf in model coordinates with mean $\mathbf{A}_k\mathbf{t}$ and covariance $\mathbf{A}_t\mathbf{C}_k\mathbf{A}_t^{\mathrm{T}}$. On the other hand, disregarding the uncertainty in the image feature position produces a Gaussian pdf in model coordinates with mean $\mathbf{A}_k\mathbf{t}$ and covariance $\mathbf{A}_k\mathbf{C}_t\mathbf{A}_k^{\mathrm{T}}$. With Gaussian uncertainty in both the image feature position and the transformation, however, the pdf in model coordinates cannot be characterized as Gaussian. At best we can approximate it as Gaussian, which we do with a mean and covariance given in $xyuv$ coordinates by

$$\mathbf{b}_{kt} = \mathbf{A}_k\mathbf{t} \tag{15}$$
$$\text{and } \mathbf{C}_{kt} \approx \mathbf{A}_t\mathbf{C}_k\mathbf{A}_t^{\mathrm{T}} + \mathbf{A}_k\mathbf{C}_t\mathbf{A}_k^{\mathrm{T}}. \tag{16}$$

The position of model feature j is also characterized by a Gaussian pdf in $xyuv$ model coordinates. Its mean $\mathbf{b}_j$ and covariance $\mathbf{C}_j$ are estimated from the series of position vectors B_j recorded by the model.[3]

We can now estimate the probability that j is paired with k according to their position pdfs in $xyuv$ model coordinates. The estimate is obtained by integrating over all positions $\mathbf{r}$ the probability that both the image feature is at $\mathbf{r}$ and the model feature matches something at $\mathbf{r}$:

$$P(\tilde{\mathbf{b}}_j = T(\mathbf{b}_k) \mid \tilde{e}_j \neq \perp, T, H) \approx \int_{\mathbf{r}} P(\tilde{\mathbf{r}}_j = \mathbf{r}) \, P(\tilde{\mathbf{r}}_{kt} = \mathbf{r}) \, d\mathbf{r}. \qquad (17)$$

Here $\mathbf{r}$ ranges over $xyuv$ model coordinates while $\tilde{\mathbf{r}}_j$ and $\tilde{\mathbf{r}}_{kt}$ are random variables drawn from the Gaussian distributions $N(\mathbf{b}_j, \mathbf{C}_j)$ and $N(\mathbf{b}_{kt}, \mathbf{C}_{kt})$. It would be costly to evaluate this integral by sampling at various $\mathbf{r}$. Fortunately, however, the integral can be rewritten as a Gaussian in $\mathbf{b}_j - \mathbf{b}_{kt}$, as can be seen from the fact that it is part of a convolution of two Gaussians. Thus it is equivalent to

$$P(\tilde{\mathbf{b}}_j = T(\mathbf{b}_k) \mid \tilde{e}_j \neq \perp, T, H) \approx G(\mathbf{b}_j - \mathbf{b}_{kt}, \mathbf{C}_j + \mathbf{C}_{kt}) \qquad (18)$$

where $G(\mathbf{x}, \mathbf{C})$ is a Gaussian with zero mean and covariance $\mathbf{C}$. In this form, the desired probability estimate is easily computed.

4. MATCHING PROCEDURE

Both recognition and learning require that we find a match between a model graph and an image graph—one that maximizes the match quality measure defined in section 3. It does not seem possible to find an optimal match through anything less than exhaustive search. In practice, however, good matches can be found quickly by *iterative alignment* [1, 13, 15]. This process hypothesizes some initial pairings between model and image features, uses those pairings to estimate the viewpoint transformation, uses the transformation estimate to evaluate and choose additional pairings, refines the transformation estimate using the additional pairings, and so on until as many features a possible have been matched.

In our version of the iterative alignment method, we explicitly represent the uncertainty in the position of each feature and the resulting uncertainty in the transformation estimate. Thus features that are well-localized contribute most to the transformation estimate, and those whose positions vary most are sought over the largest image neighborhoods. This version of iterative alignment is called *probabilistic alignment* to emphasize its basis in probability theory. It uses feature uncertainty information that has been acquired from training images and recorded in the model.

---

[3] Two practical considerations enter into the estimation of $\mathbf{C}_j$. First, when B_j contains too few samples for a reliable estimate of $\mathbf{C}_j$, the estimate that B_j yields is blended with another determined by system parameters. Second, minimum variances are imposed on $\mathbf{C}_j$ in case some dimension of B_j has zero variance.

4.1. PROBABILISTIC ALIGNMENT

To choose the initial pairings, possible pairings of higher-level features are rated according to the contribution each would make to the match quality measure. The pairing $\langle j, k \rangle$ receives the rating

$$g_j(k) = \max_T \log \mathrm{P}(\tilde{e}_j = k \mid T, H) - \log \mathrm{P}(\tilde{e}_j = k). \tag{19}$$

This rating favors pairings in which the model feature has a high likelihood of matching, the two features have similar attribute values, and the resulting transformation estimate's variance would be small. Moreover, because the component of $\mathrm{P}(\tilde{e}_j = k \mid T, H)$ that depends on T is Gaussian, its maximum over T can be computed readily.

A search is begun from each of the several highest-ranked pairings. It starts by estimating a viewpoint transformation from the initial pairing, and proceeds by repeatedly identifying additional consistent pairings, adopting the best pairings, and using those to update the transformation estimate. (A method of computing the viewpoint transformation is described in section 4.2, below.) During this search, possible pairings are rated according to the contribution each would make to the match quality measure. Provided it is consistent with pairings adopted so far, the pairing $\langle j, k \rangle$ receives the rating

$$g_j(k; T) = \log \mathrm{P}(\tilde{e}_j = k \mid T, H) - \log \mathrm{P}(\tilde{e}_j = k) \tag{20}$$

This rating considers the same criteria as the initial ratings (equation 19), while also favoring pairings whose feature positions correspond closely according to the transformation estimate.

For efficiency, a priority queue is used to manage pairing choices during a search. Each pairing is placed on the queue as it is rated so that, once all pairings have been evaluated, the queue contains a few dozen of the best pairings. Queued pairings that conflict are considered ambiguous; they are downgraded so that they will be postponed in favor of less ambiguous pairings. Finally, the highest-ranked pairings are adopted and used to update the transformation estimate. Backtracking is performed when ambiguity forces a choice among conflicting pairings, and a search branch is terminated when no additional pairings can be identified to improve the match quality measure.

From several starting hypotheses and the various search branches that result from backtracking, we obtain a number of consistent matches. As they are found only the best is retained, and its match quality measure provides a threshold for pruning subsequent search branches.

Note that the match quality measure provides an estimate of the (logarithm of the) probability that the match represents a true instance of the object in the image. One way to judge recognition, then, is to require that this probability exceeds some specified threshold. Setting the threshold to the ratio of costs of Type II and Type I decision errors produces recognition decisions that minimize the expected error cost.

4.2. ESTIMATING THE VIEWPOINT TRANSFORMATION †

The matching procedure requires that we estimate a viewpoint transformation from one or more feature pairings, with the desired estimate being that which maximizes the match quality measure for the given pairings. Fortunately, this is a linear, least-squares estimation problem for which good algorithms exist.

The estimation problem is formulated as follows. Each pairing $\langle j, k \rangle$ of model and image features is related by the transformation $\mathbf{t}$ and a residual error $\tilde{\mathbf{e}}$:

$$\mathbf{A}_k \, \mathbf{t} = \mathbf{b}_j + \tilde{\mathbf{e}}. \tag{21}$$

Here, $\mathbf{A}_k$ is the matrix representation of image feature k's mean position (see equation 1), $\mathbf{t}$ is the transformation estimate vector $[x_t\, y_t\, u_t\, v_t]$, and $\mathbf{b}_j$ is the vector representation of model feature j's mean position. The residual $\tilde{\mathbf{e}}$ is assumed to have a covariance matrix, $\mathbf{C}_j$, equal to that of the series of position vectors, B_j, recorded by the model. We can rewrite this relation so that the residual has unit variance by dividing both sides by the upper triangular square root of $\mathbf{C}_j$ (a process called *whitening*).

$$\mathbf{U}_j^{-1} \, \mathbf{A}_k \, \mathbf{t} = \mathbf{U}_j^{-1} \, \mathbf{b}_j + \tilde{\mathbf{e}}', \text{ where } \mathbf{C}_j = \mathbf{U}_j \mathbf{U}_j^{\mathsf{T}} \text{ and } \tilde{\mathbf{e}}' \sim \mathrm{N}(\mathbf{0}, \mathbf{I}). \tag{22}$$

A series of feature pairings gives us a series of such relations. From them, a linear, least-squares estimator determines both the transformation $\mathbf{t}$ that minimizes the sum of the squares of the residual errors, and its covariance $\mathbf{C}_t$.

During a match search, feature pairings are adopted sequentially. We need to refine the transformation estimate with each new pairing or group of pairings adopted so that an improved estimate can then be used to identify additional pairings. Thus a recursive estimator is used.

The square root information filter (SRIF) [4] is a recursive estimator well suited for this problem. Compared to the conventional Kalman filter it is numerically more stable and faster for batched measurements; it also has the nice property of computing the total residual error as a side effect. As its name implies, the SRIF works by updating the square root of the information matrix, which is the inverse of the estimate's covariance matrix. The initial square root $\mathbf{R}_1$ and state vector $\mathbf{z}_1$ are obtained from the first pairing $\langle j, k \rangle$ of model and image features:

$$\mathbf{R}_1 = \mathbf{U}_j^{-1} \, \mathbf{A}_k \text{ and } \mathbf{z}_1 = \mathbf{U}_j^{-1} \, \mathbf{b}_j. \tag{23}$$

Then, with each subsequent pairing $\langle j, k \rangle$, the estimate is updated by triangularizing a matrix composed of the previous estimate and data from the new pairing:

$$\begin{bmatrix} \mathbf{R}_{i-1} & \mathbf{z}_{i-1} \\ \mathbf{U}_j^{-1}\mathbf{A}_k & \mathbf{U}_j^{-1}\mathbf{b}_j \end{bmatrix} \xrightarrow{\triangle} \begin{bmatrix} \mathbf{R}_i & \mathbf{z}_i \\ 0 & \mathbf{e}_i \end{bmatrix}. \tag{24}$$

When estimates of the viewpoint transformation and its covariance are needed, they can be obtained by

$$\mathbf{t}_i = \mathbf{R}_i^{-1}\mathbf{z}_i \text{ and } \mathbf{C}_{t_i} = \mathbf{R}_i^{-1}\mathbf{R}_i^{-\mathsf{T}}. \tag{25}$$

This requires only back substitution since $\mathbf{R}_i$ is triangular. The SRIF also makes the total residual error available as $\mathbf{e}_i \mathbf{e}_i^{\mathrm{T}}$, which conveniently approximates the $\log \mathrm{P}(\tilde{\mathbf{b}}_j = T(\mathbf{b}_k) \mid \tilde{e}_j \neq \perp, T, H)$ component of our match quality measure. Thus, following each update of the transformation estimate, the match quality measure for the new transformation can be estimated easily; there is no need to re-evaluate equation 18 for the new transformation and each previous feature pairing.

5.   LEARNING PROCEDURE

The learning procedure assembles one or more model graphs from a series of training images showing various views of an object. Two tasks are required:

clustering   The learning procedure must divide the training images into clusters, each destined to form one characteristic view.

generalizing   For each cluster, it must construct a model graph summarizing the members of that cluster. The model graph represents a generalization of the cluster's contents.

Since clustering decisions ought to consider how well the resulting clusters can be generalized, the two tasks are closely related. Each will be discussed separately, however, in the following two sections.

We use $\mathcal{X}$ to denote the series of training images for one object. During learning, the object's model $\mathcal{M}$ consists of a series of clusters $\mathcal{X}_i \subseteq \mathcal{X}$, each with an associated model graph $\bar{G}_i$. Once learning is complete, only the model graphs must be retained to support recognition.

5.1.   CLUSTERING TRAINING IMAGES INTO CHARACTERISTIC VIEWS

An incremental conceptual clustering algorithm is used to create clusters among the training images. Clustering is incremental in that, as each training image is acquired, it is assigned to an existing cluster or used to form a new one. Like other conceptual clustering algorithms (e.g., COBWEB [11]), the algorithm uses a global measure of overall clustering quality to guide clustering decisions. This measure is chosen to promote and balance two somewhat-conflicting qualities. On one hand, it favors clusterings that result in simple, concise, and efficient models, while on the other hand, it favors clusterings whose resulting model graphs accurately characterize (or match) the training images.

Bayesian estimation provides a nice framework for combining these two qualities. It suggests that the learning procedure choose a model $\mathcal{M}$ that maximizes the posterior probability $\mathrm{P}(\mathcal{M} \mid \mathcal{X})$. By Bayes's theorem, this is equivalent to maximizing the product $\mathrm{P}(\mathcal{M})\mathrm{P}(\mathcal{X} \mid \mathcal{M})$. The prior distribution $\mathrm{P}(\mathcal{M})$ can be designed to favor simple models, while the conditional distribution $\mathrm{P}(\mathcal{X} \mid \mathcal{M})$ can be designed to favor models that characterize the training images accurately.

- *Prior distribution.* We apply the minimum description length (MDL) principle [22] to define a prior distribution favoring simple models. Briefly, the MDL principle provides a method of constructing a prior probability distribution over a family of statistical models by relating the probability of each to the length of its description as written in some minimal-length encoding scheme. To encode a model, we concisely enumerate its model graphs, nodes, arcs, attribute vectors, and position vectors, using a fixed number of bits for each component. With $L(\mathcal{M})$ denoting the length of $\mathcal{M}$'s encoding, the prior probability of $\mathcal{M}$ is given by $\log P(\mathcal{M}) = -L(\mathcal{M})$.

- *Conditional distribution.* We use the match quality measure to define a conditional distribution favoring accurate models. Recall that the measure is based on an estimate of the probability that the match represents a true occurrence of the modeled object in the image. For this match probability to be high, the model must accurately depict how the object appears in the image. Thus, to rate the accuracy of a model, we combine match probability estimates for each of the model's training images:

$$P(\mathcal{X} \mid \mathcal{M}) = \prod_i \prod_{X \in \mathcal{X}_i} \max_{\langle E,T \rangle} P(H \mid E, T; X, \bar{G}_i), \qquad (26)$$

where $P(H \mid E, T; X, \bar{G}_i)$ is defined by equation 4. The maximum over matches $\langle E, T \rangle$ is found by the matching procedure described in section 4.

As each training image is acquired it is assigned to an existing cluster or used to form a new one. Choices among clustering alternatives are made to maximize the resulting $P(\mathcal{M} \mid \mathcal{X})$. When evaluating an alternative, each cluster's subset of training images $\mathcal{X}_i$ is first generalized to form a model graph $\mathcal{M}_i$ as described below.

5.2. GENERALIZING TRAINING IMAGES TO FORM A MODEL GRAPH

Within each cluster, training images are merged to form a single model graph that represents a generalization of those images. An initial model graph is formed from the first training image's graph. That model graph is then matched with each subsequent training image's graph and revised after each match according to the match result. A model feature j that matches an image feature k receives an additional attribute vector $\mathbf{a}_k$ and position $\mathbf{b}_k$ for its series A_j and B_j. Some unmatched image features are used to extend the model graph, while model features that remain largely unmatched are eventually pruned. After several training images have been processed in this way the model graph nears an equilibrium, containing the most consistent features with representative populations of sample attribute vectors and positions for each.

6. EXPERIMENTAL RESULTS

A system that learns a single, characteristic view has been implemented using facilities of the Vista computer vision environment [21]; implementation of the clustering procedure needed to learn multiple views is in progress.[4] The system recognizes 3-D objects in 2-D intensity images, employing a repertoire of features designed to describe the appearance of manufactured objects. Straight and circular segments of intensity edges are the lowest-level features. These are augmented by features representing various perceptually-significant groupings, including junctions, pairs and triples of junctions, pairs of parallel segments, chains of such pairs, and convex regions. Features that are rotationally symmetric, such as straight lines, are simply represented by multiple graph nodes, one per orientation.

Experiments with this system have produced encouraging results. For example, figure 4 shows a model of a characteristic view of a stool learned from nine training images acquired over a 20-degree range of viewpoint. Figure 5 shows the result of matching that model with a cluttered test image. The match search begins with a pairing of junctions (shown with a bold × in figure 5) that is rated highly by equation 19 primarily due to the image feature's attribute values. Matching proceeds with a pairing of parallel arcs (also shown in bold) that is favored in part due to the model feature's low positional uncertainty (apparent in figure 4(d)).

We are studying the models produced to gain further insight. As evident from the model depiction in figure 4 and from the histogram in figure 6, the stool model records significant differences in the positional uncertainty of various features. Some differences are due to shifts in the relative positions of features with changing viewpoint—the seat and post remain fixed, for example, while the legs shift in various directions. Others are due to inherent differences in the accuracy of localizing various types of features—for example, a right-angle junction might be better localized than an oblique or acute one. Differences would be even greater for a flexible object.

Additional experiments have sought to determine whether the method can generalize across objects of similar appearance while still differentiating them on the basis of small distinctions. In one experiment, models were created for bottles A and B, shown in figure 7, using six training images of each. Each model was then matched with two subimages from figure 7: one containing the identical object, the other containing its counterpart. Table 1 summarizes the results. Each model matches its identical object best, meaning that the two objects are successfully distinguished; however each model also matches its counterpart to a lesser degree, meaning that each model successfully generalizes to match other objects of similar appearance.

---

[4]Since this chapter was written, a complete system capable of learning multiple-view models has been implemented and evaluated [18].

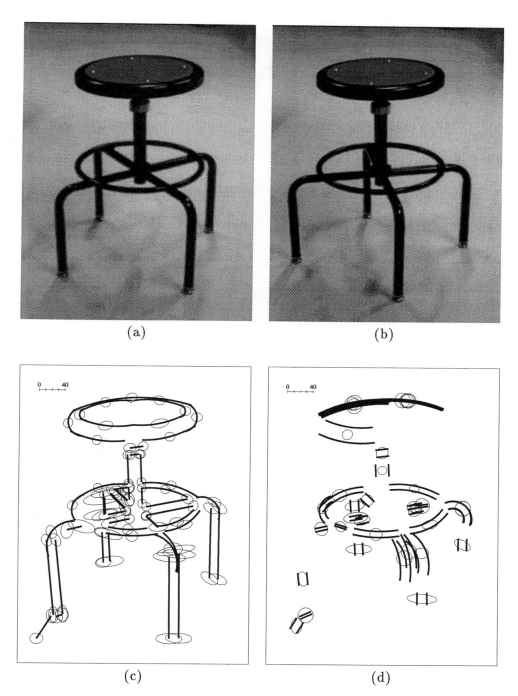

(a) (b)

(c) (d)

Figure 4: *Nine training images spanning 20 degrees of viewing angle, from (a) to (b), yield a single characteristic view model. Among model features, those denoting straight and circular segments of intensity edge are shown in (c); those denoting pairs of parallel segments are shown in (d). Ellipses depict two standard deviations of feature location uncertainty.*

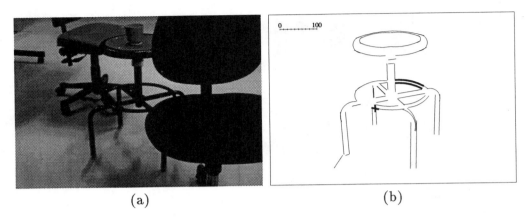

(a)   (b)

Figure 5: *A cluttered test image (a) in which the partially-occluded stool is recognized (b). Model features representing segments of intensity edge are shown projected into the image according to the final viewpoint transformation estimate. See the text for further explanation.*

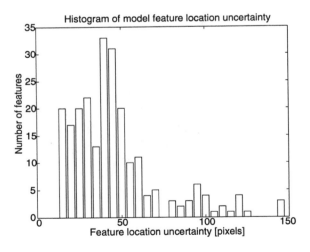

Figure 6: *Features of the stool model vary widely in positional uncertainty, as shown by this histogram of feature location uncertainty. Here, location uncertainty is measured as the area of a one-standard-deviation ellipse about the model feature's expected location.*

Figure 7: *Bottles A and B, used to test generality and specificity of models.*

Image	Model	Features Paired	Match Quality
Bottle A	Bottle A	43 / 109	60.7
Bottle A	Bottle B	20 / 56	6.7
Bottle B	Bottle A	27 / 109	-2.8
Bottle B	Bottle B	27 / 56	20.7

Table 1: *Results of matching each subimage of figure 7 with each bottle model.* Features Paired *is the proportion of model features paired.* Match Quality *is the value of the match quality measure,* $g(E, T)$. *Adapted from [19].*

In this case the specificity of the two models is due, in part, to differences in attribute value distributions. For example, each model includes a feature for its bottle's lower left corner and one attribute of that feature records the ratio of the corner's two sides. Since the two bottles have different height-to-width ratios, this feature is among those that help to differentiate the bottles. Figure 8 shows how the pdfs estimated for this attribute differ between the two models.

7. RELATED RESEARCH ON LEARNING TO RECOGNIZE OBJECTS

This section surveys other efforts to build systems that learn to recognize objects. The survey is organized according to the role that learning plays in these systems. A final section summarizes efforts to establish theoretical bounds on the learnability of object recognition.

7.1. LEARNING APPEARANCE PRIMITIVES

An object recognition system may learn new types of shape or appearance primitives to use in describing objects. Typically this is done by clustering existing primitives or groups of them, and then associating new primitives with the clusters obtained. New primitives thus represent particular configurations or abstractions of existing ones. The new configurations may improve the representation's descriptive power, and the new abstractions may allow more appropriate generalizations.

Segen [24] has demonstrated this approach with a system that learns a representation for 2-D contours. The system's lowest-level primitives are distinguished points, such as curvature extrema, found on contours in training images. Nearby points are paired, each pair is characterized by a vector of measurements, the measurement vectors are clustered, and a new primitive is invented for each cluster of significant size. Consequently, each new primitive describes a commonly observed configuration of two distinguished points. The induction process is repeated with these new primitives to generate higher-level primitives describing groups of four, eight, and more distinguished points. The Cresceptron system by Weng and his associates [31] is analogous in that it induces a hierarchy of primitives within a

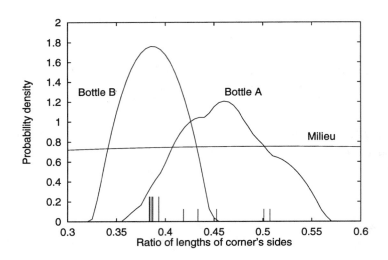

Figure 8: *Comparison of three attribute value distributions. Those labeled* **Bottle A** *and* **Bottle B** *are from model features corresponding to the lower left corners of bottles A and B. Spikes represent the two populations of sample values from which these distributions are estimated. The distribution labeled* **Milieu** *averages all corners from numerous images. From [19].*

pre-programmed framework. As these primitives are essentially templates, invariance to translation, rotation, and scaling in the image must be provided by prior segmentation or by an attentional mechanism. We would expect both these method to be sensitive to clutter in the training images and to parameters of the clustering algorithm.

Delanoy [7], Fichera [10], and their associates have described object recognition systems that induce fuzzy predicates from training images. Their systems represent models as logical formulae, and, therefore, the systems need appropriate predicates. These are invented by clustering measurements of low-level primitives that have been recovered from training images. Turk and Pentland [29] and Murase and Nayar [17] have induced features using principal component analysis. They compute the several most significant eigenvectors, or principal components, of the set of training images. Because these few eigenvectors span much of the subspace containing the training images, they can be used to concisely describe those images and others like them. However, as this is a global representation, it does not support recognition of occluded objects.

7.2. LEARNING AN APPEARANCE CLASSIFIER

The object recognition task can be characterized, in part, as a classification problem: instances represented as vectors, sets, or structures must be classified into categories corresponding to various objects. A wealth of techniques has been developed for classifying, and for inducing classifiers from training examples. For the purposes of object recognition, the important considerations distinguishing these techniques include the expressiveness and complexity of the input representation (e.g., vectors are easier to classify than structures), the generality of the categories learned, the ability to cope with noisy features, the number of training examples needed, and the sensitivity to the order in which examples are presented.

Jain and Hoffman [14] describe a system that learns rules for classifying objects in range images. The instances classified by their system are sets of shape primitives with associated measurements. The classifier applies a series of rules, each contributing evidence for or against various classifications. Each rule applies to a particular type of shape primitive and a particular range of measurements for that primitive. These rules are learned from training images by extracting primitives from the images, clustering them according to their measurements, and associating rules with the clusters that derive primarily from a single object. Because this system does not learn constraints governing the relative positions of the shape primitives, it appears to have a very limited ability to distinguish among objects that have different arrangements of similar features.

Neural networks, including radial basis function networks, have been used as trainable classifiers for object recognition (e.g., [5]). In this role, the network approximates a function that maps a vector of feature measurements to an object identifier, or to a vector of graded yes/no responses, one per object. Nearest neighbor classifiers are also commonly used. The most difficult aspect of these approaches seems to be deriving appropriate feature vectors from cluttered images, which requires consistently identifying and ordering a set of primitives. For this reason, these methods are best suited solely for indexing, as in the indexing method of Beis and Lowe [3].

7.3. LEARNING A STRUCTURAL MODEL

A structural model explicitly represents both shape primitives and their spatial relationships. Its structure is thus analogous to that of the modeled object, and it is often represented as a graph or, equivalently, as a series of predicates. In general, a structural model is learned from training images by first obtaining structural descriptions from each image, and then inducing a generalization covering those descriptions. Connell and Brady [6] have described a system that learns structural models for recognizing 2-D objects in intensity images. The system incorporates many interesting ideas. They use graphs to represent the part/whole and adjacency relations among object regions described by smoothed local symmetries (ribbon shapes). An attribute of a region, such as its elongation or curvature, is encoded symbolically by the presence or absence of additional graph nodes according to a Gray code. A structural learning procedure forms a model graph from multiple example graphs, most commonly by deleting any nodes not shared by all graphs (the well-known dropping rule for generalization). Similarity between two graphs is measured by a purely syntactic measure: simply by counting the nodes they share. Consequently, this system accords equal importance to all features, and it uses a somewhat arbitrary metric for comparing attribute values.

The approaches described below involve more powerful models that represent probability distributions over graphs. A Markov or independence condition is assumed so that the high-order, joint probability distribution can be approximated by a product of low-order distributions, one per node or arc. The probability of a particular graph instance is then defined according to a partial match between that instance and the model. Our approach is similar in that it uses a probability distributions over graphs to model objects; it differs in many aspects of how the probability distributions are defined, learned from training images, and used to accomplish matching.

Wong and You [32] represent a model as a "random graph" in which nodes represent shape primitives, arcs and hyperarcs represent relations among them, and both have attribute values characterized by discrete probability distributions. An attributed graph (i.e., a random graph's outcome) is treated as just a special case of random graph. An entropy measure is defined on random graphs, and the distance between two random graphs is defined as the increment in entropy that would result from merging the two (the minimal increment over all possible mergings). A random graph is synthesized from examples by repeatedly merging the two nearest graphs. This learning method seems to have been demonstrated only with 2-D recognition problems and clean, synthetic images. However, McArthur [16] has extended the random graph formalism to allow continuous attributes, and he has used it to learn 3-D, object-centered models from images with known viewpoints. In comparison, our formalism incorporates continuous attributes more easily using likelihoods rather than entropies, and our learning method does not require knowledge of viewpoint or feature correspondences.

In Segen's system [24] for recognizing 2-D shapes, a graph node represents a relation among shape primitives, which are oriented point features (see section 7.1). But instead of specifying a particular relation, a node in the model graph specifies a probability distribution over possible relations. For example, relations involving two features may include one that holds when the features are oriented away from each other, and another that holds when they are oriented in the same direction; a model node may specify that the first relation holds with probability 0.5, and the second, with probability 0.3. When a graph instance is matched with the model, the instance's probability can be computed by assessing the probability of each instance node according to the distribution of its corresponding model node. Recognition involves finding the most probable match. A model is learned incrementally from instances by matching it with each one successively; following each match the probabilities recorded in matching model nodes are adjusted and any unmatched instance nodes are added to the model. Whereas Segen's system reduces all measurements to global categories found by clustering, our method retains numeric measurements as attribute and position distributions that are learned individually for each model feature. As a result, we would expect our method to be capable of more precise discriminations among objects, and more appropriate generalizations.

7.4. LEARNING A SET OF CHARACTERISTIC VIEWS

In learning a model that is to be represented as a set of characteristic views, part of the task is to choose those views. This can be done by clustering training images, and choosing one characteristic view to represent each cluster. Although several researchers have clustered images rendered from CAD models and thus avoided the feature correspondence problem, a few have clustered real images. Gros [12] measures the similarity of an image pair as the proportion of matching shape features, whereas Seibert and Waxman [25] use a vector clustering algorithm with fixed-length vectors encoding global appearance. Our method, in comparison, uses a clustering measure based on objective performance criteria (accuracy and efficiency), and an appearance representation less affected by occlusion.

7.5. LEARNING A RECOGNITION STRATEGY

Draper [8] has considered how a system equipped with a variety of special-purpose representations and algorithms might learn strategies for employing those techniques to recognize specific objects. A typical recognition task would be to locate a tree by fitting a parabola to the top of its crown. For this task, an appropriate strategy is to segment the image, extract regions that are colored and textured like foliage, group these into larger regions, smooth region boundaries, and fit parabolas to the boundaries. A human supplies training examples by pointing out the desired parabolas in a series of images. The system then evaluates various strategy choices (e.g., whether to smooth region boundaries) and parameter choices (e.g., the degree of smoothing) for cost and effectiveness. From these evaluations it constructs a strategy, including alternatives, for performing the task on new images. By learning what order to try alternative recognition methods, Draper's system differs from those that just select a single set of features useful for recognition. Difficulty remains in limiting the search among strategies and parameters to achieve acceptable performance.

7.6. THEORETICAL LEARNABILITY

There have been some efforts to identify theoretical limits on what can be learned from images. These efforts are based on the analogy that learning to recognize an object from images is like learning a concept from examples. Valiant [30] has provided a useful definition for characterizing the class of concepts that can be learned by a particular algorithm: Informally, a class is probably approximately correct (PAC) learnable by an algorithm if, with high probability, the algorithm learns a concept that correctly classifies a high proportion of examples using polynomially bounded resources (and, consequently, number of training examples); the bound is a polynomial of both the accuracy and some natural parameter of the concept class (e.g., vector length for concepts defined on a vector space). Significantly, the algorithm has no prior knowledge about the distribution of examples.

Shvayster [27] has shown that some classes of concepts defined on binary images are not PAC-learnable from positive examples by any algorithm. For example, suppose a template is said to match an image when every black pixel in the template corresponds to a black pixel in the image (though not necessarily vice versa). Then the concept consisting of all instances not matching some unknown template is not PAC-learnable. Shvayster speculates that some nonlearnable concepts may become learnable, however, if some prior knowledge about the distribution of examples is available.

Edelman [9] has argued that Shvayster's negative result is not applicable to object recognition because it uses an instance representation, the binary image, that is inappropriate. If instead instances are represented by vectors of point feature locations, Edelman shows, then recognition of an object can be learned from a polynomial number of positive examples. He concludes that model learning may be practical, provided an appropriate representation is chosen.

8. SUMMARY

We have presented a method for recognizing objects using models acquired from training images. Appearance in an image is represented by an attributed graph of discrete features and their relations, with a typical object described by many features. Since one object can vary greatly in appearance when viewed under different conditions, a model is represented by a probability distribution over such graphs. The range of this distribution is divided among characteristic views, allowing a simplified representation for each view as a model graph of independent features.

A model feature is described by probability distributions for probabilities of detection, various internal attribute values, and various image positions. All three distributions are estimated from samples supplied by training images.

A match quality measure provides a principled means of evaluating a match between a model and an image. It combines probabilities that are estimated using the distributions recorded by the model. The measure leads naturally to an efficient matching procedure called probabilistic alignment. In searching for a solution, the procedure can employ constraints arising both from the topology of the model graph and from the probability distributions describing individual features.

The model learning procedure has two components. A conceptual clustering component determines clusters of training images that correspond to characteristic views by maximizing a global measure of cluster quality. That measure combines a simplicity criterion based on the minimum description length principle with a fit criterion based on the match quality measure. A generalizing component merges the images within each cluster to form a model graph representing a generalization of that cluster. It uses the matching procedure to determine correspondences among the cluster's images.

An important aspect of the recognition learning problem this work has not addressed is how a database of acquired model graphs should be organized and accessed. Possibilities include organizing the model graphs hierarchically [2, 26], or using selected high-level features and their attributes to index the collection of model graphs. This remains a topic for future study.

ACKNOWLEDGEMENTS

This research was supported by the Institute for Robotics and Intelligent Systems (IRIS), one of the Canadian Networks of Centres of Excellence. Additional support was provided by the Natural Sciences and Engineering Research Council of Canada and the Canadian Institute for Advanced Research. We wish to thank Jeffrey Beis, Alun Evans, James Little, Alan Mackworth, Daniel McReynolds, and Robert Woodham for helpful discussions.

REFERENCES

[1] N. Ayache and Olivier D. Faugeras. HYPER: A new approach for the recognition and positioning of two-dimensional objects. *IEEE Trans. Patt. Anal. Mach. Intell.*, PAMI-8(1):44–54, January 1986.

[2] R. Basri. Recognition by prototypes. In *Proc. Conf. Comput. Vision and Patt. Recognit.*, pages 161–167, 1993.

[3] Jeffrey S. Beis and David G. Lowe. Learning indexing functions for 3-D model-based object recognition. In *Proc. Conf. Comput. Vision and Patt. Recognit.*, pages 275–280, 1994.

[4] G. J. Bierman. *Factorization Methods for Discrete Sequential Estimation.* Academic Press, New York, 1977.

[5] R. Brunelli and T. Poggio. HyperBF networks for real object recognition. In *Proc. Int. Joint Conf. Artificial Intell.*, volume 2, pages 1278–1284, 1991.

[6] J. H. Connell and M. Brady. Generating and generalizing models of visual objects. *Artificial Intell.*, 31:159–183, 1987.

[7] R. L. Delanoy, J. G. Verly, and D. E. Dudgeon. Automatic building and supervised discrimination learning of appearance models of 3-D objects. In *SPIE Proc. Vol. 1708: Applications of Artificial Intell. X: Machine Vision and Robotics*, pages 549–560, 1992.

[8] B. Draper. *Learning Object Recognition Strategies.* PhD thesis, Univ. of Massachusetts, Amherst, Mass., May 1993.

[9] S. Edelman. On learning to recognize 3-D objects from examples. *IEEE Trans. Patt. Anal. Mach. Intell.*, 15(8):833–837, August 1993.

[10] O. Fichera, P. Pellegretti, F. Roli, and S. B. Serpico. Automatic acquisition of visual models for image recognition. In *Proc. IAPR Int. Conf. Patt. Recognit.*, volume 1, pages 95–98, 1992.

[11] D. H. Fisher. Knowledge acquisition via incremental conceptual clustering. *Machine Learning*, 2:139–172, 1987.

[12] P. Gros. Matching and clustering: Two steps towards automatic object model generation in computer vision. In *Proc. AAAI Fall Symp.: Machine Learning in Comput. Vision*, 1993.

[13] D. P. Huttenlocher and S. Ullman. Recognizing solid objects by alignment with an image. *Int. J. Comput. Vision*, 5(2):195–212, November 1990.

[14] A. K. Jain and R. Hoffman. Evidence-based recognition of 3-D objects. *IEEE Trans. Patt. Anal. Mach. Intell.*, 10(6):783–801, November 1988.

[15] D. G. Lowe. The viewpoint consistency constraint. *Int. J. Comput. Vision*, 1:57–72, 1987.

[16] B. A. McArthur. *Incremental Synthesis of Three-Dimensional Object Models Using Random Graphs*. PhD thesis, Univ. of Waterloo, 1991.

[17] H. Murase and S. K. Nayar. Learning and recognition of 3-D objects from brightness images. In *Proc. AAAI Fall Symp.: Machine Learning in Comput. Vision*, pages 25–29, 1993.

[18] A. R. Pope. *Learning to Recognize Objects in Images: Acquiring and Using Probabilistic Models of Appearance*. PhD thesis, Univ. of British Columbia, 1995.

[19] A. R. Pope and D. G. Lowe. Learning object recognition models from images. In *Proc. Int. Conf. Comput. Vision*, pages 296–301, 1993.

[20] A. R. Pope and D. G. Lowe. Modeling positional uncertainty in object recognition. Technical Report 94-32, Dept. of Computer Science, Univ. of B.C., November 1994. WWW http://www.cs.ubc.ca/tr/1994/TR-94-32.

[21] A. R. Pope and D. G. Lowe. Vista: A software environment for computer vision research. In *Proc. Conf. Comput. Vision and Patt. Recognit.*, pages 768–772, 1994. WWW http://www.cs.ubc.ca/nest/lci/vista/vista.html.

[22] J. Rissanen. A universal prior for integers and estimation by minimum description length. *Ann. Statist.*, 11(2):416–431, 1983.

[23] E. Saund. Labeling of curvilinear structure across scales by token grouping. In *Proc. Conf. Comput. Vision and Patt. Recognit.*, pages 257–263, 1992.

[24] J. Segen. Model learning and recognition of nonrigid objects. In *Proc. Conf. Comput. Vision and Patt. Recognit.*, pages 597–602, 1989.

[25] M. Seibert and A. M. Waxman. Adaptive 3-D object recognition from multiple views. *IEEE Trans. Patt. Anal. Mach. Intell.*, 14(2):107–124, February 1992.

[26] K. Sengupta and K. L. Boyer. Information theoretic clustering of large structural modelbases. In *Proc. Conf. Comput. Vision and Patt. Recognit.*, pages 174–179, 1993.

[27] H. Shvayster. Learnable and nonlearnable visual concepts. *IEEE Trans. Patt. Anal. Mach. Intell.*, 12(5):459–466, May 1990.

[28] B. W. Silverman. *Density Estimation for Statistics and Data Analysis*. Chapman and Hall, London, 1986.

[29] M. A. Turk and A. P. Pentland. Face recognition using eigenfaces. In *Proc. Conf. Comput. Vision and Patt. Recognit.*, pages 586–591, 1991.

[30] L. G. Valiant. A theory of the learnable. *Commun. ACM*, 27:1134–1142, 1984.

[31] J. J. Weng, N. Ahuja, and T. S. Huang. Learning recognition and segmentation of 3-D objects from 2-D images. In *Proc. Int. Conf. Comput. Vision*, pages 121–128, 1993.

[32] A. K. C. Wong and M. You. Entropy and distance of random graphs with application to structural pattern recognition. *IEEE Trans. Patt. Anal. Mach. Intell.*, 7(5):599–609, September 1985.

5   PROBABILISTIC VISUAL LEARNING FOR OBJECT REPRESENTATION

Baback Moghaddam and *Alex Pentland*
Massachusetts Institute of Technology

ABSTRACT

We present an unsupervised technique for visual learning which is based on density estimation in high-dimensional spaces using an eigenspace decomposition. Two types of density estimates are derived for modeling the training data: a multivariate Gaussian (for unimodal distributions) and a Mixture-of-Gaussians model (for multimodal distributions). These proba-bility densities are then used to formulate a maximum-likelihood *estimation framework for visual search and target detection for automatic object recognition and coding. Our learning technique is applied to the probabilistic visual modeling, detection, recognition, and coding of human faces and non-rigid objects such as hands.*

1.   INTRODUCTION

Visual attention is the process of restricting higher-level processing to a subset of the visual field, referred to as the *focus-of-attention* (FOA). The critical component of visual attention is the *selection* of the FOA. In humans this process is not based purely on bottom-up processing and is in fact goal-driven. The measure of interest or *saliency* is modulated by the behavioral state and the demands of the particular visual task that is currently active.

Palmer [24] has suggested that visual attention is the process of locating the object of interest and placing it in a *canonical* (or object-centered) reference frame suitable for recognition (or template matching). We have developed a computational technique for automatic object recognition, which is in accordance with Palmer's model of visual attention (see section 4.1). The system uses a probabilistic formulation for the estimation of the position and scale of the object in the visual field and remaps the FOA to an object-centered reference frame, which is subsequently used for recognition and verification.

At a simple level the underlying mechanism of attention during a visual search task can be based on a spatiotopic *saliency* map $S(i,j)$ which is a function of the image information in a local region R

$$S(i,j) = f\left[\{I(i+r, j+c) : (r,c) \in R\}\right] \qquad (1)$$

For example saliency maps have been constructed which employ spatio-temporal changes as cues for foveation [1] or other low-level image features such as local symmetry for detection of interest points [30]. However bottom-up techniques based on low-level features lack *context* with respect to high-level visual tasks such as object recognition. In a recognition task, the selection of the FOA is driven by higher-level goals and therefore requires internal representations of an object's appearance and a means of comparing candidate objects in the FOA to the stored object models.

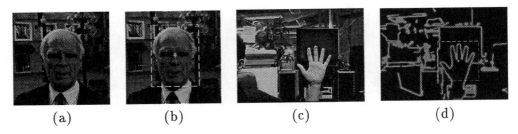

(a)   (b)   (c)   (d)

Figure 1: *(a) input image, (b) face detection, (c) input image, (d) hand detection*

In view-based recognition (as opposed to 3D geometric or invariant-based recognition), the saliency can be formulated in terms of visual similarity using a variety of metrics ranging from simple template matching scores to more sophisticated measures using, for example, robust statistics for image correlation [5]. In this paper, however, we are primarily interested in saliency maps which have a *probabilistic* interpretation as object-class membership functions or *likelihoods*. These likelihood functions are learned by applying density estimation techniques in complementary subspaces obtained by an eigenvector decomposition. Our approach to this learning problem is *view-based* — *i.e.,* the learning and modeling of the visual appearance of the object from a (suitably normalized and preprocessed) set of training imagery. Figure 1 shows examples of the automatic selection of FOA for detection of faces and hands. In each case, the target object's probability distribution was *learned* from training views and then subsequently used in computing likelihoods for detection. The face representation is based on appearance (normalized grayscale image) whereas the hand's representation is based on the shape of its contour. The maximum likelihood (ML) estimates of position and scale are shown in the figure by the cross-hairs and bounding box, respectively.

1.1. OBJECT DETECTION

The standard detection paradigm in image processing is that of normalized correlation or template matching. However this approach is only optimal in the simplistic case of a *deterministic* signal embedded in additive white Gaussian noise. When we begin to consider a target *class* detection problem — *e.g,* finding a generic human face or a human hand in a scene — we must incorporate the underlying probability distribution of the object. Subspace methods and eigenspace decompositions are particularly well-suited to such a task since they provide a compact and *parametric* description of the object's appearance and also automatically identify the *degrees-of-freedom* of the underlying statistical variability.

In particular, the eigenspace formulation leads to a powerful alternative to standard detection techniques such as template matching or normalized correlation. The reconstruction error (or residual) of the eigenspace decomposition (referred to as the "distance-from-face-space" in the context of the work with "eigenfaces" [34]) is an effective indicator of similarity. The residual error is easily computed using the projection coefficients and the original signal energy. This detection strategy is equivalent to matching with a linear combination of *eigentemplates* and allows for a greater range of distortions in the input signal (including lighting, and moderate rotation and scale). In a statistical signal detection framework, the use of eigentemplates has been shown to yield superior performance in comparison with standard matched filtering [18][26].

In [26] we used this formulation for a modular eigenspace representation of facial features where the corresponding residual — referred to as "distance-from-*feature*-space" or DFFS — was used for localization and detection. Given an input image, a saliency map was constructed by computing the DFFS at each pixel. When using M eigenvectors, this requires M convolutions (which can be efficiently computed using an FFT) plus an additional local energy computation. The global minimum of this distance map was then selected as the best estimate of the location of the target.

In this paper we will show that the DFFS can be interpreted as an estimate of a marginal component of the probability density of the object and that a complete estimate must also incorporate a second marginal density based on a complementary "distance-*in*-feature-space" (DIFS). Using our estimates of the object densities, we formulate the problem of target detection from the point of view of a maximum likelihood (ML) estimation problem. Specifically, given the visual field, we estimate the position (and scale) of the image region which is most representative of the target of interest. Computationally this is achieved by sliding an m-by-n observation window throughout the image and at each location computing the *likelihood* that the local subimage $\mathbf{x}$ is an instance of the target class Ω — *i.e.*, $P(\mathbf{x}|\Omega)$. After this probability map is computed, we select the location corresponding to the highest likelihood as our ML estimate of the target location. Note that the likelihood map can be evaluated over the entire parameter space affecting the object's appearance which can include transformations such as scale and rotation.

1.2. RELATIONSHIP TO PREVIOUS RESEARCH

In recent years, computer vision research has witnessed a growing interest in eigenvector analysis and subspace decomposition methods. In particular, eigenvector decomposition has been shown to be an effective tool for solving problems which use high-dimensional representations of phenomena which are intrinsically low-dimensional. This general analysis framework lends itself to several closely related formulations in object modeling and recognition which employ the *principal modes* or characteristic *degrees-of-freedom* for description. The identification and parametric representation of a system in terms of these principal modes is at the core of recent advances in physically-based modeling [25], correspondence and matching [32], and parametric descriptions of shape [7].

Eigenvector-based methods also form the basis for data analysis techniques in pattern recognition and statistics where they are used to extract low-dimensional subspaces comprised of statistically uncorrelated variables which tend to simplify tasks such as classification. The Karhunen-Loeve Transform (KLT) [19] and Principal Components Analysis (PCA) [14] are examples of eigenvector-based techniques which are commonly used for dimensionality reduction and feature extraction in pattern recognition.

In computer vision, eigenvector analysis of *imagery* has been used for characterization of human faces [17] and automatic face recognition using "eigenfaces" [34][26]. More recently, principal component analysis of imagery has also been applied for robust target detection [26][6], nonlinear image interpolation [3], visual learning for object recognition [22][36], as well as visual servoing for robotics [23].

Specifically, Murase and Nayar [22] used a low-dimensional *parametric* eigenspace for recovering object identity and pose by matching views to a spline-based hypersurface. Nayar *et al.* [23] have extended this technique to visual feedback control and servoing for a robotic arm in "peg-in-the-hole" insertion tasks. Pentland *et al.* [26] proposed a view-based multiple-eigenspace technique for face recognition under varying pose as well as for the detection and description of facial features. Similarly, Burl *et al.* [6] used Bayesian classification for object detection using a feature vector derived from principal component images. Weng [36] has proposed a visual learning framework based on the KLT in conjunction with an optimal linear discriminant transform for learning and recognition of objects from 2D views.

However, these authors (with the exception of [26]) have used eigenvector analysis primarily as a dimensionality reduction technique for subsequent modeling, interpolation, or classification. In contrast, our method uses an eigenspace decomposition as an integral part of an efficient technique for probability density estimation of high-dimensional data.

2. DENSITY ESTIMATION IN EIGENSPACE

In this section we present our recent work using eigenspace decompositions for object representation and modeling. Our learning method estimates the *complete* probability distribution of the object's appearance using an eigenvector decomposition of the image space. The desired target density is decomposed into two components: the density in the principal subspace (containing the traditionally-defined principal components) and its orthogonal complement (which is usually discarded in standard PCA). We derive the form for an optimal density estimate for the case of Gaussian data and a near-optimal estimator for arbitrarily complex distributions in terms of a Mixture-of-Gaussians density model.

We note that this learning method differs from *supervised* visual learning with function approximation networks [28] in which a hypersurface representation of an input/output map is automatically learned from a set of training examples. Instead, we use a probabilistic formulation which combines the two standard paradigms of *unsupervised* learning — PCA and density estimation — to arrive at a computationally feasible estimate of the class conditional density function.

Specifically, given a set of training images $\{\mathbf{x}^t\}_{t=1}^{N_T}$, from an object class Ω, we wish to estimate the class membership or *likelihood* function for this data — *i.e.*, $P(\mathbf{x}|\Omega)$. In this section, we examine two density estimation techniques for visual learning of high-dimensional data. The first method is based on the assumption of a Gaussian distribution while the second method generalizes to arbitrarily complex distributions using a Mixture-of-Gaussians density model. Before introducing these estimators we briefly review eigenvector decomposition as commonly used in PCA.

2.1. Principal component imagery

Given a training set of m-by-n images $\{I^t\}_{t=1}^{N_T}$, we can form a training set of vectors $\{\mathbf{x}^t\}$, where $\mathbf{x} \in \mathcal{R}^{N=mn}$, by lexicographic ordering of the pixel elements of each image I^t. The basis functions for the KLT [19] are obtained by solving the eigenvalue problem

$$\Lambda = \Phi^T \Sigma \Phi \qquad (2)$$

where Σ is the covariance matrix, Φ is the eigenvector matrix of Σ and Λ is the corresponding diagonal matrix of eigenvalues. The unitary matrix Φ defines a coordinate transform (rotation) which *decorrelates* the data and makes explicit the *invariant subspaces* of the matrix operator Σ. In PCA, a partial KLT is performed to identify the largest-eigenvalue eigenvectors and obtain a principal component feature vector $\mathbf{y} = \Phi_M^T \tilde{\mathbf{x}}$, where $\tilde{\mathbf{x}} = \mathbf{x} - \bar{\mathbf{x}}$ is the mean-normalized image vector and Φ_M is a submatrix of Φ containing the principal eigenvectors. PCA can be seen as a linear transformation $\mathbf{y} = \mathcal{T}(\mathbf{x}) : \mathcal{R}^N \to \mathcal{R}^M$ which extracts a lower-dimensional subspace of the KL basis corresponding to the maximal eigenvalues. These principal components preserve the major linear correlations in the data and discard the minor ones.[1]

By ranking the eigenvectors of the KL expansion with respect to their eigenvalues and selecting the first M principal components we form an orthogonal decomposition of the vector space $\mathcal{R}^N$ into two mutually exclusive and complementary subspaces: the principal subspace (or feature space) $F = \{\Phi_i\}_{i=1}^M$ containing the

---

[1]In practice the number of training images N_T is far less than the dimensionality of the imagery N, consequently the covariance matrix Σ is singular. However, the first $M < N_T$ eigenvectors can always be computed (estimated) from N_t samples using, for example, a Singular Value Decomposition [12].

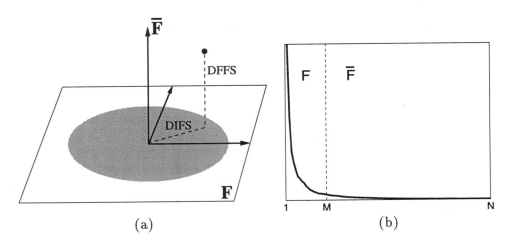

Figure 2: *(a) Decomposition into the principal subspace F and its orthogonal complement $\bar{F}$ for a Gaussian density, (b) a typical eigenvalue spectrum and its division into the two orthogonal subspaces.*

principal components and its orthogonal complement $\bar{F} = \{\Phi_i\}_{i=M+1}^{N}$. This orthogonal decomposition is illustrated in Figure 2(a) where we have a prototypical example of a distribution which is embedded entirely in F. In practice there is always a signal component in $\bar{F}$ due to the minor statistical variabilities in the data or simply due to the observation noise which affects every element of $\mathbf{x}$.

In a partial KL expansion, the residual reconstruction error is defined as

$$\epsilon^2(\mathbf{x}) \;=\; \sum_{i=M+1}^{N} y_i^2 \;=\; ||\tilde{\mathbf{x}}||^2 \;-\; \sum_{i=1}^{M} y_i^2 \tag{3}$$

and can be easily computed from the first M principal components and the L_2 norm of the mean-normalized image $\tilde{\mathbf{x}}$. Consequently the L_2 norm of every element $\mathbf{x} \in \mathcal{R}^N$ can be decomposed in terms of its projections in these two subspaces. We refer to the component in the orthogonal subspace $\bar{F}$ as the "distance-from-feature-space" (DFFS) which is a simple Euclidean distance and is equivalent to the residual error $\epsilon^2(\mathbf{x})$ in Eq.(3). The component of $\mathbf{x}$ which lies *in* the feature space F is referred to as the "distance-in-feature-space" (DIFS) but is generally not a distance-based norm, but can be interpreted in terms of the probability distribution of y in F.

2.2. GAUSSIAN DENSITIES

We begin by considering an optimal approach for estimating high-dimensional Gaussian densities. We assume that we have (robustly) estimated the mean $\bar{\mathbf{x}}$

and covariance Σ of the distribution from the given training set $\{\mathbf{x}^t\}$.[2] Under this assumption, the likelihood of an input pattern $\mathbf{x}$ is given by

$$P(\mathbf{x}|\Omega) = \frac{\exp\left[-\frac{1}{2}(\mathbf{x} - \bar{\mathbf{x}})^T\Sigma^{-1}(\mathbf{x} - \bar{\mathbf{x}})\right]}{(2\pi)^{N/2}\,|\Sigma|^{1/2}} \tag{4}$$

The sufficient statistic for characterizing this likelihood is the *Mahalanobis* distance

$$d(\mathbf{x}) = \tilde{\mathbf{x}}^T\Sigma^{-1}\tilde{\mathbf{x}} \tag{5}$$

where $\tilde{\mathbf{x}} = \mathbf{x} - \bar{\mathbf{x}}$. However, instead of evaluating this quadratic product explicitly, a much more efficient and robust computation can be performed, especially with regard to the matrix inverse Σ^{-1}. Using the eigenvectors and eigenvalues of Σ we can rewrite Σ^{-1} in the diagonalized form

$$
\begin{aligned}
d(\mathbf{x}) &= \tilde{\mathbf{x}}^T\Sigma^{-1}\tilde{\mathbf{x}} \\
&= \tilde{\mathbf{x}}^T\left[\Phi\Lambda^{-1}\Phi^T\right]\tilde{\mathbf{x}} \\
&= \mathbf{y}^T\Lambda^{-1}\mathbf{y}
\end{aligned}
\tag{6}
$$

where $\mathbf{y} = \Phi^T\tilde{\mathbf{x}}$ are the new variables obtained by the change of coordinates in a KLT. Because of the diagonalized form, the *Mahalanobis* distance can also be expressed in terms of the sum

$$d(\mathbf{x}) = \sum_{i=1}^{N}\frac{y_i^2}{\lambda_i} \tag{7}$$

In the KLT basis, the *Mahalanobis* distance in Eq.(5) is conveniently *decoupled* into a weighted sum of uncorrelated component energies. Furthermore, the likelihood becomes a *product* of independent separable Gaussian densities. Despite its simpler form, evaluation of Eq.(7) is still computationally infeasible due to the high-dimensionality. We therefore seek to *estimate* $d(\mathbf{x})$ using only M projections. Intuitively, an obvious choice for a lower-dimensional representation is the principal subspace indicated by PCA which captures the major degrees of statistical variability in the data.[3] Therefore, we divide the summation into two independent parts corresponding to the principal subspace $F = \{\Phi_i\}_{i=1}^{M}$ and its orthogonal complement $\bar{F} = \{\Phi_i\}_{i=M+1}^{N}$

$$d(\mathbf{x}) = \sum_{i=1}^{M}\frac{y_i^2}{\lambda_i} + \sum_{i=M+1}^{N}\frac{y_i^2}{\lambda_i} \tag{8}$$

---

[2]In practice, a full rank N-dimensional covariance Σ can not be estimated from N_T independent observations when $N_T < N$. But as we shall see our estimator does not require the full covariance, but only its first M principal eigenvectors where $M < N_T$.

[3]We will see shortly that given the typical eigenvalue spectra observed in practice (*e.g.*, Figure 2(b)), this choice is optimal for a different reason: it minimizes the information-theoretic *divergence* between the true density and our estimate of it.

We note that the terms in the first summation can be computed by projecting $\mathbf{x}$ onto the M-dimensional principal subspace F. The remaining terms in the second sum $\{y_i\}_{i=M+1}^{N}$, however, can not be computed explicitly in practice because of the high-dimensionality. However, the *sum* of these terms is available and is in fact the DFFS quantity $\epsilon^2(\mathbf{x})$ which can be computed from Eq.(3). Therefore, based on the available terms, we can formulate an estimator for $d(\mathbf{x})$ as follows

$$
\begin{aligned}
\hat{d}(\mathbf{x}) &= \sum_{i=1}^{M} \frac{y_i^2}{\lambda_i} + \frac{1}{\rho}\left[\sum_{i=M+1}^{N} y_i^2\right] \\
&= \sum_{i=1}^{M} \frac{y_i^2}{\lambda_i} + \frac{\epsilon^2(\mathbf{x})}{\rho}
\end{aligned}
\tag{9}
$$

where the term in the brackets is $\epsilon^2(\mathbf{x})$, which as we have seen can be computed using the first M principal components. We can therefore write the form of the likelihood estimate based on $\hat{d}(\mathbf{x})$ as the product of two marginal and independent Gaussian densities

$$
\begin{aligned}
\hat{P}(\mathbf{x}|\Omega) &= \left[\frac{\exp\left(-\frac{1}{2}\sum_{i=1}^{M}\frac{y_i^2}{\lambda_i}\right)}{(2\pi)^{M/2}\prod_{i=1}^{M}\lambda_i^{1/2}}\right] \cdot \left[\frac{\exp\left(-\frac{\epsilon^2(\mathbf{x})}{2\rho}\right)}{(2\pi\rho)^{(N-M)/2}}\right] \\[2mm]
&= P_F(\mathbf{x}|\Omega)\,\hat{P}_{\bar{F}}(\mathbf{x}|\Omega)
\end{aligned}
\tag{10}
$$

where $P_F(\mathbf{x}|\Omega)$ is the true marginal density in F-space and $\hat{P}_{\bar{F}}(\mathbf{x}|\Omega)$ is the estimated marginal density in the orthogonal complement $\bar{F}$-space. The optimal value of ρ can now be determined by minimizing a suitable cost function $J(\rho)$. From an information-theoretic point of view, this cost function should be the Kullback-Leibler divergence or *relative entropy* [9] between the true density $P(\mathbf{x}|\Omega)$ and its estimate $\hat{P}(\mathbf{x}|\Omega)$

$$
J(\rho) = \int P(\mathbf{x}|\Omega)\,\log\frac{P(\mathbf{x}|\Omega)}{\hat{P}(\mathbf{x}|\Omega)}\,d\mathbf{x} = \mathrm{E}\left[\log\frac{P(\mathbf{x}|\Omega)}{\hat{P}(\mathbf{x}|\Omega)}\right]
\tag{11}
$$

Using the diagonalized forms of the *Mahalanobis* distance $d(\mathbf{x})$ and its estimate $\hat{d}(\mathbf{x})$ and the fact that $\mathrm{E}[y_i^2] = \lambda_i$, it can be easily shown that

$$
J(\rho) = \frac{1}{2}\sum_{i=M+1}^{N}\left[\frac{\lambda_i}{\rho} - 1 + \log\frac{\rho}{\lambda_i}\right]
\tag{12}
$$

The optimal weight ρ^* can be then found by minimizing this cost function with respect to ρ. Solving the equation $\frac{\partial J}{\partial \rho} = 0$ yields

$$
\rho^* = \frac{1}{N-M}\sum_{i=M+1}^{N}\lambda_i
\tag{13}
$$

which is simply the arithmetic average of the eigenvalues in the orthogonal subspace $\bar{F}$. [4] In addition to its optimality, ρ^* also results in an *unbiased* estimate of the *Mahalanobis* distance — *i.e.*, $\mathrm{E}[\hat{d}(\mathbf{x}; \rho^*)] = \mathrm{E}[d(\mathbf{x})]$. This derivation shows that once we select the M-dimensional principal subspace F (as indicated, for example, by PCA), the optimal estimate of the sufficient statistic $\hat{d}(\mathbf{x})$ will have the form of Eq.(9) with ρ given by Eq.(13).

It is interesting to consider the minimal cost $J(\rho^*)$

$$J(\rho^*) \;=\; \frac{1}{2} \sum_{i=M+1}^{N} \log \frac{\rho^*}{\lambda_i} \tag{14}$$

from the point of view of the $\bar{F}$-space eigenvalues $\{\lambda_i : i = M + 1, \cdots, N\}$. It is easy to show that $J(\rho^*)$ is minimized when the the $\bar{F}$-space eigenvalues have the *least* spread about their mean ρ^*. This suggests a strategy for selecting the principal subspace: choose F such that the eigenvalues associated with its orthogonal complement $\bar{F}$ have the least absolute deviation about their mean. In practice, the higher-order eigenvalues typically decay and stabilize near the observation noise variance. Therefore this strategy is usually consistent with the standard PCA practice of discarding the higher-order components since these tend to correspond to the "flattest" portion of the eigenvalue spectrum (see Figure 2(b)). In the limit, as the $\bar{F}$-space eigenvalues become exactly equal, the divergence $J(\rho^*)$ will be zero and our density estimate $\hat{P}(\mathbf{x}|\Omega)$ approaches the true density $P(\mathbf{x}|\Omega)$.

We note that in most applications it is customary to simply discard the $\bar{F}$-space component and simply work with $P_F(\mathbf{x}|\Omega)$. However, the use of the DFFS metric or equivalently the marginal density $P_{\bar{F}}(\mathbf{x}|\Omega)$ is critically important in formulating the likelihood of an observation $\mathbf{x}$ — especially in an object detection task — since there are an infinity of vectors which are *not* members of Ω which can have likely F-space projections. Without $P_{\bar{F}}(\mathbf{x}|\Omega)$ a detection system can result in a significant number of false alarms.

2.3. MULTIMODAL DENSITIES

In the previous section we assumed that probability density of the training images was Gaussian. This lead to a likelihood estimate in the form of a product of two independent multivariate Gaussian distributions (or equivalently the sum of two *Mahalanobis* distances: DIFS + DFFS). In our experience, the distribution of samples in the feature space is often accurately modeled by a single Gaussian distribution. This is especially true in cases where the training images are accurately aligned views of similar objects seen from a standard view (*e.g.,* aligned frontal views of human faces at the same scale and orientation). However, when the training set represents multiple views or multiple objects under varying illumination conditions, the distribution of training views in F-space is no longer

---

[4]Cootes *et al.* [8] have used a similar decomposition of the Mahalanobis distance but instead use an ad-hoc parameter value of $\rho = \frac{1}{2}\lambda_{M+1}$ as an approximation.

unimodal. In fact the training data tends to lie on complex and non-separable low-dimensional manifolds in image space. One way to tackle this multimodality is to build a view-based (or object-based) formulation where separate eigenspaces are used for each view [26]. Another approach is to capture the complexity of these manifolds in a universal or *parametric* eigenspace using splines [22], or local basis functions [3].

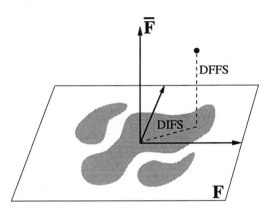

Figure 3: *Decomposition into the principal subspace F and its orthogonal complement $\bar{F}$ for an arbitrary density.*

If we assume that the $\bar{F}$-space components are Gaussian and independent of the principal features in F (this would be true in the case of pure observation noise in $\bar{F}$) we can still use the separable form of the density estimate $\hat{P}(\mathbf{x}|\Omega)$ in Eq.(10) where $P_F(\mathbf{x}|\Omega)$ is now an *arbitrary* density $P(\mathbf{y})$ in the principal component vector $\mathbf{y}$. Figure 3 illustrates the decomposition, where the DFFS is the residual $\epsilon^2(\mathbf{x})$ as before. The DIFS, however, is no longer a simple *Mahalanobis* distance but can nevertheless be interpreted as a "distance" by relating it to $P(\mathbf{y})$ — *e.g.*, as DIFS $= -\log P(\mathbf{y})$.

The density $P(\mathbf{y})$ can be estimated using a parametric mixture model. Specifically, we can model arbitrarily complex densities using a Mixture-of-Gaussians

$$P(\mathbf{y}|\Theta) \;=\; \sum_{i=1}^{N_c} \pi_i \, g(\mathbf{y}; \mu_i, \Sigma_i) \tag{15}$$

where $g(\mathbf{y}; \mu, \Sigma)$ is an M-dimensional Gaussian density with mean vector μ and covariance Σ, and the π_i are the mixing parameters of the components, satisfying $\sum \pi_i = 1$. The mixture is completely specified by the parameter $\Theta = \{\pi_i, \mu_i, \Sigma_i\}_{i=1}^{N_c}$. Given a training set $\{\mathbf{y}^t\}_{t=1}^{N_T}$ the mixture parameters can be estimated using the ML principle

$$\Theta^* \;=\; \text{argmax} \left[\prod_{t=1}^{N_T} P(\mathbf{y}^t|\Theta) \right] \tag{16}$$

This estimation problem is best solved using the Expectation-Maximization (EM) algorithm [11] which consists of the following two-step iterative procedure:

- E-step:

$$h_i^k(t) = \frac{\pi_i^k g(\mathbf{y}^t; \mu_i^k, \Sigma_i^k)}{\sum_{j=1}^{N_c} \pi_j^k g(\mathbf{y}^t; \mu_j^k, \Sigma_i^k)} \tag{17}$$

- M-step:

$$\pi_i^{k+1} = \frac{\sum_{t=1}^{N_T} h_i^k(t)}{\sum_{i=1}^{N_c} \sum_{t=1}^{N_T} h_i^k(t)} \tag{18}$$

$$\mu_i^{k+1} = \frac{\sum_{t=1}^{N_T} h_i^k(t)\mathbf{y}^t}{\sum_{t=1}^{N_T} h_i^k(t)} \tag{19}$$

$$\Sigma_i^{k+1} = \frac{\sum_{t=1}^{N_T} h_i^k(t)(\mathbf{y}^t - \mu_i^{k+1})(\mathbf{y}^t - \mu_i^{k+1})^T}{\sum_{t=1}^{N_T} h_i^k(t)} \tag{20}$$

The E-step computes the *a posteriori* probabilities $h_i(t)$ which are the *expectations* of "missing" component labels $z_i(t) = \{0, 1\}$ which denote the membership of $\mathbf{y}^t$ in the i-th component. Once these expectations have been computed, the M-step maximizes the joint likelihood of the data *and* the "missing" variables $z_i(t)$. The EM algorithm is monotonically convergent in *likelihood* and is thus guaranteed to find a local maximum in the total likelihood of the training set. Further details of the EM algorithm for estimation of mixture densities can be found in [29].

Given our operating assumptions — that the training data is M-dimensional (at most) and resides solely in the principal subspace F with the exception of perturbations due to white Gaussian measurement noise, or equivalently that the $\bar{F}$-space component of the data is itself a separable Gaussian density — the estimate of the complete likelihood function $P(\mathbf{x}|\Omega)$ is given by

$$\hat{P}(\mathbf{x}|\Omega) = P(\mathbf{y}|\Theta^*) \, \hat{P}_{\bar{F}}(\mathbf{x}|\Omega) \tag{21}$$

where $\hat{P}_{\bar{F}}(\mathbf{x}|\Omega)$ is a Gaussian component density based on the DFFS, as before.

3.   Maximum likelihood detection

The density estimate $\hat{P}(\mathbf{x}|\Omega)$ can be used to compute a local measure of target saliency at each spatial position (i, j) in an input image based on the vector $\mathbf{x}$ obtained by the lexicographic ordering of the pixel values in a local neighborhood R

$$S(i, j; \Omega) = \hat{P}(\mathbf{x}|\Omega) , \quad \mathbf{x} = \downarrow [\{I(i + r, j + c) : (r, c) \in R\}] \tag{22}$$

where $\downarrow [\bullet]$ is the operator which converts a subimage into a vector. The ML estimate of position of the target Ω is then given by

$$(i, j)^{\text{ML}} = \text{argmax } S(i, j; \Omega) \tag{23}$$

This ML formulation can be extended to estimate object scale with *multiscale* saliency maps. The likelihood computation is performed (in parallel) on linearly scaled versions of the input image $I^{(\sigma)}$ corresponding to a pre-determined set of scales $\{\sigma_1, \sigma_2, \cdots \sigma_n\}$

$$S(i, j, k; \Omega) = \hat{P}\left(\downarrow \{I^{(\sigma_k)}(\sigma_k i + r, \sigma_k j + c) : (r, c) \in R\} \mid \Omega \right) \tag{24}$$

where the ML estimate of the spatial and scale indices is defined by

$$(i, j, k)^{\text{ML}} = \text{argmax } S(i, j, k ; \Omega) \tag{25}$$

4.   Applications

The above ML detection technique has been tested in the detection of complex natural objects including human faces, facial features (*e.g.,* eyes), and non-rigid articulated objects such as human hands. In this section we will present several examples from these application domains.

4.1.   Faces

Over the years, various strategies for facial feature detection have been proposed, ranging from edge map projections [15], to more recent techniques using generalized symmetry operators [30] and multilayer perceptrons [35]. In any robust face processing system this task is critically important since a face must be first geometrically normalized by aligning its features with those of a stored model before recognition can be attempted.

The eigentemplate approach to the detection of facial features in "mugshots" was proposed in [26], where the DFFS metric was shown to be superior to standard template matching for target detection. The detection task was the estimation of the position of facial features (the left and right eyes, the tip of the nose and the center of the mouth) in frontal view photographs of faces at fixed scale. Figure 4 shows examples of facial feature training templates and the resulting detections on the MIT Media Laboratory's database of 7,562 "mugshots".

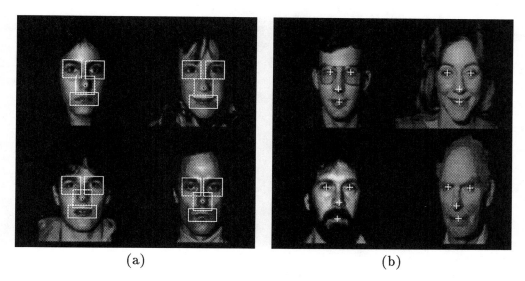

(a) (b)

Figure 4: *(a) Examples of facial feature training templates and (b) the resulting typical detections.*

We have compared the detection performance of three different detectors on approximately 7,000 test images from this database: a sum-of-square-differences (SSD) detector based on the average facial feature (in this case the left eye), an eigentemplate or DFFS detector and a ML detector based on $S(i, j; \Omega)$ as defined in section 2.2. Figure 5(a) shows the *receiver operating characteristic* (ROC) curves for these detectors, obtained by varying the detection threshold independently for each detector. The DFFS and ML detectors were computed based on a 5-dimensional principal subspace. Since the projection coefficients were unimodal a Gaussian distribution was used in modeling the true distribution for the ML detector as in section 2.2. Note that the ML detector exhibits the best detection vs. false-alarm tradeoff and yields the highest detection rate (95%). Indeed, at the *same* detection rate the ML detector has a false-alarm rate which is nearly 2 orders of magnitude lower than the SSD.

Figure 5(b) provides the geometric intuition regarding the operation of these detectors. The SSD detector's threshold is based on the *radial* distance between the average template (the origin of this space) and the input pattern. This leads to hyperspherical detection regions about the origin. In contrast, the DFFS detector measures the orthogonal distance to F, thus forming planar acceptance regions about F. Consequently to accept valid object patterns in Ω which are very different from the mean, the SSD detector must operate with high thresholds which result in many false alarms. However, the DFFS detector can not discriminate between the object class Ω and non-Ω patterns in F. The solution is provided by the ML detector which incorporates both the $\bar{F}$-space component (DFFS) and the F-space likelihood (DIFS). The probabilistic interpretation of Figure 5(b) is

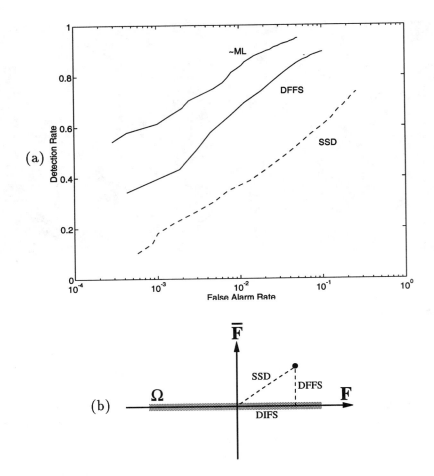

Figure 5: *(a) Detection performance of an SSD, DFFS and a ML detector, (b) geometric interpretation of the detectors.*

as follows: SSD assumes a *single* prototype (the mean) in additive white Gaussian noise whereas the DFFS assumes a *uniform* density in F. The ML detector, on the other hand, uses the complete probability density for detection.

We have incorporated and tested the multiscale version of the ML detection technique in a face detection task. This multiscale head finder was tested on the ARPA FERET database where 97% of 2,000 faces were correctly detected. Figure 6 shows examples of the ML estimate of the position and scale on these images. The multiscale saliency maps $S(i, j, k; \Omega)$ were computed based on the likelihood estimate $\hat{P}(\mathbf{x}|\Omega)$ in a 10-dimensional principal subspace using a Gaussian model (section 2.2). Note that this detector is able to localize the position and scale of the head despite variations in hair style and hair color, as well as presence of sunglasses. Illumination invariance was obtained by normalizing the input subimage $\mathbf{x}$ to a zero-mean unit-norm vector.

Figure 6: *Examples of multiscale face detection.*

4.1.1. USING ML DETECTION FOR CODING

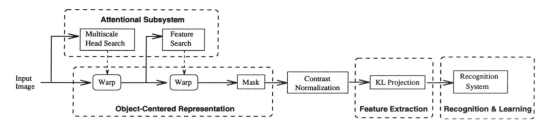

Figure 7: *The face processing system.*

We have also used the multiscale version of the ML detector as the *attentional* component of an automatic system for recognition and model-based coding of faces. The block diagram of this system is shown in Figure 7 which consists of a two-stage object detection and alignment stage, a contrast normalization stage, and a feature extraction stage whose output is used for both recognition and coding. Figure 8 illustrates the operation of the detection and alignment stage on a natural test image containing a human face. The function of the face finder is to locate regions in the image which have a high likelihood of containing a face.

The first step in this process is illustrated in Figure 8(b) where the ML estimate of the position and scale of the face are indicated by the cross-hairs and bounding box. Once these regions have been identified, the estimated scale and position are used to normalize for translation and scale, yielding a standard "head-in-the-box" format image (Figure 8(c)). A second feature detection stage operates at this fixed scale to estimate the position of 4 facial features: the left and right eyes, the tip of the nose and the center of the mouth (Figure 8(d)). Once the facial features have been detected, the face image is warped to align the geometry and shape of the face with that of a canonical model. Then the facial region is extracted (by applying a fixed mask) and subsequently normalized for contrast.

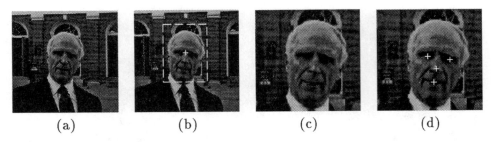

Figure 8: *(a) original image, (b) position and scale estimate, (c) normalized head image, (d) position of facial features.*

The geometrically aligned and normalized image (shown in Figure 9(a)) is then projected onto a custom set of eigenfaces to obtain a feature vector which is then used for recognition purposes as well as facial image coding.

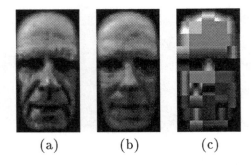

Figure 9: *(a) aligned face, (b) eigenspace reconstruction (85 bytes) (c) JPEG reconstruction (530 bytes).*

Figure 9 shows the normalized facial image extracted from Figure 8(d), its reconstruction using a 100-dimensional eigenspace representation (requiring only 85 bytes to encode) and a comparable non-parametric reconstruction obtained using a standard transform-coding approach for image compression (requiring 530 bytes to encode). This example illustrates that the eigenface representation used for recognition is also an effective *model-based* representation for data compression. The first 8 eigenfaces used for this representation are shown in Figure 10.

4.1.2. USING ML DETECTION FOR RECOGNITION

Figure 11 shows the results of a similarity search in an image database tool called Photobook [27]. Each face in the database was automatically detected and aligned by the face processing system in Figure 7. The normalized faces were then projected onto a 100-dimensional eigenspace. The image in the upper left is the one searched on and the remainder are the ranked nearest neighbors in the FERET

Figure 10: *The first 8 eigenfaces.*

database. The top three matches in this case are images of the same person taken a month apart and at different scales. The recognition accuracy (defined as the percent correct rank-one matches) on a database of 155 individuals is 99% [21].

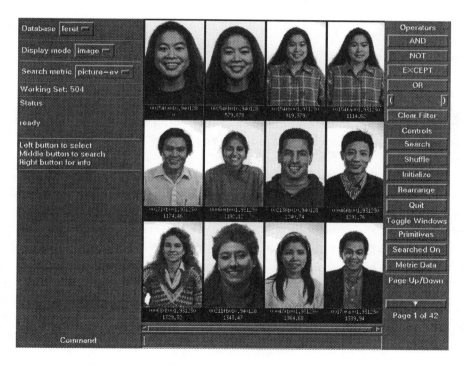

Figure 11: *Photobook: FERET face database.*

4.1.3. RECOGNITION ON LARGE DATABASES

In order to have an estimate of the recognition performance on much larger databases, we have conducted tests on a database of 7,562 images of approximately 3,000 people. The images were collected in a small booth at a Boston photography show, and include men, women, and children of all ages and races. Head position was controlled by asking people to take their own picture when they were lined up with the camera. Two LEDs placed at the bottom of holes adjacent to the camera allowed them to judge their alignment; when they could see both LEDs then they were correctly aligned.

The eigenfaces for this database were approximated using a principal components analysis on a representative sample of 128 faces. Recognition and matching was subsequently performed using the first 20 eigenvectors.

To assess the average recognition rate, 200 faces were selected at random, and a nearest-neighbor rule was used to find the most-similar face from the entire database. If the most-similar face was of the same person then a correct recognition was scored. In this experiment the eigenvector-based recognition system produced a recognition accuracy of 95%. This performance is somewhat surprising because the database contains wide variations in expression, and has relatively weak control of head position and illumination. In a *verification* task, our system yielded a false rejection rate of 1.5% at a false acceptance rate of 0.01%.

4.1.4. VIEW-BASED RECOGNITION

The problem of face recognition under general viewing conditions (change in pose) can also be approached using an eigenspace formulation. There are essentially two ways of approaching this problem using an eigenspace framework. Given N individuals under M different views, one can do recognition and pose estimation in a universal eigenspace computed from the combination of NM images. In this way a single "parametric eigenspace" will encode both identity as well as pose. Such an approach, for example, has recently been used by Murase and Nayar [22] for general 3D object recognition.

Alternatively, given N individuals under M different views, we can build a "view-based" set of M distinct eigenspaces, each capturing the variation of the N individuals in a common view. The view-based eigenspace is essentially an extension of the eigenface technique to multiple sets of eigenvectors, one for each combination of scale and orientation. One can view this architecture as a set of parallel "observers" each trying to explain the image data with their set of eigenvectors (see also Darrell and Pentland [10]). In this view-based, multiple-observer approach, the first step is to determine the location and orientation of the target object by selecting the eigenspace which best describes the input image. This can be accomplished by calculating the likelihood estimate using each viewspace's eigenvectors and then selecting the maximum.

The key difference between the view-based and parametric representations can be understood by considering the geometry of facespace. In the high-dimensional vector space of an input image, multiple-orientation training images are represented by a set of M distinct regions, each defined by the scatter of N individuals. Multiple views of a face form non-convex (yet connected) regions in image space [2]. Therefore the resulting ensemble is a highly complex and non-separable manifold.

The parametric eigenspace attempts to describe this ensemble with a projec-

Figure 12: *Some of the images used to test accuracy at face recognition despite wide variations in head orientation. Average recognition accuracy was 92%, the orientation error had a standard deviation of 15°.*

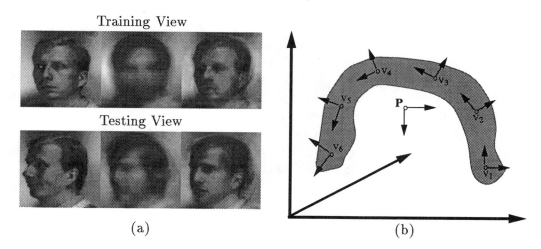

(a)

(b)

Figure 13: *(a) parametric vs. view-based eigenspace reconstructions for a training view and a novel testing view. The input image is shown in the left column. The middle and right columns correspond to the parametric and view-based reconstructions, respectively. All reconstructions were computed using the first 10 eigenvectors. (b) a schematic representation of the two approaches.*

tion onto a single low-dimensional linear subspace (corresponding to the first n eigenvectors of the NM training images). In contrast, the view-based approach corresponds to M independent subspaces, each describing a particular region of the facespace (corresponding to a particular view of a face). The relevant analogy here is that of modeling a complex distribution by a single cluster model or by the union of several component clusters. Naturally, the latter (view-based) representation can yield a more accurate representation of the underlying geometry.

This difference in representation becomes evident when considering the quality of reconstructed images using the two different methods. Figure 13 compares reconstructions obtained with the two methods when trained on images of faces at multiple orientations. In Figure 13(a) we see first an image in the training set, followed by reconstructions of this image using first the parametric eigenspace and then the view-based eigenspace. Note that in the parametric reconstruction neither the pose nor the identity of the individual is adequately captured. The view-based reconstruction, on the other hand, provides a much better characterization of the object. Similarly, in Figure 13(b) we see a novel view ($+68°$) with respect to the training set ($-90°$ to $+45°$). Here, both reconstructions correspond to the nearest view in the training set ($+45°$) but the view-based reconstruction is seen to be more representative of the individual's identity. Although the quality of the reconstruction is not a direct indicator of the recognition power, from an information-theoretic point-of-view the multiple eigenspace representation is a more accurate representation of the signal content.

We have evaluated the view-based approach with data similar to that shown in Figure 12. This data consists of 189 images consisting of nine views of 21 people. The nine views of each person were evenly spaced from $-90°$ to $+90°$ along the horizontal plane. In the first series of experiments the *interpolation* performance was tested by training on a subset of the available views $\{\pm90°, \pm45°, 0°\}$ and testing on the intermediate views $\{\pm68°, \pm23°\}$. A 90% average recognition rate was obtained. A second series of experiments tested the *extrapolation* performance by training on a range of views (*e.g.*, $-90°$ to $+45°$) and testing on novel views outside the training range (*e.g.*, $+68°$ and $+90°$). For testing views separated by $\pm23°$ from the training range, the average recognition rates were 83%. For $\pm45°$ testing views, the average recognition rates were 50% (see [26] for further details).

4.1.5.   MODULAR RECOGNITION

The eigenface recognition method is easily extended to facial features as shown in Figure 14(a). This leads to an improvement in recognition performance by incorporating an additional layer of description in terms of facial features. This can be viewed as either a modular or layered representation of a face, where a coarse (low-resolution) description of the whole head is augmented by additional (higher-resolution) details in terms of salient facial features.

The utility of this layered representation (eigenface plus eigenfeatures) was tested on a small subset of our large face database. We selected a representative

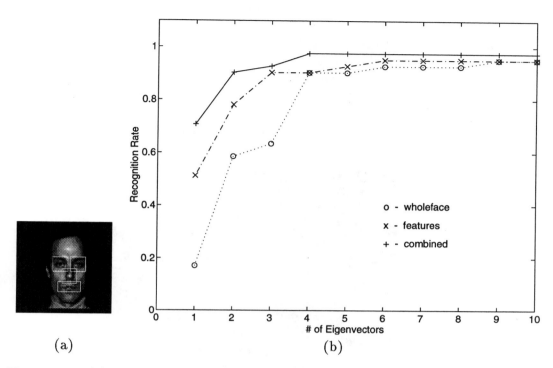

(a) (b)

Figure 14: *(a) facial eigenfeature regions, (b) recognition rates for eigenfaces, eigenfeatures and the combined modular representation.*

sample of 45 individuals with two views per person, corresponding to different facial expressions (neutral vs. smiling). These set of images was partitioned into a training set (neutral) and a testing set (smiling). Since the difference between these particular facial expressions is primarily articulated in the mouth, this feature was discarded for recognition purposes.

Figure 14(b) shows the recognition rates as a function of the number of eigenvectors for eigenface-only, eigenfeature-only and the combined representation. What is surprising is that (for this small dataset at least) the eigenfeatures alone were sufficient in achieving an (asymptotic) recognition rate of 95% (equal to that of the eigenfaces). More surprising, perhaps, is the observation that in the lower dimensions of eigenspace, eigenfeatures outperformed the eigenface recognition. Finally, by using the combined representation, we gain a slight improvement in the asymptotic recognition rate (98%). A similar effect was reported by Brunelli and Poggio [4] where the cumulative normalized correlation scores of templates for the face, eyes, nose and mouth showed improved performance over the face-only templates.

A potential advantage of the eigenfeature layer is the ability to overcome the shortcomings of the standard eigenface method. A pure eigenface recognition system can be fooled by gross variations in the input image (hats, beards, etc.).

Figure 15(a) shows additional testing views of 3 individuals in the above dataset of 45. These test images are indicative of the type of variations which can lead to false matches: a hand near the face, a painted face, and a beard. Figure 15(b) shows the nearest matches found based on standard eigenface matching. Neither of the 3 matches correspond to the correct individual. On the other hand, Figure 15(c) shows the nearest matches based on the eyes and nose, and results in correct identification in each case. This simple example illustrates the potential advantage of a modular representation in disambiguating low-confidence eigenface matches.

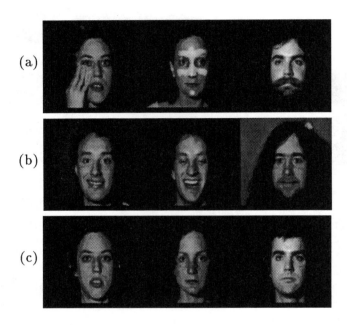

Figure 15: *(a) Test views, (b) Eigenface matches, (c) Eigenfeature matches.*

4.1.6. RECOGNITION USING EDGE-BASED FEATURES

We have also extended the normalized eigenface representation into an edge-based domain for facial description. We simply run the normalized facial image through a Canny edge detector to yield an edge map as shown in Figure 16(a). Such an edge map is simply an alternative representation which imparts mostly *shape* (as opposed to texture) information and has the advantage of being less susceptible to illumination changes. The recognition rate of a pure edge-based normalized eigenface representation (on a FERET database of 155 individuals) was found to be 95% which is surprising considering that it utilizes what appears to be (to humans at least) a rather impoverished representation. The slight drop in recognition rate is most likely due to the increased dimensionality of this representation space and its greater sensitivity to expression changes, *etc.*

Interestingly, we can combine both texture and edge-based representations

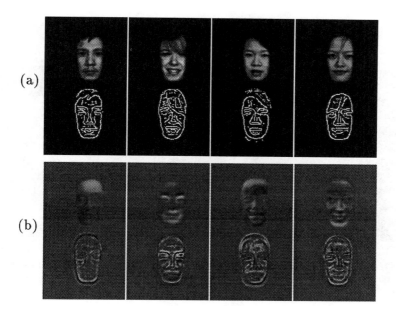

Figure 16: *(a) Examples of combined texture/edge-based face representations and (b) few of the resulting eigenvectors.*

of the object by simply performing a KL expansion on the augmented images shown in Figure 16. The resulting eigenvectors conveniently decorrelate the joint representation and provide a basis set which optimally spans both domains simultaneously. With this bimodal representation, the recognition rate was found to be 97%. Though still less than a normalized grayscale representation, we believe a bimodal representation can have distinct advantages for tasks other than recognition, such as detection and image interpolation.

4.2. HANDS

We have also applied our eigenspace density estimation technique to articulated and non-rigid objects such as hands. In this particular domain, however, the original intensity image is an unsuitable representation since, unlike faces, hands are essentially textureless objects. Their identity is characterized by the variety of *shapes* they can assume. For this reason we have chosen an edge-based representation of hand shapes which is invariant with respect to illumination, contrast and scene background. A training set of hand gestures was obtained against a black background. The 2D contour of the hand was then extracted using a Canny edge-operator. These binary edge maps, however, are highly uncorrelated with each other due to their sparse nature. This leads to a very high-dimensional principal subspace. Therefore to reduce the intrinsic dimensionality, we *induced* spatial correlation via a *diffusion* process on the binary edge map, which effectively broadens

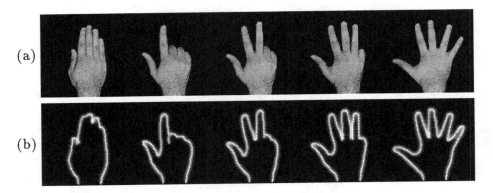

Figure 17: *(a) Examples of hand gestures and (b) their diffused edge-based representation.*

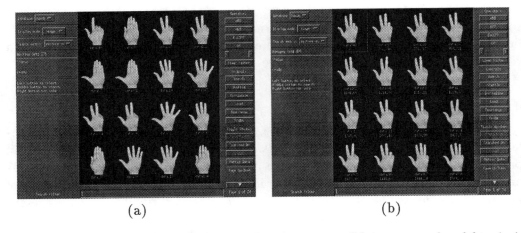

(a)   (b)

Figure 18: *(a) a random collection of hand gestures (b) images ordered by similarity (left-to-right, top-to-bottom) to the image at the upper left.*

and "smears" the edges, yielding a continuous-valued contour image which represents the object shape in terms of the spatial distribution of edges. Figure 17 shows examples of training images and their diffused edge map representations. We note that this *spatiotopic* representation of shape is biologically motivated and therefore differs from methods based purely on computational considerations (*e.g.,* moments [13], Fourier descriptors [20], "snakes" [16], Point Distribution Models [7], and modal descriptions [32]).

It is important to verify whether such a representation is adequate for discriminating between different hand shapes. Therefore we tested the diffused contour image representation in a recognition experiment which yielded a 100% rank-one accuracy on 375 frames from an image sequence containing 7 hand gestures. The matching technique was a nearest-neighbor classification rule in a 16-dimensional principal subspace. Figure 18(a) shows some examples of the various hand gestures used in this experiment. Figure 18(b) shows the 15 images that are most similar to the "two" gesture appearing in the top left. Note that the hand gestures judged most similar are all objectively the same shape.

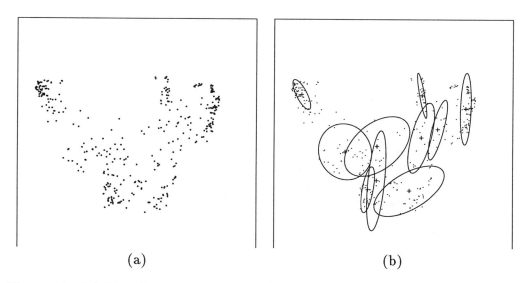

(a)   (b)

Figure 19: *(a) Distribution of training hand shapes (shown in the first two dimensions of the principal subspace) (b) Mixture-of-Gaussians fit using 10 components.*

Naturally, the success of such a recognition system is critically dependent on the ability to find the hand (in any of its articulated states) in a cluttered scene, to account for its scale and to align it with respect to an object-centered reference frame prior to recognition. This localization was achieved with the same multiscale ML detection paradigm used with faces, with the exception that the underlying image representation of the hands was the diffused edge map rather the grayscale image.

The probability distribution of hand shapes in this representation was auto-

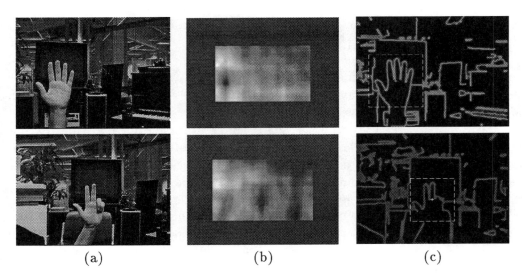

(a)   (b)   (c)

Figure 20: *(a) Original grayscale image, (b) negative log-likelihood map (at most likely scale) and (c) ML estimate of position and scale superimposed on edge map.*

matically learned using our eigenspace density estimation technique. In this case, however, the distribution of training data is *multimodal* due to the different hand shapes. Therefore the multimodal density estimation technique in section 2.3 was used. Figure 19(a) shows a projection of the training data on the first two dimensions of the principal subspace F (defined in this case by $M = 16$) which exhibit the underlying multimodality of the data. Figure 19(b) shows a 10-component Mixture-of-Gaussians density estimate for the training data. The parameters of this estimate were obtained with 20 iterations of the EM algorithm. The orthogonal $\bar{F}$-space component of the density was modeled with a Gaussian distribution as in section 2.3.

The resulting complete density estimate $\hat{P}(\mathbf{x}|\Omega)$ was then used in a detection experiment on test imagery of hand gestures against a cluttered background scene. In accordance with our representation, the input imagery was first pre-processed to generate a diffused edge map and then scaled accordingly for a multiscale saliency computation. Figure 20 shows two examples from the test sequence, where we have shown the original image, the negative log-likelihood saliency map, and the ML estimates of position and scale (superimposed on the diffused edge map). Note that these examples represent two different hand gestures at slightly different scales.

To better quantify the performance of the ML detector on hands we carried out the following experiment. The original 375-frame video sequence of training hand gestures was divided into 2 parts. The first (training) half of this sequence was used for learning, including computation of the KL basis and the subsequent EM clustering. For this experiment we used a 5-component mixture in a 10-

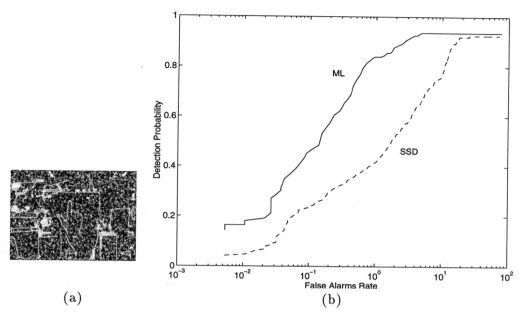

(a)   (b)

Figure 21: *(a) Example of test frame containing a hand gesture amidst severe background clutter and (b) ROC curve performance contrasting SSD and ML detectors.*

dimensional principal subspace. The second (testing) half of the sequence was then embedded in the background scene, which contains a variety of shapes. In addition, severe noise conditions were simulated as shown in Figure 21(a).

We then compared the detection performance of an SSD detector (based on the mean edge-based hand representation) and a probabilistic detector based on the complete estimated density. The resulting negative-log-likelihood detection maps were passed through a valley-detector to isolate local minimum candidates which were then subjected to a ROC analysis. A correct detection was defined as a below-threshold local minimum within a 5-pixel radius of the ground truth target location. Figure 21(b) shows the performance curves obtained for the two detectors. We note, for example, that at an 85% detection probability the ML detector yields (on the average) 1 false alarm per frame, where as the SSD detector yields an order of magnitude more false alarms.

5. DISCUSSION

In this paper we have described an eigenspace density estimation technique for unsupervised visual learning which exploits the *intrinsic* low-dimensionality of the training imagery to form a computationally simple estimator for the complete likelihood function of the object. Our estimator is based on a subspace decomposition and can be evaluated using only the M-dimensional principal component vector. We derived the form for an optimal estimator and its associated expected cost for the case of a Gaussian density. In contrast to previous work on learning and characterization — which uses PCA primarily for dimensionality reduction and/or feature extraction — our method uses the eigenspace decomposition as an integral part of estimating *complete* density functions in high-dimensional image spaces. These density estimates were then used in a maximum likelihood formulation for target detection. The multiscale version of this detection strategy was demonstrated in applications in which it functioned as an attentional subsystem for object recognition. The performance was found to be superior to existing detection techniques in experiments with large numbers of test data.

We note that from a probabilistic perspective, the class conditional density $P(\mathbf{x}|\Omega)$ is the most important object representation to be learned. This density is the critical component in detection, recognition, prediction, interpolation and general inference. For example, having learned these densities for several object classes $\{\Omega_1, \Omega_2, \cdots, \Omega_n\}$, one can invoke a Bayesian framework for classification and recognition:

$$P(\Omega_i|\mathbf{x}) = \frac{P(\mathbf{x}|\Omega_i)P(\Omega_i)}{\sum\limits_{j=1}^{n} P(\mathbf{x}|\Omega_j)P(\Omega_j)} \qquad (26)$$

where now a maximum *a posteriori* (MAP) classification rule can be used for object/pose identification.

Such a framework is also important in detection. In fact, the ML detection framework can be extended using the notion of a "not-class" $\bar{\Omega}$, resulting in *a posteriori* saliency maps of the form

$$S(i, j, k; \Omega) = P(\Omega|\mathbf{x}) = \frac{P(\mathbf{x}|\Omega)P(\Omega)}{P(\mathbf{x}|\bar{\Omega})P(\bar{\Omega}) + P(\mathbf{x}|\Omega)P(\Omega)} \qquad (27)$$

where now a maximum *a posteriori* (MAP) rule can be used to estimate the position and scale of the object. One difficulty with such a formulation is that the "not-class" $\bar{\Omega}$ is, in practice, too broad a category and is therefore multimodal and very high-dimensional. One possible approach to this problem is to use ML detection to identify the particular subclass of $\bar{\Omega}$ which has high likelihoods (*e.g.,* false alarms) and then to estimate this distribution and use it in the MAP framework. This can be viewed as a probabilistic approach to learning using positive as well as *negative* examples.

In fact, such a MAP framework can be viewed as a Bayesian formulation of some neural network approaches to target detection. Perhaps the most closely related is the neural network face detector of Sung and Poggio [33] which is essentially a trainable nonlinear binary pattern classifier. They too learn the distribution of the object class with a Mixture-of-Gaussians model (using an elliptical k-means algorithm instead of EM). Instead of likelihoods, however, input patterns are represented by a set of distances to each mixture component (similar to a combination of the DIFS and DFFS), thus forming a feature vector indicative of the overall class membership. In addition, Sung and Poggio explicitly model the "not-class" by learning the distribution of nearby *non-face* patterns. The set of distances to both classes are then used to train a neural network to discriminate between face and non-face patterns (similar to computing a likelihood ratio in MAP). Another recent example of a neural network technique for object detection which also utilizes negative examples is the face-finder system of Rowley *et al.* [31]. The experimental results obtained with these methods clearly demonstrate the need for incorporating negative examples in building robust detection systems.

ACKNOWLEDGEMENTS

The FERET database was provided by the US Army Research Laboratory. The multiple-view face database was provided by Westinghouse Electric Systems.

REFERENCES

[1] Anderson, C.H., Burt, P.J., and Van der Wall, G.S., "Change Detection and Tracking Using Pyramid Transform Techniques," *Proc. of SPIE Conf. on Intelligence, Robots and Computer Vision*, vol. 579, pp. 72-78, 1985.

[2] Bichsel, M., and Pentland, A., "Human Face Recognition and the Face Image Set's Topology," *CVGIP: Image Understanding*, vol. 59, no. 2, pp. 254-261, 1994.

[3] Bregler, C., and Omohundro, S.M., "Surface Learning with Applications to Lip Reading," in *Advances in Neural Information Processing Systems 6*, eds. J.D. Cowan, G. Tesauro and J. Alspector, Morgan Kaufman Publishers, San Fransisco, pp. 43-50, 1994.

[4] Brunelli, R., and Poggio, T., "Face Recognition: Features vs. Templates,", *IEEE Trans. on Pattern Analysis and Machine Intelligence,*, vol. 15, no. 10, Oct. 1993.

[5] Brunelli, R., and Messelodi, S., "Robust Estimation of Correlation: An Application to Computer Vision," *IRST Tech. Report no. 9310-015*, October 1993.

[6] Burl, M.C., *et al.*, "Automating the Hunt for Volcanos on Venus," *Proc. IEEE Conf. on Computer Vision & Pattern Recognition*, Seattle, WA, June 21-23, 1994.

[7] Cootes, T.F. and Taylor, C.J., "Active Shape Models: Smart Snakes," in *Proc. British Machine Vision Conf.*, Springer-Verlag, pp. 9-18, 1992.

[8] Cootes, T.F., Hill, A., Taylor, C.J. and Haslam, J., "Use of Active Shape Models for Locating Structures in Medical Images," *Image and Vision Computing*, vol. 12, no. 6, pp. 355-365, July/August 1994.

[9] Cover, M. and Thomas, J.A., *Elements of Information Theory*, John Wiley & Sons, New York, 1994.

[10] Darrell, T., and Pentland, A., "Space-Time Gestures," *Proc. IEEE Conf. on Computer Vision & Pattern Recognition*, New York, NY, June 1993.

[11] Dempster, A.P., Laird, N.M., Rubin, D.B., "Maximum Likelihood from Incomplete Data via the EM Algorithm," *Journal of the Royal Statistical Society B*, vol. 39, 1977.

[12] Golub, G.H. and Van Loan, C.F., *Matrix Computations*, Johns Hopkins Press, 1989.

[13] Hu, M.K., "Visual Pattern Recognition by Moment Invariants," *IEEE Trans. on Information Theory*, vol. 8, pp. 179-187, 1962.

[14] Jolliffe, I.T., *Principal Component Analysis*, Springer-Verlag, New York, 1986.

[15] Kanade, T., "Picture Processing by Computer Complex and Recognition of Human Faces," Tech. Report, Kyoto University, Dept. of Information Science, 1973.

[16] Kass, M., Witkin, A., and Terzopoulos, D., "Snakes: Active Contour Models," *Int'l Journal of Computer Vision*, vol. 1, no. 4, pp. 321-331, 1987.

[17] Kirby, M., and Sirovich, L., "Application of the Karhunen-Loeve Procedure for the Characterization of Human Faces," *IEEE Trans. Pattern Analysis and Machine Intelligence*, vol. 12, no. 1, Jan. 1990.

[18] Kumar, B., Casasent, D., and Murakami, H., "Principal Component Imagery for Statistical Pattern Recognition Correlators," *Optical Engineering*, vol. 21, no. 1, Jan/Feb 1982.

[19] Loeve, M.M., *Probability Theory*, Van Nostrand, Princeton, 1955.

[20] McElroy, T., Wilson, E., and Anspach, G. "Fourier Descriptors and Neural Networks for Shape Classification," in *Proc. of Int'l Conf. on Acoustics, Speech and Signal Processing*, Detroit, MI, May 1995.

[21] Moghaddam, B. and Pentland, A., "Face Recognition Using View-Based and Modular Eigenspaces," in *Automatic Systems for the Identification and Inspection of Humans*, SPIE vol. 2277. 1994.

[22] Murase, H., and Nayar, S.K., "Visual Learning and Recognition of 3D Objects from Appearance," *Int'l Journal of Computer Vision*, vol. 14, no. 1, 1995.

[23] Nayar, S.K., Murase, H., and Nene, S.A., "General Learning Algorithm for Robot Vision," in *Neural & Stochastic Methods in Image & Signal Processing*, SPIE vol. 2304, July 1994.

[24] Palmer, S.E., "The Psychology of Perceptual Organization: A Transformational Approach," in *Human and Machine Vision*, J. Beck, B. Hope and A. Rosenfeld (eds.), Academic Press, 1983.

[25] Pentland, A. and Sclaroff, S., "Closed-Form Solutions for Physically Based Shape Modeling and Recovery," *IEEE Trans. Pattern Analysis and Machine Intelligence*, vol. 13, no. 7, pp. 715–729, July 1991.

[26] Pentland, A., Moghaddam, B. and Starner, T., "View-based and Modular Eigenspaces for Face Recognition," *Proc. of IEEE Conf. on Computer Vision & Pattern Recognition*, Seattle, WA, June 1994.

[27] Pentland, A., Picard, R., and Sclaroff, S., "Photobook: Tools for Content-Based Manipulation of Image Databases," in *Storage and Retrieval of Image and Video Databases II*, SPIE vol. 2185, San Jose, Feb 6-10, 1994.

[28] Poggio, T. and Girosi, F., "Networks for Approximation and Learning," *Proceedings of the IEEE*, vol. 78, no. 9, pp. 1481-1497, 1990.

[29] Redner, R.A., and Walker, H.F., "Mixture Densities, Maximum Likelihood and the EM Algorithm," *SIAM Review*, vol. 26, no. 2, pp. 195-239, 1984.

[30] Reisfeld, D., Wolfson, H., and Yeshurun, Y., "Detection of Interest Points Using Symmetry,", *Proc. of Int'l Conf. on Computer Vision*, Osaka, Japan, Dec. 1990.

[31] Rowley, H., Baluja, S. and Kanade, T., "Human Face Detection in Visual Scenes," Technical Report CMU-CS-95-158, Carnegie Mellon University, July 1995.

[32] Sclaroff, S. and Pentland, A., "Modal Matching for Correspondence and Recognition," *IEEE Trans. on Pattern Analysis & Machine Intelligence*, vol. 17, no. 6, pp. 545-561, 1995.

[33] Sung, K., and Poggio, T., "Example-based Learning for View-based Human Face Detection," in *Proc. of Image Understanding Workshop*, Monterey, CA, November 1994.

[34] Turk, M., and Pentland, A., "Eigenfaces for Recognition," *Journal of Cognitive Neuroscience*, vol. 3, no. 1, 1991.

[35] Vincent, J. M., Waite, J. B., and Myers, D. J, "Automatic Location of Visual Features by a System of Multilayered Perceptrons," *IEE Proceedings,* vol. 139, no. 6, Dec. 1992.

[36] Weng, J.J., "On Comprehensive Visual Learning," in *Proc. NSF/ARPA Workshop on Performance vs. Methodology in Computer Vision,* Seattle, WA, June 24-25, 1994.

Parametric Appearance Representation

Shree K. Nayar
Columbia University

Hiroshi Murase
NTT Basic Research Laboratory

Sameer A. Nene
Columbia University

Abstract

In contrast to the traditional approach, the recognition problem is formulated as one of matching appearance rather than shape. For any given vision task, all possible appearance variations define its visual workspace. A set of images is obtained by coarsely sampling the workspace. The image set is compressed to obtain a low-dimensional subspace, called the eigenspace, in which the visual workspace is represented as a continuous appearance manifold. Given an unknown input image, the recognition system first projects the image to eigenspace. The parameters of the vision task are recognized based on the exact position of the projection on the appearance manifold. The proposed appearance representation has several applications in visual perception. As examples, a real-time recognition system with 20 complex objects, an illumination planning technique for robust object recognition, and a real-time visual positioning and tracking system are described. The simplicity and generality of the proposed ideas have led to the development of a comprehensive software library for appearance modeling and matching.

1. Introduction

Vision research has placed significant emphasis on the development of compact and descriptive shape representations for object recognition [39, 3, 23]. This has lead to the creation of a variety of novel representations, including, generalized cylinders [4], superquadrics [2][33], extended gaussian images [10], parametric bicubic patches [23] and differential geometric representations [5], only to name a few. While these representations are all useful in specific application domains, each has been found to have its own drawbacks. This has kept researchers in search for more powerful representations.

Will shape representation suffice? After all, vision deals with brightness images that are functions not only of shape but also other intrinsic scene properties such as reflectance and perpetually varying factors such as illumination. This observation has led to the exploration of view-based approaches to object recognition (see [37][43][14][44][38] for examples). It motivates us to take an extreme approach to visual representation. What we seek is not a representation of shape but rather appearance [19], encoded in which are brightness variations caused by three-dimensional shape, surface reflectance properties, sensor parameters, and illumination conditions. Given the number of factors at work, it is immediate that an appearance representation that captures all possible variations is simply impractical. Fortunately, there exist a wide collection of vision applications where pertinent variables are few and hence compact appearance representation in a low-dimensional space is indeed possible.

An added drawback of shape representation emerges when a vision programmer attempts to develop a practical recognition system. Techniques for automatically acquiring shape models from sample objects are only being researched. For now, a vision programmer is forced to select an appropriate shape representation, design object models using the chosen representation, and then manually input this information into the system. This procedure is cumbersome and impractical when dealing with large sets of objects, or objects with complex shapes. It is clear that recognition systems of the future must be capable of acquiring object models without human assistance. It turns out that the appearance representation proposed here is easier to acquire through an automatic learning phase than to create manually.

The appearance of an object is the combined effect of its shape, reflectance properties, pose in the scene, and the illumination conditions. While shape and reflectance are intrinsic properties that do not change for any rigid object, pose and illumination vary from one scene to the next. We approach the visual learning problem as one of acquiring a compact model of the object's appearance under different poses and illumination directions. The object is "shown" to the image sensor in several orientations and lighting conditions. This can be accomplished using, for example, two robot manipulators; one rotates the object while the other varies the illumination direction. The result is a large set of object images. These images could either be used directly or after being processed to enhance object characteristics. Since all images in the set are of the same object, consecutive images are correlated to a large degree. The problem then is to compress this large image set to a low-dimensional representation of object appearance.

A well-known image compression or coding technique is based on principal component analysis, also known as the Karhunen-Loéve transform [32] [9]. It uses the eigenvectors of an image set as orthogonal bases for representing individual images in the set. Though a large number of eigenvectors may be required for very accurate reconstruction of an object image, only a few are generally sufficient to capture the significant appearance characteristics of an object, as shown in [42][43]. These eigenvectors constitute the dimensions of what we refer to as the *eigenspace*. From the perspective of machine vision, the eigenspace has an attractive property. If any two images from the set are projected to the eigenspace, the distance between the corresponding points in eigenspace is the best approximation to correlation between the images.

We have proposed a continuous and compact representation of object appearance that is parametrized by the variables, namely, object pose and illumination. This representation is referred to as the *parametric eigenspace* [18][19]. We have shown that parametric eigenspaces are useful not only for object recognition but a variety of other vision tasks. In object recognition, first an image set of the object is obtained by varying pose and illumination in small increments. The image set is then normalized in brightness and scale to achieve invariance to sensor magnification and illumination intensity. The eigenspace for the image set is constructed and all object images (learning samples) are projected to it to obtain a set of points. These points lie on a *manifold* that is parametrized by pose and illumination. The manifold is constructed from the discrete points by spline interpolation [19]. For the class of objects with linear reflectance models, we have analyzed the effect of illumination on the structure of the manifold [26]. In was shown that, in the case of an ideal diffuse object with arbitrary texture, three illumination directions are sufficient to construct the entire illumination manifold. This result drastically reduces the number of images required in the learning stage.

Recognition and pose estimation can be summarized as follows. Given an image consisting of an object of interest, we assume that the object is not occluded and can be segmented from the remaining scene. The segmented image region is normalized in scale and brightness, such that it has the same size and brightness range as the images used in the learning stage. This normalized image is projected to eigenspace. The closest manifold reveals the identity of the object and exact position of the closest point on the manifold determines pose and illumination direction. Two different techniques have been tested for determining the closest manifold point, one is based on binary search [30] and other uses an input-output mapping network [15]. We have achieved further speed-up in recognition by developing a comprehensive theory and a novel algorithm for pattern rejection [1].

Will appearance representation suffice? Given the large number of parameters that affect appearance, it does not suggest itself as a replacement for shape representation. In fact, our experiments on recognition and robot tracking show that appearance models are in many ways complementary to shape models. Appearance representation proves extremely effective when the task variables are few; it is efficient and circumvents time-consuming and often unreliable operations such as feature detection. On the other hand, when occlusion effects are not negligible, shape models offer solutions in the form of partial matching that is more challenging in the case appearance matching [22].

Parametric appearance models have been applied to a variety of problems besides object recognition, such as, illumination planning for robust recognition [20] [21], visual positioning and tracking [25], and temporal inspection of complex parts [27]. These applications have demonstrated that the techniques underlying appearance modeling and matching are general. This has motivated us to develop a comprehensive software package [31] for appearance matching that is presently being used at several research institutions. We conclude with a brief discussion on the salient features of appearance matching and our most recent results on the topic.

2. COMPUTING APPEARANCE MODELS

We begin by presenting a general procedure for acquiring appearance models. In subsequent sections, this procedure is applied to a few vision problems.

2.1. THE VISUAL WORKSPACE

Each appearance model is parametrized by the variables of the vision task at hand. In the case of object recognition, these could include object pose and illumination parameters. If the objects are non-rigid, deformation parameters would serve as additional variables. In the case of visual tracking applications, the coordinates of a hand-eye system with respect to a moving object would be pertinent variables. Without loss of generality, we define the variables of a vision task as the *visual degrees of freedom* (DOF):

$$\mathbf{q} = [q_1, q_2, \ldots, q_m]^{\mathrm{T}} \tag{1}$$

where m is the total number of DOF at work. For any vector $\mathbf{q}$, the vision sensor produces an image vector:

$$\mathbf{i} = [i_1, i_2, \ldots, i_N]^{\mathrm{T}} \tag{2}$$

In a given application, $\mathbf{q}$ has lower and upper bounds and its continuous set of values within these bounds map to a continuous domain of images $\mathbf{i}(\mathbf{q})$. This range of appearances is what we refer to as the *visual workspace* of the task. Our approach is to acquire an image set by coarsely sampling the visual workspace and then produce a compact representation of the image set that can be used not only to recognize the discrete appearances in the image set but also those that lie in between the ones in the set, i.e. a continuous representation of the entire visual workspace.

To achieve scale invariance we force all images in an acquired image set to be of the same size. For instance, in a recognition task an object region is segmented from the scene and scale normalized [18] to fit a predetermined image size. This ensures that the recognition system is invariant to magnification, i.e.

the distance of the object from the image sensor. It is also desirable that appearance representation and recognition be unaffected by variations in the intensity of illumination or the aperture of the imaging system. This can be achieved by normalizing each acquired image such that the total energy contained within is unity: $\hat{\mathbf{i}}_j = \mathbf{i}_j / \| \mathbf{i}_j \|$.

Let the number of discrete samples obtained for each degree of freedom q_l be R_l. Then the total number of images is $M = \Pi_{l=1}^m R_l$. The complete image set

$$\{ \hat{\mathbf{i}}_1, \ldots, \hat{\mathbf{i}}_2, \ldots, \hat{\mathbf{i}}_M \} \tag{3}$$

can be a uniform or non-uniform sampling of the visual workspace.

Note that the above vectors, $\hat{\mathbf{i}}_j$, represent unprocessed brightness images (barring the scale and brightness normalizations). Alternatively, processed images such as smoothed images, first derivatives, second derivatives, Laplacian, or even the power spectrum of each image may be used instead. In applications that employ depth sensors, the images could be range maps. The image type is selected based on its ability to capture distinct appearance characteristics of the task workspace. Here, for the purpose of description we use raw brightness images, bearing in mind that appearance models can in principle be constructed for any image type.

2.2. COMPUTING EIGENSPACES

Images in the set tend to be correlated to a large degree since visual displacements between consecutive images are small. The obvious step is to take advantage of this and compress the large set to a low-dimensional representation that captures the key appearance characteristics of the visual workspace. A suitable compression technique is based on principal component analysis [32], where the eigenvectors of the image set are computed and used as orthogonal bases for representing individual images. Principal component analysis has been previously used in computer vision for deriving basis functions for feature detection [12] [13], representing human face images [42], and recognizing face images [43] [34]. Though, in general, all the eigenvectors of an image set are required for perfect reconstruction of any particular image, only a few are sufficient for visual recognition. These eigenvectors constitute the dimensions of the *eigenspace*, or image subspace, in which the visual workspace is compactly represented.

First, the average $\mathbf{c}$ of all images in the set is subtracted from each image. This would ensure that the eigenvector with the largest eigenvalue represents the subspace dimension in which the variance of images is maximum in the correlation sense. In other words, it is the most important dimension of the eigenspace. An image matrix is constructed by subtracting $\mathbf{c}$ from each image and stacking the resulting vectors column-wise:

$$\mathbf{P} \triangleq \left\{ \hat{\mathbf{i}}_1 - \mathbf{c}, \ \hat{\mathbf{i}}_2 - \mathbf{c}, \ \ldots, \ \hat{\mathbf{i}}_M - \mathbf{c} \right\} \tag{4}$$

P is $N \times M$, where N is the number of pixels in each image and M is the total number of images in the set. To compute eigenvectors of the image set we define the *covariance matrix*:

$$\mathbf{Q} \overset{\triangle}{=} \mathbf{P}\,\mathbf{P}^{\mathrm{T}} \tag{5}$$

Q is $N \times N$, clearly a very large matrix since a large number of pixels constitute an image. The eigenvectors $\mathbf{e}_k$ and the corresponding eigenvalues λ_k of **Q** are determined by solving the well-known eigenstructure decomposition problem:

$$\lambda_k\,\mathbf{e}_k = \mathbf{Q}\,\mathbf{e}_k \tag{6}$$

Calculation of the eigenvectors of a matrix as large as **Q** is computationally intensive. Fast algorithms for solving this problem have been a topic of active research in the area of image coding/compression and pattern recognition. A few of the representative algorithms are summarized in Appendix A. In some of our systems we have used a fast implementation [31] of the algorithm proposed by Murakami and Kumar [16] and in others the STA algorithm of Murase and Lindenbaum [17]. On a Sun IPX workstation, for instance, 20 eigenvectors of a set of 100 images (each 128x128 in size) can be computed in about 3 minutes, and 20 eigenvectors of a 1000 image set in less than 4 hours. Workstations are fast gaining in performance and these numbers are expected to diminish quickly.

The result of eigenstructure decomposition is a set of eigenvalues $\{\,\lambda_k \mid k = 1, 2, ..., K\,\}$ where $\{\,\lambda_1 \geq \lambda_2 \geq ..... \geq \lambda_K\,\}$, and a corresponding set of orthonormal eigenvectors $\{\,\mathbf{e}_k \mid k = 1, 2, ..., K\,\}$. Note that each eigenvector is of size N, i.e. the size of an image. These K eigenvectors constitute our eigenspace; it is an approximation to a complete Hilbert space with N dimensions. A variety of criteria have been suggested for selecting K for any given image set [32]. In most of our applications, we have found eigenspaces of 20 or less dimensions to be more than adequate.

2.3. PARAMETRIC EIGENSPACE REPRESENTATION

Each workspace sample $\hat{\mathbf{i}}_j$ in the image set is projected to eigenspace by first subtracting the average image **c** from it and finding the inner product of the result with each of the K eigenvectors. The result is a point $\mathbf{f}_j$ in eigenspace:

$$\mathbf{f}_j = [\mathbf{e}_1, \mathbf{e}_2, ..., \mathbf{e}_K]^{\mathrm{T}}\,(\hat{\mathbf{i}}_j - \mathbf{c}) \tag{7}$$

By projecting all images in this manner, a set of discrete points is obtained. Since consecutive images are strongly correlated, their projections are close to one another. Hence, the discrete points obtained by projecting all the discrete samples of the workspace can be assumed to lie on a manifold that represents a *continuous* appearance function. The discrete points are interpolated to obtain this manifold. In our implementation, we have used a standard quadratic B-spline interpolation algorithm [41]. The resulting manifold can be expressed as:

$$\mathbf{f}(\mathbf{q}) = \mathbf{f}(q_1, q_2, ..., q_m) \tag{8}$$

It resides in a low-dimensional space and therefore is a compact representation of appearance as a function of the task DOF $\mathbf{q}$. The exact number of task DOF is of course application dependent. It is worth pointing out that multiple visual workspaces (for instance, multiple objects in a recognition task) can be represented in the same eigenspace as set of manifolds $F=\{\mathbf{f}^1, \mathbf{f}^2, ..., \mathbf{f}^P\}$. In this case, the eigenspace is computed using image sets of all the visual workspaces. The above representation is called the *parametric eigenspace.*

2.4.   CORRELATION AND DISTANCE IN EIGENSPACE

Before we proceed to describe appearance recognition, it is worthwhile to discuss some relevant properties of the eigenspace representation. Consider two images $\hat{\mathbf{i}}_m$ and $\hat{\mathbf{i}}_n$ that belong to the image set used to compute an eigenspace. Let the points $\mathbf{f}_m$ and $\mathbf{f}_n$ be the eigenspace projections of the two images. It is well-known in pattern recognition theory [32] that each of the images can be expressed in terms of its projection:

$$\hat{\mathbf{i}}_m = \sum_{i=1}^{N} f_{mi}\, \mathbf{e}_i + \mathbf{c} \tag{9}$$

where $\mathbf{c}$ is once again the average of the entire image set. The above expression simply states that the image $\hat{\mathbf{i}}_m$ can be exactly represented as a weighted sum of all N eigenvectors of the image set. The individual weights f_{mi} are the co-ordinates of the point $\mathbf{f}_m$. Note that our eigenspaces are composed of only K eigenvectors. Since these correspond to the largest eigenvalues, they represent the most significant variations within the image set. Hence, $\hat{\mathbf{i}}_m$ can be approximated by the first K terms in the above summation:

$$\hat{\mathbf{i}}_m \approx \sum_{i=1}^{K} f_{mi}\, \mathbf{e}_i + \mathbf{c} \tag{10}$$

As a result of the brightness normalization described in section 2.1, $\hat{\mathbf{i}}_m$ and $\hat{\mathbf{i}}_n$ are unit vectors. The similarity between the two images can be determined by finding the *sum-of-squared-difference* (SSD) between brightness values in the images. This measure is extensively used in machine vision for template matching, establishing correspondence in binocular stereo, and feature tracking in motion estimation. It is known that SSD is related to correlation $\hat{\mathbf{i}}_m^{\mathrm{T}} \hat{\mathbf{i}}_n$ between the images as:

$$\begin{aligned} \| \hat{\mathbf{i}}_m - \hat{\mathbf{i}}_n \|^2 &= (\hat{\mathbf{i}}_m - \hat{\mathbf{i}}_n)^{\mathrm{T}} (\hat{\mathbf{i}}_m - \hat{\mathbf{i}}_n) \\ &= 2 - 2\hat{\mathbf{i}}_m^{\mathrm{T}} \hat{\mathbf{i}}_n \end{aligned} \tag{11}$$

Maximizing correlation, therefore, corresponds to minimizing SSD and thus maximizing similarity between the images. Alternatively, the SSD can be expressed in terms of the eigenspace points $\mathbf{f}_m$ and $\mathbf{f}_n$ using (10):

$$\| \hat{\mathbf{i}}_m - \hat{\mathbf{i}}_n \|^2 \approx \| \sum_{i=1}^{K} f_{mi}\,\mathbf{e}_i - \sum_{i=1}^{K} f_{ni}\,\mathbf{e}_i \|^2 \tag{12}$$

The right-hand side of the above expression can be simplified to obtain:

$$\| \sum_{i=1}^{K} f_{mi}\,\mathbf{e}_i - \sum_{i=1}^{K} f_{ni}\,\mathbf{e}_i \|^2 = \| \sum_{i=1}^{K} (f_{mi} - f_{ni})\,\mathbf{e}_i \|^2$$

$$= \| \mathbf{f}_m - \mathbf{f}_n \|^2 \tag{13}$$

The last simplification results from the eigenvectors being orthonormal; $\mathbf{e}_i^{\mathrm{T}}\,\mathbf{e}_j = 1$ when $i = j$, and 0 otherwise. From (12) and (13), we get:

$$\| \hat{\mathbf{i}}_m - \hat{\mathbf{i}}_n \|^2 \approx \| \mathbf{f}_m - \mathbf{f}_n \|^2 \tag{14}$$

The above relation implies that the square of the Euclidean distance between points $\mathbf{f}_m$ and $\mathbf{f}_n$ is an approximation to the SSD between images $\hat{\mathbf{i}}_m$ and $\hat{\mathbf{i}}_n$. In other words, the closer the projections are in eigenspace, the more highly correlated are the images. This property of the eigenspace makes it appealing from the perspective of computational vision, where, correlation is frequently used as a measure of similarity between images.

3.   IMAGE RECOGNITION

Our goal here is to develop an efficient method for recognizing an unknown input image $\hat{\mathbf{i}}_c$. A brute force solution would be to compare the input image with all images corresponding to discrete workspace samples. Such an approach is equivalent to exhaustive template matching. Clearly, this is impractical from a computational perspective given the large number of images we are dealing with. Further, the input image $\hat{\mathbf{i}}_c$ may not correspond exactly to any one of the images obtained by sampling the visual workspace; $\hat{\mathbf{i}}_c$ may lie in between discrete samples.

The parametric eigenspace representation enables us to accomplish image matching in a very efficient manner. Since the eigenspace is optimal for computing correlation between images, we can project the current image to eigenspace and simply look for closest point on the appearance manifold. Image recognition proceeds as follows. We will assume that $\hat{\mathbf{i}}_c$ has already been normalized in scale and brightness to suit the invariance requirements of the application. The average $\mathbf{c}$ of the visual workspace is subtracted from $\hat{\mathbf{i}}_c$ and the resulting vector is projected to eigenspace to obtain the point:

$$\mathbf{f}_c = [\,\mathbf{e}_1, \mathbf{e}_2, ..., \mathbf{e}_K\,]^{\mathrm{T}} (\hat{\mathbf{i}}_c - \mathbf{c}) \tag{15}$$

The matching problem then is to find the minimum distance d_r between $\mathbf{f}_c$ and the manifold $\mathbf{f}(\mathbf{q})$:

$$d_r = {\min_{\mathbf{q}}} \| \mathbf{f}_c - \mathbf{f}(\mathbf{q}) \| \tag{16}$$

If d_r is within some pre-determined threshold value (selected based on the noise characteristics of the image sensor), we conclude that $\hat{\mathbf{i}}_c$ does belong to the appearance manifold $\mathbf{f}$. Then, parameter estimation is reduced to finding the coordinate $\mathbf{q}_c$ on the manifold corresponding to the minimum distance d_r. In practice, the manifold is stored in memory as a list of K-dimensional points obtained by densely resampling $\mathbf{f}(\mathbf{q})$. Therefore, finding the closest point to $\mathbf{f}_c$ on $\mathbf{f}(\mathbf{q})$ (or even a set of manifolds, F) is reduced to the classical nearest-neighbor problem.

4. FINDING THE CLOSEST MANIFOLD POINT

Mapping an input image to eigenspace is computationally simple. As mentioned earlier, the eigenspaces are typically less than 20 in dimensions. The projection of an input image to a 20-D space requires 20 dot products of the image with the orthogonal eigenvectors that constitute the space. This procedure can easily be done in real-time (frame-rate of a typical image digitizer) using simple and inexpensive hardware. What remains to be addressed is an efficient way of finding the closest manifold point. One approach is to use an exhaustive search algorithm. This is clearly inefficient both in memory and time; all the sampled manifold points need to be stored, and the distance of the input point with respect to each manifold point must be computed. The computational complexity is $O(Kn)$ where n is the number of manifold points and K is the dimensionality of the eigenspace.

We have implemented two alternative schemes. The first is an efficient technique for binary search in multiple dimensions [30]. This algorithm uses a carefully designed data structure to facilitate quick search through the multi-dimensional eigenspace in $O(k\,log_2\,n)$. This approach is particularly effective when the number of manifold points is relatively small. The second approach [15] uses three-layered radial basis function (RBF) networks proposed by Poggio and Girosi [36] to learn the mapping between input points and manifold parameters (object number and pose). The complexity of the network approach depends on the number of networks used and their sizes. In [15] a new framework is introduced that uses the wavelet integral transform for finding the smallest RBF network to accomplish any given input-output mapping. The performance of the network based scheme is generally comparable to that of the binary search approach. The network implicitly interpolates, or reconstructs, manifolds from the discrete eigenspace points $\mathbf{f}_j$ and therefore does not require the use of spline interpolation followed by the resampling of manifolds. This advantage however comes with a slight sacrifice in parameter estimation accuracy [15].

5. OBJECT RECOGNITION AND POSE ESTIMATION

We have used appearance models for 3-D object recognition and pose estimation [18] [19]. During model acquisition, each object is placed on a computer-controlled turntable (see Fig.1) and its pose is varied about a single axis, namely, the axis

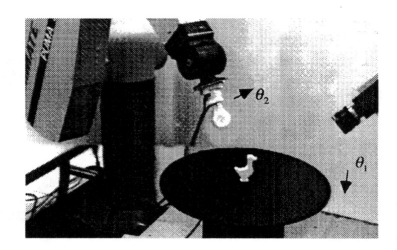

Figure 1: *Setup used to automatically acquire object appearance models for recognition and pose estimation. The object is placed on a motorized turntable.*

of rotation of the turntable. Most objects have a finite number of stable configurations when placed on a planar surface. For such objects, the turntable is adequate as it can be used to vary pose for each of the object's stable configurations. The object is illuminated by the ambient lighting of the environment that is expected to remain more or less unchanged between model acquisition and recognition stages. This ambient illumination is of relatively low intensity. The main source of brightness is an additional light source whose direction can vary. Illumination is varied using a 6 DOF robot manipulator (see Fig.1) with a light source mounted on its end-effector. Images of the object are sensed using a 512×480 pixel CCD camera and digitized using an Analogics frame-grabber board. Fig.2 shows four toys and their respective appearance models. For each object, 90 poses and 5 source directions were used (a total of 450 images, each 128x128 pixels in size after segmentation and scale normalization). The manifolds reside in 10-D eigenspaces and are parameterized by a single pose parameter θ_1 and a single illumination direction parameter θ_2.

Several experiments were conducted to verify the accuracy of recognition and pose estimation [19]. For the four objects in Fig.2. a total of 1080 test images were used. These images were taken at object poses that lie in between the ones used to obtain the learning samples. We define *recognition rate* as the percentage of test images for which the object in the image is correctly recognized. Figs.3(a) and (b) summarize the recognition results for the four objects. Fig.3(a) illustrates the sensitivity of recognition rate to the number of eigenspace dimensions. Clearly, the discriminating power of the eigenspace is expected to increase with the number of dimensions. The recognition rate is found to be poor if less than 4 dimensions

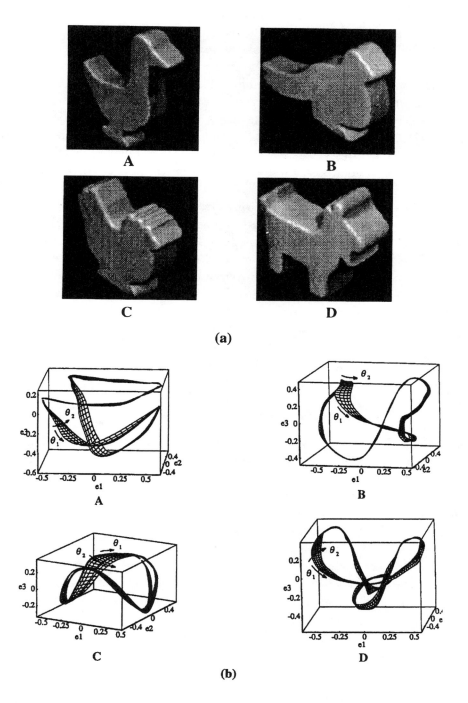

Figure 2: *(a) Four objects and (b) their parametric appearance manifolds (from [19]). The manifolds reside in 10-D eigenspace but are displayed here in 3-D. They are parametrized by object pose (θ_1) and illumination direction (θ_2).*

are used but approaches unity as the dimensionality is increased to 10.

Fig.3(b) shows the relationship between recognition rate and the number of poses used for each object. If the pose increments used in the learning stage are small, we obtain a larger number of learning samples and hence a larger number of discrete points on the parametric manifold. Since each manifold is obtained by interpolating these discrete points, the accuracy of the manifold representation increases with the number of learning poses used. For the four objects, 30 poses of each object (12 degree increments of the turntable position) are sufficient to obtain recognition rates close to unity. If a smaller number of learning poses are used, recognition tends to be unreliable when the test images correspond to poses that lie in between the learning poses.

The 1080 test images of the four objects were also used to determine the accuracy of pose estimation. Since these images were taken using the controlled turntable, the actual pose in each image is known. Figs.3(c) and (d) show histograms of pose errors (in degrees) computed for the 1080 test images. In Fig.3(c), 450 learning samples (90 poses and 5 source directions) were used to compute an 8-D eigenspace. In Fig.3(d), 90 learning samples (18 poses and 5 source directions) were used. The pose estimation results in both cases are found to be very accurate. In the first case, the average absolute pose error computed using all 1080 images is 0.5 degrees, while in the second case the average error is 1.0 degree. The sensitivity of recognition to image noise and segmentation error is analyzed in [21].

6.   AUTOMATED REAL-TIME RECOGNITION SYSTEM

Based on the above results, we implemented a recognition system with 20 objects in its database (see Fig.4). These objects vary from smoothly curved shapes with uniform reflectance, to fairly complex shapes with intricate textures and specularities. Developing CAD models of such objects could prove extremely cumbersome and time consuming. Both learning and recognition are done in a laboratory environment where illumination remains more or less unchanged. As a result, appearance manifolds are reduced to curves parametrized by just object pose. Each object image set includes 72 learning images (5 degree increments in pose), resulting in a set of 1440 images. The object appearance curves were constructed in a 20-D eigenspace. The entire learning process, including, image acquisition, computation of eigenvectors, and construction of appearance curves was completed in less than 12 hours using a Sun SPARC workstation.

The recognition system automatically detects significant changes in the scene, waits for the scene to stabilize, and then digitizes an image. In the present implementation, objects are presented to the system one at a time and a dark background is used to alleviate object segmentation. The complete recognition process, including, segmentation, scale and brightness normalization, image projection in eigenspace, and search for the closest object and pose is accomplished in less than 1 second on the Sun workstation. The robustness of this system was tested using

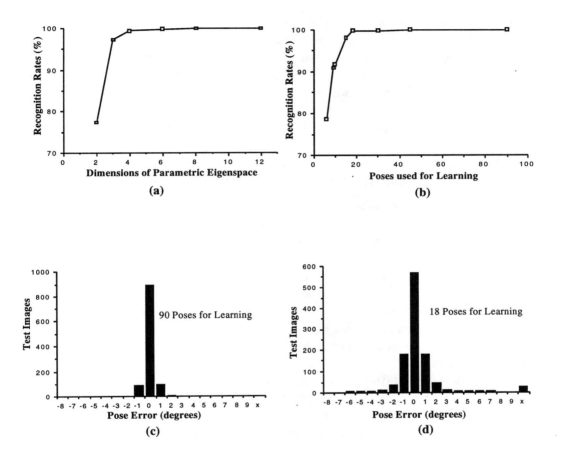

Figure 3: *Recognition and pose estimation results for the object set shown in Fig.2 (from [19]). (a) Recognition rate plotted as a function of the number of eigenspace dimensions used. (b) Recognition rate plotted as a function of the number of discrete poses of each object used in the learning stage. In both cases recognition rates were computed using 1080 test images that differ from the ones used for learning. Histogram of error in computed object pose when (c) 90 poses are used for learning and (d) 18 poses used for learning. The average absolute pose error is 0.5 degrees in the first case and 1.0 degree in the second case.*

320 test images of the 20 objects taken at randomly selected but known poses of the objects. All test images were correctly identified by the system. A histogram of the absolute pose error is shown in Fig.4(c); the average and standard deviation of the absolute pose error were found to be 1.59 degrees and 1.53 degrees, respectively.

Recently, we have extended the capability of the above system [28]. It now includes 100 objects in its database and uses as input vectors the three bands of a color image sensor. This allows the system to distinguish between objects that are identical in shape but differ in spectral characteristics. In addition, the segmentation algorithm was modified to ensure that multiple objects (not occluding one another) can be placed in the scene and recognized simultaneously. The system is now operational and is being constantly interacted with by passers-by.

7.   STRUCTURAL PROPERTIES OF APPEARANCE MANIFOLDS

In the context of large systems, the primary bottleneck in appearance matching could turn out to be the learning stage which includes the acquisition of large image sets, the computation of eigenspaces from large covariance matrices, and the construction of parametric appearance manifolds. As described in the previous section, each object is represented as a separate manifold in eigenspace that is parametrized by pose and illumination parameters. The efficiency of the learning stage is determined by the number of sample images needed to compute an accurate appearance manifold. This brings us to the following question: What is the smallest number of images needed for constructing the appearance manifold for any given object?

The answer lies in the structural properties of appearance manifolds. The structure of an object's manifold is closely related to its geometric and reflectance properties. In special cases, such as solids of high symmetry and solids of revolution, one can make concrete statements regarding the dimensionality of the manifold. For instance, given a fixed illumination direction and viewpoint, the manifold for a sphere of uniform reflectance is simply a point since the sphere appears the same in all its poses. This unfortunately is an extreme instance of little practical value. Under perspective projection, the relation between object shape and manifold structure is complex to say the least. A general expression that relates object pose to manifold structure would be much to hope for.

In contrast, the function space associated with object reflectance is more concise and hence conducive to analysis. It is possible to establish, under certain reflectance assumptions, a closed-form relationship between illumination parameters and manifold structure [26]. Given that the eigenspaces we use are linear subspaces, the class of linear reflectance functions [35][40] is of particular interest to us. It turns out that for this reflectance class the structure of the illumination manifold is completely determined from a small number of samples of the manifold. In particular, for Lambertian surfaces of arbitrary texture, the en-

(a) Object set

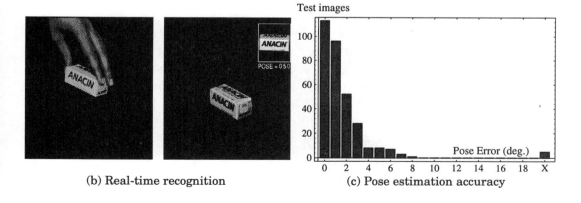

(b) Real-time recognition   (c) Pose estimation accuracy

Figure 4: *A real-time recognition system with 20 objects in the database [19]. A complete recognition and pose estimation cycle takes less than 1 second on a Sun IPX workstation without the use of any customized hardware.*

tire illumination manifold can be constructed from just three images taken using known illuminants. Alternatively, the dimensionality of the illumination manifold is exactly 3. This result is supported by a detailed empirical investigation reported recently in [8]. In [26] we use the above bound on the manifold dimensionality to show that novel images of the object can be recognized from just three projections on the illumination manifold without the explicit construction of the manifold. In addition, the validity of the above results for illumination by multiple sources and in the presence of interreflections caused by concave surfaces is demonstrated. This last property results from the fact that a concave Lambertian surface with all its interreflections behaves exactly like another Lambertian surface without interreflections but with a different set of normals and albedo values [24].

For ideal diffuse objects, these results have direct implications on the efficiency of both learning and recognition, as they dramatically reduce the number of images needed for appearance representation. These results stem from the observation that the image of a diffuse object under any illumination can be expressed as a linear combination of images taken using three independent basis illuminants. Such a linear combination does not generally exist for objects with nonlinear reflectance functions. For instance, a pure specular object would produce only strong highlights for each of the basis illuminants. The highlights produced by a novel source cannot in general be expressed as a linear combination of basis images. In fact, it is hard to envision non-trivial upper bounds on the dimensionality of a vector space containing illumination manifolds for the class of nonlinear reflectance functions.

8.   ILLUMINATION PLANNING FOR OBJECT RECOGNITION

In structured environments, vision systems are used to perform a variety of tasks, such as, inspect manufactured parts, recognize objects and sort them, or aid a robot in assembly operations. In each of these cases, the illumination of the environment can be selected to enhance the reliability and accuracy of the vision system. For instance, the robustness of the recognition system described in section 5 can be maximized by selecting a source direction that makes the objects of interest maximally different from each other in the correlation sense [20] [21].

Consider two objects, say p and q, from the set used to compute the eigenspace. For each light source direction l, we compute parametric curves for the two objects:

$$\mathbf{f}_l^{(p)}(\theta_1^{(p)}) \quad \text{and} \quad \mathbf{f}_l^{(q)}(\theta_1^{(q)}) \tag{17}$$

Here, the parameters $\theta_1^{(p)}$ and $\theta_1^{(q)}$ represent the poses of p and q, respectively. The shortest Euclidean distance between the two curves in eigenspace is computed as:

$$d_l^{(p,q)} = \min_{\theta_1^{(p)}, \theta_1^{(q)}} \| \mathbf{f}_l^{(p)}(\theta_1^{(p)}) - \mathbf{f}_l^{(q)}(\theta_1^{(q)}) \| \tag{18}$$

The $\theta_1^{(p)}$ and $\theta_1^{(q)}$ values that produce the minimum distance $d_l^{(p,q)}$, correspond to poses of the two objects for which the objects appear most similar (in correlation) when illuminated by source l (see Fig.5). The illumination planning problem is formulated as follows: Find the source direction $\tilde{l}$ that maximizes the minimum distance $d_l^{(p,q)}$ between the object curves. This *max-min* strategy yields the safest illumination direction for the worst case poses that make the two objects appear most similar.

The above example includes only two objects. The *max-min* strategy is easily extended to a set of P objects. For a given illumination direction l, we now have P curves in eigenspace. The minimum distance $d_l^{(p,q)}$ is computed for all pairs of objects, resulting in P^2 minimum distances. The minimum of all these distances, say d_l, represents the worst case for the entire object set. The source direction $\tilde{l}$ that maximizes d_l is then the *optimal source direction* for the object set. Fig.5 shows eigenspace curves of two objects used in our experiments [21], for a particular illumination direction. The solid line segment illustrates the shortest distance between the two curves. If in a particular application the poses of the objects are fixed, the eigenspace representation of each object, for a given illumination, is reduced from a curve to a point. In that case, the optimal source direction maximizes the minimum distance between points in eigenspace that represent different objects. In [20], the above planning strategy was used to optimize the robustness of a recognition system similar to the one described in section 5.

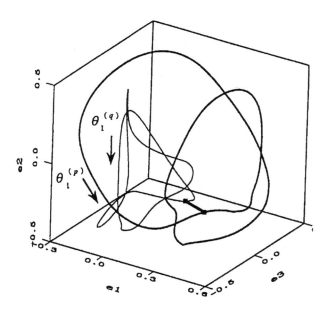

Figure 5: *Parametric eigenspace curves of two different objects obtained for a given illumination direction [21]. The shortest distance (thick line segment) between the two curves represents the worst case poses for which the objects appear most similar in the correlation sense. The optimal illumination maximizes the minimum distance between all pairs of object appearance manifolds.*

Though we have posed the planning problem as one of finding the optimal source direction, several other source characteristics such as size, distance, and spectral distribution, can be incorporated into the planning process. For instance, in [20] optimization of illumination color is described and demonstrated. The planning approach can also be used to simultaneously optimize multiple parameters. The only requirement is that these parameters be varied during the acquisition of the planning image set. Clearly, for multiple parameters, acquiring image sets, computing parametric eigenspaces, and determining the optimal parameter values can be time consuming. The planning method tends to prove impractical when more than three illumination parameters need to be jointly optimized. A small number of parameters, however, can be easily accommodated since illumination planning is typically done off-line and only once. As a result, it is generally not subject to severe time constraints.

9.   ROBOT POSITIONING AND TRACKING

For a robot to be able to interact in a precise and intelligent manner with its environment, it must rely on sensory feedback. Vision serves as a powerful component of such a feedback system. It can enable a manipulator to handle task uncertainties, react to a varying environment, and gracefully recover from failures. A problem of substantial relevance to robotics is visual servoing; the ability of a robot to either automatically position itself at a desired location with respect to an object, or accurately follow an object as it moves along an unknown trajectory.

The parametric appearance representation has been used to develop an effective solution to the visual servoing problem [25]. Our implementation uses the hand-eye system shown in Fig.6. First, a sizable image window is selected that represents the appearance of the object when the robot is in the desired position. A large set of object images is then obtained by incrementally perturbing the robot's end-effector (hand-eye system) with respect to the desired position. The appearance manifold in this case represents the mapping between camera image and robot displacement, i.e. it is parametrized by the DOF of the robot end-effector.

In a positioning or tracking application, each new image is projected to eigenspace and the location of the projection on the manifold determines the robot displacement (error) with respect to the desired position. This information is relayed to the robot controller to drive it to the desired coordinates. In contrast to most previous visual servoing schemes, positioning and tracking are achieved without prior knowledge of the object's shape or reflectance, the robot's kinematic parameters, and the vision sensor's intrinsic and extrinsic parameters.

We have conducted several positioning experiments using the Adept robot and hand-eye system shown in Fig.6. Fig.7(a) shows a printed circuit board. The box shown is the image area (128x128 pixels) used for learning and positioning. Note that the image is rather complex and includes a variety of subtle features. In this experiment, robot displacements were restricted to two dimensions (x and

sensing modality (color, infrared, range, etc.) that captures the primary visual features of a task may be used. The input vectors could even be locations and properties of features computed in images. The integration of the present scheme with previously developed geometry based recognition techniques is an interesting and open problem.

- **Shape and Reflectance:** An appealing feature of the proposed scheme is that it does not require any knowledge of the shape and reflectance properties of objects. By varying object pose and illumination (or end-effector coordinates in servoing applications), we capture the combined effect of both shape and reflectance. In addition, the appearance for any given pose and illumination may include specular highlights and complex interreflections between points on the object surface. All of these phenomena together produce the overall appearance of the object. Since it is appearance itself that we are representing, such phenomena need not be modeled or analyzed in isolation.

- **Segmentation and Occlusion:** We have seen that applications such as visual positioning and tracking are often not confronted with the problems of segmentation and occlusion. In such cases, it is assumed that the manipulator is close to the desired position and hence a fixed image window may be used that is more or less guaranteed to lie within the confines of the object of interest. In object recognition, learning and classification require the segmentation of object regions. In structured environments, the background can be controlled, in which case, simple thresholding is sufficient for robust segmentation. In the case of moving objects, simple background subtraction algorithms can be effective for segmentation [19]. In the context of general scenes, however, segmentation poses serious problems. The method, as described here, also requires that the objects not be occluded. Since it is based on direct appearance matching, it cannot handle substantial degrees of occlusion. Segmentation and occlusion therefore present challenging research directions for appearance based recognition. Our initial investigation of this topic has resulted in a technique that performs partial matching followed by appearance voting [22].

- **Computations for Learning:** For problems that involve multiple workspaces (as in object recognition) or a large number of workspace parameters, the appearance manifolds can be expensive to compute both in time and memory requirements. It is therefore not a viable approach for the general recognition problem faced in entirely unstructured environments. However, as we have seen, it can prove as a practical approach for a variety of well-defined applications that involve a small number of parameters. Using any popular workstation, problems that involve three or less parameters can be handled with ease. Needless to say, the power and versatility of appearance matching is commensurate with the performance of the machine it is executed on. Its application domain therefore can be safely expected to broaden with time. Further, when assumptions regarding surface reflectance are feasible, we have shown that upper bounds on the dimensionality of the appearance manifold can be derived and the learning samples reduced [26].

- **Computations for Recognition:** Though the learning process poses large memory requirements and is computationally intensive, it is done off-line. The time taken to learn a visual workspace is generally not as crucial as the time needed for image recognition. In contrast to learning, recognition and parameter estimation are simple and computationally very efficient, requiring only the projection of the input image to eigenspace and search for the closest manifold point. Recognition of 100 or more objects can therefore be accomplished in real-time (frame-rate of 30 Hz) using simple and inexpensive hardware [28]. In contrast, most 3-D CAD model based recognition algorithms are too slow for practical applications. The simplicity and efficiency of appearance matching makes it an attractive approach for a variety of real-world applications.

- **Efficient Pattern Rejection:** Despite the inherent efficiency of appearance matching, the present approach has complexity that at times is linear in the number of manifolds stored in the database. Recently, it was shown that the notion of *pattern rejection* [1] can be used to very quickly eliminate a large fraction of classes (manifolds) stored in the database. The result is a small set of candidates that can be viewed as a substantially reduced database for the input vector (pattern) in question. This theory of pattern rejection is applicable to not only appearance matching but in fact a large variety of well-known classification problems. It can be viewed as a complementary precursor to pattern recognition.

- **Generalized Feature Detection:** A large number of local visual features are parametric in nature, including, edges, lines, corners, and junctions. The concept of appearance matching can be used as a general framework for the design and implementation of detectors for parametrized features [29]. For robustness, the features are modeled in detail to precisely capture their appearances in the physical world. In addition, optical and sensing artifacts are incorporated to achieve realistic feature models in image domain. Each feature is then represented as a densely sampled parameterized manifold in Hilbert space. The concepts of parameter reduction by normalization, dimension reduction, pattern rejection, and efficient search are employed to achieve compact feature manifolds and efficient detection. Detectors have been implemented [29] for five specific features, namely, step edge, roof edge, line, corner, and circular disc. The tools discussed in this chapter have allowed us to generate all five of these detectors using the same procedure by simply inputing different feature models. Detailed experiments on the robustness of detection and the accuracy of parameter estimation are reported in [29].

APPENDIX

A. COMPUTING EIGENVECTORS OF LARGE IMAGE SETS

Let $\mathbf{P}$ be an $N \times M$ image matrix, where M is the total number of images and N the number of pixels in each image. We are interested in finding the eigenvectors of the covariance matrix $\mathbf{Q} = \mathbf{P}\mathbf{P}^T$, an $N \times N$ matrix. The calculation of the eigenvectors of such a large matrix is computationally intensive. Fast algorithms for solving this problem have been a topic of active research in the area of image coding and compression. Here, we briefly describe three algorithms. We refer to these as the conjugate gradient, singular value decomposition, and spatial temporal adaptive algorithms. Each algorithm may be viewed as a modification of the previous one. The first two of these algorithms are described in detail in [32].

Conjugate Gradient:

A practical approach to computing the eigenvectors of large matrices is to use iterative methods. A reasonably efficient iterative scheme that suggests itself is the conjugate gradient method. There are several variations to the conjugate gradient approach [45]. The problem is formulated as one of finding the eigenvalues and eigenvectors that maximize a scalar function. A function that is often used is the Raleigh quotient $F(\mathbf{e})$:

$$F(\mathbf{e}) = \frac{(\mathbf{e}^T \mathbf{Q} \mathbf{e})}{(\mathbf{e}^T \mathbf{e})} \tag{19}$$

Conjugate gradient is used to find the vector $\mathbf{e}_1$ that maximizes F. The corresponding value of the Raleigh quotient, $F(\mathbf{e}_1)$, is the largest eigenvalue λ_1 of the covariance matrix $\mathbf{Q}$. Once the largest eigenvalue and the corresponding eigenvector are computed in this manner, $\mathbf{Q}$ is modified to remove the dimension associated with the computed eigenvector. The Raleigh quotient is then used with the modified covariance matrix to determine the next largest eigenvalue and corresponding eigenvector. The iterative modification of $\mathbf{Q}$ can be summarized as:

$$\begin{aligned} \mathbf{Q}_1 &= \mathbf{Q} \\ \mathbf{Q}_s &= \mathbf{Q}_{s-1} - \lambda_{s-1} \mathbf{e}_{s-1} \mathbf{e}_{s-1}{}^T \end{aligned} \tag{20}$$

The above procedure can be repeated until a desired number of eigenvectors of $\mathbf{Q}$

are computed. Since in our case $\mathbf{Q}$ is a very large matrix ($N \times N$), each iteration of the conjugate gradient algorithm can prove expensive.

Singular Value Decomposition:

If the number of images M is much smaller than the number of pixels N in each image, a much more efficient algorithm may be used. This algorithm, described by Murakami and Kumar [16], uses the implicit covariance matrix $\tilde{\mathbf{Q}}$, where:

$$\tilde{\mathbf{Q}} = \mathbf{P}^{\mathrm{T}} \mathbf{P} \tag{21}$$

Note that $\tilde{\mathbf{Q}}$ is an $M \times M$ matrix and therefore much smaller than $\mathbf{Q}$ when the number of images in $\mathbf{P}$ is smaller than the number of pixels in each image. Using the conjugate gradient algorithm described above, the M eigenvectors of $\tilde{\mathbf{Q}}$ can be computed. These can be computed much faster than the first M eigenvectors of $\mathbf{Q}$ due to the disparity in the sizes of the two matrices. Using singular value decomposition (SVD), Murakami and Kumar [16] show that the M largest eigenvalues and the corresponding eigenvectors of $\mathbf{Q}$ can be determined from the M eigenvalues and eigenvectors of $\tilde{\mathbf{Q}}$ as:

$$\begin{aligned} \lambda_i &= \tilde{\lambda}_i \\ \mathbf{e}_i &= \tilde{\lambda}_i^{-\frac{1}{2}} \mathbf{P} \, \tilde{\mathbf{e}}_i \end{aligned} \tag{22}$$

Here, λ_i and $\mathbf{e}_i$ are the ith eigenvalue and eigenvector of $\mathbf{Q}$, while $\tilde{\lambda}_i$ and $\tilde{\mathbf{e}}_i$ are the ith eigenvalue and eigenvector of $\tilde{\mathbf{Q}}$. Since we are only interested in the first k eigenvectors of $\mathbf{Q}$, where $k < M$, the SVD algorithm can be used. It is not viable, however, when more than M eigenvectors are needed.

Spatial Temporal Adaptive:

Murase and Lindenbaum [17] have proposed the spatial temporal adaptive (STA) algorithm that takes the above SVD algorithm one step further to achieve substantial improvements in computational efficiency. They observe that the computation of $\tilde{\mathbf{Q}}$ from the image matrix $\mathbf{P}$ is itself expensive. Therefore, each image in $\mathbf{P}$ is divided into "blocks" and image data in each block is compressed using the discrete cosine transform (DCT) [6]. Due to spatial correlation within an image, each image block is typically represented by a small number of DCT coefficients. Further, blocks at the same location in consecutive images are often highly correlated and have the same DCT coefficients. A set of such blocks are referred to as a "superblock" and is represented by the DCT coefficients of a single block. In this manner, the image matrix $\mathbf{P}$ is compressed to obtain a small number of DCT coefficients. Individual elements of $\tilde{\mathbf{Q}}$ can then be computed from the DCT coefficients of the blocks and superblocks of $\mathbf{P}$. This procedure of computing $\tilde{\mathbf{Q}}$ saves substantial computations. Next, the conjugate gradient algorithm is used to compute the eigenvalues and eigenvectors of $\tilde{\mathbf{Q}}$. These eigenvalues and eigenvectors are used to compute the eigenvectors $\mathbf{e}_i$ and eigenvalues λ_i of the original covariance matrix $\mathbf{Q}$ by applying the SVD technique (equation 22). This step also requires the use of $\mathbf{P}$ which is now compressed using the DCT. Computations are once again saved by determining $\mathbf{e}_i$ in DCT domain and then transforming it back to spatial domain using the inverse DCT.

Murase and Lindenbaum have compared the performance of the STA algorithm with the conjugate gradient and SVD algorithms described previously. Their results show the STA algorithm to be superior in performance to both algorithms, often 10 or more times faster than the SVD algorithm.

ACKNOWLEDGEMENTS

This research was conducted at the Center for Research in Intelligent Systems, Department of Computer Science, Columbia University. It was supported in parts by the NSF National Young Investigator Award, the ARPA Grant under Contract No. DACA 76-92-C-0007, and the David and Lucile Packard Fellowship. Hiroshi Murase was supported by the NTT Basic Research Laboratory.

REFERENCES

[1] S. Baker and S. K. Nayar, "A Theory of Pattern Rejection," Tech. Rep. CUCS-013-95, Dept. of Computer Science, Columbia Univ., May 1995.

[2] A. H. Barr, "Superquadric and Angle Preserving Transformations," *IEEE Computer Graphics and Applications,* Vol. 1, No. 1, pp. 11-23, Jan. 1981.

[3] P. J. Besl and R. C. Jain, "Three-Dimensional Object Recognition," *Computing Surveys,* Vol. 17, No. 1, pp. 75-145, Mar. 1985.

[4] T. O. Binford, "Generalized Cylinder Representation," *Encyclopedia of Artificial Intelligence,* S. C. Sahpiro, Ed., John Wiley & Sons, New York, pp. 321-323, 1987.

[5] M. Brady, J. Ponce, A. Yuille, and H. Asada, "Describing Surfaces," *Computer Vision, Graphics, and Image Processing,* Vol. 32, pp. 1-28, 1985.

[6] W. H Chen, H. Smith, and S. C. Fralick, "A Fast Computational Algorithm for the Discrete Cosine Transform," *IEEE Transactions on Communications,* Vol. 25, pp. 1004-1009, 1977.

[7] R. T. Chin and C. R. Dyer, "Model-Based Recognition in Robot Vision," *ACM Computing Surveys,* Vol. 18, No. 1, pp. 67-108, 1986.

[8] R. Epstein, P. W. Hallinan, and A. L. Yuille, "5±2 Eigenimages Suffice: An Empirical Investigation of Low-Dimensional Lighting Models," *Proc. of*

IEEE Workshop on Physics Based Modeling in Computer Vision, pp. 108-116, Boston, June 1995.

[9] K. Fukunaga, *Introduction to Statistical Pattern Recognition*, Academic Press, London, 1990.

[10] B. K. P. Horn, "Extended Gaussian Images," *Proceedings of the IEEE*, Vol. 72, No. 12, pp. 1671-1686, Dec. 1984.

[11] A. S. Householder, *The theory of matrices in numerical analysis*, Dover Publications, New York, 1964.

[12] R. A. Hummel, "Feature Detection Using Basis Functions," *Computer Graphics and Image Processing*, Vol. 9, pp. 40-55, 1979.

[13] R. Lenz, "Optimal Filters for the Detection of Linear Patterns in 2-D and Higher Dimensional Images," *Pattern Recognition*, Vol. 20, No. 2, pp. 163-172, 1987.

[14] N. K. Logothetis, J. Pauls, H. H. Bulthoff, and T. Poggio, "View-dependent object recognition by monkeys," *Current Biology*, Vol. 4, No. 5, pp. 401-414, 1994.

[15] S. Mukherjee and S. K. Nayar, "Optimal RBF Networks for Visual Learning," *Proc. of Fifth Int'l. Conf. on Computer Vision*, Boston, June 1995.

[16] H. Murakami and V. Kumar, "Efficient Calculation of Primary Images from a Set of Images," *IEEE Trans. on Pattern Analysis and Machine Intelligence*, Vol. 4, No. 5, pp. 511-515, Sept. 1982.

[17] H. Murase and M. Lindenbaum, "Spatial Temporal Adaptive Method for Partial Eigenstructure Decomposition of Large Images," *NTT Technical Report No. 6527*, Mar. 1992.

[18] H. Murase and S. K. Nayar, "Learning Object Models from Appearance," *Proc. of AAAI*, Washington D. C., July 1993.

[19] H. Murase and S. K. Nayar, "Visual Learning and Recognition of 3D Objects from Appearance," *International Journal of Computer Vision*, Vol. 14, No. 1, pp. 5-24, 1995.

[20] H. Murase and S. K. Nayar, "Illumination Planning for Object Recognition in Structured Environments," *Proc. of IEEE Conf. on Computer Vision and Pattern Recognition*, Seattle, pp. 31-38, June 1994.

[21] H. Murase and S. K. Nayar, "Illumination Planning for Object Recognition Using Parametric Eigenspaces," *IEEE Trans. on Pattern Analysis and Machine Intelligence,* Vol. 16, No. 12, pp. 1219-1227, Jan. 1995.

[22] H. Murase and S. K. Nayar, "Image Spotting of 3D Objects Using the Parametric Eigenspace Representation," *Proc. of 9th Scandinavian Conference on Image Analysis,* pp. 325-332, June 1995.

[23] V. S. Nalwa, *A Guided Tour of Computer Vision,* Addison Wesley, 1993.

[24] S. K. Nayar, K. Ikeuchi, and T. Kanade, "Shape from Interreflections," *International Journal of Computer Vision,* Vol. 2, No. 3, pp. 173-195, 1991.

[25] S. K. Nayar, H. Murase, and S. A. Nene, "Learning, Positioning, and Tracking Visual Appearance," *Proc. of IEEE Int'l. Conf. on Robotics and Automation,* San Diego, May 1994.

[26] S. K. Nayar and H. Murase, "On the Dimensionality of Illumination in Eigenspace," Tech. Rep. CUCS-021-94, Dept. of Computer Science, Columbia Univ., Aug. 1994. Revised Sept. 1995.

[27] S. K. Nayar, S. A. Nene, and H. Murase, "Subspace Methods for Robot Vision," *IEEE Trans. on Robotics and Automation,* Special issue on "Vision-Based Control of Robot Manipulators," to appear in 1996. Also Tech. Rep. CUCS-06-95, Dept. of Computer Science, Columbia Univ., Mar. 1995.

[28] S. K. Nayar, S. A. Nene, and H. Murase, "Real-Time 100 Object Recognition System," Tech. Rep. CUCS-021-95, Dept. of Computer Science, Columbia Univ., Sept. 1995.

[29] S. K. Nayar, S. Baker, and H. Murase, "Parametric Feature Detection," Tech. Rep. CUCS-028-95, Dept. of Computer Science, Columbia Univ., Oct. 1995.

[30] S. A. Nene and S. K. Nayar, "Algorithm and Architecture for High Dimensional Search," Tech. Rep. CUCS-030-95, Dept. of Computer Science, Columbia Univ., Oct. 1995.

[31] S. A. Nene, S. K. Nayar, H. Murase, "SLAM: A Software Library for Appearance Matching," *Proc. of ARPA IU Workshop,* Monterey, Nov. 1994.

[32] E. Oja, *Subspace methods of Pattern Recognition,* Res. Studies Press, Hertfordshire, 1983.

[33] A. P. Pentland, "Perceptual Organization and the Representation of Natural Form," *Artificial Intelligence,* Vol. 28, pp. 293-331, 1986.

[34] A. Pentland, B. Moghaddam, and T. Starner, "View-Based and Modular Eigenspaces for Face Recognition," *Proc. of IEEE Conf. on Computer Vision and Pattern Recognition*, Seattle, June 1994.

[35] A. P. Petrov, "Color and Grassman-Cayley coordinates of shape," in *Human Vision, Visual Processing and Digital Display II*, SPIE Proc., Vol. 1453, pp. 342-352, 1991.

[36] T. Poggio and F. Girosi, "Networks for Approximation and Learning," *Proc. of the IEEE*, Vol. 78, No. 9, pp. 1481-1497, Sept. 1990.

[37] T. Poggio and S. Edelman, "A network that learns to recognize 3D objects," *Nature*, Vol. 343, pp. 263–266, 1990.

[38] A. R. Pope and D. G. Lowe, "Learning Object Recognition Models from Images," *Proc. of Fourth Int'l. Conf. on Computer Vision*, pp. 296-301, Berlin, May 1993.

[39] A. A. G. Requicha, "Representation of Rigid Solids: Theory, Methods and Systems," *Computing Surveys*, Vol. 12, No. 4, pp. 1-437-464, Dec. 1980.

[40] A. Shashua, "On Photometric Issues in 3D Visual Recognition from a Single 2D Image," Tech. Rep., Artificial Intelligence Lab., MIT, 1993.

[41] D. F. Rogers, *Mathematical Elements for Computer Graphics*, 2nd ed., McGraw-Hill, New York, 1990.

[42] L. Sirovich and M. Kirby, "Low dimensional procedure for the characterization of human faces," *Journal of Optical Society of America*, Vol. 4, No. 3, pp. 519-524, 1987.

[43] M. A. Turk and A. P. Pentland, "Face Recognition Using Eigenfaces," *Proc. of IEEE Conf. on Computer Vision and Pattern Recognition*, pp. 586-591, June 1991.

[44] J. Weng, N. Ahuja, and T. S. Huang, "Learning recognition and segmentation of 3-d objects from 2-d images," *Proc. of Fourth Int'l Conf. on Computer Vision*, pp. 121–128, Berlin, May 1993.

[45] X. Yang, T. K. Sarkar, and E. Arvas, "A Survey of Conjugate Gradient Algorithms for Solution of Extreme Eigen-Problems of a Symmetric Matrix," *IEEE Trans. on Acoustics, Speech and Signal Processing*, Vol. 37, No. 10, pp. 1550-1555, Oct. 1989.

7   Neural Network Vision for Robot Driving

Dean Pomerleau
Carnegie Mellon University

Abstract

Many real world problems require a degree of flexibility that is difficult to achieve using hand programmed algorithms. One such domain is vision-based autonomous driving. In this task, the dual challenges of a constantly changing environment coupled with a real time processing constrain make the flexibility and efficiency of a machine learning system essential. This chapter describes just such a learning system, called ALVINN (Autonomous Land Vehicle In a Neural Network). It presents the neural network architecture and training techniques that allow ALVINN to drive in a variety of circumstances including single-lane paved and unpaved roads, multilane lined and unlined roads, and obstacle-ridden on- and off-road environments, at speeds of up to 55 miles per hour.

1. Introduction

Autonomous navigation is a difficult problem for traditional vision and robotic techniques, primarily because of the noise and variability associated with real world scenes. Autonomous navigation systems based on traditional image processing and pattern recognition techniques often perform well under certain conditions but have problems with others. Part of the difficulty stems from the fact that the processing performed by these systems remains fixed across various environments.

Artificial neural networks have displayed promising performance and flexibility in other domains characterized by high degrees of noise and variability, such as handwritten character recognition [17] and speech recognition[1] and face recognition[4]. ALVINN (Autonomous Land Vehicle In a Neural Network) is a system that brings the flexibility of connectionist learning techniques to the task of autonomous robot navigation. Specifically, ALVINN is an artificial neural network designed to control the Navlab, Carnegie Mellon's autonomous driving test vehicle (See Figure 1).

This chapter describes the architecture, training and performance of the AL-VINN system. It demonstrates how simple connectionist networks can learn to

Figure 1: *The CMU Navlab Autonomous Navigation Testbed.*

precisely guide a mobile robot in a wide variety of situations when trained appropriately. In particular, this chapter presents training techniques that allow ALVINN to learn in under 5 minutes to autonomously control the Navlab by watching a human driver's response to new situations. Using these techniques, ALVINN has been trained to drive in a variety of circumstances including single-lane paved and unpaved roads, multilane lined and unlined roads, and obstacle-ridden on- and off-road environments, at speeds of up to 55 miles per hour.

2. NETWORK ARCHITECTURE

The basic network architecture employed in the ALVINN system is a single hidden layer feedforward neural network (See Figure 2). The input layer now consists of a single 30x32 unit "retina" onto which a sensor image from either a video camera or a scanning laser rangefinder is projected. Each of the 960 input units is fully connected to the hidden layer of 4 units, which is in turn fully connected to the output layer. The 30 unit output layer is a linear representation of the currently appropriate steering direction which may serve to keep the vehicle on the road or to prevent it from colliding with nearby obstacles[1]. The centermost output unit represents the "travel straight ahead" condition, while units to the left and right of center represent successively sharper left and right turns. The units on the extreme left and right of the output vector represent turns with a 20m radius to the left and right respectively, and the units in between represent turns which decrease linearly in their curvature down to the "straight ahead" middle unit in

---

[1]The task a particular driving network performs depends on the type of input sensor image and the driving situation it has been trained to handle.

the output vector.

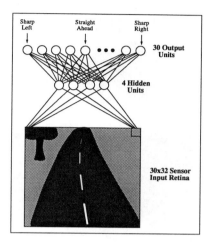

Figure 2: *Neural network architecture for autonomous driving.*

To drive the Navlab, an image from the appropriate sensor is reduced to 30x32 pixels and projected onto the input layer. After propagating activation through the network, the output layer's activation profile is translated into a vehicle steering command. The steering direction dictated by the network is taken to be the center of mass of the "hill" of activation surrounding the output unit with the highest activation level. Using the center of mass of activation instead of the most active output unit when determining the direction to steer permits finer steering corrections, thus improving ALVINN's driving accuracy.

3. NETWORK TRAINING

The network is trained to produce the correct steering direction using the back-propagation learning algorithm [7]. In backpropagation, the network is first presented with an input and activation is propagated forward through the network to determine the network's response. The network's response is then compared with the known correct response. If the network's actual response does not match the correct response, the weights between connections in the network are modified slightly to produce a response more closely matching the correct response.

Autonomous driving has the potential to be an ideal domain for a supervised learning algorithm like backpropagation since there is a readily available teaching signal or "correct response" in the form of the human driver's current steering direction. In theory it should be possible to teach a network to imitate a person as they drive using the current sensor image as input and the person's current steering direction as the desired output. This idea of training "on-the-fly" is depicted in Figure 3.

Training on real images would dramatically reduce the human effort required to develop networks for new situations, by eliminating the need for a hand-

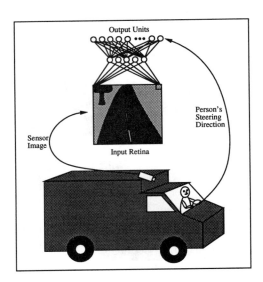

Figure 3: *Schematic representation of training "on-the-fly". The network is shown images from the onboard sensor and trained to steer in the same direction as the human driver.*

programmed training example generator. On-the-fly training should also allow the system to adapt quickly to new situations.

3.1. POTENTIAL PROBLEMS

There are two potential problems associated with training a network using live sensor images as a person drives. First, since the person steers the vehicle down the center of the road during training, the network will never be presented with situations where it must recover from misalignment errors. When driving for itself, the network may occasionally stray from the road center, so it must be prepared to recover by steering the vehicle back to the middle of the road. The second problem is that naively training the network with only the current video image and steering direction may cause it to overlearn recent inputs. If the person drives the Navlab down a stretch of straight road at the end of training, the network will be presented with a long sequence of similar images. This sustained lack of diversity in the training set will cause the network to "forget" what it had learned about driving on curved roads and instead learn to always steer straight ahead.

Both problems associated with training on-the-fly stem from the fact that back-propagation requires training data which is representative of the full task to be learned. The first approach we considered for increasing the training set diversity was to have the driver swerve the vehicle during training. The idea was to teach the network how to recover from mistakes by showing it examples of the person steering the vehicle back to the road center. However this approach was deemed impractical for two reasons. First, training while the driver swerves would require turning learning off while the driver steers the vehicle off the road, and then back on when he swerves back to the road center. Without this ability to toggle the state of learning, the network would incorrectly learn to imitate the person swerving off the road as well as back on. While possible, turning learning on and off would require substantial manual input during the training process, which we wanted to avoid. The second problem with training by swerving is that it would require swerving in many circumstances to enable the network to learn a general representation. This would be time consuming, and also dangerous when training in traffic.

3.2. SOLUTION - TRANSFORM THE SENSOR IMAGE

To achieve sufficient diversity of real sensor images in the training set, without the problems associated with training by swerving, we have developed a technique for transforming sensor images to create additional training exemplars. Instead of presenting the network with only the current sensor image and steering direction, each sensor image is shifted and rotated in software to create additional images in which the vehicle appears to be situated differently relative to the environment (See Figure 4). The sensor's position and orientation relative to the ground plane are known, so precise transformations can be achieved using perspective geometry.

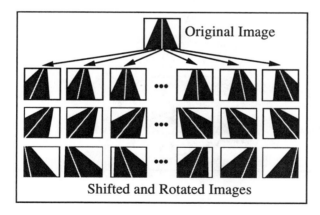

Figure 4: *The single original video image is shifted and rotated to create multiple training exemplars in which the vehicle appears to be at different locations relative to the road.*

The image transformation is performed by first determining the area of the ground plane which is visible in the original image, and the area that should be visible in the transformed image. These areas form two overlapping trapezoids as illustrated by the aerial view in Figure 5. To determine the appropriate value for a pixel in the transformed image, that pixel is projected onto the ground plane, and then back-projected into the original image. The value of the corresponding pixel in the original image is used as the value for the pixel in the transformed image. One important thing to realize is that the pixel-to-pixel mapping which implements a particular transformation is constant. In other words, assuming a planar world, the pixels which need to be sampled in the original image in order to achieve a specific shift and translation in the transformed image always remain the same. In the actual implementation of the image transformation technique, ALVINN takes advantage of this fact by precomputing the pixels that need to be sampled in order to perform the desired shifts and translations. As a result, transforming the original image to change the apparent position of the vehicle simply involves changing the pixel sampling pattern during the image reduction phase of preprocessing. Therefore, creating a transformed low resolution image takes no more time than is required to reduce the image resolution to that required by the ALVINN network. Obviously the environment is not always flat. But the elevation changes due to hills or dips in the road are small enough so as not to significantly violate the planar world assumption.

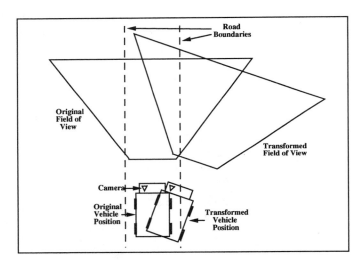

Figure 5: *An aerial view of the vehicle at two different positions, with the corresponding sensor fields of view. To simulate the image transformation that would result from such a change in position and orientation of the vehicle, the overlap between the two field of view trapezoids is computed and used to direct resampling of the original image.*

3.2.1. EXTRAPOLATING MISSING PIXELS

The less than complete overlap between the trapezoids of Figure 5 illustrates the need for one additional step in the image transformation scheme. The extra step involves determining values for pixels which have no corresponding pixel in the original image. Consider the transformation illustrated in Figure 6. To make it appear that the vehicle is situated one meter to the right of its position in the original image requires not only shifting pixels in the original image to the left, but also filling in the unknown pixels along the right edge. Notice the number of pixels per row whose value needs to be extrapolated is greater near the bottom of the image than at the top. This is because the one meter of unknown ground plane to the right of the visible boundary in the original image covers more pixels at the bottom than at the top. We have experimented with two techniques for extrapolating values for these unknown pixels (See Figure 7).

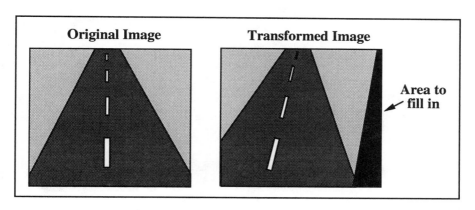

Figure 6: *A schematic example of an original image, and a transformed image in which the vehicle appears one meter to the right of its initial position. The black region on the right of the transformed image corresponds to an unseen area in the original image. These pixels must be extrapolated from the information in the original image.*

In the first technique, to determine the value for a pixel that projects to the ground plane at point A in the transformed image, the closest ground plane point in the original viewing trapezoid (point B) is found. This point is then back-projected into the original image to find the appropriate pixel to sample. The image in the top right shows the sampling performed to fill in the missing pixel using this extrapolation scheme. The problem with this technique is that it results in the "smearing" of the image approximately along rows of the image, as illustrated in the middle image of Figure 8. In this figure, the leftmost image represents an actual reduced resolution image of a two-lane road coming from the camera. Notice the painted lines delineating the center and right boundaries of the lane. The middle image shows the original image transformed to make it appear that the vehicle is one meter to the right of its original position using the extrapolation technique described above. The line down the right side of the road can be seen smearing to the right where it intersects the border of the original image. Because the length of this smear is highly correlated with the correct steering direction, the network learns to depend on the size of this smear to predict the correct steering direction. When driving on its own however, this lateral smearing of features is not present, so the network performs poorly.

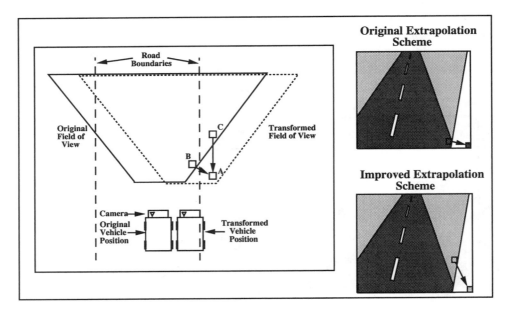

Figure 7: *An aerial view (left) and image based view (right) of the two techniques used to extrapolate the values for unknown pixels. See text for explanation.*

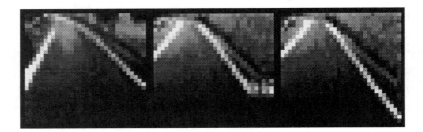

Figure 8: *Three reduced resolution images of a two-lane road with lines painted down the middle and right side. The left image is the original coming directly from the camera. The middle image was created by shifting the original image to make it appear the vehicle was situated one meter to the right of its original position using the first extrapolation technique described in the text. The right image shows the same shift of the original image, but using the more realistic extrapolation technique.*

To eliminate this artifact of the transformation process, we implemented a more realistic extrapolation technique which relies on the fact that interesting features (like road edges and painted lane markers) normally run parallel to the road, and hence parallel to the vehicle's current direction. With this assumption, to extrapolate a value for the unknown pixel A in Figure 7, the appropriate ground plane point to sample from the original image's viewing trapezoid is not the closest point (point B), but the nearest point in the original image's viewing trapezoid along the line that runs through point A and is parallel to the vehicle's original heading (point C).

The effect this improved extrapolation technique has on the transformed image can be seen schematically in the bottom image on the right of Figure 7. This technique results in extrapolation along the line connecting a missing pixel to the vanishing point, as illustrated in the lower right image. The realism advantage this extrapolation technique has over the previous scheme can be seen by comparing the image on the right of Figure 8 with the middle image. The line delineating the right side of the lane, which was unrealistically smeared using the previous method, is smoothly extended in the image on the right, which was created by shifting the original image by the same amount as in the middle image, but using the improved extrapolation method.

The improved transformation scheme certainly makes the transformed images look more realistic, but to test whether it improves the network's driving performance, we did the following experiment. We first collected actual two-lane road images like the one shown on the left side of Figure 8 along with the direction the driver was steering when the images were taken. We then trained two networks on this set of images. The first network was trained using the naive transformation scheme and the second using the improved transformation scheme. The magnitude of the shifts and rotations, along with the buffering scheme used in the training process are described in detail below. The networks were then tested on a disjoint set of real two-lane road images, and the steering direction dictated by the networks was compared with the person's steering direction on those images. The network trained using the more realistic transformation scheme exhibited 37% less steering error on the 100 test images than the network trained using the naive transformation scheme. In more detail, the amount of steering error a network produces is measured as the distance, in number of units (i.e. neurons), between the peak of the network's "hill" of activation in the output vector and the "correct" position, in this case the direction the person was actually steering in. This steering error measurement is illustrated in Figure 9. In this case, the network trained with the naive transformation technique had an average steering error across the 100 test images of 3.5 units, while the network trained with the realistic transformations technique had an average steering error of only 2.2 units.

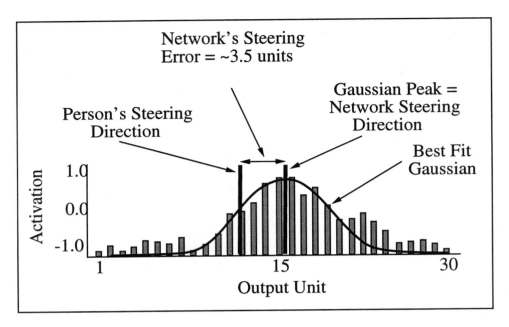

Figure 9: *To calculate a network's steering error the best fit gaussian is found to the network's output activation profile. The distance between the peak of the best fit gaussian and the position in the output vector representing the reference steering direction (in this case the person's steering direction) is calculated. This distance, measured in units or neurons between the two positions, is defined to be the network's steering error.*

3.3. TRANSFORMING THE STEERING DIRECTION

As important as the technique for transforming the input images is the method used to determine the correct steering direction for each of the transformed images. The correct steering direction as dictated by the driver for the original image must be altered for each of the transformed images to account for the altered vehicle placement. This is done using a simple model called pure pursuit steering [15]. In the pure pursuit model, the "correct" steering direction is the one that will bring the vehicle to a desired location (usually the center of the road) a fixed distance ahead. The idea underlying pure pursuit steering is illustrated in Figure 10. With the vehicle at position A, driving for a predetermined distance along the person's current steering arc would bring the vehicle to a "target" point T, which is assumed to be in the center of the road.

After transforming the image with a horizontal shift s and rotation θ to make it appear that the vehicle is at point B, the appropriate steering direction according to the pure pursuit model would also bring the vehicle to the target point T. Mathematically, the formula to compute the radius of the steering arc that will take the vehicle from point B to point T is

$$r = \frac{l^2 + d^2}{2d}$$

where r is the steering radius l is the lookahead distance and d is the distance from point T the vehicle would end up at if driven straight ahead from point B for distance l. The displacement d can be determined using the following formula:

$$d = \cos\theta \cdot (d_p + s + l\tan\theta)$$

where d_p is the distance from point T the vehicle would end up if it drove straight ahead from point A for the lookahead distance l, s is the horizontal distance from point A to B, and θ is the vehicle rotation from point A to B. The quantity d_p can be calculated using the following equation:

$$d_p = r_p - \sqrt{r_p^2 - l^2}$$

where r_p is the radius of the arc the person was steering along when the image was taken.

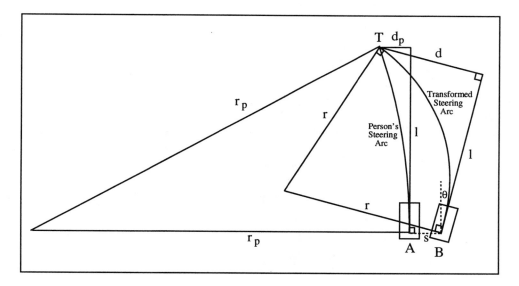

Figure 10: *Illustration of the "pure pursuit" model of steering. See text for explanation.*

The only remaining unspecified parameter in the pure pursuit model is l, the distance ahead of the vehicle to select a point to steer towards. Empirically, I have found that over the speed range of 5 to 55 mph, accurate and stable vehicle control can be achieved using the following rule: look ahead the distance the vehicle will travel in 2-3 seconds.

Interestingly, with this empirically determined rule for choosing the lookahead distance, the pure pursuit model of steering is a fairly good approximation to how people actually steer. Reid, Solowka and Billing [11] found that at 50km/h, human subjects responded to a 1m lateral vehicle displacement with a steering radius ranging from 511m to 1194m. With a lookahead equal to the distance the vehicle will travel in 2.3 seconds, the pure pursuit model dictates a steering radius of 594m, within the range of human responses. Similarly, human subjects reacted to a 1 degree heading error relative to the current road direction with a steering radius ranging from 719m to 970m. Again using the 2.3 second travel distance for lookahead, the pure pursuit steering model's dictated radius of 945m falls within the range of human responses.

Like the image transformation scheme, the steering direction transformation technique uses a simple model to determine how a change in the vehicle's position and/or orientation would affect the situation. In the image transformation scheme, a planar world hypothesis and rules of perspective projection are used to determine how changing the vehicle's position and/or orientation would affect the sensor image of the scene ahead of the vehicle. In the steering direction transformation technique, a model of how people drive is used to determine how a particular vehicle transformation should alter the correct steering direction. In both cases, the transformation techniques are independent of the driving situation. The person could be driving on a single lane dirt road or a multi lane highway: the transformation techniques would be the same.

Anthropomorphically speaking, transforming the sensor image to create more training images is equivalent to telling the network "I don't know what features in the image are important for determining the correct direction to steer, but whatever they are, here are some other positions and orientations you may see them in". Similarly, the technique for transforming the steering direction for each of these new training images is equivalent to telling the network "whatever the important features are, if you see them in this new position and orientation, here is how your response should change". Because it does not rely on a strong model of what important image features look like, but instead acquires this knowledge through training, the system is able to drive in a wide variety of circumstances, as will be seen later in the chapter.

These weak models are enough to solve the two problems associated with training in real time on sensor data. Specifically, using transformed training patterns allows the network to learn how to recover from driving mistakes that it would not otherwise encounter as the person drives. Also, overtraining on repetitive images is less of a problem, since the transformed training exemplars maintain variety in the training set.

3.4. ADDING DIVERSITY THROUGH BUFFERING

As additional insurance against the effects of repetitive exemplars, the training set diversity is further increased by maintaining a buffer of previously encountered training patterns. When new training patterns are acquired through digitizing and transforming the current sensor image, they are added to the buffer, while older patterns are removed. We have experimented with four techniques for determining which patterns to replace. The first is to replace oldest patterns first. Using this scheme, the training pattern buffer represents a history of the driving situations encountered recently. But if the driving situation remains unchanged for a period of time, such as during an extended right turn, the buffer will loose its diversity and become filled with right turn patterns. The second technique is to randomly choose old patterns to be replaced by new ones. Using this technique, the laws of probability help ensure somewhat more diversity than the oldest pattern replacement scheme, but the buffer will still become biased during monotonous stretches.

The next solution we developed to encourage diversity in the training was to replace those patterns on which the network was making the lowest error, as measured by the sum squared difference between the network's output and the desired output. The idea was to eliminate the patterns the network was performing best on, and leave in the training set those images the network was still having trouble with. The problem with this technique results from the fact that the human driver doesn't *always* steer in the correct direction. Occasionally he may have a lapse of attention for a moment and steer in an incorrect direction for the current situation. If a training exemplar was collected during this momentary lapse, under this replacement scheme it will remain there in the training buffer for a long time, since the network will have trouble outputting a steering response to match the person's incorrect steering command. In fact, using this replacement technique, the only way the pattern would be removed from the training set would be if the network learned to duplicate the incorrect steering response, obviously not a desired outcome. I considered replacing both the patterns with the lowest error *and* the patterns with the highest error, but decided against it since high network error on a pattern might also result on novel input image with a correct response associated with it. A better method to eliminate this problem is to add a random replacement probability to all patterns in the training buffer. This ensured that even if the network never learns to produce the same steering response as the person on an image, that image will eventually be eliminated from the training set.

While this augmented lowest-error-replacement technique did a reasonable job of maintaining diversity in the training set, we found a more straightforward way of accomplishing the same result. To make sure the buffer of training patterns does not become biased towards one steering direction, we add a constraint to ensure that the mean steering direction of all the patterns in the buffer is as close to straight ahead as possible. When choosing the pattern to replace, I select the pattern whose replacement will bring the average steering direction closest to straight. For instance, if the training pattern buffer had more right turns than left, and a left turn image was just collected, one of the right turn images in the buffer would be chosen for replacement to move the average steering direction towards straight ahead. If the buffer already had a straight ahead average steering direction, then an old pattern requiring a similar steering direction the new one would be replaced in order to maintain the buffer's unbiased nature. By actively compensating for steering bias in the training buffer, the network never learns to consistently favor one steering direction over another. This active bias compensation is a way to build into the network a known constraint about steering: in the long run right and left turns occur with equal frequency.

3.5. TRAINING DETAILS

The final details required to specify the training on-the-fly process are the number and magnitude of transformations to use for training the network. The following quantities have been determined empirically to provide sufficient diversity to allow networks to learn to drive in a wide variety of situations. The original sensor image is shifted and rotated 14 times using the technique describe above to create 14 training exemplars. The size of the shift for each of the transformed exemplars is chosen randomly from the range -0.6 to +0.6 meters, and the amount of rotation is chosen from the range -6.0 to +6.0 degrees. In the image formed by the camera on the Navlab, which has a 42 degree horizontal field of view, an image with a maximum shift of 0.6m results in the road shifting approximately 1/3 of the way across the input image at the bottom.

Before the randomly selected shift and rotation is performed on the original image, the steering direction that would be appropriate for the resulting transformed image is computed using the formulas given above. If the resulting steering direction is sharper than the sharpest turn representable by the network's output (usually a turn with a 20m radius), then the transformation is disallowed and a new shift distance and rotation magnitude are randomly chosen. By eliminating extreme and unlikely conditions from the training set, such as when the road is shifted far to the right and vehicle is heading sharply to the left, the network is able to devote more of its representation capability to handling plausible scenarios.

The 14 transformed training patterns, along with the single pattern created by pairing the current sensor image with the current steering direction, are inserted into the buffer of 200 patterns using the replacement strategy described above. After this replacement process, one forward and one backward pass of the back-propagation algorithm is performed on the 200 exemplars to update the network's weights, using a learning rate of 0.01 and a momentum of 0.8. The entire process is then repeated. Each cycle requires approximately 2.5 seconds on the three Sun Sparcstations onboard the vehicle. One of the Sparcstation performs the sensor image acquisition and preprocessing, the second implements the neural network simulation, and the third takes care of communicating with the vehicle controller and displaying system parameters for the human observer. The network requires approximately 100 iterations through this digitize-replace-train cycle to learn to drive in the domains that have been tested. At 2.5 seconds per cycle, training takes approximately four minutes of human driving over a sample stretch of road. During the training phase, the person drives at approximately the speed at which the network will be tested, which ranges from 5 to 55 miles per hour.

4. PERFORMANCE IMPROVEMENT USING TRANSFORMATIONS

The performance advantage this technique of transforming and buffering training patterns offers over the more naive methods of training on real sensor data is illustrated in Figure 11. This graph shows the vehicle's displacement from the road center measured as three different networks drove at 4 mph over a 100 meter section of a single lane paved bike path which included a straight stretch and turns to the left and right. The three networks were trained over a 150 meter stretch of the path which was disjoint from the test section and which ended in an extended right turn.

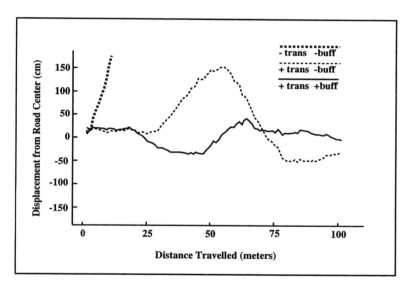

Figure 11: *Vehicle displacement from the road center as the Navlab was driven by networks trained using three different techniques.*

The first network, labeled "-trans -buff", was trained using just the images coming from the video camera. That is, during the training phase, an image was digitized from the camera and fed into the network. One forward and backward pass of back-propagation was performed on that training exemplar, and then the process was repeated. The second network, labeled "+trans -buff", was trained using the following technique. An image was digitized from the camera and then transformed 14 times to create 15 new training patterns as described above. A forward and backwards pass of back-propagation was then performed on each of these 15 training patterns and then the process was repeated. The third network, labeled "+trans +buff" was trained using the same transformation scheme as the second network, but with the addition of the image buffering technique described above to prevent overtraining on recent images.

Note that all three networks were presented with the same number of images. The transformation and buffering schemes did not influence the quantity of data the networks were trained on, only its distribution. The "-trans -buff" network was trained on closely spaced actual video images. The "+trans -buff" network was presented with 15 times fewer actual images, but its training set also contained 14 transformed images for every "real" one. The "+trans +buff" network collected even fewer live images, since it performed a forward and backward pass through its buffer of 200 patterns before digitizing a new one.

The accuracy of each of the three networks was determined by manually measuring the vehicle's lateral displacement relative to the road center as each network drove. The network trained on only the current video image quickly drove off the right side of the road, as indicated by its rapidly increasing displacement from the road center. The problem was that the network overlearned the right turn at the end of training and became biased towards turning right. Because of the increased diversity provided by the image transformation scheme, the second network performed much better than the first. It was able to follow the entire test stretch of road. However it still had a tendency to steer too much to the right, as illustrated in the graph by the vehicle's positive displacement over most of the test run. In fact, the mean position of the vehicle was 28.9cm right of the road center during the test. The variability of the errors made by this network was also quite large, as illustrated by the wide range of vehicle displacement in the "+trans -buff" graph. Quantitatively, the standard deviation of this network's displacement was 62.7cm.

The addition of buffering previously encountered training patterns eliminated the right bias in the third network, and also greatly reduced the magnitude of the vehicle's displacement from the road center, as evidenced by the "+trans +buff" graph. While the third network drove, the average position of the vehicle was 2.7cm right of center, with a standard deviation of only 14.8cm. This represents a 423% improvement in driving accuracy.

A separate test was performed to compare the steering accuracy of the network trained using both transformations and buffering with the steering accuracy of a human driver. This test was performed over the same stretch of road as the previous one, however the road was less obscured by fallen leaves in this test, resulting in better network performance. Over three runs, with the network driving at 5 miles per hour along the 100 meter test section of road, the average position of the vehicle was 1.6cm right of center, with a standard deviation of 7.2cm. Under human control, the average position of the vehicle was 4.0cm right of center, with a standard deviation of 5.47cm. The average distance the vehicle was from the road center while the person drove was 5.70cm. It appears that the human driver, while more consistent than the network, had an inaccurate estimate of the vehicle's centerline, and therefore drove slightly right of the road center. Studies of human driving performance have found similar steady state errors and variances in vehicle lateral position. Blaauw [2] found consistent displacements of up to 7cm were not uncommon when people drove on highways. Also for highway driving, Blaauw reports standard deviations in lateral error up to 16.6cm.

5. RESULTS AND COMPARISON

The competence of the ALVINN system is also demonstrate by the range of situations in which it has successfully driven.

The training on-the-fly scheme gives ALVINN a flexibility which is novel among autonomous navigation systems. It has allowed me to successfully train individual networks to drive in a variety of situations, including a single-lane dirt access road, a single-lane paved bicycle path, a two-lane suburban neighborhood street, and a lined two-lane highway (See Figure 12). Using other sensor modalities as input, including laser range images and laser reflectance images, individual ALVINN networks have been trained to follow roads in total darkness, to avoid collisions in obstacle rich environments, and to follow alongside railroad tracks. ALVINN networks have driven without intervention for distances of up to 22 miles. In addition, since determining the steering direction from the input image merely involves a forward sweep through the network, the system is able to process 15 images per second, allowing it to drive at up to 55 miles per hour. This is over four times faster than any other sensor-based autonomous system using the same processing hardware, has driven the Navlab [5] [10].

Figure 12: *Video images taken on three of the road types ALVINN modules have been trained to handle. They are, from left to right, a single-lane dirt access road, a single-lane paved bicycle path, and a lined two-lane highway.*

The level of flexibility across driving situations exhibited by ALVINN would be difficult to achieve without learning. It would require the programmer to 1) determine what features are important for the particular driving domain, 2) program detectors (using statistical or symbolic techniques) for finding these important features and 3) develop an algorithm for determining which direction to steer from the location of the detected features. As a result, while hand programmed systems have been developed to drive in some of the individual domains ALVINN can handle [5] [10] [12] [8], none have duplicated ALVINN's flexibility.

ALVINN is able to *learn* for each new domain what image features are important, how to detect them and how to use their position to steer the vehicle. Analysis of the hidden unit representations developed in different driving situations shows that the network forms detectors for the image features which correlate with the correct steering direction. When trained on multi-lane roads, the network develops hidden unit feature detectors for the lines painted on the road, while in single-lane driving situations, the detectors developed are sensitive to road edges and road-shaped regions of similar intensity in the image. For a more detailed analysis of ALVINN's internal representations see [14] [13].

This ability to utilize arbitrary image features can be problematic. This was the case when ALVINN was trained to drive on a poorly defined dirt road with a distinct ditch on its right side. The network had no problem learning and then driving autonomously in one direction, but when driving the other way, the network was erratic, swerving from one side of the road to the other. After analyzing the network's hidden representation, the reason for its difficulty became clear. Because of the poor distinction between the road and the non-road, the network had developed only weak detectors for the road itself and instead relied heavily on the position of the ditch to determine the direction to steer. When tested in the opposite direction, the network was able to keep the vehicle on the road using its weak road detectors but was unstable because the ditch it had learned to look for on the right side was now on the left. Individual ALVINN networks have a tendency to rely on *any* image feature consistently correlated with the correct steering direction. Therefore, it is important to expose them to a wide enough variety of situations during training so as to minimize the effects of transient image features.

On the other hand, experience has shown that it is more efficient to train several domain specific networks for circumstances like one-lane vs. two-lane driving, instead training a single network for all situations. To prevent this network specificity from reducing ALVINN's generality, we are currently implementing connectionist and non-connectionist techniques for combining networks trained for different driving situations. Using a simple rule-based priority system similar to the subsumption architecture [3], we have combined a road following network and an obstacle avoidance network. The road following network uses video camera input to follow a single-lane road. The obstacle avoidance network uses laser rangefinder images as input. It is trained to swerve appropriately to prevent a collision when confronted with obstacles and to drive straight when the terrain ahead is free of obstructions. The arbitration rule gives priority to the road following network when determining the steering direction, except when the obstacle avoidance network outputs a sharp steering command. In this case, the urgency of avoiding an imminent collision takes precedence over road following and the steering direction is determined by the obstacle avoidance network. Together, the two networks and the arbitration rule comprise a system capable of staying on the road and swerving to prevent collisions.

To facilitate other rule-based arbitration techniques, we have adding to AL-VINN a non-connectionist module which maintains the vehicle's position on a map [6]. Knowing its map position allows ALVINN to use arbitration rules such as "when on a stretch of two lane highway, rely primarily on the two lane highway network". This symbolic mapping module also allows ALVINN to make high level, goal-oriented decisions such as which way to turn at intersections and when to stop at a predetermined destination.

Finally, we are experimenting with connectionist techniques, such as the task decomposition architecture [16] and the meta-pi architecture [9], for combining networks more seamlessly than is possible with symbolic rules. These connectionist arbitration techniques will enable ALVINN to combine outputs from networks trained to perform the same task using different sensor modalities and to decide when a new expert must be trained to handle the current situation.

6. DISCUSSION

A truly autonomous mobile vehicle must cope with a wide variety of driving situations and environmental conditions. As a result, it is crucial that an autonomous navigation system possess the ability to adapt to novel domains. Supervised training of a connectionist network is one means of achieving this adaptability. But teaching an artificial neural network to drive based on a person's driving behavior presents a number of challenges. Prominent among these is the need to maintain sufficient variety in the training set to ensure that the network develops a sufficiently general representation of the task. Two characteristics of real sensor data collected as a person drives which make training set variety difficult to maintain are temporal correlations and the limited range of situations encountered. Extended intervals of nearly identical sensor input can bias a network's internal representation and reduce later driving accuracy. The human trainer's high degree of driving accuracy severely restricts the variety of situations covered by the raw sensor data.

The techniques for training "on-the-fly" described in this chapter solve these difficulties. The key idea underlying training on-the-fly is that a model of the process generating the live training data can be used to augment the training set with additional realistic patterns. By modeling both the imaging process and the steering behavior of the human driver, training on-the-fly generates patterns with sufficient variety to allow artificial neural networks to learn a robust representation of individual driving domains. The resulting networks are capable of driving accurately in a wide range of situations.

ACKNOWLEDGEMENTS

Support for this work was from ARPA, under contract DACA76-89-C0014, "Perception for Outdoor Navigation", and from the DOT/National Highway Traffic Safety Admin, under contract DTNH22-93-C-07023, "Run-Off-Road Counter

Measures". This research was also funded in part by a grant from Fujitsu Corporation.

REFERENCES

[1] G. Hinton K. Shikano A. Waibel, T. Hanazawa and K. Lang. Phoneme recognition: Neural networks vs. hidden markov models. In *Proceedings from Int. Conf. on Acoustics Speech and Signal Processing*, New York, New York, 1988.

[2] G.J. Blaauw. Driving experience and task demands in simulator and instrumented car: A validation study. *Human Factors*, 24:473–486, 1982.

[3] R.A. Brooks. A robust layered control system for a mobile robot. *IEEE Journal of Robotics and Automation*, RA-2(1):14–23, 1986.

[4] G.W. Cottrell. Extracting features from faces using compression networks: Face identity emotion and gender recognition using holons. In *Connectionist Models: Proc. of the 1990 Summer School*, pages 328–337, San Mateo California, 1990. Morgan Kaufmann Publishers.

[5] J.D. Crisman and C.E. Thorpe. Color vision for road following. In C.E. Thorpe, editor, *Vision and Navigation: The CMU Navlab*. Kluwer Academic Publishers, Boston Massachusetts, 1990.

[6] J. Gowdy D.A. Pomerleau and C.E. Thorpe. Combining artificial neural networks and symbolic processing for autonomous robot guidance. *Engineering Applications of Artificial Intelligence*, 4(4):279–285, 1991.

[7] G.E. Hinton D.E. Rumelhart and R.J. Williams. Learning internal representations by error propagation. In D.E. Rumelhart and J.L. McClelland, editors, *Parallel Distributed Processing: Explorations in the Microstructures of Cognition*, volume 1. Bradford Books/MIT Press, Cambridge Massachusetts, 1986.

[8] E.D. Dickmanns and A. Zapp. Autonomous high speed road vehicle guidance by computer vision. In *Proceedings of the 10th World Congress on Automatic Control*, volume 4, Munich Germany, 1987.

[9] J.B. Hampshire and A.H. Waibel. The meta-pi network: Building distributed knowledge representations for robust pattern recognition. Technical Report CMU-CS-89-166-R, Carnegie Mellon University, 5000 Forbes Ave., Pittsburgh PA 15213, August 1989.

[10] K. Kluge and C.E. Thorpe. Explicit models for robot road following. In C.E. Thorpe, editor, *Vision and Navigation: The CMU Navlab*. Kluwer Academic Publishers, Boston Massachusetts, 1990.

[11] E.N. Solowka L.D. Reid and A.M. Billing. A systematic study of driver steering behaviour. *Ergonomics*, 24:447–462, 1981.

[12] K.D. Gremban M.A. Turk, D.G. Morgenthaler and M. Marra. Vits – a vision system for autonomous land vehicle navigation. *IEEE Transactions on Pattern Analysis and Machine Intelligence*, 10, 1988.

[13] D.A. Pomerleau, editor. *Neural network perception for mobile robot guidance.* Kluwer Academic Publishing, 1993.

[14] D.A. Pomerleau and D.S. Touretzky. Understanding neural network internal representations through hidden unit sensitivity analysis. In *Proceedings of the International Conference on Intelligent Autonomous Systems*, Amsterdam, 1993. IOS Publishers.

[15] C. Thorpe H. Moravec W. Whittaker R. Wallace, A. Stentz and T. Kanade. First results in robot road-following. In *Proceedings of Int. Joint Conf. on Artificial Intelligence*, 1985.

[16] A.G. Barto R.A. Jacobs, M.I. Jordan. Task decomposition through competition in a modular connectionist architecture: The what and where vision tasks. Technical Report 90-27, Univ. of Massachusetts Computer and Information Science Department, March 1990.

[17] J.S. Denker D. Henderson R.E. Howard W. Hubbard Y. LeCun, B. Boser and L.D. Jackel. Backpropagation applied to handwritten zip code recognition. *Neural Computation*, 1(4), 1989.

CRESCEPTRON AND SHOSLIF: TOWARD COMPREHENSIVE VISUAL LEARNING

John J. Weng
Michigan State University

ABSTRACT

Comprehensive visual learning concerns a unified theory and methodology for computer vision systems to comprehensively learn the visual world with only minimal hand-crafted rules about the world. This chapter explains why comprehensive learning is crucial for a vision system to be capable of operating in complex real-world environments; how to automatically select the most useful features; and how to automatically organize visual information using a coarse-to-fine space partition tree which results in a very low, logarithmic time complexity for retrieving from a large visual knowledge base. A new system SHOSLIF, along with its predecessor the Cresceptron, is described to indicate how a core-shell model was used as a unified approach to comprehensive visual learning for several major vision tasks, such as recognition, motion understanding and autonomous navigation.

1. COMPREHENSIVE VS. RESTRICTED LEARNING

Despite the power of modern computers, whose principle was first introduced in 1936 by Alan Turing in his now celebrated paper [20], we have seen a paradoxical picture of artificial intelligence: Computers have done very well in those areas that are typically considered very difficult (by humans), such as playing chess games; but they have done poorly in areas that are commonly considered easy, such as vision. It seems a relatively simpler task to write a program to learn how to solve a symbolic problem that has been well-defined mathematically while the input to the program is clean, preprocessed symbolic data. For example, the rules for playing chess have been well defined, and the input to a chess playing program is typically a certain kind of symbolic representation for the piece placement. However, it is very difficult for a computer to solve a problem that is not easily definable in a symbolic form and to deal with data in the original form that the nature enforces on our eyes, such as a picture of a chess board scattered with sculptural pieces. In fact, it is still a very difficult task for a machine to play a chess game *visually.*

A fundamental problem to solve for any fully autonomous intelligent system is to deal with visual information directly, without relying on humans to preprocess data. The concept of *comprehensive learning* is introduced for this objective. It consists of two basic requirements:

1. Comprehensive coverage of the visual world. The system should be able to learn *comprehensive* visual world with virtually no restriction on the type of object or scene it can handle.

2. Comprehensive coverage of the system. Learning takes a comprehensive rule in the system, and virtually all the major stages of the vision system are based on learning.

Fig. 1 gives an illustration of the concept. Restricted learning (or noncomprehen-

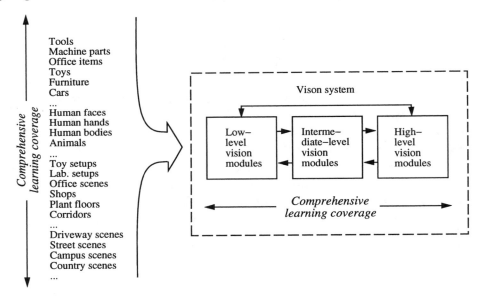

Figure 1: *The concept of comprehensive learning implies two coverages: comprehensive coverages over both the visual world and the vision system.*

sive learning) means that either the method assumes only a small class of objects or scene type to be dealt with, or only a small part of the vision algorithm is based on learning.

1.1. RESTRICTED LEARNING

Machine learning is not a new concept. Various learning techniques have been developed in the areas of pattern recognition and machine learning. However, in many cases, learning has been used only in a restricted sense.

In restricted visual learning, feature types are typically determined by human experts. It is also common to assume that feature vectors are already provided somehow, each vector corresponding to a single object. The learning process is then to classify feature vectors. Methods for this type of classification problem can be roughly divided into two types: statistical pattern recognition methods and symbolic methods. Statistical pattern recognition methods include parameter estimation based on Bayesian decision theory, non-parametric k-nearest-neighbor rule, linear discriminant functions, clustering techniques, etc. Symbolic methods may involve use of decision trees, production rules, etc. [16] [2] [12].

The capability of a system is very limited if its algorithm designer pre-defines the features to be used. Although a pre-designed set of features may be enough to classify a small number of objects, it becomes insufficient when more and more objects must be classified. Furthermore, a pre-determined set of features may be suited for some conditions but not for others, due to the human designer's limited capability to predict real world conditions. Therefore, unless the environmental condition is well controlled, manually imposing feature types results in a brittle system when it is exposed to the complex real world, since there is no effective and automatic way to check if the conditions are met.

In addition, the requirement that each feature vector is from a single object is often difficult to be met by a fully automatic system. As we know, segmenting image regions into meaningful objects is a major task. It is not always practical to assume that segmentation is done by a human. If a human is available to segment the objects of interest from images, then why not let him or her perform the entire recognition task! Segmenting an object from the background is not necessarily easier than recognizing it, and the two are not independent. The former task depends very much on the latter. If feature vectors are provided for the entire image without identifying which features belong to a single object, no traditional learning technique can work.

1.2. COMPREHENSIVE LEARNING

The comprehensive world coverage and the comprehensive system coverage are two indispensable components in the concept of comprehensive learning. Without the former, the system cannot handle general scenes and thus is brittle. Without the latter, the vision algorithm lacks adaptability due to the restrictions brought about by the hand-crafted rules.

The first coverage calls for visual learning algorithms that are suited for general real-world environments. Generality has a direct implication on the robustness of a vision system. In fact, the brittleness of many vision algorithms is due to more a lack of generality than a lack of capability of handling outliers in the sense of Hubert [9]. So far, there have been few reported works that deal with recognition from general real-world scenes. This situation can be attributed to the lack of a comprehensive visual learning scheme.

The second coverage calls for a drastically different methodology for vision algorithm design. In the field of computer vision, a lot of effort has been spent to investigate relationships that exist in image formation — from lighting, to surface geometry, to surface reflectance, to viewing geometry. Such investigations gave some mathematically manageable relations, provided that various conditions and restrictions are met. Then, hand-crafted rules are designed with various assumptions, conditions and simplifications. A typical vision algorithm is realized by coding these hand-crafted rules into an algorithm. Learning has been used in only few stages of the algorithm, if it has been used at all. Due to severe limitation of these relations in modeling the extremely complex visual perception, such an algorithm is unlikely to be successful in a general real-world setting.

The biological structure of our brain's cortex at birth is probably independent of whether the brain will store a medical doctor's knowledge or a computer designer's knowledge. The structure makes storage and retrieval of various knowledge possible, but it does not model (i.e., restrict) the knowledge itself. Therefore, in developing a vision system for the complex real world, it seems not appropriate for the vision algorithm itself to model visual knowledge, such as image formation process, object shape, etc. A more reasonable alternative approach is to design the way in which the system organizes itself according to whatever is seen, leaving the task of actually organizing the system to the process of machine learning.

The challenging task raised by comprehensive learning is to develop a unified theory and methodology for a vision system to learn from any visual world and to self-organize effectively and efficiently. All knowledge-level rules can be learned, instead of hand-crafted, to ensure generality and applicability of the rules. Theories for developing artificial intelligent machines may concentrate on representation and modeling at signal-level instead of knowledge level so that the method can represent virtually any knowledge that is too complex to be represented and handled effectively by existing knowledge-level tools.

A few recent works have a capability of learning directly from sensors, without imposing much restriction on the type of input, such as Pomerleau's use of neural network in ALVINN [15], applying the principle component analysis (PCA) directly on images by Turk and Pentland [21], the Cresceptron [24] [25] to be explained in this chapter, use of (PCA) for illumination planning [13], and the SHOSLIF described in this chapter.

The following sections describe two systems for comprehensive learning. Section 2 describes the Cresceptron, which appears to be the first work that is capable of learning directly from natural images and performing the task of general recognition *and* segmentation from images of the complex real world, virtually without limiting the type of objects that the system can deal with. A more complete account of the Cresceptron can be found in [24]. Section 4 describes its successor, the SHOSLIF, which targets at a low time complexity.

2. THE CRESCEPTRON

The term "Cresceptron" was coined from Latin *cresco* (grow) and *perceptio* (perception). Like the Neocognitron by Fukushima [7] for numeral recognition, the Cresceptron uses multi-level retinotopic layers of artificial neurons. However, it is fundamentally different from the Neocognitron in that the network configuration of the Cresceptron is *automatically* determined during learning, among many other structural differences. The Cresceptron has been designed primarily for recognition and segmentation of 3-D objects from 2-D images.

2.1. MAJOR CHARACTERISTICS
The following are some major characteristics of the Cresceptron.

1. The Cresceptron uses unsupervised learning from automatic hierarchical image *analysis* and hierarchical structural concepts derived therefrom (see Fig. 2). During learning, new concepts (image feature combinations) are

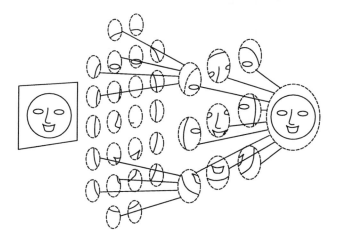

Figure 2: *A schematic illustration of hierarchical feature grouping in the Cresceptron. In the figure, not all the connections are shown.*

   automatically detected and the network structures are incrementally created to memorize new concepts with previously learned concepts. Knowledge sharing occurs automatically at every level of the network.

2. Tolerance to shape deviation is made hierarchical, smaller at a lower level and larger at a higher level. This makes it possible to handle many perceptually similar objects from a relatively small set of training samples.

3. The learning is based on hierarchical *analysis* instead of back-propagation. The structure of the object is analyzed in a bottom-up fashion before a decision is made. Therefore, the problem of local minima with the back-propagation methods is avoided.

4. Segmentation and recognition are tightly coupled. No foreground extraction is necessary, which is achieved by backtracking the response of the network through the hierarchy to the image parts contributing to the recognition.

5. The network is locally and sparsely connected. This is a crucial restriction one must impose for computational tractability with a large network.

2.2. NETWORK STRUCTURE

The network consists of multiple levels, as indicated in Fig. 3. Each level has 2 or

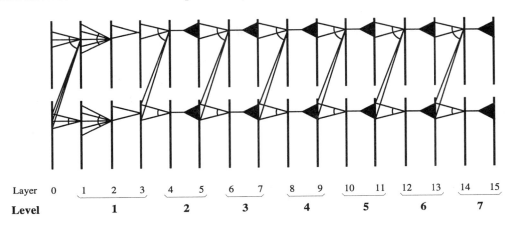

Figure 3: *A schematic illustration of the selected framework for a multi-level network. A thick vertical line represents an edge-on view of a neural plane. For each neural plane, only partial connections are shown. In the illustration, a plane being connected to two lower-layer planes means that every plane in this layer can be connected to several planes during learning. Otherwise, it accepts input from only one lower-layer plane. Layers 1,2,4,6,8,10,12,14 are pattern-detection layers; layter 3 is a node-reduction layer and layers 5,7,9,11,13,15 are blurring layers.*

3 layers. The output of a lower layer l is the input to the next higher layer $l + 1$. At each layer l, there are many neural planes. Each neural plane consists of a square of $k(l) \times k(l)$ nodes. Since each neural plane represents a concept and the response at a certain location on the neural plane indicates the presence of the concept, all the locations in a neural plane use the same sigmoidal function and the same set of synaptic weights. The nodes at layer $l = 0$ correspond to pixels in the input (fovea) image.

Basic network components serve as building blocks of the network. These components are: (1) The pattern-detection layer, whose purpose is to detect the presence of a feature. (2) The node-reduction layer, which is used to reduce the number of nodes in a neural plane for spatial efficiency. (3) The blurring layer, which blurs the input so that shape generalization is realized. It has been proved that the structure of the Cresceptron guarantees *recallability* in the sense that if a pattern is learned at a position on the fovea, then the same pattern is recognized no matter where it appears on the fovea.

2.3. THE LEARNING AND PERFORMANCE PHASES

To better handle lighting variations, the version implemented uses directional edges instead of image intensity values. Fig. 4 shows the user interface of the

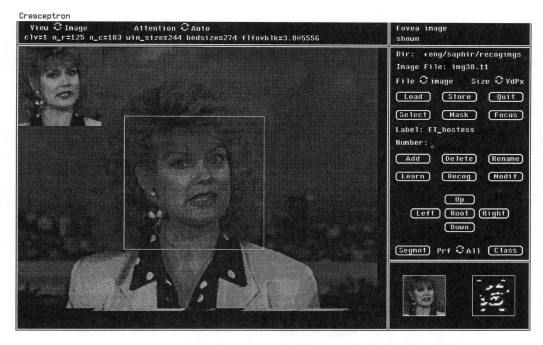

Figure 4: *Interface console of the Cresceptron.*

Cresceptron. During the learning phase, the user selects the object to learn by interactively drawing a polygon in the fovea image, to outline the object. A click on the button "learn" triggers the learning process which performs automatic new concept detection, network updating and increment, recursively from low level to high level through the network. The network grows only to memorize the innovation that it needs to learn. The user names the object by assigning a label. The system can also learn several samples as members of a single class. To do this, the user identifies the top neural plane that represents this class and then clicks the button "class" instead of "learn".

In the performance phase, a new image is presented to the Cresceptron. The step of selecting attention image is as follows. Each attention fixation defines a square attention window. Its objective is to scale the part of the image covered by the square attention window down to the size of the *attention image* (i.e., with a fixed number of pixels) as input to the neural network. In our experiment, the attention image is a square of 64×64 pixels. The size of the attention window changes from large to small. With each fixed size, the attention window scans the image at a set of grid points, whose density is inversely proportional to the window size. At each scanning position, the part of the input image covered by the attention window is scaled to the fovea image of 64×64 pixels. The network is then applied to this fovea image for recognition. Obviously, this way of selecting attention image is still computationally expensive. A future work is to develop an attention selector that itself is a learner.

At the top layer of the Cresceptron, the network reports all the response values (confidence values) higher than 0.5. A click on button "segment" instructs the system to segment the recognized object.

3. EXPERIMENTS WITH THE CRESCEPTRON

Here we show the result of an automatically generated network which has learned 21 classes of objects: faces of 10 different persons plus 11 other classes of object, including path scenes, street cars, dogs, fire hydrants, walking human figures, stop signs, parked cars, telephones, chairs, and computers. The result shown in Fig. 5 indicates the *tolerance*. Fig. 6 shows some of the 10 different faces, to show its

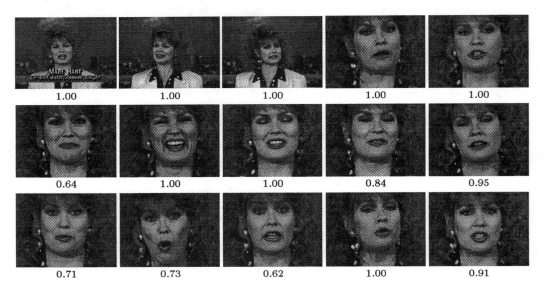

Figure 5: *The first 15 face expressions in the 35 "ET Hostess" face images tested by the Cresceptron. The first three images were used to train the network. The number under each image is the response value (or confidence value) of the recognition, i.e., the response value at the corresponding node at the top layer.*

discrimination power. Some of the 11 classes of nonface objects are shown in Fig. 7 which indicate the *versatility* of the Cresceptron.

The system was trained with 25 images from 20 classes, 10 face classes and 10 nonface classes, some of which are shown in Figs. 5 to 7. Another set of 68 images, none of which was used in the training, was used for testing, resulting in a correct recognition rate 100%. Every reported class (i.e., those with confidence > 0.5) was *unique*, except two cases in which a second candidate class was reported. For example, one of the two cases is the "stop sign" shown in Fig. 7, where a "dog" was reported from the top half of the stop sign with a confidence value 0.66, but the top choice is the correct "stop sign" with a confidence value 0.97.

Although the recognition performance of the Cresceptron looks positive with the set of images tested, the Cresceptron has a high computational complexity in terms of the number of objects learned. This raises the need for optimal feature selection and a fast indexing scheme for retrieval from a huge visual knowledge base. Its successor, the SHOSLIF addresses these critical issues from a task-independent point of view.

4. SHOSLIF

SHOSLIF stands for the *S*elf-organizing *H*ierarchical *O*ptimal *S*ubspace *L*earning and *I*nference *F*ramework.

4.1. THE CORE-SHELL MODEL

In order to systematically develop the task-independent part of intelligent learning and control, SHOSLIF uses a core-shell model, as shown in Fig. 8.

The core is task-independent. It accomplishes basic functionality of intelligence, such as memory, recall, reasoning, and inference. The SHOSLIF core $C = (N, L, R)$ has three components: a network N as a knowledge base, a learning procedure L, and a knowledge retrieval procedure R. The knowledge base defines a function $Y = N(X)$, where $X = (S, M)$ contains a sensor data item S, as well as mission vector M which specifies the requirement from the shell. The output from the knowledge base $Y = (E, P, A)$ contains an explanation E (e.g., pointers to text strings that describe the object or event's name, event's prediction etc.), a parameter vector P (e.g., object's image size, 3-D viewing angle, event speed, etc.), and an effector control vector A for control.

For each input vector X, the retrieval procedure R finds matches in the knowledge base N and gives the corresponding output vector $Y = (E, P, A)$.

The knowledge base N is empty before learning, denoted by N_0. The learning procedure L updates the current knowledge base N_{i-1} using a set of training data T_i to give an updated knowledge base $N_i = L(N_{i-1}, T_i)$. This is a sequential learning formulation. Each training set T_i contains one or more training data items $T_i = (D_1, D_2, \cdots, D_{n_i})$ where $D_j = (X_j, Y_j, V_j)$ consists of the input and outout pair (X_j, Y_j) as well as the learning specification vector V_j which specifies the learning requirement from the shell[1].

---

[1]For example, V_j may give an error tolerance in Y: If N_{i-1} without learning D_j can already give an output Y within the tolerance of error given by V_j, then L will not use D_j to further increase the size of the knowledge base, avoiding over-learning.

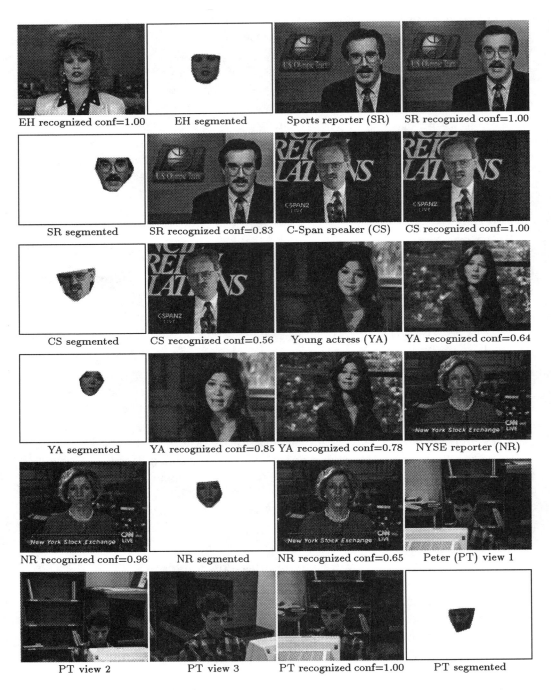

Figure 6: *Some examples of trained and tested 11 human face images with segmentation results. An image with class label only is a training image. An image with a given confidence value is a test image. An image with a word "segmented" is the result of segmentation from the previous test image.*

Figure 7: *Some examples of the result for 11 other nonface objects.*

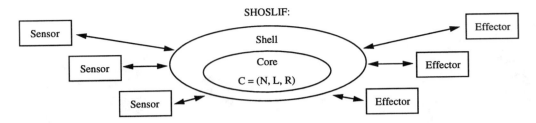

Figure 8: *A layer of SHOSLIF's shell and core, with sensors and effectors. Several such layers can be grouped and nested.*

The shell is task-dependent. Its functionalities include: (1) task-specific data management; (2) data collection and generation; (3) learning by invoking the core; (4) retriving knowledge by invoking the core.

With this core-shell structure, the core is independent of specific tasks. The same core can be used for many different tasks. The shell applies the core to different types of sensory data and different instances of knowledge base. The outputs of several knowledge bases can be grouped as a higher-level input vector to train a higher level knowledge base using another level of core-shell structure. In other words, the core-shell structure can be grouped and nested to solve low-level and high-level problems. For example, object recognition can be a low-level problem; motion understanding (i.e., spatiotemporal event recognition) can be a middle-level problem since it requires the result of object recognition; and mobile robot path planning can be a high-level problem since it requires the results from recognition and motion understanding. The core-shell model facilitates the systematic design, development, training and testing.

4.2. An overview of the SHOSLIF
The SHOSLIF uses the core-shell model to organize various tasks.

4.2.1. Global invariance and local invariance
As an example for discussion, consider the task of object recognition. The first stage is to determine where to look and the scale of attention, or in other words, to select visual attention, as shown in Fig. 9. Suppose a recognition network is trained so that the recognition is successful as long as the image is admissible, i.e., the object size and position are within a certain variation range (e.g., 10%) from those of a learned image. Then, the second stage is to generate an admissible image by fixating at the face with a proper scale. The third stage is to recognize the object from the admissible image.

From the above example, we can see that a very difficult recognition problem can be decomposed into several stages. An earlier stage must deal with global (large scale) variations but only needs to give very rough results. A later stage must give more specific results but only needs to deal with local (small scale)

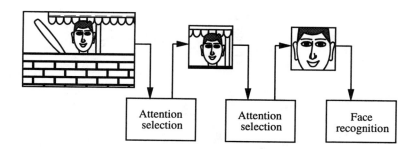

Figure 9: *Attention selection as subtasks of finding an object of interest and fixating with a proper scale.*

variations. A single core-shell structure can accomplish one or more such stages, depending on the nature of the problem.

4.2.2. SEVERAL FIXATIONS ON THE INPUT DATA

The above process corresponds to a single fixation on the input data. Typically, several eye fixations are needed to confidently recognize an object. This is particularly true when the object is partially occluded. Therefore, the result of attention selection can be a series of fixations.

Fig. 10 shows attention fixations of the SHOSLIF. The hierarchical network is invoked several times (3 in the figure) according to the visual saccades sequence specified by the human operator during the learning phase. Within each network, the coarse-to-fine hierarchy recursively classifies the visual object into finer and finer subclasses. The darkened paths in Fig. 10 are traversed nodes. In actuality, each tree is not necessarily a complete tree. The final confidence for recognizing an object can be measured by the product of the probabilities computed from every invocation. In case of occlusion, the final probability can be the maximum of those computed from several fixations. This integration of fixation seems better to be accomplished by another core-shell layer.

4.2.3. REPRESENTATION

We consider the problem of the core, which is to give a desired output given an input. The representation must be very general in order to reach the wide coverage of the visual world, as required by the comprehensive learning principle. With this motivation, we represent an image by a vector. A digital image with r pixel rows and c pixel columns can be denoted by a vector $\mathbf{X}$ in (rc)-dimensional space [21] [23] [13]. In order to deal with an astronomical number of images that can be present in an application, we regard observed input image vector $\mathbf{X}$ as a random sample. The second order statistics between pixels are represented by the corresponding covariance matrix of the random vector $\mathbf{X}$. Therefore, treating a two-dimensional image as a one-dimensional vector $\mathbf{X}$ is just for notational

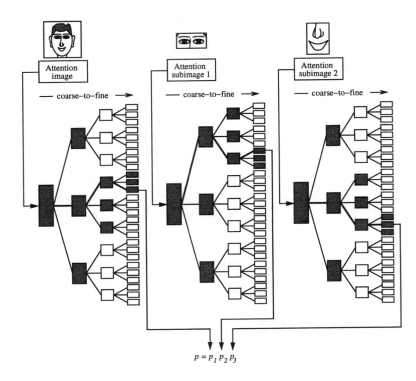

Figure 10: *Multiple fixations by the SHOSLIF.*

convenience and the representation itself does not lose any two-dimensional information.

Our objective of constructing a navigator is equivalent to approximating function $f : S \mapsto C$ by another function $\hat{f} : S \mapsto C$. The error of approximation can be indicated by certain measures of the error $\hat{f} - f$. One such measure is the mean square error

$$E\|\hat{f} - f\|^2 = \int_{\mathbf{X} \in S} \|\hat{f}(\mathbf{X}) - f(\mathbf{X})\|^2 dF(\mathbf{X})$$

where $F(\mathbf{X})$ is the probability distribution function of $\mathbf{X}$ in S.

A powerful method of constructing $\hat{f}$ is using case-based learning. Specifically, a series of cases is acquired as the learning data set:

$$L = \{(\mathbf{X}_i, f(\mathbf{X}_i)) \mid i = 1, 2, \cdots, n\}. \tag{1}$$

Then, the task of learning is to construct $\hat{f}$ based on L. One powerful method is *case-based learning* using the nearest-neighbor principle, i.e., $\hat{f}(\mathbf{X}) = f(\mathbf{X}_i))$ if $\mathbf{X}_i$ is the nearest neighbor of $\mathbf{X}$ in S among all the sample points in L. A very desirable property of the nearest-neighbor principle is that its does not suffer from the *local minima problem*. However, a straight forward application is not possible because of the low efficiency when the number of samples n is huge. This is dealt with by the following method.

4.3. THE HIERARCHICAL SPACE PARTITION

The space S is automatically partitioned into cells at every level, according to the training samples. as shown in Fig. 11(a). At the first level, the space is

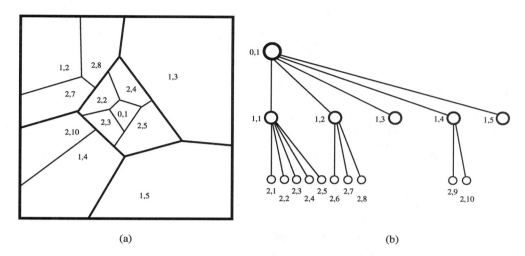

(a)   (b)

Figure 11: A 2-D illustration of a hierarchical Dirichlet partition and the corresponding recursive partition tree (RPT). (a) The partition, where the label indicates the center of a cell. The label of the child to which its parent's center belongs is not shown due to the lack of space. (b) The recursive partition tree.

partitioned into large cells. Each large cell is recursively partitioned into smaller and smaller cells at deeper levels. A cell is a leaf if only one learning sample falls into it. The partition is represented by what is called a recursive partition tree (RPT) as illustrated in Fig. 11(b). Each leaf keeps a training sample $\mathbf{X}$ and the corresponding desired output $f(\mathbf{X})$. In this way, regions in which f is not defined or with a low probability are approximated very roughly by a few coarse cells, but regions of high density are approximated in detail by many small cells for a high accuracy.

In the performance phase, given an input $\mathbf{X}'$, the retriever recursively searches for the nearest cell at each level and explore its children to find the nearest cell, until a leaf is found and its stored $f(\mathbf{X})$ is retrieved.

4.4. INTERPOLATION

Although such a hierarchical partition allows a very fast retrieval algorithm, the final partition determined by the leaf nodes is not a Dirichlet partition (or Voronoi diagram) in general, as indicated in the example shown in Fig. 11. Therefore, it is not guaranteed that the nearest-neighbor leaf can be found by the above single-path search method.

Our way of dealing with this problem is to explore $k > 1$ competitive paths down the RPT. At each level, top k nearest cells are explored. It is likely that the correct path that leads to the nearest neighbor is included in these k active paths. At the end, the corresponding output values of the k competitive leaves will be used in a weighted interpolation according to the distance from $\mathbf{X}'$ to each of the k competitive leaves. This is the basic idea behind the k-competitor distance-based (KCDB) approximator to be used. Such a k-path search method with interpolation has a very desirable property: it allows interpolation among reached leaf nodes so that even if the nearest neighbor is not among them, the interpolated result is typically reasonably good. The interpolation also enables inference to be discussed in Section 4.7.

4.4.1. RETRIEVAL COMPLEXITY

For simplicity, consider a complete tree having l levels and a branching factor b. The number of learning samples stored by the tree corresponds to the number of leaf nodes, which is $n = b^l$. The number of total nodes is equal to $1+b+b^2+...+b^l = (b^{l+1} - 1)/(b - 1) = O(b^l) = O(n)$. Suppose an input is given for search for a match. With the RPT, given an input, k top matched nodes are explored further at each level. Thus, the number of nodes visited is equal to $kbl = O(\log_b(n))$. To appreciate this extremely low complexity, let us consider a numerical example: Suppose that $b = l = 10$ and $k = 4$. Then, to search for a match in a RPT of $n = 10^{10} = 10$ billions stored items, only about $k\log_b(n) = 400$ nodes need to be traversed. This tremendous saving is brought about by the coarse-to-fine hierarchical decomposition of the space. In general, with n objects, a complexity of order $O(\log(n))$ is expected for search with the RPT.

4.5. THE MOST EXPRESSIVE FEATURES

The dimensionality of the RPT will be equal to the dimensionality of the input vector, if no dimension reduction is done. This dimension is too large for a high dimensional problem, such as recognition from images or image sequences. Since each cell represents only an extremely small part of the entire space, its sample space typically is well represented by a low dimensional space. The process of determining the basis of this low dimensional space is also a process of finding features, as we will see below.

Images of objects in a category (e.g., human faces) can be considered as samples represented by an n-dimensional random vector $\mathbf{X}$. $\mathbf{X}$ can be expanded exactly by n orthonormal vectors, $\mathbf{v}_1, \mathbf{v}_2, ..., \mathbf{v}_n$, so that

$$\mathbf{X} = \sum_{i=1}^{n} y_i\mathbf{v}_i = V\mathbf{Y} \tag{2}$$

where V is an orthogonal $n \times n$ square matrix consisting of orthonormal column vectors $\mathbf{v}_i$. Without loss of generality, we assume that the mean of the random vector $\mathbf{Y}$ is a zero vector, since we can always redefine $\mathbf{Y} - E\mathbf{Y}$ as the new feature vector.

We expect that a relatively small number of features is sufficient to characterize a class. Suppose we use m features, where each is a component of $\mathbf{Y}$. The approximate representation is $\hat{\mathbf{X}}(m) = \sum_{i=1}^{m} y_i \mathbf{v}_i$. It has been proved [11] that the best $\mathbf{v}_1 \ \mathbf{v}_2 \ ... \ \mathbf{v}_m$ that minimize the mean square error of the approximation

$$\epsilon^2(m) = E\|\mathbf{X} - \hat{\mathbf{X}}(m)\|^2 \tag{3}$$

are the m unit eigenvectors of the covariance matrix of $\mathbf{X}$, $\Sigma_X = E[(\mathbf{X} - E\mathbf{X})(\mathbf{X} - E\mathbf{X})^t]$, associated with the m largest eigenvalues. After the $\mathbf{v}_i$'s are computed, these m feature values, y_i, can be computed from

$$y_i = \mathbf{v}_i^t \mathbf{X} \qquad i = 1, 2, ..., m \tag{4}$$

or $\mathbf{Y} = V^t \mathbf{X}$, where $V = [\mathbf{v}_1 \ \mathbf{v}_2 \ ... \ \mathbf{v}_n]$. This is known as the Karhunen-Loeve projection [11] or the principal component analysis (PCA) [10]. Turk and Pentland used the PCA to represent and recognize human face images [21]. Murase and Nayar used the PCA to estimate the illumination direction [13].

Since the m features, $\mathbf{v}_i$'s in (4), give the minimum mean-square error, we can call them the *most expressive features* (MEF) in that they best describe the sample population in the sense of a linear transformation. We choose m so that the ratio of the mean-square error over the total variance, is smaller than a given percentage:

$$\frac{\sum_{i=m+1}^{d} \lambda_i}{\sum_{i=1}^{d} \lambda_i} \leq \tau \tag{5}$$

(e.g. $\tau = 5\%$).

If we are given k discrete training images, $\mathbf{X}_1, \mathbf{X}_2, ..., \mathbf{X}_k$, Σ_X is approximated by scatter matrix

$$S = \sum_{i=1}^{k} (\mathbf{X}_i - \mathbf{m})(\mathbf{X}_i - \mathbf{m})^t = UU^t \tag{6}$$

where $U = [\mathbf{U}_1 \ \mathbf{U}_2 \ ... \ \mathbf{U}_k]$, and $\mathbf{U}_i = \mathbf{X}_i - \mathbf{m}$, $\mathbf{m} = (1/k) \sum_{i=1}^{k} \mathbf{X}_i$. Typically, the number of training images, k, is smaller than n because n is very large. Instead of dealing with a very large UU^t directly, we can find the eigenvector and eigenvalues of a smaller $k \times k$ matrix $U^t U$, which has the same non-zero eigenvalues as $S = UU^t$. If $\mathbf{w}_i$ is an eigenvector of $U^t U$ associated with the eigenvalue λ_i, then $\mathbf{v}_i = U\mathbf{w}_i$ is the eigenvector of $S = UU^t$ associated with the same eigenvalue.

4.6. THE MOST DISCRIMINATING FEATURES
4.6.1. WEAKNESS OF THE MEF's FOR CLASSIFICATION

The MEF's are, in general, not the best ones for classification, because the features that describe some major variations in the class may be irrelevant to how the subclasses are divided, as shown in Fig. 12. Although the variation along z_1 is not large, it catches the major feature that is crucial for classifying subclasses. A threshold for the projection onto z_1 can be used to separate the two subclasses.

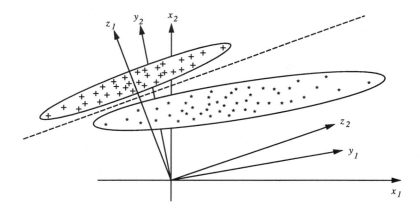

Figure 12: *The most discriminating features (MDF) for two subclasses. The MDF is the vector along z_1 and the MEF is the vector along y_1. The MEF along y_1 cannot separate the two subclasses but the MDF can.*

However, the MEF, represented by y_1, cannot separate the two subclasses, nor can the direction along the difference of the two subclass means. The theory for this issue is called discriminant analysis in mathematical statistics.

4.6.2. HYPERPLANES ARE SUFFICIENT FOR SPACE DECOMPOSITION

A natural question which arises here is whether the classes are linearly separable. Note that we want to use hyperplanes to obtain hierarchical space decomposition as shown in Fig. 11, instead of separating two pre-defined classes. The region of a class can be approximated to within any given accuracy by the union of a number of hyper-plane defined cells (i.e., polyhedrons) at proper levels, although the number of cells could be large.

Of course, we would like to decompose the space in an efficient way. If visually similar objects mostly fall into the same cell, the network tends to be small because relatively few nodes at a coarse level can cover the type of objects in the training set. Therefore, the MDF is also useful for reducing the network size.

4.6.3. FISHER'S DISCRIMINANT ANALYSIS AND THE MDF'S

Suppose a sample $\mathbf{Y}$ is an m-dimensional random vector drawn from c classes. The ith class has a probability p_i, a mean vector $\mathbf{m}_i$ and a scatter matrix Σ_i. The *within-class scatter matrix* is defined by

$$S_w = \sum_{i=1}^{c} p_i E\{(\mathbf{Y} - \mathbf{m}_i)(\mathbf{Y} - \mathbf{m}_i)^t \mid \omega_i\} = \sum_{i=1}^{c} p_i \Sigma_i \qquad (7)$$

The *between-class scatter matrix* is $S_b = \sum_{i=1}^{c} p_i (\mathbf{m}_i - \mathbf{m})(\mathbf{m}_i - \mathbf{m})^t$ where $\mathbf{m}$ is the grand mean defined as $\mathbf{m} = E\mathbf{Y} = \sum_{i=1}^{c} p_i \mathbf{m}_i$. The *mixture scatter matrix* is defined by $S_m = E\{(\mathbf{Y} - \mathbf{m})(\mathbf{Y} - \mathbf{m})^t\} = S_w + S_b$. Suppose we use k-dimensional linear features $\mathbf{Z} = W^t\mathbf{Y}$ where W is an $m \times k$ rectangular matrix whose column vectors are linearly independent. The above mapping represents a linear projection from m-dimensional space to k-dimensional space. We want to find $m \times k$ matrix W to maximize the between-class scatter while minimizing the within-class scatter in the space of $\mathbf{Z}$. In the multidimensional multiclass discriminant analysis [27], an objective function we wish to maximize is

$$\text{trace}\{S_{Zw}^{-1}S_{Zb}\} \tag{8}$$

where S_{Zw} and S_{Zb} are the within-class and between-class scatter matrices of $\mathbf{Z}$, respectively. Alternatively, we can also consider another objective function. Note that $\det\{S_{Zw}\}$ and $\det\{S_{Zb}\}$ measure the hyperellipsoidal scattering volume of S_{Zw} and S_{Zb}, respectively. We may maximize their ratio

$$\frac{\det\{S_{Zb}\}}{\det\{S_{Zw}\}} = \frac{\det\{W^tS_{Yb}W\}}{\det\{W^tS_{Yw}W\}} \tag{9}$$

It has been proved that both objective functions (8) and (9) lead to the same projection matrix W whose column vectors are the eigenvectors of $S_{Yw}^{-1}S_{Yb}$ associated with the first k largest eigenvalues. The column vectors of W are called *the most discriminating features* (MDF). Since the rank of S_{Yb} is at most $c - 1$, we know that only at most $c - 1$ features are needed and others do not contribute to the maximum of the objective functions. Note that although $S_{Yw}^{-1}S_{Yb}$ is generally not a symmetric matrix, its eigenvectors and eigenvalues can be computed from eigenvalue decomposition for symmetric matrices.

4.6.4. THE DKL PROJECTION

The discriminant analysis procedure breaks down when the within-class scatter matrix S_w becomes degenerate, which is true when the dimensionality of the input image is larger than the number of learning samples.

In fact, the discriminant analysis can be performed in the space of the Karhunen-Loeve projection (i.e., MEF space), where the degeneracy typically does not occur. Thus, the new overall discriminant projection consists of two projections, the Karhunen-Loeve projection followed by the discriminant projection. To do this, we first project the d-dimensional $\mathbf{X}$-space onto m-dimensional MEF space ($\mathbf{Y}$-space) using the Karhunen-Loeve projection. Then, we project $\mathbf{Y}$-space onto the k-dimensional MDF space ($\mathbf{Z}$-space). For notational convenience, we define the *DKL projection* (short for Discriminant Karhunen-Loeve projection) from the d-dimensional space of $\mathbf{X}$ to the k-dimensional space of $\mathbf{Z}$ as $\mathbf{Z} = W^tV^t\mathbf{X}$. It appears that the need for the DKL projection has not been raised by classical pattern recognition problems where the dimensionality of the feature space is typically much smaller than the number of available samples.

We must determine the dimensionality m of $\mathbf{Y}$ so that S_w is not degenerate. Given s samples from c classes, the maximum rank of S_w is $s - c$. Therefore, in order to make S_w nondegenerate, the input space of MDF projection m (i.e., the size of S_w) cannot be larger than $s - c$. That is, $m \leq s - c$. This means that, in the MEF projection, we need to discard $(s - c + 1)$th up to $(s - 1)$th eigenvalues of Σ_X (i.e., the $c - 1$ smallest ones). As we can expect, these eigenvalues are typically extremely small, because the $(s - 1)$th eigenvalue is the smallest among all the nonzero eigenvalues. In practice, we would like to discard more because it is very unlikely that they are important for classification either. On the other hand, m cannot be smaller than the number of classes c. Therefore we have $k < c \leq m \leq s - c$. Typically, s is much larger than c and thus, m can be chosen as an integer value in $[c, s - c]$ which also satisfies the variation criterion in (5).

4.7. INVARIANT RECOGNITION AS LEARNING-BASED INFERENCE

Invariant recognition is the ability to infer and deal with various variations of an object class. Variations fall into two categories, image-plane geometric variation and general variation.

4.7.1. IMAGE-PLANE GEOMETRIC VARIATION

The parameters for image-plane geometric variation include, size, position and orientation.

Once the input images are reduced to a low dimensional MDF space, a training sample is represented by a point in the MDF space. We need to estimate the parameters of the input subimage. It is reasonable to assume that the MDF values vary continuously and slowly with these parameters, especially with certain amount of image blurring corresponding to each RPT level. Fig. 13 gives a schematic illustration.

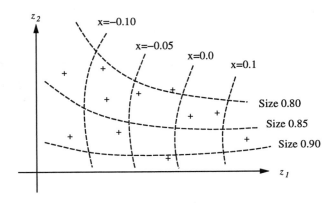

Figure 13: *Geometric inference via function fitting and interpolation in the MDF space. The plus signs indicate training samples.*

We define a vector-valued function $\mathbf{S(Z)}$ which maps from MDF space to the parameter space. Given any $\mathbf{Z}$, $\mathbf{S(Z)}$ is approximated by a set of points $\mathbf{Z}_{n_i}$, $i = 1, 2, ...n$, where $\mathbf{Z}_{n_i}$ is the i-th nearest neighbor of $\mathbf{Z}$ in the MDF space. One such approximation is

$$\mathbf{S}(\mathbf{Z}) = \frac{1}{\sum_{i=1}^{k} w_i} \sum_{i=1}^{k} w_i \mathbf{S}(\mathbf{Z}_{n_i}) \tag{10}$$

where $w_i = w(\mathbf{Z}, \mathbf{Z}_{n_1}, \mathbf{Z}_{n_i})$ is the value of a scalar weighting function. As an example, the weighting function $w(\mathbf{Z})$ can take the form

$$w(\mathbf{Z}, \mathbf{Z}_{n_1}, \mathbf{Z}_{n_i}) = \alpha^{-\|\mathbf{Z}-\mathbf{Z}_{n_i}\|^2/(\epsilon+\|\mathbf{Z}-\mathbf{Z}_{n_1}\|^2)} \tag{11}$$

where ϵ is a small positive number to avoid a zero denominator when $\mathbf{Z} = \mathbf{Z}_{n_1}$. The value of α determines how fast the weight decreases for other runners up. A point $\mathbf{Z}_{n_i}$ at twice the distance compared to that of the nearest neighbor $\mathbf{Z}_{n_1}$ will have its weight decreased by a factor of $1/\alpha$ from that of the nearest neighbor. For example, $\alpha = 10$ is a reasonable choice for α.

There is a very rich collection of interpolation methods, e.g., the generalized Gaussian radial basis function [14], and various generalized multiquadratics interpolants surveyed by Stead [17]. Our interpolation function in (10) is adaptive to local sample density without need of a manually chosen scale σ for a Gaussian radial basis function. Its interpolated value is guaranteed to be bounded above and below by the maximum and minimum values of the sample points, respectively. Thus, it does not suffer from the well-known over-fitting problem in function fitting.

4.7.2. GENERAL VARIATION

While the above geometric inference is for 2-D variations, general variation deals all the other variations, such as 3-D viewing angle, illumination, face expressions, etc. The major difference between the two types of variation is that for the former, we need also estimates of the parameters; but for the latter, we typically do not have, or do not need to have, a parameterization at all, such as the effect of illumination variation.

The interpolation scheme in the above section can be modified to handle general variations. To simplify the discussion, let us consider variation of 3-D azimuth viewing angle in recognition. The manifold of an object is defined by a curved axis in the feature space, as indicated in Fig. 14 by a thick dashed trajectory. For general case, the manifold may have a higher dimension. Due to variations of many other factors, the manifold may have certain width and probably several branches, with a high probability on the axis and with a decreasing probability when the observed feature vector moves away from the axis. The manifold may go through several cells (i.e., nodes in the network) at a certain level.

We use the interpolation function $f(\mathbf{Z})$ in the same form as (10)

$$f(\mathbf{Z}) = \frac{1}{\sum_{i=1}^{k} w_i} \sum_{i=1}^{k} w_i f(\mathbf{Z}_{n_i}) \tag{12}$$

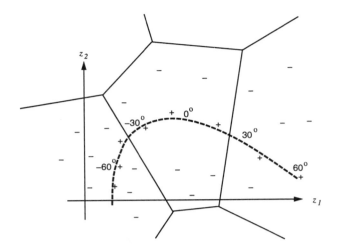

Figure 14: *General inference using decision-boundary learning. The boundary of the cells is indicated by line segments. The thick dashed curve indicates the axis of the manifold of an object class. Plus and minus signs indicate positive and negative samples, respectively.*

where $f(\mathbf{Z})$ is the confidence (or probability) value for input $\mathbf{Z}$ to arise from the object class under consideration. The function $f(\mathbf{Z})$ is such that $f(\mathbf{Z}) \approx 1$ means that $\mathbf{Z}$ represents a sample of the object class with a high confidence; $f(\mathbf{Z}) \approx -1$ means that it surely does not belong to the class; and $f(\mathbf{Z}) \approx 0$ implies a lack of confidence, either positive or negative. The function $f(\mathbf{Z})$ uses both positive and negative samples to approximate the complex manifold of the class in the MDF space. The interpolated value is always between -1 and 1 because of the weighting function in (11). The decision boundary is defined by $f(\mathbf{Z}) = c$ for a relatively small c (e.g., $c = 0$).

Clearly, to construct such a function, the samples near the boundary of the manifold are useful and faraway negative samples are not (there are a lot of them for each class!). For the sack of efficiency, we should not use faraway negative samples for interpolation in (12). Periodically, the system tries to delete each sample point $\mathbf{Z}_i$. If the resulting tree makes no error at $\mathbf{Z}_i$, the sample point $\mathbf{Z}_i$ is deleted from the tree. When the number of learned objects is very large, such a local fitting and interpolation using decision-boundary learning is very important to contain the storage cost.

In summary, the interpolation function can be used to infer various types of output from a set of nearby sample points. The output can represent a numerical class label, an attribute-parameter vector, a control vector, or the confidence for giving such an output. Obviously, the success of such an interpolation scheme depends very much on the density of the available training samples as will as the nature of the application problem.

Table 1: *Experimental data of SHOSLIF-O*

Type	Training set	Classes	Test set	Top 1	Top 15
Face	1206 images	477 classes	258 images	92.6%	98.8%
Nonface	109 images	48 classes	41 images	92.7%	97.6%
All	1315 images	525 classes	299 images	92.6%	98.7%

5. SOME EXPERIMENTAL APPLICATIONS OF THE SHOSLIF

To show the generality of the SHOSLIF, we present some experimental results of SHOSLIF for three major vision and robotic tasks: object recognition, motion understanding, and autonomous navigation. The SHOSLIF is currently also being applied to hand-eye coordinated learning for robot manipulators in project SHOSLIF-R, SHOSLIF for robot manipulators [8].

5.1. SHOSLIF-O: SHOSLIF FOR OBJECT RECOGNITION

SHOSLIF-O consists of the SHOSLIF core and a SHOSLIF shell for object recognition. The experiment presented here does not include the functionality of attention selection. All the images used for the experiment were "well-framed" in the sense that each object of interest is centered in the image and has an appropriate size. A total of 1315 images were used for training, among which there are 1206 face images and 109 images of other objects, such as cars, chairs, cups, desks, dogs, auto parts, telephones, human bodies, traffic signs, etc. For each test image, top 15 best matches found through the automatically generated RPT were reported with the similarity measure. Table 1 summaries the result of training and test. Note that none of the test images was present in the training set. A test set that consists of all the 1315 training images resulted in 100% correct recognitions all as top 1 choice. Therefore, the performance of an open-ended learning system like SHOSLIF hinges on its learning experience. The more images that have been learned, the better the performance will be.

An as example to indicate major differences between MEF and MDF in selecting the most discriminating features, Fig. 15 shows sample images represented by points in the space of the best (in terms of the largest eigenvalues) two MEFs and MDFs, respectively, which were computed from 11 classes of face images and 8 classes of other objects (2 learning samples were used for each class). As indicated by Fig. 15, in the MDF space the samples in the same class are much tightly clustered and samples from different classes are wider separated than the case of MEF. This implies that MDFs have a significantly higher capability to catch major differences between classes and discount factors that are not related to classification. More detailed result can be found in [18] [19].

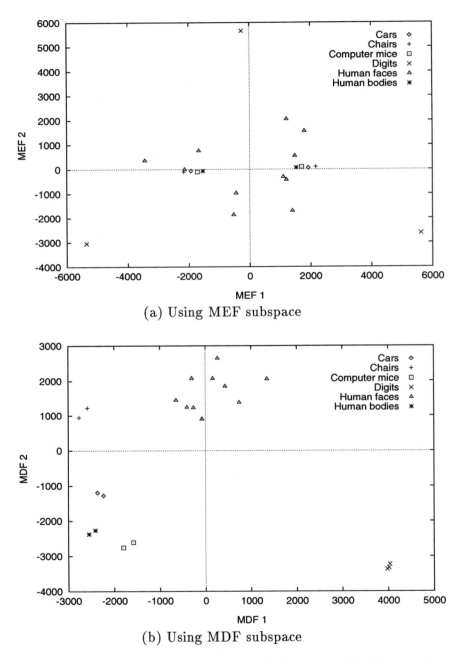

(a) Using MEF subspace

(b) Using MDF subspace

Figure 15: *Distribution of the samples using the best two (the first two) features in the MEF and the MDF subspaces. In the MDF subspace, objects of the same class are clustered much more tightly than in the MEF subspace.*

5.2. SHOSLIF-M: SHOSLIF FOR MOTION UNDERSTANDING

SHOSLIF-M is a subsystem for motion understanding, i.e., spatiotemporal event recognition. In the example shown here, the SHOSLIF-M was applied to hand sign recognition.

Each spatiotemporal event is recorded by an image sequence. To understand such an event, the system needs to recognize spatial content as well as temporal content. In hand sign recognition, for example, the system needs to recognize hands of different gestures. Motion of a hand and change of its gesture indicate a hand sign.

The SHOSLIF-M operates in the following stages. (1) Inter-frame motion information is used to generate a motion clip, which consists of an image sequence in which some motion occurs from the beginning to the end. (2) Hand is recognized and segmented from each frame of the sequence, based on various learned hand shapes and gestures. This process includes an invocation of the SHOSLIF core with a network for hand recognition. (3) Each subimage that includes the hand is stacked along time axis to give a cropped and normalized sequence, which define a vector of $s_x s_y s_t$ dimensions, where s_x, s_y and s_t are the sizes of the sequence in width, height, and time, respectively. The global motion parameters of the hand are represented in the x- and y- coordinates, which define a separate 2-D global motion vector. The combination of the cropped sequence and the global motion vector defines a new vector called *fovea vector*, which is of $s_x s_y s_t + 2$ dimensions. (4) The core is called to learn and recognize from the fovea vectors. The motive of the above procedures is to effectively use global motion parameters and to reduce the dimensionality from original image sequences. This is an example where two core-shell structures are nested, one for spatial recognition and one for spatiotemporal recognition from fovea vectors.

Hand sign classes used for training and testing are "angry," "any," "boy," "yes," "cute," "fine," "funny," "girl," "happy," "hi," "high," "hot," "later," "low," "no," "nothing," "of course," "ok," "parent," "pepper," "smart," "sour," "strange," "sweet," "thank you," "thirsty," "welcome," and "wrong," as defined in American Sign Language [1]. Fig. 16 shows a few examples of these 28 hand signs, with the result of automatic segmentation from the spatial recognition.

For each of the 28 hand sign classes, 36 sample sequences were acquired, a half of which was used for training and the other half for testing, which brought the total numbers of training and testing sequences to $18 \times 28 = 504$, respectively. The system correctly recognized 98% of the test sequence and declared "unknown" for the rest (2%) without misclassification, i.e., without accepting any sequence as an incorrect hand sign. On a SUN SPARC-10, average time for the RPT network retrieval was 3.57 seconds. Of course, it does not cover the motion detection and hand segmentation which are much slower. A more detailed report of the experiment is available in [4] [5]. The current method cannot deal with situations where the background is complex. In the experiment, only a simple background is used. The task of segmenting hand from a complex background is investigated

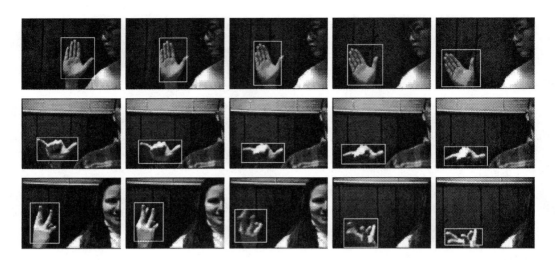

Figure 16: *Sequences of "hi" (upper row), "of course" (middle rrow) and "wel-come" (lower row). The result of hand-recognition gives the segmentation shown by the white rectangles.*

in [6].

5.3. SHOSLIF-N: SHOSLIF FOR AUTONOMOUS NAVIGATION

SHOSLIF-N's task is to control a mobile robot to navigate autonomously in an unstructured (i.e., unknown) environment based on only visual images. No active sensors, such as sonar or infrared proximity sensors, can be used.

The program was run on a SUN SPARC-1 on board of Rome, a mobile robot built on a Labmate platform from TRC. A test site for our navigation experiments is located inside of the Engineering Building at MSU. The selected experimental area consists of several typical hallway sections with various turns. In the learning phase, ROME was controlled manually to take pictures at different positions for learning. At each position, a set of five images with different heading directions were obtained: two left headings (5 and 10 degrees), two right headings (-5 and -10 degrees) and the straight-ahead direction. The corresponding corrected heading directions were also recorded. At turns, learning images were taken during sample drives controlled manually using a joystick. A total of 318 images were collected for training. Some of the sample training images are shown in Fig. 17.

For comparison purpose, two trees MEF RPT (one that uses MEF only) and MDF RPT were automatically constructed from the learning set of 318 images. The tree sizes shown in Table 2 indicates that the number of nodes in the MDF RPT is just about 10% of that of the MEF RPT. Given an input, the average retrieval time from the larger MEF tree took about 0.128 sec.

Fig. 18 shows the distribution of error in retrieved heading direction with a set of 204 test images that were not used in the learning set. Comparing Fig. 18(a)

Figure 17: *Some sample training images in a straight hallway (upper row) and a turn (lower row).*

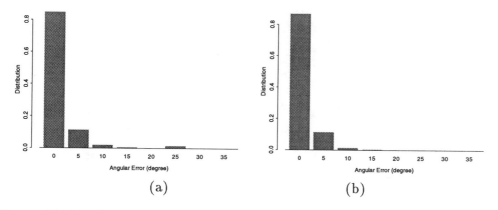

(a)   (b)

Figure 18: Distribution of absolute angular error (degree) of retrieved heading directions. These plots are based on queries using a test set of 204 images, of which 170 are from a straight hallway and 34 from the learned corner. (a) Using an MDF RPT with $k = 1$. (b) Using an MDF RPT with $k = 4$.

Table 2: *Comparision of the MEF and MDF tree sizes*

Tree Type	Total number of nodes
MEF RPT	635 nodes
MDF RPT	69 nodes

and Fig. 18(b), we can see that the errors in retrieving from the MDF tree are generally smaller, especially for the bin of 5-degree error. With multiple tree paths ($k = 4$), the cases with large errors virtually disappear, as shown in Fig. 18(c).

In the performance phase, we let Rome navigate autonomously along three straight hallways and two turns, including two trained hall ways and one trained turn. In more than 30 test drives Rome has performed so far, Rome has always successfully navigated, even along the straight section and the turn that it has not learned. During these over 30 tests, there were people walking along the hallways, but that did not bother Rome because it recognizes the entire scene instead of a particular type of landmark (e.g., road edges). Fig. 19 shows a diagram of a sample navigation and Fig. 20 shows some images of the navigational environment. For

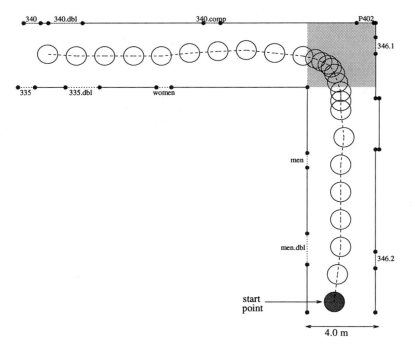

Figure 19: *Sample navigation in the trained hallway: two straight hallways and one turn. The circles indicate the locations where images are taken.*

each input image, it took only 0.128 seconds on average for the SPARC-1 on board to retrieve from the SHOSLIF tree, which explains why real-time navigation speed has been easily reached, due to the logarithmic time complexity of the SHOSLIF.

Figure 20: *ROME with SHOSLIF-N navigates automatically with a walking speed, along hallways, turning at corners and passing through a hallway door. The real-time computation is accomplished by an on-board Sun SPARC-1 workstation and a SunVideo image digitizer, without any other special-purpose image processing hardware.*

For more details of the study, the reader is referred to [3] [26]. Further work is under way for a much larger variety of scenes, both indoor and outdoor.

6. CONCLUDING REMARKS

The scope of the work accomplished so far is still very limited. First, the system does not make any high-level inference, which probably requires several nested SHOSLIF networks instead of one. It is still an open issue as to how to automatically build nested SHOSLIF networks to perform high-level learning and inference. Second, the ability to handle various variations has not yet been fully investigated. Motivated by generality, the system does not use pre-defined invariants and thus, it does not intrinsically generalize for size, position, orientation, lighting, etc. Existing invariants [22] have only limited invariance properties and are not applicable to general situations, as explained in [23]. The SHOSLIF approach deals with all variations in a unified way — through learning experience. Only variations that are present in the environment will be learned. Instead of performing expensive *search* for the right size, position, orientation, etc, as with the Cresceptron, it seems faster to *retrieve* a correct case from the memory, as with the SHOSLIF, once a logarithmic complexity is achieved. Third, it is an open question as to how to more effectively learn a potentially infinite number of cases with a large, but finite memory by forgetting most sensed information and keeping only information that is essential. All these are very important future research issues.

A lot of efforts that have been spent in computer vision can be described as to build a "learned brain" by loading computers with many pieces of hand-crafted vision rules. Learning has mostly been used in a very restricted sense, with various assumptions about the visual world. The concept of comprehensive visual learning introduced here is to build a fully adaptive "visual brain" that does not know how to "see" (i.e., understand) at the beginning but can learn, memorize, generalize and infer how to "see" through its interaction with the complex real world. The unified and systematic approach of SHOSLIF has shown its strength with several major vision tasks and also unveiled exciting directions for future research.

ACKNOWLEDGEMENTS

The work was supported by NSF Grant IRI 9410741 and ONR grant No. N00014-95-1-0637. The author would like to thank Shaoyun Chen, Yuntao Cui, Sally Howden and Dan Swets for discussions and development of SHOSLIF-N, SHOSLIF-M, SHOSLIF-O and SHOSLIF-R, respectively, and Laura Blackwood for proofreading the manuscript.

REFERENCES

[1] H. Bornstein and K. Saulnier. *The Signed English Starter*. Clerc Books, Gallaudet University Press, Washington, D.C., 1989.

[2] L. Breiman, J. Friedman, R. Olshen, and C. Stone. *Classification and Regression Trees*. Wadsworth, CA, 1984.

[3] S. Chen and J. Weng. Autonomous navigation through case-based learning. In *IEEE Int'l Symposium on Computer Vision*, Coral Gables, FL, Nov. 20-22 1995.

[4] Y. Cui, D. Swets, and J. Weng. Learning-based hand sign recognition using shoslif-m. In *Proc. Int'l Conf. Comptuer Vision*, pages 631–636, Cambridge, MA, June 20-23 1995.

[5] Y. Cui and J. Weng. SHOSLIF-M: SHOSLIF for motion understanding (phase I for hand sign recognition). Technical Report Technical Report CPS 94-68, Department of Computer Science, Michigan State University, East Lansing, MI, Dec. 1994.

[6] Y. Cui and J. Weng. Learning-based object segmentation for fovea images. In *Proc. 2nd Asian Conf. on Computer Vision,*, Singapore, Dec. 5-8 1995.

[7] K. Fukushima. Neocognitron: A self-organizing neural network model for a mechanism of pattern recognition unaffected by shift in position. *Biological Cybernetics*, 36:193–202, 1980.

[8] S. Howden and J. Weng. Hand-eye coordinated learning using hierarchical space tessellation. Technical Report Technical Report CPS-94-29, Department of Computer Science, Michigan State University, East Lansing, MI, April 1994.

[9] P. J. Hubert. *Robust Statistics*. Wiley, New York, NY, 1981.

[10] A. K. Jain and R. C. Dubes. *Algorithms for Clustering Data.* Prentice-Hall, New Jersey, 1988.

[11] M. M. Loeve. *Probability Theory.* Van Nostrand, Princeton, NJ, 1955.

[12] R. Michalski, I. Mozetic, J. Hong, and N. Lavrac. The multi-purpose incremental learning system AQ15 and its testing application to three medical domains. In *Proc. Fifth Annual National Conf. Artificial Intelligence*, pages 1041–1045, Philadelphia, PA, 1986.

[13] H. Murase and S. K. Nayar. Illumination planning for object recognition in structured environments. In *Proc. IEEE Conf. Comp. Vision Pattern Recognition*, pages 31–38, Seattle, WA, June 1994.

[14] T. Poggio and S. Edelman. A network that learns to recognize three-dimensional objects. *Nature*, 343:263–266, 1990.

[15] D. A. Pomerleau. Efficient training of artificial neural networks for autonomous navigation. *Neural Computation*, 3(1):88–97, 1991.

[16] J. Quinlan. Introduction of decision trees. *Machine Learning*, 1:81–106, 1986.

[17] S. E. Stead. *Smooth multistage multivariate approximation.* PhD thesis, Department of Math., Brown University, 1983.

[18] D. Swets and J. Weng. Efficient content-based image retrieval using automatic feature selection. In *Proc. IEEE Int'l Symposium on Computer Vision*, Coral Gables, FL, Nov. 20-22 1995.

[19] D. Swets and J. Weng. SHOSLIF-O: SHOSLIF for object recognition (Phase II). Technical Report Technical Report CPS 94-64, Department of Computer Science, Michigan State University, East Lansing, MI, Oct. 1995.

[20] A. M. Turing. On computable numbers with an application to the Entscheidungsproblem. *Proc. London Math. Soc.*, 2(42):230–265, 1936.

[21] M. Turk and A. Pentland. Eigenfaces for recognition. *Journal of Cognitive Neuroscience*, 3(1):71–86, 1991.

[22] I. Weiss. Geometric invariants and object recognition. *Int'l Journal of Computer Vision*, 10(3):207–231, 1993.

[23] J. Weng. On comprehensive visual learning. In *Proc. NSF/ARPA Workshop on Performance vs. Methodology in Computer Vision*, pages 152–166, Seattle, WA, June 1994.

[24] J. Weng, N. Ahuja, and T. S. Huang. Learning recognition and segmentation of 3-d objects from 2-d images. In *Proc. 4th Int'l Conf. Computer Vision*, pages 121–128, May 1993.

[25] J. Weng, N. Ahuja, and T. S. Huang. Learning recognition using the cresceptron. *Int'l Journal of Computer Vision*, 1996. to appear.

[26] J. Weng and S. Chen. SHOSLIF-N: SHOSLIF for autonomous navigation (phase II). Technical Report Technical Report CPS 95-22, Department of Computer Science, Michigan State University, East Lansing, MI, May 1995.

[27] S. S. Wilks. *Mathematical Statistics*. Wiley, New York, NY, 1963.

9   MEMORIZATION LEARNING FOR OBJECT RECOGNITION

Randal C. Nelson
University of Rochester

ABSTRACT

We consider the fundamental complexity of intelligent systems, and argue that some form of learning is essential in order to acquire the amount of information necessary to specify such a system. In this view, learning is essentially a means of acquiring large amounts of structured information by relatively simple recoding of information flowing down high-bandwidth channels (the senses) from a pre-existing source of structured information (the world). This chapter considers the case of visual learning. We argue that, of the known methods of computational learning, the only technique that can effectively assemble the very large amount of information needed to specify visual intelligence amounts to the construction of an indexed memory. We show how an associative memory organization coupled with the use of robust, semi-invariant features can lead to reliable 3-D object recognition.

1.   INTELLIGENCE, COMPUTATION, AND PERCEPTION

There has been an ongoing endeavor, at least since the industrial revolution, to construct machines that can do some of what people can do, only faster, better, and more cheaply. In terms of physical processes, this effort has been enormously successful, and the resultant reduction in the amount of human labor required to produce physical artifacts has been largely responsible for the increase in the so-called standard of living that has occurred in the last two centuries. There is, however, a group of tasks that require abilities that are loosely thought of as intelligence, e.g., reasoning or sophisticated sensing. Performing such tasks seems to involve, fundamentally, a complexity that is not practical to implement in a macroscopic mechanical device. With the advent of digital computers, however, came the idea that the required complexity might be reducible to information processing operations. For performing such operations, electronic devices can be built that are many orders of magnitude faster, more compact, more reliable, and less expensive than macroscopic mechanical devices, and it is still not clear where the limits are. Moreover, a large body of theoretical knowledge concerning information processing has been accumulated that is directly applicable to the capabilities of the electronic devices. Thus was born the field of artificial intelligence. Its creed was that the essence of intelligence is some sort of information processing; more precisely, that the primary complexity in an intelligent mechanism can be modeled as and implemented with an information processing system. (This position has been challenged, e.g. [19] but no persuasive alternatives have been proposed.)

As researchers attempted to emulate intelligent processes, it rapidly became clear that the information processing associated with intelligent abilities was extremely complex compared to the sort of processing that had proved useful for other tasks, such as numerical modeling. Particularly surprising was the complexity required to implement even rudimentary sensory abilities, especially visual ones. Prior to these sorts of investigations, basic visual skills such as recognition and navigation had not been considered particularly intelligent processes. However, by all we know currently, building a machine to recognize even simple objects visually in real world contexts is considerably harder than building one to play an excellent game of chess. These sorts of results gradually led to the recognition of basic sensory processes as fundamental intelligent abilities.

A second realization was that, although the main complexity in an intelligent mechanism might well be expressible in terms of information processing, information processing in itself did not constitute intelligence. Rather, intelligence exists in the context of a mechanism that exhibits intelligent behavior in a physical world. In other words, intelligence does not exist as a mathematical abstraction, but only embodied in a functioning mechanism. This might seem either an obvious or a purely philosophical point, but it led to the development of what is termed the behavioral vision paradigm [3, 1, 17] where the notion of functional behavior is used as a structuring element for creating visual systems. The particular statement in this case, is that vision (being a form of intelligence) cannot be considered independent of its embodiment in a behaving system.

1.1. COMPLEXITY AND INFORMATION ACQUISITION

One of the advantages to using the formalisms of information processing in attempting to describe a complex process such as intelligence is that there are a number of theoretical measures that can be used to discuss the complexity of a system. One of the most fundamental is *Kolmogorov complexity*. The basic idea is that the fundamental complexity of an object, say a number or a function, is the length of the shortest program (in some language for some formal system) that generates it. One of the basic results of K-complexity is that it does not matter much what the formal descriptive system is; the K-complexity is about the same in any case. More precisely, as long as two systems are Turing equivalent, then the shortest description lengths will differ by at most a constant value. The proof essentially involves tacking on a translator. If we believe that whatever neurons contribute to intelligence is modelable computationally, and that the rules for translating from the neural specification to a standard computational form are short (compared to the amount of state information in the brain), then bits of brain state and bits of computer state are more or less equivalent when discussing the complexity of a mechanism. Of course no one knows yet how to describe brain state, or what its translation is; nevertheless, the above propositions are widely accepted. It is also pretty much impossible to determine the actual K-complexity of an object. However, the notion is useful because it can be used to set bounds on the complexity of certain classes of objects, and to find limits on the way that certain objects might be created.

Returning to visual intelligence, if we look at the information processing problem from a superficial standpoint, neglecting the complicating factor of time and temporal change, we find ourselves considering functions of, say 10^6 variables (the number of fibers in the optic nerve). The number of possible such functions, even if only binary values are considered, is absurdly large; so large that the average K-complexity of these functions enormously exceeds the amount of information that could be packed into the observable universe with any known physical process (this statement is true even for functions of 1000 variables). Thus is is non-sensical to consider the brain as implementing some arbitrary function of a large number of variables. The only functions the brain is capable of implementing must have astonishingly low K-complexity compared to arbitrary functions of the input.

On the other hand, the K-complexity of the information handling mechanism in the brain may be quite large in human terms. Estimates of the amount of computationally significant state in the human brain run as high as 2^{50} bits (and keep increasing). This is a large amount of information relative to the biggest current computer systems, which contain on the order of 2^{40} bits. If the K-complexity of the system is anything approaching this value, and there are reasons to believe that the information is not redundant by more than an order of magnitude or so (at least not in a computationally feasible way), then there is no way to create such a system without providing a very large amount of structured information. Where does this information come from? It can't come directly from the genome, which contains only a few times 2^{30} bits, (though somehow this must guide the acquisition of the information). Nor, as far as we know, is there any direct copying process that maps information from one individual onto another. The obvious source of structured information is the world, loaded over the relatively high-bandwidth channels that are the senses. The process of mapping this information into the mechanism specification is learning, which we have got to, finally.

1.2. GOING ARTIFICIAL

There is an analogous situation for artificial intelligent systems. If we want to create a system that has anything approaching human intelligent capabilities, in any but the most constrained domains, it is probable that the system description will be too large to be entered efficiently by the designer typing it in. Again, the world is an obvious source of structured information, and artificial senses can provide high bandwidth channels. The job of the designer is in specifying how this information is to be obtained, structured, and used. Thus a designer of intelligences must understand learning processes; what sort of information they are and are not capable of supplying, and the efficiency with which various learning processes operate. We do not yet know the answers to all these questions. This chapter considers some of what is known about various learning processes, and how they can and cannot be applied to the creation of intelligent mechanisms, and by extension, how such processes may contribute to the development of intelligent mechanisms in nature.

Put another way, our primary problem is how to bootstrap an artificially intelligent system, specifically visual perception, into existence. In light of the above discussion, entering the entire description directly appears infeasible simply because of its size. Copying the information from an existing biological intelligence requires both understanding of biological representations, and transcription technologies that do not yet exist. Letting the system evolve itself from scratch also seems likely to be infeasible. Thus somehow, we must discover how to make use of pre-existing structured information.

A companion question is, what can we learn about how to solve our problem by looking at how biological intelligences bootstrap themselves? In broad overview, the development of biological intelligence appears to involve three distinct, though somewhat interwoven processes. At the bottom level, there is the process of *evolution*, that over the course of four billion years with the resources of the planet has generated the seed information packets known as genomes. Despite recent interest in search methods modeled on genetic selection and transcription, we think that evolutionary processes are too slow to produce efficiently the algorithmic seed information (what is analogous to the genome) for a sophisticated artificial system. We believe that this sort of information will ultimately be supplied by the system designers (i.e. typed in), and that it will be obtained from basic understanding of physical science, the desired functionality, and perhaps also information about how biological systems really operate, since they are working models of some of the abilities that we wish to achieve. The amount of information in the human genome is within the capacity of a modest team of programmers to produce over a period of several years (say a few times 2^{30} bits).

Through the poorly understood process of *development* information in the genome is translated into a system that has the capability to acquire, through a third process that we will refer to as *learning*, new structural information from the world, increasing its essential complexity by many orders of magnitude (say to 2^{50} bits).

In this chapter we describe a memory-based learning process for 3-D object recognition that is consistent with the huge amount of additional information required for the specification of an intelligence. It is our position that the only method of learning that has the potential to supply very large amounts of structured information amounts essentially to the memorization, in an indexed store, of large amounts of (translated and screened) sensory data. Moreover, the translation and screening algorithms must be essentially supplied a-priori, either by development of the genome or by the designer.

Optimization processes of the sort that are popular in the learning literature can play, at most, a minor role in the acquisition of the huge amount of extragenetic information that defines an intelligence. The basic argument is that, on computational grounds, no optimization approach that requires even N^2 work in the size of the result is feasible when the size of the result is 2^{50} bits. Approaches such as backpropagation, simulated annealing, reinforcement learning, and genetic algorithms all tend to require at least N^2 work to find reasonable solutions. However, a locally optimized indexed memory can be constructed with NlogN work. Hence we are driven to consider memory-based approaches as the primary information acquisition system.

As a final comment, it is interesting to note that, although the amount of information in a typical vertebrate genome is to large to be practically acquired through an N^2 optimization process from a human perspective, it is within the reach of an N^2 process operating over the surface of the planet over geological time. (The genome is a few billion bits, and geological history involves at least billions of individuals operating over at least a billion generations).

2. MEMORY-BASED SHAPE RECOGNITION: AN EXAMPLE OF VISUAL LEARNING

In this section we describe a method of 3-D object recognition based on two stage use of a general purpose associative memory and a principal views representation. In accordance with the ideas laid out in the introduction, the basic processing used to extract visual features, and the overall organization and method of use of the memory is specified a-priori (in this case by the programmer rather than a genome and development). The object models, however, which give the system both its capabilities and its "personality" so to speak, and which in a large scale system would constitute most of the information, are learned via the same sensory system that feeds the recognition process. Because the amount of information to be acquired may be very large, we cannot use an optimization process to organize this information. This was argued in the introduction to this chapter. Rather, the memory is formed simply by storing the appropriately processed incoming information into an efficiently accessible, content addressable structure. Duplication of information can be efficiently avoided, but no attempt to make more general optimizations is made.

The basic object recognition strategy is to make use of semi-invariant sensory objects called *keys*. A key is any robustly extractable feature that has sufficient information content to specify a 2-D configuration of an associated object (location, scale, orientation) plus sufficient additional parameters to provide efficient indexing and meaningful verification. The recognition system utilizes an associative memory organized so that access via a key feature evokes associated hypotheses for the identity and configuration of all previously seen objects that could have produced it. These hypothesis are fed into a second stage associative memory, which maintains a probabilistic estimate of the likelihood of each hypothesis based on statistics about the occurrence of the keys in the primary database. Because it is based on a merged percept of local features rather than global properties, the method is expected to be robust to occlusion and background clutter, and does not require prior object segmentation. We have implemented a version of the system that allows arbitrary definitions for key features, and describe experiments using keys based on perceptual groups of line segments to recognize different polyhedral objects from arbitrary viewing angles in clutter.

2.1. THE VISUAL RECOGNITION PROBLEM

Object recognition is probably the single most studied problem in machine vision. It is also one of the most ill defined. The standard intuitive definition typically involves establishing a correspondence between some internal model of an object, and 2-D patterns of light produced by an imaging system. Attempts to formalize this notion, however, generally lead to problem statements that are either unsolvable, or so restrictive as to be practically useless. There remains a pervasive intuition, stemming from human subjective visual experience, that visual recognition works, and that the bad cases, even in the general statement, are somehow pathological. This leads to a belief that a problem statement of the sort "the ability to recognize an image of an arbitrary normal object from any natural viewpoint in any reasonable environment most of the time" makes sense. The difficulty, of course, is making scientific sense of words such as "normal", "natural", and "reasonable".

The operative word in the above paragraph is "works", because it leads to the question "works for what?". The behavioral idea is to interpret "works" in the context of a particular problem or problem area. The subjective terms in the previous paragraph can then be given meaning. A natural viewpoint is thus one that is expected to occur in the context of the application, a normal object is one whose identification is important, and a reasonable environment is one in which the application must be carried out. In this context, recognition appears less as a process of solving a geometric or optical puzzle and more as a matter of using sensory information to get at stored state that permits the system to interact with the environment successfully, however success is defined.

2.2. PREVIOUS WORK

Addressing vision from the standpoint of behavior and memory is not a new idea. In fact, prior to the development of electronic computers, behavioral description was the only avenue available for investigating the phenomenon of vision. This precomputational work is epitomized by Gibson (e.g., [9]) who advanced the central postulate that vision was essentially a modality that allowed biological systems to react to invariants in the structure of the world. What Gibson overlooked, however, was the complexity of computing the visual invariants used as primitives. The first influential theory of computational vision, due to Marr [14], essentially defined vision as the problem of determining what is where, and focussed almost entirely on the computational and representational aspects of the problem. Marr's theory of vision essentially described a staged computational architecture leading from image, to primal sketch, to 2-1/2 D sketch to invariant object centered descriptions. The processing hierarchy however, was static, and provided no structure for incorporating behavioral constraints. Moreover, the final, critical step, from 2-1/2 D image to object centered representation proved problematical, suggesting that something important was missing.

What distinguishes the recent interest in behavioral vision from the historical efforts is the commitment to establish it within a computational framework. The resurgence of interest in the behavioral aspects of intelligence is perhaps most clearly illustrated by the subsumption architecture proposed by Brooks [5]. This paradigm is rather rigorously Gibsonian in that it explicitly disavows the notion of internal representation, relying instead on purely reactive strategies. The architecture works quite well for implementing low-level behaviors such as walking using simple sensors; however it now seems clear that higher level behaviors and more sophisticated sensory modalities such as vision, require some form of representation.

Recent work on active vision [2, 3] has focussed on how directed control of the sensor characteristics (e.g. eyes, or tactile receptors) can simplify the process of obtaining the desired information. Most work to date has focussed on the effect of the ability to move the sensor [7] or dynamically change an internal focus of attention [22, 23]. Work on purposive or behavioral vision [17] attempts to take the context of the task explicitly into account.

Much previous work in 3-D vision has focussed on model-based systems, on which there is a large literature. Notable recent examples are [13, 12, 11]. The indexing techniques used in several of these systems have been recently analyzed, and the sensitivity of the techniques to various perturbations determined [10]. Most model acquisition strategies have focussed on CAD-like techniques. The models are either entered by hand, or via a geometric reconstruction.

There is little work on direct acquisition of 3-D representation from visual exploration, or on implicit representation of 3-D structure, though there is some research on world and object representations that can be refined during navigation by a mobile robot [4]. A rigid body representation that is implicitly encoded in linear combinations of three views, and thus is in principle automatically acquirable, is described in [24], but seems not to have been implemented. Work on automatic acquisition of 2-D representation has been more successful, since all the information is present (e.g. [8]) We expect these techniques to be useful here, since we essentially propose utilizing a collection of augmented 2-D representations.

Some recent work has a memory-based flavor. Rao and Ballard [21] describe an approach based on the memorization of the responses of a set of steerable filters centered on, or located at key points of an object. Mel [15] takes a somewhat similar approach using a database of stored feature vectors representing multiple low-level cues. Three-dimensional wireframes can be recognized by a neural net that effectively memorizes and interpolates between several training views [20]. Frontal face recognition using a variant of template matching can outperform feature-based methods [6]. Murase and Nayar [16] find the major principal components of an image dataset, and use the projections of unknown images onto these as indices into a recognition memory. The common theme behind all these approaches is extraction of a medium-sized set of parameters that are expected to vary slowly with changes in orientation, lighting, etc. followed by indexing into some set of examples organized by the same indices. Three dimensional structure is handled by using multiple examples. Our approach is along similar basic lines, but we index on robustly extractable parts and add a second indexing stage in order to accumulate evidence.

2.3. THE METHOD

The visual recognition learning technique proposed here is based on two stage use of a general purpose associative memory, and a principal views representation of three dimensional objects. The experiments described below concern the application of the technique to the recognition of rigid 3-D objects, but the underlying principles are not dependent on rigid geometry, and we anticipate extending the system to handle non-rigid and statistical objects as well.

The approach makes use of semi-invariant objects we call *keys*. A key is any robustly extractable part or feature that has sufficient information content to specify a configuration of an associated object plus enough additional parameters to provide efficient indexing and meaningful verification.   Configuration is a general term for descriptors that provide information about where in appearance space an image of an object is situated. For rigid objects, configuration generally implies location and orientation, but more general interpretations can be used for other object types. Semi-invariant means that over all configurations in which the object of interest will be encountered, a matchable form of the feature will be present a significant proportion of the time. Robustly extractable means that in any scene of interest containing the object, the feature will be in among the best features found a significant proportion of the time. The descriptions and processing associated with keys and configurations are not learned, but are part of the seed information provided to the system - in this case by the programmer.

The basic idea is to utilize an associative memory organized so that access via a key feature evokes associated hypotheses for the identity and configuration of all objects that could have produced it. These hypothesis are fed into a second stage associative memory, keyed by the configuration, which maintains a probabilistic estimate of the likelihood of each hypothesis based on statistics about the occurrence of the keys in the primary database. The idea is similar to a multidimensional Hough transform without the space problems. Efficient access to the associative memories is achieved using a hashing scheme.

The approach has several advantages. First, because it is based on a merged percept of local features rather than global properties, the method is robust to background clutter, and does not require prior segmentation. We also expect the method to exhibit robustness to occlusion, but have not tested this property extensively. This is an advantage over systems based on principal components template analysis, which are sensitive to occlusion and clutter. Second, entry of objects into the memory is an active, automatic procedure. Essentially, the system explores the object visually from different viewpoints, accumulating 2-D views, until it has seen enough not to mix it up with any other object it knows about. Third, the method lends itself naturally to multi-modal recognition. Because there is no single, global structure for the model, evidence from different kinds of keys can be combined as easily as evidence from multiple keys of the same type. The only requirement is that the configuration descriptions evoked by the different keys have enough common structure to allow evidence combination procedures to be used. This is an advantage over conventional alignment techniques, which typically require a prior 3-D model of the object. Finally, the probabilistic nature of the evidence combination scheme, coupled with the formal definitions for semi-invariance and robustness allow quantitative predictions of the reliability of the system to be made.

2.3.1. GENERAL ASSOCIATIVE MEMORY

We have been advocating a memory-based approach to recognition, but have not described just what is meant by the term. To some extent, all recognition algorithms employ memory in the recognition process, if only in the form of stored 3-D models. What distinguishes a memory-based approach, is that memory-lookup operations account for a large proportion of the computation employed in the recognition procedure (as opposed to, say, geometric operations or graph search), and that the automatically acquired memory constitutes a large proportion of the total system specification information.

Since our approach is based on an efficient associative memory, one of the first steps was to design and implement such a memory and verify that it satisfies our requirements. The basic operation we need is partial match association over heterogeneous keys. More specifically, we want a structure into which we can store and access (key, association) pairs where the key and association objects may be any of a number of disparate types. Associated with each object type employed as a key is a distance metric. The ideal query operation takes a reference key and returns all stored (key, association) pairs where the key is of the correct type and within a specified distance of the reference key in the appropriate metric. In practice, this ideal may have to be modified somewhat for efficiency reasons. In particular, highly similar association pairs may be merged in storage, and we may place a bound on the number of associations that are returned for any given query, or on the maximum separation that can be handled.

Our overall approach to the design of the memory was leave it as flexible as possible. In the current implementation, the memory is just a large array of buckets each of which can hold a variable number of (key, association) pairs. This allows a number of different access schemes to coexist. In particular, hashing, array indexing and tree search can all be implemented efficiently. Associated with each key type are functions defining a distance metric and a search procedure for locating keys in the memory. Thus if a certain key type has an efficient indexing method, it can be implemented for this type, rather than using a uniform but less efficient policy. This allows a large amount of flexibility in the system, and also permits new key types to be added efficiently in a modular fashion.

2.3.2. KEY FEATURES

The recognition technique is based on the the assumption that robustly extractable, semi-invariant keys can be efficiently recovered from image data. More specifically, the keys must posses the following characteristics. First, they must be complex enough not only to specify the configuration the object, but to have parameters left over that can be used for indexing. Second, the keys must have a substantial probability of detection if the object containing them occupies the region of interest (robustness). Third, the index parameters must change relatively slowly as the object configuration changes (semi-invariance). Many classical features do not satisfy these criteria. Line segments are not sufficiently complex, full object contours are not robustly extractable, and simple templates are not semi-invariant. We believe that features with the necessary properties can be found for a large number of situations. It may be necessary, however, to take the particular task and context into consideration. For example, in some applications, color cues may be sufficient. In others, where it is important to recognize orientation, shape features may be more important.

One conflict that must be resolved is that between feature complexity and robust detectability. In order to reduce multiple matches, key features must be fairly complex. However, if we consider complex features as arbitrary combinations of simpler ones, then the number of potential high-level features undergoes a combinatorial increase as the complexity increases. This is clearly undesirable from the standpoint of robust detectability, as we do not wish to consider or store exponentially many possibilities. The solution is not to use arbitrary combinations, but to base the higher level feature groups on structural heuristics such as adjacency and good continuation. Such *perceptual grouping* processes have been extensively researched in the last few years.

The use of semi-invariance represents another necessary compromise. From a computational standpoint, true invariance is desirable, and a lot of research has gone into looking for invariant features. Unfortunately, such features seem to be hard to design, especially for 2-D projections of general 3-D objects. We settle for semi-invariance and compensate by a combination of two strategies. First, we take advantage of the statistical unlikelihood of close matches for complex patterns (another advantage of relatively complex keys). Second, the memory-based recognition strategy provides what amounts to multiple representations of an object in that the same physical attribute of the object may evoke several different associations as the object appears in different configurations. The semi-invariance prevents this number from being too large. Possible keys for recognition of rigid 3-D objects include robust contour fragments, feature normalized templates, keyed color histograms, and normalized texture vectors.

Our current implementation is designed to recognize 3-D polyhedral objects on the basis of their shape, using a set of 2-D views as the underlying representation. This particular context derives from a robot assembly system we are implementing that servos off shape and geometric relationships between parts. The prototype manipulates a set of polyhedral pieces, which have no distinguishing markings aside from their shape. The vision system requirements are an ability to recognize which of several parts is present in a scene, and to localize important geometric features of the part. A shape-based description thus seemed appropriate. The keys we chose for our initial tests are based on chains of line segments, variously referred to in the literature as polylines or supersegments. In particular, we first run a line segment finder on the image, and then extract perceptual groups of three segments whose properties are consistent with the hypothesis that they form a section of a 3-D boundary. We call such groups *3-chains*. The base segment of a 3-chain provides enough information to determine the 2-D configuration of any view of which it might be a part. In addition, associated with each 3-chain are two angles and two length ratios, which are absolute invariants for rigid 2-D transformations, and semi-invariant for 3-D rigid transformation of the projected object (see Figure 1). This use of segment chains is somewhat similar to the structural indexing of Stein and Medioni [8].

Very recently, we have also run tests using key features based on edge orientation templates normalized by segmented curves. The performance of the system using these keys is considerably superior to that using segment groups, and can be applied to curved objects. However, extensive tests have not yet been completed, so we mention this only briefly in the experimental section.

2.4. Recognition algorithms

The basic recognition procedure consists of four steps. First, potential key features are extracted from the image using low and intermediate level visual routines. In the second step, these keys are used to access the associative memory and retrieve information about what objects could have produced them, and in what relative configuration. The third step uses this information, in conjunction with geometric parameters factored out of the key features such as position, orientation, and scale, to produce hypotheses about the identity and configuration of potential objects. Finally, these hypotheses are themselves used as keys into a second stage associative memory, which is used to accumulate evidence for the various hypotheses.

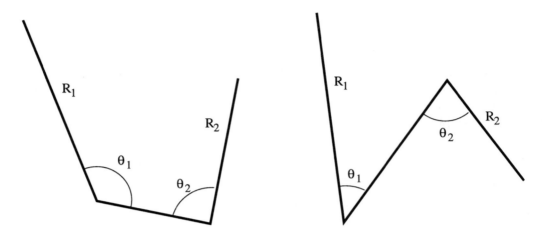

Figure 1: *Examples of 3-chains showing invariant angles and length ratios.*

In the first step, the extraction of key features, one of the most significant issues involves the idea of active or selective processing. In general an object recognition algorithm will perform better if the search domain is restricted — that is, if the system is handed a region of interest thought to be more or less filled by some recognizable object, rather than simply being asked what recognizable objects occur in the scene. This is essentially the "what" task in the "what/where" dichotomy. The design of attentional operators that efficiently tag regions of high interest on the basis of low-level processing is consequently an important subject. A number of global or task-independent cues have been suggested, including gray-level blob detection, closed contour analysis, color contrast analysis, motion segmentation, and scale entropy measures. When incorporated into an autonomous system, such interest measures must be provided. For the purposes of testing the recognition system, we can have a user provide a window.

Such considerations raise the question, however, whether task-independent cues are always what is desired. All the previously mentioned cues already make an implicit assumption about the task - namely that we are looking for discrete physical objects. Perhaps the pre-attentive cues should be tailored to the task. Carried to its logical extreme, this idea suggests tailoring an attentional mechanism to respond best to a particular object, or even a particular configuration of an object. This is essentially the "where" task in the "what/where" dichotomy The associative memory system proposed can be used to solve this task as well as the "forward what" task. One interesting approach is to use a reverse association to obtain the keys likely to be associated with an object or class of objects. These could then be used to design an optimal filtering process.

In the final step, an important issue is the method of combining evidence. The simplest technique is to use an elementary voting scheme - each piece of evidence contributes equally to the total. This is clearly not well founded, as a feature that occurs in many different situations is not as good an indicator of the presence of an object as one that is unique to it. An evidence scheme that takes this into account would probably display improved performance. The question is how to evaluate the quality of various pieces of evidence. An obvious approach in our case is to use statistics computed over the information contained in the associative memory to evaluate the quality of a piece of information. Having said this, it is clear that the optimal quality measure, which would rely on the full joint probability distribution over keys, objects and configurations is infeasible to compute, and we must use some approximation.

A simple example would be to use the first order feature frequency distribution over the entire database, and this is what we do. The actual algorithm is to accumulate evidence proportional to $\log(1 + 1/(kx))$ where x is the probability of making the particular matching observation as approximated from database statistics, and k is a proportionality constant that attempts to estimate the actual geometric probability associated with the prediction of a pose from a key. The underlying model is that the evidence represents the log of the reciprocal of the probability that the particular combination of features is due to chance. The procedure used makes an independence assumption which is unwarranted in the real world, with the result that the evidence values actually obtained are serious overestimates if actually interpreted as probabilities. However, the rank ordering of the values is fairly robust to distortion due to this independence assumption. Since only the rank ordering enters into the decisions made by the system, we are more comfortable with the scheme than might be expected.

Once a well founded evidence combination scheme is defined, the use of multi-modal information is relatively simple to implement. All that needs to be done is to define a new key type, and hook in the various routines needed to implement it. Issues of relative importance are subsumed by the evidence combination scheme. This easy use of multiple source of information was a primary factor in choosing to look at memory-based recognition. Characterization of the usefulness of the various key classes in different applications is an important piece of information for the integration system.

2.5. MODEL ACQUISITION

In the preceding discussion we have assumed that the associative memory already existed in the requisite form. However, one of the primary attractions of a memory-based recognition system is that it can be trained efficiently from image data. The basic process of model acquisition is simply a matter of providing images of the object to the system, running the key detection procedures on these images, and storing the resulting (key, association) pairs. The number of images needed may vary from one, for simple 2-D applications, to several tens for rigid object recognition, and possibly more for complicated non-rigid objects. This procedure has a number of advantages over existing schemes. First, it does not require a pre-existing 3-D model; just access to imagery of the object. It is even possible to use imagery that contains occluded or cluttered views of the object, though this requires some modification of the process. Second, the process is efficient. It essentially runs in time proportional to the number of pairs stored in memory. This is in contrast to many learning algorithms that scale poorly with the the number of stored items. Note that the term model acquisition is actually something of a misnomer since the representation of a particular object is typically distributed over many memory locations, and there is not necessarily any single structure that might be called a model gluing together all the parts.

Despite the simplicity of the basic procedure, there are a number of interesting research issues associated with the model acquisition process. First, the basic process may be modified somewhat. The most obvious modification would be to merge duplicate or near duplicate entries in the memory in order to conserve space. This is easily done by accessing a key in the database and examining the current associations before storing a new one.

A rather more interesting issue has to do with a tie-in to active vision. The necessary information for a two dimensional object can theoretically be obtained from a single image. In contrast, several views are needed for rigid 3-D objects. One way of getting these is simply for a human operator to guess at how many views are needed and from what angles, provide them, and then test the resulting system to make sure it is reliable. A more interesting approach however, is to use an active agent to explore the object and acquire the necessary views automatically. The basic idea is for the agent to examine the object in various configurations, adding new information whenever its current memory does not recognize the object. Doing this randomly would yield reasonably good performance quickly, however finding low-probability problematical configurations could take a long time. There is considerable room in this case for knowledge directed exploration. For instance, the system could make use of knowledge that end-on views of highly elongated objects are apt to cause trouble. For non-rigid objects, the problem is even more interesting. Here, we have the possibility of not only active exploration for model acquisition, but for recognition as well. For example, in the case of a highly articulated object with no distinctive rigid subparts, an approach to recognition would be to attempt to manipulate it into a canonical form (e.g. stretched out) which would be more easily recognizable.

2.6. EXPERIMENTS

Using the principles described above, we implemented a memory-based recognition system for polyhedral objects using 3-chains, and recently curve-keyed edge templates, as the basic keys. Component segments were extracted using a stick-growing method developed recently at Rochester [18], and organized into chains. For objects entered into the database, the best 10 chains were selected to represent the object. The threshold on the distance metric between chains was adjusted so that it would tolerate approximately 15-20 degrees deviation in the appearance of a frontal plane (less for oblique ones). The practical considerations leading to

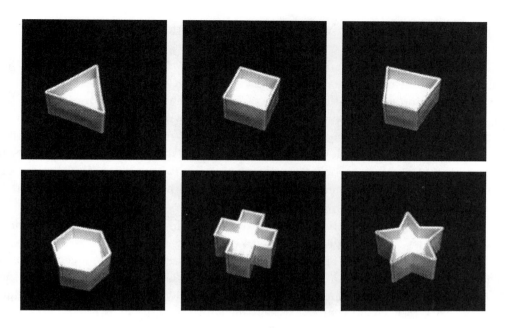

Figure 2: *Six of the seven polyhedral objects used in the test set.*

this selection were to allow the system to discriminate pentagons from hexagons without requiring more than about 50 views for an object.

We performed experiments using a set of 7 polyhedral objects from a child's toy. Some of these are shown in Figure 2, and from the top they appear as a triangle, a square, a trapezoid, a pentagon, a hexagon, a star, and a cross. Note, however that the objects are not simple prisms, but have an H-shaped cross section. This produces interesting edges and shadow effects when the objects are viewed from any angle other than straight down.

We obtained a training database of approximately 150 views of these objects from different directions ranging from 12 for the hexagon, to 60 for the trapezoid, and covering all viewing angles except straight-on from the side, since from that point of view a number of the objects are indistinguishable without measurements accurate to a few percent. The variation in the number of views needed is due to varying degrees of symmetry in the objects. All training images were acquired under normal room illumination, with the objects in isolation against a dark background. The training database was used to compile a segment-based associative memory for recognition of the objects.

We then subjected the recognition system to a series of increasingly stringent tests. Recall that the geometric design of the geometric indexing system ensures invariance to 2-D translation, rotation, and scale down to the point where there are insufficient pixels to provide a good estimate of segment attributes. Invariance to out-of-plane rotations is provided by the combination of slightly flexible match criteria for the chain features coupled with multiple views. Robustness against clutter and occlusion is provided by the representation in terms of multiple features. The experiments were designed to test various aspects of this design.

A basic assumption made during these tests is that some other process has isolated a region of the image where a recognizable object may occur. We do not assume prior segmentation, but we do assume that only one, or at most a few objects of interest (as opposed to tens or hundreds) will occur in a window handed to the system. The system has a certain capability to state that it recognizes nothing in a window, and, in fact, tended to do this when given windows in which none of the known objects appeared. However, we have not statistically grounded this ability and hence the results reported here should be considered to be essentially forced choice experiments.

The first test, was simply to identify top down views of the objects, in various positions, scales, and rotations. This was essentially a test of the 2-D invariance built into the geometry. The system was tested first with a reduced database generated from 7 top down views (one for each object), and then with the full 3-D database, to ensure that the additional information stored did not produce enough cross talk to interfere with the recognition. Object presentations were under ordinary room lighting, with the objects isolated against a dark background. The system performed as expected in both cases, with no mistakes.

For the second test, we acquired 14 additional views of the objects, two of each, again isolated against a dark background, and taken from viewpoints intermediate between the ones in the database. The idea here is to test the 3-D rotation invariance. No errors were made in the 14 test cases, even between similar objects such as the square and the trapezoid, or the pentagon and the hexagon, despite the fact that we had anticipated some confusion in these cases. These results alone allow us to say that the system is probably at least 90 percent accurate in situations of this type. Results from other tests lead us to believe that the actual performance is, in fact, somewhat better.

In the third test we took a number of images containing multiple objects viewed from modest angles (45 degrees or less from overhead) under normal lighting against a dark background. An example is shown in Figure 3. We then supplied the system with windows containing one object and parts of others. Since the system performs no explicit segmentation of its own, the intent of this experiment is to test robustness against minor clutter. Examples of the sort of windows passed to the system are shown in Figure 4. In twenty plus tests, we observed no errors due to clutter. We did have one failure, but it was due to an object in the image being too small for the segment finder to find good boundary sets. We also tried examples with two objects in the window. In this case, the system typically identified one of the objects, and when asked what else was there identified the second as well.

The fourth experiment was a more severe clutter test. Here we took pictures of different objects held in a robot hand at various angles. Examples are shown in Figure 5. This was a hard problem for the segment-based system, and we obtained

Figure 3: *View of a group of objects.*

Figure 4: *A set of windows containing objects and minor clutter. The central object was correctly identified in all these cases.*

Figure 5: *A set of windows containing objects held by a robot hand representing moderate clutter. The system successfully identified the object in all cases except the example in the lower right.*

recognition rates only on the order of 75 percent - i.e. we saw a significant number of failures. On analysis, we found that the primary reason for failure was not crosstalk in the memory caused by clutter, but poor performance of the low-level feature identification process caused by the added complexity in the image. Thus the memory index has nothing to work on. Potential solutions involve improving the segment finder, which at present is strictly bottom up, and does no local grouping of its own, or using other features. Figure 6 shows a degree of clutter that broke the system based on segment groups completely. Recognition in windows from this image was essentially at the level of chance. Again, the failure is in the low-level processes.

Processing times were dominated by the low-level feature extraction. On a typical window containing one object plus clutter, the indexing process in the full database took a couple of seconds on a SPARC1. The low level processing could take a few tens of seconds, depending on the complexity of the image.

Very recent experiments using a different set of key features, based on normalized edge orientation templates surrounding single segmented curves rather than groups of line segments, thus decreasing the sensitivity to good low-level performance brought performance on the robot hand type pictures to above 90 percent, and performance on the dinosour image to above 80 percent. We have not completed experiments with this key type, which can be applied not only to polyhedral, but to curved objects, hence these results should be considered

Figure 6: *An image with substantial clutter. Performance of the segment-based system on windows drawn from this image was only slightly above chance level (2 out of 6 identified correctly). However, a modified system using curve-keyed edge orientation templates performed above 80 percent.*

preliminary.

2.7. Conclusions and future work

In this section we have argued for a memory-access interpretation of recognition, and proposed a general framework for memory-based recognition using a 2-stage association process. We have illustrated the concept by implementing a memory-based recognition system for 3-D polyhedral objects using chains of line segments as memory keys. The system actually performs quite well for a small database of 3-D shapes, and exhibits a certain amount of robustness against clutter. When the algorithm fails, it is not due to crosstalk in the memory, but to failure of the low-level processes to extract robust features. We are currently engaged in embedding the system into a robotic manipulation system that we will use for assembly tasks.

The next step we plan to take is to generalize the system to use keys based on boundary curves rather than just straight segments. We also plan to incorporate multi-modal features into the database, including color and texture as well as shape information. We anticipate that this will give us a capability to recognize less well structured objects such as leaves or clothing in addition to objects having a strictly defined shape.

There is also the issue of dealing with hierarchical classification of objects. As described above, the system handles object classes in a flat manner. There is no way of specifying that a particular small portion of an object may, in some application, be crucial for making a distinction (e.g. the license plate of a car). Similarly, there is no explicit way of dealing with multiple scales of structure in a single object. Adapting a memory-based recognition system to deal effectively with hierarchical class/subclass distinctions and multi-resolution structure is an important area for future research. As argued in the introduction to this chapter, we believe it is unlikely that computational learning techniques will be able to provide much in the way of such high-level organizational principles, and that this is the appropriate domain for a system designer to operate.

Acknowledgements

This material is based on work supported by the National Science Foundation under Grants numbered CDA-8822724 and IRI-9202816. The government has certain rights in this material.

References

[1] Y. Aloimonos. *Active Perception*. Lawrence Erlbaum, 1993.

[2] Y. Aloimonos, A. Bandyopadhyay, and I. Weiss. Active vision. In *First International Conference on Computer Vision*, pages 35–54, June 1987.

[3] D. H. Ballard and C. M. Brown. Principles of animate vision. *CVGIP*, 56(1):3–21, July 1992.

[4] A. F. Bobick and R. C. Bolles. Representation space: An approach to the integration of visual information. In *Proc. CVPR*, pages 492–499, San Diego CA, June 1989.

[5] R. A. Brooks. A robust layered control system for a mobile robot. *IEEE Journal of Robotics and Automation*, 2:14–23, April 1986.

[6] R. Brunelli and T. Poggio. Face recognition: Features versus templates. *IEEE Trans. PAMI*, 15(10):1042–1062, 1993.

[7] D. J. Coombs and C. M. Brown. Real-time binocular smooth pursuit. *International Journal of Computer Vision*, pages 147 – 164, October 1993.

[8] F.Stein and G. Medioni. Efficient 2-dimensional object recgnition. In *Proc. ICPR*, pages 13–17, Atlantic City NJ, June 1990.

[9] J. J. Gibson. *The Perception of the Visual World*. Houghton Mifflin, Boston, 1950.

[10] W. E. L. Grimson and D. P. Huttenlocher. On the sensitivity of geometric hashing. In *3rd International Conference on Computer Vision*, pages 334–338, 1990.

[11] D. P. Huttenlocher and S. Ullman. Recognizing solid objects by alignment with an image. *International Journal of Computer Vision*, 5(2):195–212, 1990.

[12] Y. Lamdan and H. J. Wolfson. Geometric hashing: A general and efficient model-based recognition scheme. In *Proc. International Conference on Computer Vision*, pages 238–249, Tampa FL, December 1988.

[13] D. G. Lowe. Three-dimensional object recognition from single two-dimensional images. *Artificial Intelligence*, 31:355–395, 1987.

[14] D. C. Marr. *Vision*. W. H. Freeman and Co., 1982.

[15] B. Mel. Object classification with high-dimensional vectors. In *Proc. Telluride Workshop on Neuromorphic Engineering*, Telluride CO, July 1994.

[16] H. Murase and S. K. Nayar. Learning and recognition of 3d objects from appearance. In *Proc. IEEE Workshop on Qualitative Vision*, pages 39–50, 1993.

[17] R. C. Nelson. Vision as intelligent behavior: Research in machine vision at the university of rochester. *International Journal of Computer Vision*, 7(1):5–9, November 1991.

[18] R. C. Nelson. Finding line segments by stick growing. *IEEE Trans PAMI*, 16(5):519–523, May 1994.

[19] R. Penrose. *The Emperor's New Mind: Concerning Computation, Minds, and the Laws of Nature*. Oxford University Press, 1989.

[20] T. Poggio and S. Edelman. A network that learns to recognize three-dimensional objects. *Nature*, 343:263–266, 1990.

[21] R. P.N. Rao. Top-down gaze targeting for space-variant active vision. In *Proc. ARPA Image Understanding Workshop*, pages 1049–1058, Monterey CA, November 1994.

[22] R. D. Rimey and C. M. Brown. Controlling eye movements with hidden markov models. *International Journal of Computer Vision*, 7(1):47–66, November 1991.

[23] R. D. Rimey and C. M. Brown. Control of selective perception using bayes nets and decision theory. *International Journal of Computer Vision*, 12(2,3):173–208, April 1994.

[24] S. Ullman and R. Basri. Recognition by linear combinations of models. *IEEE Trans. PAMI*, 13(10), 1991.

10   Learning to Catalog Science Images

Usama M. Fayyad, Padhraic J. Smyth, Michael C. Burl, and *Pietro Perona*
California Institute of Technology

Abstract

In astronomy, remote sensing, and medicine, as well as in other fields of science and engineering, large databases of images have become commonplace. However, the speed with which scientists can analyze such databases has not kept pace with their size. Hence, vast amounts of potentially useful data are never examined. This chapter presents our progress in developing tools for exploring image databases. We first present SKICAT, a system being used for the reduction and analysis of a 3 terabyte astronomy data set. SKICAT integrates techniques from image processing, data classification, and database management. Machine learning played a powerful and enabling role in SKICAT, permitting us to solve a difficult, real-world, scientifically significant classification problem. A more ambitious project called JARtool targets the development of a trainable tool for object recognition. This application involves automatically locating all small volcanoes in the Magellan SAR imagery of the planet Venus, which consists of over 30,000 images and contains an estimated one million small volcanoes. The primary challenge is to construct volcano detectors from a small set of training examples provided by the scientists.

1. Introduction

In astronomy and space sciences, we currently face a data glut crisis. The problem of dealing with huge volumes of data accumulated from a variety of sources, of correlating the data and extracting and visualizing the important trends, is now fully recognized. Database sizes are already being measured in terabytes (10^{12} bytes) and this problem will only become more acute with the advent of new telescopes, sensors, and space missions. We face a critical need for information processing technologies and methodologies to manage this data avalanche. The future of scientific information processing hinges upon the development of intelligent tools that enable the user to interact effectively with large image databases. Paradigms that have emerged from the fields of machine learning, computer vision, statistical pattern recognition, and related areas can provide some solutions. The focus of the work presented here is to approach the problem of data analysis strictly from a "learning from examples" perspective. We believe that such an approach offers a natural interface between a scientist and a large data set: the scientist simply provides the system with examples of what to look for. In addition, when successful, such an approach avoids the need to write customized detectors for different tasks, and can thus have more general applicability.

Across a variety of disciplines, two-dimensional digital image data is now a fundamental component of routine scientific investigation. The proliferation of image acquisition hardware such as multi-spectral remote-sensing platforms, medical imaging sensors, and high-resolution cameras has led to the widespread use of image data in fields such as atmospheric studies, planetary geology, ecology, agriculture, glaciology, forestry, astronomy, and diagnostic medicine, to name but a few. The common factor across all of these disciplines is the following: the image data for each application, whether it be a Landsat image or an ultrasound scan, is only a means to an end. The investigator is interested in using the image data to infer some facts about the physical properties of the target being imaged. Hence, the image data merely serves as an intermediate representation that facilitates the scientific process of inferring a conclusion from the available evidence.

In the past, both in planetary science and astronomy, images were painstakingly analysed by hand and much investigative work was carried out using hardcopy photographs or photographic plates. However, the image databases that are currently being acquired are so large that simple manual cataloging is no longer practical, especially *if all of the available data is to be utilized*. This chapter focuses on two such databases: (1) the Second Palomar Observatory Sky Survey (POSS-II), and (2) the SAR imagery of Venus returned by the Magellan spacecraft. As will be argued below, both of these image databases defy manual/visual analysis capabilities and provide good examples of the need for intelligent image analysis tools.

This chapter deals with the basic problems that arise if one is to use a learning approach for performing object recognition in science image databases. Two familiar issues are at the heart of the problem: (1) transforming (reducing) the data from pixels to meaningful or useful features, and (2) recognizing (classifying) the detected objects in feature space. Rather than requiring the user to design and implement a classification algorithm to achieve the second step, a machine learning approach may be used to automatically construct the classifier based on training examples provided by the user. Not only does this eliminate the burden of programming from the user, it also provides a mechanism for tackling the often difficult problem of recognizing objects in feature space. The discussion in this chapter is embedded in the context of two illustrative case studies.

The first case study is intended to demonstrate the benefits of using a learning approach in a context where the transformation from pixel space to feature space is well-understood. When the basic image processing (segmentation) to detect the objects (or regions of interest) is straightforward, the remaining problem is one of recognition (classification). Scientists often find it easier to define features of objects of interest than to produce recognizers (models, classifiers) of these objects. Hence one premise is that feature definition and measurement is an easier problem than modelling and recognition. Note that the transformation to feature space often leaves one with a significant classification problem to solve. This is especially true if the dimensionality of the resulting feature space is still high. Our first case study is meant to illustrate exactly that problem: solving the classification problem in the high-dimensional feature space derived from elaborate features which in turn result from significant knowledge of the domain of study. The second case study deals with a case where the basic image processing is not well-understood, and the domain experts are unable to provide much information beyond labeling objects in noisy images. In this case, robust approaches to focus of attention, feature extraction, and classification learning need to be developed.

1.1. A TALE OF TWO APPLICATIONS

Two current projects at JPL and Caltech involving the development of image exploration algorithms and tools are presented in this chapter. The first is an application of decision tree learning to classification. The SKICAT system, which was developed to address the automated processing and analysis of images from POSS-II, demonstrates the effectiveness of machine learning in a context where the users (in this case, astronomers) were able to provide an effective transformation for reducing the data from pixel space to feature space.

The second project represents ongoing work which targets the more ambitious problem of dealing with domains in which the basic reduction from pixels to features is not straightforward. The Magellan spacecraft transmitted back to earth a data set consisting of over 30,000 high resolution radar images of the Venusian surface. This data set is greater than that gathered by all previous planetary missions combined — planetary scientists are literally swamped by data. However, the study of volcanic processes is essential to an understanding of the geologic evolution of the planet [6], and volcanoes are by far the single most visible geologic feature in the Magellan data set. In fact, there are estimated to be on the order of 10^6 visible volcanoes scattered throughout the 30,000 images [1]. Central to any volcanic study is a catalog identifying the location, size, and characteristics of each volcano. Such a catalog would enable scientists to use the data to support various scientific theories and analyses. For example, the volcanic spatial clustering patterns could be correlated with other known and mapped geologic features such as mean planetary radius to provide evidence for (or against) particular theories of geologic evolution. However, it has been estimated that manually producing such a catalog of volcanoes would require 10 man-years of a planetary geologist's time.

1.2. Scope and outline

The Magellan-Venus data set is an example of a currently familiar pattern in the remote-sensing and astronomy communities — a new image data set becomes available but the size of the data set precludes the use of simple manual methods for exploration. Hence, scientists are beginning to express a need for automated tools which can assist them in navigating through large sets of images.

We shall first present the application in astronomy, whose focus is classifier learning in a human-defined feature space. We then proceed to cover the Venus volcano recognition problem which starts at the lowest possible level: labelled examples on raw pixel images and proceeds without using much knowledge of the domain.

Note that in this chapter the type of problem being addressed differs from the types of problems typically addressed by classical work in machine vision. Machine vision work has focused primarily on image understanding, parsing, and segmentation, with a particular emphasis on detecting and analysing *man-made* objects in the scene of interest. The focus of our work is on the detection of *natural*, as opposed to *man-made*, objects. The distinction is important because, in the context of image analysis, natural objects tend to possess much greater variability in appearance than man-made objects. Hence, we shall focus primarily on the use of algorithms that "learn by example" as the basis for image exploration. The primary alternative, the model-based approach, will not be dealt with except in passing. The "learn by example" approach is potentially more generally applicable since domain scientists find it relatively easier to provide examples of what they are searching for, compared to the process of describing a model. However, it should be pointed out that the "prior models" and "learning by example" approaches should be viewed as two ends of a spectrum of methods rather than dichotomous points of view.

2. The SKICAT system

The Sky Image Cataloging and Analysis Tool: SKICAT (pronounced sky-cat) has been developed for use on the images resulting from the POSS-II conducted by Caltech. The photographic plates are digitized via high-resolution scanners resulting in about 3,000 digital images of $23,040 \times 23,040$ pixels each (16 bits/pixel), totaling over three terabytes of data. When complete, the survey will cover the entire northern sky in three colors, detecting virtually every sky object down to a B magnitude of 22 (a normalized measure of object brightness). This is at least one magnitude fainter than previous comparable photographic surveys. We estimate that at least 5×10^7 galaxies and 2×10^9 stellar objects (including over 10^5 quasars) will be detected. This data set will be the most comprehensive large-scale imaging survey produced to date and will not be surpassed in scope until the completion of a fully digital all-sky survey.

The purpose of SKICAT is to facilitate the extraction of meaningful information from such a large database in an efficient and timely manner. The first step in analyzing the results of a sky survey is to identify, measure, and catalog the detected objects in the image into their respective classes. Once the objects have been classified, further scientific analysis can proceed. For example, the resulting catalog may be used to test models of the formation of large-scale structure in the universe, probe galactic structure from star counts, perform automatic identifications of radio or infrared sources, and so forth [3, 26, 27]. Reducing the images to catalog entries is an overwhelming task which inherently requires an automated approach. The goal of our project is to automate this process, providing a consistent and uniform methodology for reducing the data sets. This will provide the means for objectively performing tasks that formerly required subjective and visually-intensive manual analysis.

An important goal of this work is to classify objects whose intensity (isophotal magnitude) is too faint for recognition by inspection, hence requiring an automated classification procedure. Faint objects constitute the majority of objects on any given plate. We target the classification of objects that are at least one magnitude fainter than objects classified in previous surveys using comparable photographic material.

2.1. CLASSIFYING SKY OBJECTS

Existing computational methods for classifying the images would preclude the identification of the majority of objects in each image since they are at levels too faint for traditional recognition algorithms or even manual inspection and analysis approaches. A principal goal of SKICAT is to provide an effective, objective, and examinable basis for classifying sky objects at levels beyond the limits of existing technology.

Figure 1 depicts the overall data processing scheme used by SKICAT for plate catalog construction and classification. Each of the 3,000 digital images, consisting of $23,040^2$ 16-bit pixels, is subdivided into a set of partially overlapping frames. Low-level image processing and object separation is performed by a modified version of the FOCAS image processing software [15, 24]. Attributes are then measured based on this segmentation. The total number of attributes measured for each object by SKICAT is 40, including magnitudes, areas, sky brightness, peak values, and intensity-weighted and unweighted pixel moments. The base-level attributes measured are generic quantities typically used in astronomical analyses [24], including:

- isophotal, aperture, core, and asymptotic "total" magnitudes
- isophotal and "total" areas
- sky brightness and sigma (variance)
- peak, intensity weighted, and unweighted positions: xc, yc, icx, icy, cx, cy
- intensity weighted and unweighted image moments: ir1, ir2, ir3, ir4, r1, r2, ixx, iyy, ixy, xx, yy, xy

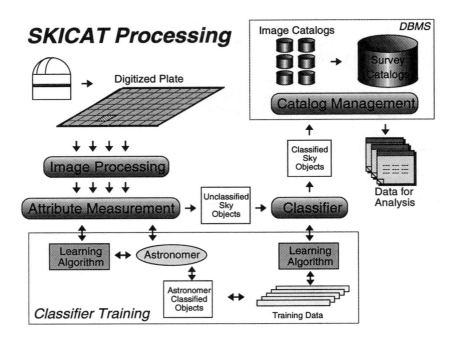

Figure 1: *Overview of SKICAT Cataloguing and Classification Process.*

- ellipticity and position angle (orientation)

Once all attributes, including normalized and non-linear combinations of these attributes, are measured for each object, final classification is performed on the catalog. Our current goal is to classify objects into four major categories, following the original scheme in FOCAS: *star, star with fuzz, galaxy,* and *artifact*[1].

2.2. CLASSIFYING FAINT SKY OBJECTS

In addition to the scanned photographic plates, we have access to CCD images that span several small regions in some of the frames. The main advantage of a CCD image is higher resolution and higher signal-to-noise ratio at fainter levels. Hence, many of the objects that are too faint to be classified by inspection on a photographic plate are easily classifiable in a CCD image. In addition to using these images for photometric calibration of the photographic plates, we make use of CCD images for two machine learning purposes: they enable us (1) to obtain class labels for faint objects in the photographic plates, and (2) to accurately assess the classification results.

In order to produce a classifier that classifies faint objects correctly, the learning algorithm needs training data consisting of faint objects labeled with the appropriate class. The class label is therefore obtained by examining the CCD

---

[1]an artifact represents anything that is not a sky object, e.g. satellite or airplane trace, film aberrations, and so forth.

frames. Once trained on properly labeled objects, the learning algorithm produces a classifier that is capable of properly classifying objects based on the values of the attributes provided by FOCAS. Hence, in principle, the classifier will be able to classify objects in the photographic image that are simply too faint for an astronomer to classify by inspection. Using the class labels, the learning algorithms are basically being used to solve the more difficult problem of separating the classes in the multi-dimensional space defined by the set of attributes derived via image processing. We target the classification of sky objects that are at least one magnitude fainter than objects classified in photographic all-sky surveys to date.

3. Background on Decision Tree Based Learning Algorithms

A particularly efficient method for extracting classifiers from data is to generate a decision tree [2, 18]. A decision tree consists of nodes that represent tests on attribute values. The outgoing branches of a node correspond to all the possible outcomes of the test at the node, thus partitioning the examples at a node along the branches. A well-known algorithm for generating decision trees is Quinlan's ID3 [18] with extended versions called C4 [19]. ID3 starts with all the training examples at the root node of the tree. An attribute is selected to partition the data. For each value of the attribute, a branch is created and the corresponding subset of examples that have the attribute value specified by the branch are moved to the newly created child node. The algorithm is applied recursively to each child node until either all examples at a node are of one class, or all the examples at that node have the same values for all the attributes. Every leaf in the decision tree represents a classification rule. Note that the critical decision in such a top-down decision tree generation algorithm is the choice of attribute at a node. Attribute selection in ID3 and C4 is based on minimizing an information entropy measure applied to the examples at a node. The measure favors attributes that result in partitioning the data into subsets that have low class entropy. A subset of data has low class entropy when the majority of examples in it belong to a single class. For a detailed discussion of the information entropy selection criterion see [18, 23, 10].

3.1. The GID3* and O-Btree algorithms

The attribute selection criterion clearly determines whether a "good" or "bad" tree is generated by a greedy algorithm (see [9, 23] for the details of what we formally mean by one decision tree being better than another). Since making the globally optimal attribute choice is computationally infeasible, ID3 utilizes a heuristic criterion which favors the attribute that results in the partition having the least information entropy with respect to the classes. There are weaknesses inherent in algorithms like ID3/C4.5 due to the fact that a branch is created for each value of the attribute chosen for branching. This overbranching is problem-

atic since in general it may be the case that only a subset of values of an attribute
are of relevance to the classification task while the rest of the values may not have
any special predictive value for the classes. The GID3* algorithm was designed
mainly to overcome this problem. We generalized the ID3 algorithm so that it
does not necessarily branch on each value of the chosen attribute. GID3* can
branch on arbitrary individual values of an attribute and "lump" the rest of the
values in a single default branch representing a subset of values of an attribute.
Unnecessary subdivision of the data may thus be reduced. See [23, 8] for more
details.

The O-Btree algorithm [10] was designed to overcome problems with the information entropy selection measure itself. O-Btree creates strictly binary trees
and utilizes a measure from a different family of measures that detect class separation rather than class impurity. Information entropy is a member of the class
of impurity measures. O-Btree employs an orthogonality measure rather than entropy for branching. For details on problems with entropy measures and empirical
evaluation of O-Btree, the interested reader is referred to [23, 10].

Both O-Btree and GID3* differ from ID3 and C4 in one additional aspect:
the discretization algorithm used at each node to locally discretize continuous-
valued attributes. Whereas ID3 and C4 utilize a binary interval discretization
algorithm, we utilize a generalized version of that algorithm which derives multiple
intervals rather than strictly two. For details and empirical tests showing that
this algorithm does indeed produce better trees see [23, 11]. We have found that
this capability improves performance considerably in several domains.

3.2.   The RULER system: extracting rules from multiple trees

There are limitations to decision tree generation algorithms that derive from the
inherent fact that the classification rules they produce originate from a single
tree. This fact was recognized by practitioners early on [2, 18]. Tree pruning
is used to overcome overspecialization. The very reason which makes decision
tree generation efficient (the fact that data is quickly partitioned into ever smaller
subsets) is also the reason why overspecialization or incorrect classification occurs.
It is our philosophy that once we have good, efficient decision tree generators, they
could be used to generate multiple trees, keeping only the best rules in each tree.

Figure 2 shows the process used by RULER for generating robust rules by
statistically optimizing over multiple decision trees. In multiple passes, RULER
partitions a training set randomly into a training subset and test subset. A
decision tree is generated from the training set and its rules are tested on the
corresponding test set. Using Fisher's exact test [13] (the exact hyper-geometric
distribution) RULER evaluates each condition in a given rule's preconditions for
relevance to the class predicted by the rule. Ruler estimates the probability that
the condition is correlated with the class by chance, and if it is higher than a small
threshold (say 0.01), the condition is deemed irrelevant and is pruned. Recall that

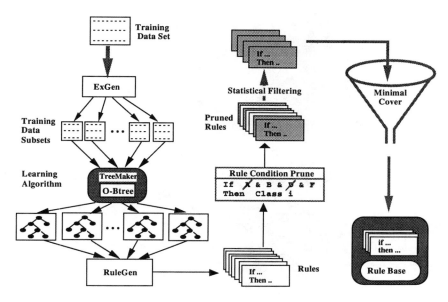

Figure 2: *Architecture of the RULER Rule Learning System.*

the Chi-square test is actually an approximation to Fisher's exact test when the number of test examples is large. We use Fisher's exact test because it is robust for both small and large data sets. In addition, RULER also measures the merit of the entire rule by applying the test to the entire precondition as a unit. This process serves as a filter which passes only robust, general, and correct rules.

By gathering a large number of redundant rules through iterating on randomly subsampled training sets, RULER builds a large rule base of robust rules that collectively cover the entire original data set of examples. A greedy covering algorithm is then employed to select a minimal subset of rules that covers the examples. The set is minimal in the sense that no rule could be removed without losing complete coverage of the original training set. Using RULER, we can typically produce a robust set of rules that has fewer rules than any of the original decision trees used to create it. The fact that decision tree algorithms constitute a fast and efficient method for generating a set of rules allows us to generate many trees without requiring extensive amounts of time and computation.

4. SKICAT CLASSIFICATION RESULTS

The training and test data consisted of objects collected from four different plates from regions for which we had CCD image coverage (since this is data for which accurate classification is available). The learning algorithms are trained on a data set from 3 plates and tested on data from the remaining plate for cross validation. This estimates our accuracy in classifying objects across plates. Note that the plates cover different regions of the sky and that CCD frames cover multiple, very small portions of each plate. The training data consisted of 1,688 objects that

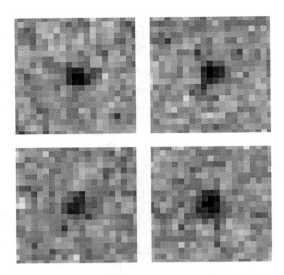

Figure 3: *A sampling of four faint objects.*

were classified manually by an astronomer by examining the corresponding CCD frames. It is noteworthy that for the majority of these objects, the astronomer would not be able to reliably determine the classes by examining the corresponding survey (digitized photographic) images. All attributes used by the learning algorithms are derived from the survey images and not, of course, from the higher resolution CCD frames. The classification results are as follows:

Learning Algorithm:	ID3	GID3*	O-Btree	RULER
Classification Accuracy:	75.6%	90.1%	91.2%	94.2%

Note that such high classification accuracy results could only be obtained after expending significant effort on defining more robust attributes that captured sufficient invariances between various plates. When the same experiments were conducted using only the base-level attributes measured by FOCAS, the results were significantly worse. The error rates jumped above 20% for O-BTree, above 25% for GID3*, and above 30% for ID3. The respective sizes of the trees grew significantly as well [12].

In order to demonstrate the difficulty and significance of the classification results presented so far, consider the example shown in Figure 3. This figure shows four image patches each centered about a faint sky object that was classified by SKICAT. These images were obtained from a plate that was not provided to SKICAT in the training cycle and the objects are part of a region in the sky containing the Abell 1551 cluster of galaxies near the North Galactic Pole. SKICAT classified the top two objects as stars and the bottom two as galaxies. According to astronomers we questioned, the objects shown in Figure 3 are too faint for reliable classification. As a matter of fact, an astronomer visually inspecting these images would be hard pressed to decide whether the object in the lower right hand corner is a star or galaxy. The object in the upper right hand corner appears as a galaxy based on visual inspection. Upon retrieving the corresponding higher resolution CCD images of these objects, it was clear that the SKICAT classification was indeed correct. Note that SKICAT produced the prediction based on the lower resolution survey images (shown in the figure). This example illustrates how the SKICAT classifier can correctly classify the majority of faint objects which even the astronomers cannot classify. Indeed, the results indicate that SKICAT performs this task with an accuracy better than 91% (for the faintest objects in the survey).

5. Summary and benefits of SKICAT

The SKICAT project represents a step towards the development of an objective, reliable automated sky object classification method. The results of our effort to automate sky object classification in order to automatically reduce the images produced by POSS-II to sky catalogs are very encouraging. Using machine learning techniques, SKICAT classifies objects that are at least one magnitude fainter than objects cataloged in previous surveys. This results in a 200% increase in the number of classified sky objects available for scientific analysis in the resulting sky catalog database. Furthermore, we have exceeded our initial accuracy target of 90%. This level of accuracy is required for the data to be useful in testing or refuting theories on the formation of large structure in the universe and theories on other phenomena of interest to astronomers. SKICAT is now being employed to both reduce and analyze the survey images as they arrive from the digitization instrument [28, 16]. We are also beginning to explore the application of SKICAT to the analysis of other surveys planned by NASA and other institutions.

A consequence of the SKICAT work is a fundamental change in the notion of a sky catalog from the classical static entity "in print", to a dynamic, ever growing, ever improving, on-line database. An important feature of the survey analysis system will be to facilitate such detailed interactions with the catalogs. The catalog generated by SKICAT will eventually contain about a billion entries representing hundreds of millions of sky objects. We view our effort as targeting the development of a new generation of intelligent scientific analysis tools [27, 3]. Without the availability of these tools for the first survey (POSS-I) conducted over four decades ago, no objective and comprehensive analysis of the data was possible. In contrast, we are targeting a comprehensive sky catalog that will be available on-line for the use of the scientific community.

6. Volcano detection in Magellan-Venus data

The Magellan-Venus data set constitutes yet another example of the large volume of data that current imaging systems can collect. This data set covers more than 95% of the surface of Venus and provides more detail than was previously available from Pioneer Venus, Venera 15/16, or ground-based radar observations put together [17]. We are initially targeting the automated detection of the "small-shield" volcanoes (less than 15km in diameter) that constitute the most abundant visible geologic feature [5] in the more than 30,000 1-Mbyte synthetic aperture radar (SAR) images of the surface of Venus. It has been extrapolated from previous studies and knowledge of the underlying geologic processes that there should be on the order of 10^6 of these volcanoes visible in the Magellan data [1, 7]. Generating a comprehensive catalog including the size, location, and other relevant information about each volcano is clearly a prerequisite for more advanced studies such as cluster analysis of the volcano locations. Such analysis could provide insight into eruption mechanics, the relationship between volcanoes and local tectonic structure, and the pattern of heat flow within the planet. Automatically generating a volcano catalog from the Magellan image database presents a significant challenge to current pattern recognition and machine learning capabilities; however, the alternative approach of manually locating volcanoes is simply not feasible.

Our long-term goal is to develop a general system for locating patterns of interest in image data. Toward this goal we have developed a prototype system, based on classical filtering and statistical pattern recognition techniques, for finding volcanoes. The system is called JARtool (JPL Adaptive Recognition Tool). Training for the specific volcano-detection task is obtained from examples provided by experts. The absence of absolute "ground truth" leads to some practical problems for training and performance evaluation that are discussed in Section 6.2 The system is described in Section 6.3, with preliminary results on a small set of images given in Section 7

6.1. MAGELLAN IMAGERY

A fundamental objective of the Magellan mission was to provide global mapping of the surface of Venus. The mapping was performed using synthetic aperture radar (SAR) because of its ability to penetrate the dense cloud cover surrounding Venus. A complete description of the Magellan SAR imaging system is given in [17], so here only the most important characteristics are summarized:

- Wavelength: 12.6cm
- Frequency: 2.385 GHz–S band
- Incidence Angle: 15°–45° (nominal)
- Range resolution: 120m - 360m
- Azimuth resolution: 120m
- Pixel-spacing: 75m (full resolution)
- Number of looks: 5–16

Figure 4 shows a 30km × 30km area imaged by Magellan (illumination from the lower-left). This area is located near latittude 30°N, longtitude 332°, at an

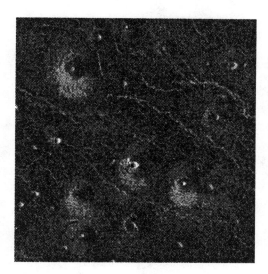

Figure 4: Magellan SAR sub-image (30km × 30km region).

incidence angle of ≈ 40°, contains several small volcanoes. Observe that the larger volcanoes in this figure have the classic radar signature one would expect based on the topography; that is, the upward sloping surface of the volcano in near-range (close to the radar) scatters more energy back to the sensor than the surrounding flat plains and therefore appears bright. The downward sloping surface of the volcano in far-range scatters energy away from the sensor and therefore appears dark. Together, these effects cause the volcano to appear as a left-to-right *bright-dark pair* within a circular planimetric outline. Near the center of the volcanoes, there is usually a summit pit that appears as a *dark-bright* pair because the radar energy backscatters strongly from the far-range rim. Pits which are sized on the order of, or less than, the 75m resolution of the imaging instrument may appear as only a bright point in the image or not be visible at all.

The topography-induced features described above are the primary visual cues that geologists use to locate volcanoes. However, there are a number of other, more subtle cues. The apparent brightness of an area in a radar image depends not only on the macroscopic topography but also on the surface roughness relative to the radar wavelength. Thus, if the flanks of a volcano have different roughness properties than the surrounding plains, the volcano may appear as a bright or dark circular area instead of as a bright-dark pair. Volcanoes may also appear as radial flow patterns, texture differences, or disruptions of graben[2].

---

[2]Graben are ridges or grooves in the planet surface, which appear as bright lines in the radar imagery — see Figure 4.

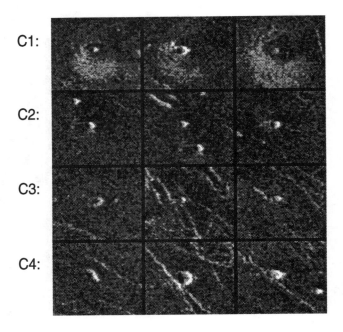

C1:

C2:

C3:

C4:

Figure 5: *A selection of ROIs as labeled by the geologists showing categories 1–4.*

6.2. GROUND TRUTH

In the volcano-location problem, as in many pattern recognition applications, real ground truth data may not exist. No one has ever been to Venus, and despite the fact that the Magellan data is the best imagery ever obtained of Venus, scientists cannot always determine with 100% certainty (due to factors such as image resolution, signal-to-noise level, etc.) whether a particular image feature is indeed a volcano.

Thus, to provide training data for a supervised learning system in domains where real ground truth does not exist, one must carefully design a scheme for collecting the training data in a manner that is consistent with the practical realities. This adds two important dimensions to the traditional classification learning problem which we discuss in Sections 6.2.1 and 6.2.2

6.2.1. ATTACHING UNCERTAINTY LABELS TO THE TRAINING EXAMPLES

Using JARtool's graphical labelling interface, the geologists provide the system with training data. The scientists can indicate size information by fitting circles (or other shapes) around each region of interest (ROI). The problem of labeling uncertainty is handled by asking the scientists to give a subjective estimate of the probability that each object is actually a volcano. To avoid the pitfalls of biased subjective estimates, we allow the fewest necessary degrees of freedom in representing these probabilities. Through discussions with the scientists, we decided to quantize the confidence attached to each ROI into four levels:

Category 1: definitely a volcano, with all primary visual cues present; this represents a subjective probability in the range $[0.95 - 1.0]$.

Category 2: very likely to be a volcano, a non-essential visual cue is missing; subjective probability in the range $[0.75 - 0.95]$.

Category 3: possibly a volcano, at least two of the primary cues are missing; subjective probability roughly in the range $[0.5 - 0.7]$.

Category 4: only a pit is showing; likely to be a volcano but more evidence is needed: subjective probability roughly in the range $[0.5 - 0.7]$.

The scientists believe that this quantization is both reasonable and appropriate. Note that Class 3 and Class 4 are not strictly ordered in the sense that a three is not necessarily more volcano-like than a four. They both indicate uncertain volcanoes, but the uncertainty is generally due to different factors. Figure 5 illustrates some typical volcanoes from each category.

6.2.2. PERFORMANCE EVALUATION WITH UNCERTAIN GROUND TRUTH

Given that the scientists cannot classify each object with 100% confidence, how can we assess how well our algorithms are performing? The basic idea is to measure the performance of individual scientists with respect to a "consensus ground truth", where the consensus data is generated by several scientists working together discussing the merits of each candidate volcano (see Figure 6). The performance of an algorithm is considered to be satisfactory if, compared to consensus ground truth, its performance is as good as that of an individual scientist. The philosophy here is that if a single scientist is qualified to perform the analysis, then it is sufficient if our algorithms perform comparably.

We evaluated the individual performance of two scientists in the following way. Each was asked to label separately the volcanoes in a collection of four images using the subjective probability categories described above. Approximately one week later, the two scientists jointly labeled the same images starting anew, i.e., they did not directly use their previous individual labelings. Figure 7 shows the confusion matrices comparing each scientist's labeling to the consensus.

The (i, j) entry in the confusion matrix is interpreted as the number of volcanoes labeled i by an individual scientist that were in fact labeled j in the consensus. Thus, scientist A labeled 5 volcanoes as category 2 that were listed in the consensus as category 1. The last row of the confusion matrix shows the number of volcanoes the scientist completely missed. The last column shows the number of false alarms by the scientist. The $(0, 0)$ entry is defined to be 0. The confusion matrices can also be shown graphically as in the plots at the right in Figure 7. Notice the significant number of of off-diagonal elements. We will return to the scientists' labeling performance in Section 7 when we evaluate the performance of our algorithms.

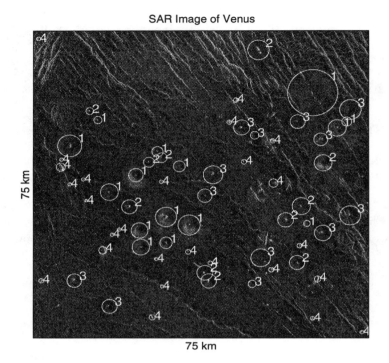

Figure 6: *Magellan SAR image of Venus with consensus ground truth showing location, size, and category of small volcanoes.*

6.3. STRUCTURE OF THE ALGORITHM

In this section, we provide an overview of the algorithm we have developed for finding small volcanoes on Venus. The algorithm operates in two distinct phases: (1) the learning phase and (2) the production phase. Figure 8 illustrates the learning phase. The production phase is obtained by removing the shaded boxes and gray arrows. The main function of the learning phase is to develop models of the objects of interest based on a number of examples and counter-examples. Three components in the system are constructed using learning from training data: the focus of attention (FOA) component, the feature learning component, and the classification learning (CL) component. The FOA is intended to select candidate regions of interest with minimal computational effort. Use of the FOA eliminates the need to examine uninteresting areas in extensive detail. Based on comparison with the ground truth, the FOA candidates are separated into a set of examples (actual instances of the desired pattern) and counter-examples (false alarms). The FOA is discussed in detail in Section 6.4.

The examples and counter-examples produced by the FOA algorithm are then processed by a feature learning algorithm. This component attempts to derive a set of relevant features based on the examples and counter-examples. In our

		Consensus				
		1	2	3	4	0
	1	28	11	6	1	0
A	2	5	9	8	9	9
07-93	3	1	2	20	8	31
	4	1	2	5	26	13
	0	0	6	11	4	0

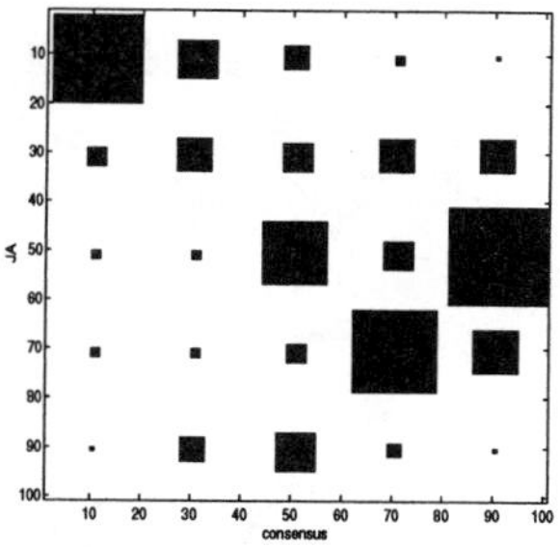

		Consensus				
		1	2	3	4	0
	1	19	6	6	3	1
B	2	9	5	9	4	6
07-93	3	4	13	18	6	37
	4	0	3	3	25	18
	0	3	3	14	10	0

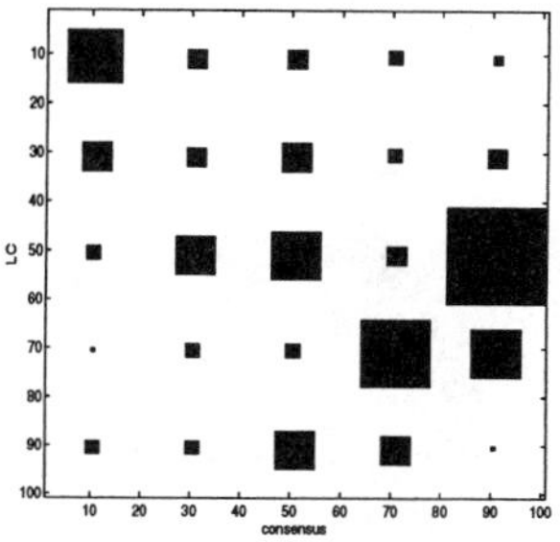

Figure 7: *Single scientist performance compared to 'consensus' ground-truth: confusion matrices for two scientists, A and B; depicted graphically on the right.*

approach each feature is a linear combination of the pixel values in an image region. The vectors of combination coefficients (which may be seen either as 'templates' or as kernels of linear filters) are generated using principal component analysis of the examples (Section 6.5) [14].

Measuring the feature values for a particular region of interest (ROI) involves only a simple dot-product or cross-correlation of the ROI with each template. This projects an ROI down to low-dimensional feature vectors which hopefully encode the essential or relevant information contained in each ROI. The final stage of the learning phase is the classification learning component. The purpose of this component is to construct a mapping from the space of features to a class label. Based on the features associated with an ROI, the classifier declares the ROI to be either: (1) an actual object of interest or (2) a false alarm. The classifier will compensate for the FOA's tendency to respond to weak candidates (high false alarm rate). We use a quadratic classifier (also known as the Gaussian classifier [4]) in the experiments that we present in later sections. We have experimented with a number of other well-established supervised learning methodologies including decision trees, neural networks, and kernel density estimation methods with similar results. The particular choice of classifier technology is not critical provided that the features are the right ones.

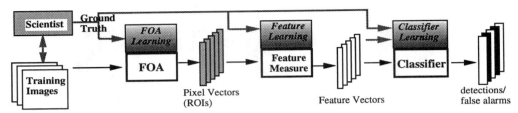

Figure 8: *A block diagram showing the overall structure of the system.*

6.4. FOCUS OF ATTENTION

The main goal of the FOA component is to detect as many volcanoes as possible in a quick and efficient pass. The inputs to the FOA are the full 'raw' images (eg. the SAR images of the surface of Venus); its output is a discrete set of fixed-size image neighborhoods containing an object of interest with some probability. The FOA is by design intended to be aggressive; i.e., it is acceptable for the FOA to generate a significant number of false alarms, as long as it misses very few actual targets. The constraints of computational efficiency and low miss-rate suggest that a linear filtering operation should be used for this component. The problem of finding the best linear filter to detect a deterministic signal in white noise is well-known. The solution is the matched filter; i.e., the filter whose shape matches the shape of the signal one is trying to find. To find a random signal with non-zero mean in white noise, the filter should be matched to the mean of the signal.

A matched filter is constructed by forming an average template from all the volcanoes in the training set. Let $\mathbf{v}_i$ denote the $k \times k$ pixels in a window around the i-th volcano rearranged as a k^2-dimensional vector. Before computing the average, we first normalize each volcano with respect to the local DC (μ) and local contrast level (σ, the standard deviation of the pixels in $\mathbf{v}_i$). Each region of interest in the training dataset is then normalized as follows:

$$\tilde{\mathbf{v}}_i = \frac{\mathbf{v}_i - \mu \cdot \mathbf{1}}{\sigma} \tag{1}$$

where $\mathbf{1}$ is a $k^2 \times 1$ vector of ones. The matched filter $\mathbf{f}$ is constructed simply by averaging the normalized examples. Although the resulting filter is guaranteed to have the zero DC property, we must renormalize the contrast to one.

The matched filter response is computed as the normalized cross-correlation between $\mathbf{f}$ and each image patch (i.e., each image patch is normalized as in Equation 1 prior to computing the dot product with $\mathbf{f}$). The response is equivalent to the statistical cross-correlation between $\mathbf{f}$ and the image patch; thus, response values close to one indicate that the image patch is strongly correlated with the filter. Substantial savings in the computation of the cross-correlation can be achieved using separable kernel methods to approximate the 2-D kernel $\mathbf{f}$ as a sum of 1-D outer products.

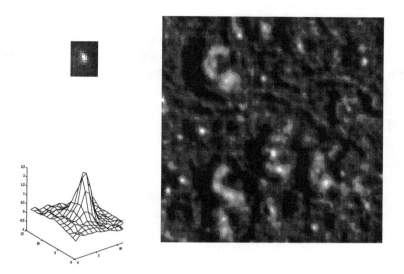

Figure 9: *Left: The matched filter, right: response of the matched filter on the area shown in Figure 4.*

The matched filter response image is thresholded at a level determined from training images. Nearby pixels that are above the threshold are clustered into a single candidate location. Although there are quite a few false alarms, recall that the goal of the FOA component is to achieve a low-miss rate while reducing the amount of data to be processed by later stages. The FOA algorithm is successful in detecting all the volcanoes from Categories 1 and 2, but misses a few from Categories 3 and 4.

We have experimented with several variations of the matched filter. One variation, which we call the size-binned matched filter, attempts to account for size information. With this approach, the training volcanoes are grouped into four size ranges based on the scientist-fitted diameters. A separate matched filter is constructed for each size range. The candidate locations identified by each matched filter are merged and consolidated into a master list of candidates. We also considered a version of the matched filter that takes into account the subjective uncertainty of the scientists. This filter is constructed in the same way as the original FOA scheme, except each training volcano is multiplied by the scientists subjective probability when averaging. Provided the subjective probabilities are unbiased, this method can be shown to have useful asymptotic properties [20].

6.5. FEATURE SYNTHESIS

Determining features from examples is essential to developing a domain-independent algorithm. The feature learning component uses examples generated by the FOA algorithm to synthesize a number of features to be used for classification. As mentioned before, these examples are in the form of fixed-size image neighborhoods (ROIs). One must note that in the present application, generating features automatically is an underconstrained problem: the dimensionality of the space of all possible features is much too high relative to the number of examples that are available. The search must therefore be restricted to a family of potentially useful features; the choice of the family is of course essential to the success of the application. Given the unstructured nature of our data we have chosen to generate features using the classical technique of projecting the ROI onto a low dimensional subspace. Each feature is a coordinate in this space and may be obtained as a linear combination of the ROI pixel values; this is equivalent to selecting an ROI-sized kernel for each feature and computing the inner product of the ROI with the kernel. Having selected this computational strategy, our problem is now one of determining the dimension q of the subspace on which to project and finding q basis vectors (i.e., the appropriate kernels) that span the subspace.

If one takes a probabilistic point of view, the Karhunen-Loève transform yields the 'best' subspace on which to project the data. This subspace is spanned by the highest-eigenvalue eigenvectors of the data covariance matrix. The full covariance matrix unfortunately cannot be computed reliably from the number of examples we typically have available. However, since we are only interested in the highest-eigenvalue eigenvectors, the approximate K-L basis vectors can be found by the method of principal components. This technique has been used already in visual pattern recognition, for example, by Turk and Pentland for face recognition [22].

Despite its intuitive appeal, there are a number of arguments against using such a simple image-based approach for recognition: most notably, it is not invariant with respect to translation, rotation, scaling and direction of illumination. For the volcano problem these limitations are not critical since the FOA algorithm 'centers' the volcanoes well, and the angle of illumination of the SAR is known and roughly constant. However, for the general problem these invariance issues must be addressed systematically and eventually resolved.

The principal components can be determined as follows. Each normalized example is placed as a column in an $n \times m$ matrix X, where n is the number of pixels in each ROI and m the number of examples (ROIs). Using the singular value decomposition, we can factor X as follows:

$$X = USV^T \tag{2}$$

For notational convenience, we will assume m is less than n since this is usually the case. Then in Equation 2, U is an $n \times m$ matrix such that $U^T U = I_{m \times m}$, S is $m \times m$ and diagonal with the elements on the diagonal (the singular values) in descending order, and V is $m \times m$ with $V^T V = VV^T = I_{m \times m}$. Notice that any column of

X (equivalently, any ROI) can be written exactly as a linear combination of the columns of U. Furthermore, if the singular values decay quickly enough, then the columns of X can be very closely approximated using only linear combinations of the first few columns of U. That is, the first few columns of U serve as an approximate basis for the entire set of examples in X.

The columns of U are, in fact, the principal component vectors which will serve in place of the K-L vectors. These are shown in Figure 10 reshaped into ROIs. Notice that the first ten or so exhibit structure, while the remainder appear very random. This suggests that we should use a subspace of dimension $q = 10$. The singular values plotted in the figure indicate that 6 to 10 features capture most of the information in the examples.

Once we have determined the appropriate number q of features to use, we can calculate the feature values for an ROI as follows:

$$\mathbf{y} = \begin{bmatrix} \mathbf{u}_1 & \mathbf{u}_2 & \ldots & \mathbf{u}_q \end{bmatrix}^T \mathbf{x} \tag{3}$$

where $\mathbf{x}$ is the ROI reshaped as an n-dimensional vector of pixels and $\mathbf{y}$ is a q-dimensional vector of features. The feature vectors $\mathbf{y}$ serve as the input to the classification algorithm.

A final point to note about the feature learning algorithm is that like the FOA algorithm, the scientist's subjective probabilities can be taken into account during training. Since the principal components are the eigenvectors of the sample covariance matrix, the subjective probabilities are used to calculate a modified covariance matrix as follows:

$$\Sigma_p = \frac{\sum_{i=1}^{m} p_i \, \mathbf{x}_i \mathbf{x}_i^T}{\sum_{i=1}^{m} p_i} \tag{4}$$

where p_i is the probability that example $\mathbf{x}_i$ corresponds to a true volcano. Note that this formula also encompasses the deterministic labeling method in which each p_i is simply equal to 1. The probabilities can be taken into account directly in the matrix X by multiplying column i by $\sqrt{p_i/p}$, where p is the denominator of Equation 4.

6.6.   CLASSIFICATION

The quadratic classifier is the optimal classifier (in the Bayes sense for the zero-one loss matrix) if the class-conditional probability densities of the feature vector $\mathbf{y}$ are multivariate Gaussian, i.e., if

$$\begin{aligned} p(\mathbf{y}|\omega_1) &\sim N(\mu_1, \Sigma_1) \\ p(\mathbf{y}|\omega_2) &\sim N(\mu_2, \Sigma_2) \end{aligned} \tag{5}$$

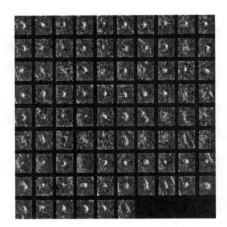 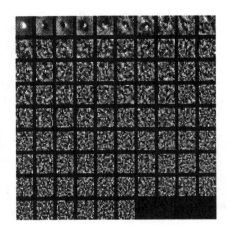

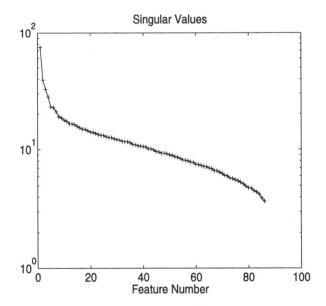

Figure 10: *A collection of volcanoes used for feature synthesis (upper left), principal components derived from the examples (upper right), and singular values curve (bottom).*

Even if the Gaussian assumption does not strictly hold, the quadratic classifier usually performs well provided the densities are unimodal. There are two common interpretations of the algorithm, both of which are useful. The first interpretation is that the algorithm estimates posterior probability densities of the two classes given the feature vector $\mathbf{y}$. For example, the class 1 posterior probability is estimated as:

$$p(\omega_1|\mathbf{y}) = \frac{p(\mathbf{y}|\omega_1)p(\omega_1)}{p(\mathbf{y}|\omega_1)p(\omega_1) + p(\mathbf{y}|\omega_2)p(\omega_2)} \tag{6}$$

where $p(\omega_1)$ and $p(\omega_2)$ are the prior probabilities for each class. Training the quadratic classifier is particularly easy, since the class-conditional densities are completely determined from the class mean and covariance matrix. Thus, we simply have to estimate these parameters from the training data.

The other common interpretation of the quadratic classifier is as a nearest distance classifier, where the distance metric is the Mahalanobis distance:

$$d_i(\mathbf{y}) = (\mathbf{y} - \mu_i)^T \Sigma_i^{-1} (\mathbf{y} - \mu_i) \tag{7}$$

An unknown sample $\mathbf{y}$ is assigned to the class i for which $d_i(\mathbf{y})$ is the smallest. As seen from Equation 7, the minimum distance rule corresponds to using a quadratic hyper-surface to separate the two classes.

7. EXPERIMENTAL PERFORMANCE RESULTS

The experiments reported in this chapter were performed on four 1024×1024 images using a cross-validation paradigm. That is, three images were used to train the algorithm, while the fourth image was reserved for testing. This process was repeated four times with each image serving as the test image. All results were scored relative to the consensus ground truth treating the subjective labels 1, 2, 3, and 4 as true volcanoes. The figure of merit that we measure is the number of detections (true volcanoes identified) versus the number of false alarms (non-volcanoes mistakenly identified as volcanoes) summed over the four test images. In all the performance plots, detection and false alarm rates are expressed *as a percentage relative to the number of true volcanoes (163) in the four images*. Thus, the detection rate is bounded above by 100%, while the false alarm rate can be arbitrarily large. The use of percentages allows one to easily compare results across different images and across different labeling strategies. For most of the algorithm variations we have considered, there is a parameter that can be adjusted to make the algorithm more or less aggressive in declaring volcanoes. Varying this parameter generates a curve comparable to a standard ROC (receiver operating characteristic) curve.

As a basis for comparison (see Section 6.2.2), we evaluated the labeling performance of three scientists, who are all familiar with the Magellan data and with the appearance of volcanoes in the data. The detection/false alarm (DFA) point

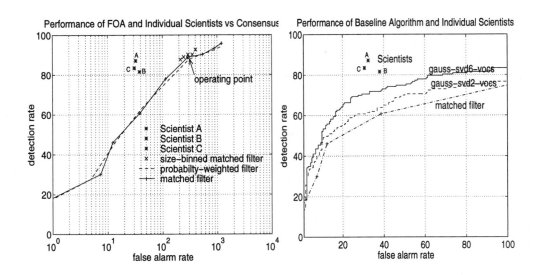

Figure 11: *(Left) FOA algorithm performance: 3 variants of matched filter vs. 3 scientists. (Right) Performance of the overall algorithm vs. individual scientists.*

for each scientist is shown as a labeled asterisk in Figure 11. Note that the x-axis is logarithmic. Figure 11 also shows the performance of the matched filter focus of attention algorithm (solid line). The matched filter algorithm has one free parameter (a threshold), which can be adjusted to make the algorithm more or less aggressive in declaring volcanoes. Since the purpose of the FOA is to provide a low rate of missed volcanoes, the threshold was selected to make the algorithm operate at the point ($f \approx 300\%$, $d \approx 90\%$).

The performance of the size-binned matched filtering scheme of Section 6.4 was also evaluated. The idea behind this experiment was to examine the effect of ignoring scale information in the original single-scale matched filter scheme. For the size-binned algorithm however, it is difficult to obtain a performance *curve* because there are multiple thresholds — one for each size matched filter; nevertheless, the performance for several threshold combinations can easily be determined. The corresponding DFA points are shown in Figure 11 with **x**'s. Observe that the size-binned matched filter improves only slightly upon the performance of the single-scale matched filter. The size-binned algorithm, however, requires considerably more computation time, is more difficult to synthesize, and has more parameters to adjust than the single-scale version. Hence, we continue to use the single-scale matched filter as the baseline focus of attention algorithm. Like the size-binned matched filter, the probability-weighted matched filter did not yield any improvement in performance over the original matched filter. In fact, the probability-weighted filter performed slightly worse, which may indicate that the scientist's probability estimates are not well-calibrated.

Next we evaluated the end-to-end performance of the baseline algorithm. Recall that each candidate ROI is mapped from pixel space to feature space by measuring the values of the features that were learned by the feature learning stage during training. Candidates are then classified as volcano or not-volcano by the quadratic (Gaussian) classifier of Section 6.6. The overall performance of the baseline algorithm is presented in Figure 11. The performance is shown for two cases: (1) six features and (2) two features. The performance with six features is approaching that of the scientists for this task. *In particular, the algorithm detection rate is within 10% of Scientist B's detection rate at the same false alarm rate.*

Also shown on Figure 11 is the FOA curve. One might be curious as to whether the whole volcano labeling task could have been performed using the matched filter (as in [29]). This figure clearly shows, however, that the FOA alone is significantly worse than the combination of an aggressive FOA followed by classification. This raises an interesting question. Since the features learned by the feature learning stage are linear filters, these features could be computed at *every* pixel in an image simply by convolution. The classification algorithm could then attempt to classify each pixel as volcano or non-volcano. How would the performance of the classifier-only algorithm compare to the FOA-classifier combination? If there is an improvement in performance, would it be substantial enough to offset the significant increase in computational costs? We intend to address these questions in future research.

Another question that arises is whether the detection vs false alarm rate (DFA) curves can be parameterized in some manner that will provide summary statistics by which different algorithms can be compared. We have derived the result that under moderate assumptions, the DFA curves can be expressed as a function of two parameters r and ν. The key assumption is that an algorithm makes decisions based on a scalar quantity (e.g., the log-likelihood discriminant function), which is class-conditionally Gaussian distributed. Designating (μ_1, σ_1) and (μ_2, σ_2) as the parameters for these class-conditional Gaussian models (for volcanoes and non-volcanoes respectively), we can define r and ν as follows:

$$\nu = \frac{\mu_1 - \mu_2}{\sigma_2} \tag{8}$$

$$r = \frac{\sigma_1}{\sigma_2} \tag{9}$$

For fixed r, ν can be interpreted as a figure of merit for how well the class densities are separated in feature-space: for small ν (ν near 1 or less) there is much overlap and classification is difficult: as ν increases, the class densities become more separated and classification is easier. The theoretical DFA function is then given approximately by:

$$d \approx \frac{100\frac{N_1}{K}}{1 + \left(e^{-\alpha\nu} \cdot \left(\frac{100N_2}{Kf} - 1\right)\right)^{\frac{1}{r}}} \tag{10}$$

where d is the detection rate, f is the false alarm rate (both expressed in the usual way as percentages relative to the total number of volcanoes K), α is a constant approximately equal to $2.4/\sqrt{2}$, and N_1, N_2 are the number of volcanoes and false alarms in the data after the FOA stage. We have found that Equation 10 provides an excellent fit to our experimentally-obtained DFA curves. The best-fit values of ν and r can be used to characterize the empirical DFA curves more compactly, which is useful when comparing many DFA curves.

Figure 11 indicates that using six SVD features provides better classification than two features. This result was to be expected based on the singular value decay curve shown in Figure 10. Clearly, more than two of the singular values have significant energy; the best number of features to use for detection appears to be between six and ten. We performed an experiment to determine empirically how many SVD features would yield the best performance. The results are shown in two different ways. Figure 12(a) shows the measured detection rate versus the number of SVD components at a few selected false alarm rates. Figure 12(b) shows the fitted DFA performance parameters ν and r. Notice that ν (defined in Equation 8) is relatively flat across the whole range of SVD number, although it is somewhat better (larger) between 4 and 13. Since both the detection curves and figure of merit ν appear to be quite flat over a broad range of the number of svd features, we conclude that the performance is relatively insensitive to the exact number of features, as long as at least four are used. Beyond ten features, the classifier may recognize that the features are very noisy and don't carry much information, which explains the flatness of the curves versus number of features. However, if too many noisy features are included, the performance begins to degrade.

We have performed a preliminary experiment to determine whether using the scientists subjective labels in feature learning would yield an improvement in performance. The results shown in Figure 13 indicate that the performance actually degraded slightly. (We also found the same result when using the probabilities for FOA). There are several possible explanations that we are investigating. The subjective probabilities stated by the scientists may be uncalibrated: in related work we have shown how the subjective labelling noise of each labeller can be estimated and accounted for based on a statistical model of noisy labelling [21]. When scoring the algorithms, we treat all categories in the consensus as true volcanoes; however, in training, the weighting emphasizes features that are useful for category 1 and category 2. The end result may be that we do better classifying the good volcanoes but worse on the marginal ones. Finally, small sample size may be a factor contributing to the degraded performance.

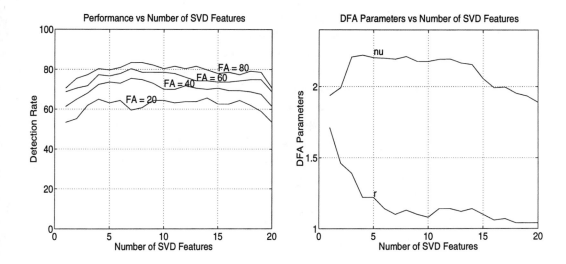

Figure 12: *Performance versus number of SVD features: (a) detection rates vs number of features at four false alarm rates (left) and (b) parameters fitted to DFA curves as a function of the number of features used (right).*

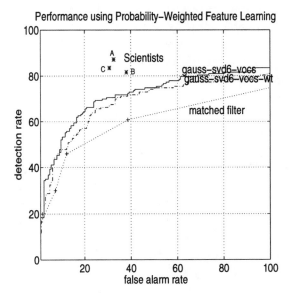

Figure 13: *Performance of the SVD algorithm with probabilistic weightings.*

8.   DISCUSSION AND CONCLUSION

In this chapter, two applications of learning-based approaches to object recognition for science image analysis tasks were presented. In both applications, the
size of the data sets and the numbers of objects involved make manual analysis
approaches infeasible. This explosion in the sizes of data sets acquired is becoming
the norm, not only in science, but in medical imaging, in finance, in entertainment,
in security and defense applications, and in a host of other fields.

Significant resources and time are spent in order to collect data sets such
as the ones we presented in this chapter. A sky survey is conducted by many
astronomers over a period of 5-10 years and costs millions of dollars. Similarly, the
design, construction, and launch of a spacecraft like Magellan requires considerable
resources, not to mention the subsequent costs of operation, data collection, and
distribution. It would be a shame not to utilize the collected data as extensively
as possible. An automated approach to the analysis of the data is a necessity.
Furthermore, since different scientists/users will be interested in searching for
different objects in the data, a learning-from-examples approach offers a natural
solution that does not require the users to be expert programmers. Furthermore,
hand-coding customized object recognizers is a difficult, and sometimes untenable
proposition.

The SKICAT application demonstrates this notion very strongly. The problem
of separating stars from galaxies at faint levels has been an important standing
problem. Several approaches to writing classification programs (see [25, 28] for
a coverage of these) have resulted in discouraging results. Using classification
learning, and labeled training data from limited higher-resolution CCD images,
we were able to obtain reliable classifiers on data over a magnitude fainter than
previous methods. The problem humans faced was that accurate classification
required the use of up to 8 dimensions at once. Manual classifier design methods in astronomy were based on working in two dimensional (sometimes up to
four dimensional) feature space. No robust classifier in those low dimensions exists. Decision tree learning algorithms were able to extract the important eight
dimensions out of the 40 available features.

It is noteworthy that SKICAT is not only able to solve the sky object identification problem with high accuracy, but that it can outperform humans in
classifying faint objects. The reason for this is that the feature set (defined by
humans) captures the necessary information from the underlying pixel space. The
human visual system is apparently unable to extract this discriminating information, however.

The JARtool system developed for the analysis of the Magellan data set illustrates a more difficult setting where even the low-level image processing is not
well-understood. The system we developed is based on classical filtering and pattern recognition techniques. It is being applied to the problem of locating small
volcanoes in the Magellan SAR imagery of Venus. Tests conducted on four images
(containing 163 small volcanoes and covering an area 150km × 150km) show that

our system is performing nearly as well as trained human observers. These results should, of course, be considered preliminary being based on just four images (out of 30,000); further experiments are underway.

In the applications we covered, a key advantage to automating the analysis, beyond making comprehensive analysis of the data possible, is the fact that the resulting catalog of identified objects is obtained via a consistent, systematic, repeatable process. This is in contrast to the manual approach to analysis which not only utilizes only a small portion of the data, but is subject to the day-to-day variation due to human error and various factors affecting human analysts in their daily lives.

As we mentioned at the outset, our long-term goal is to develop a trainable pattern recognition tool that can be applied to various remote-sensing and visual inspection problems without reprogramming. The prototype system described in this chapter is trained completely from examples and appears to work well for finding volcanoes. However, there are a number of technical issues that remain to be addressed. Achieving invariance to translation, scaling, rotation, and illumination without renouncing the advantages of filter-based processing is foremost. (Recall that these issues were not critical for the volcano problem.) Effectively using counter-examples and allowing the scientists to enter "hints" such as "find this object at any scale" are important open issues. Finally, we note that a general system will likely incorporate a variety of pattern recognition techniques, each more or less suited to particular types of problems.

ACKNOWLEDGEMENTS

The SKICAT work is a collaboration between U. Fayyad (JPL), N. Weir and S. Djorgovski (Caltech Astronomy). The work on JARtool is a collaboration between the authors and the domain scientists: J. Aubele and L. Crumpler, Department of Geological Sciences, Brown University. We thank Maureen Burl, Joe Roden, and the SKICAT and JARtool teams for significant help on implementation and experimentation work. Major funding for both projects has been provided by NASA's Office of Space Access and Technology (Code X). The work described in this paper was carried out in part by the Jet Propulsion Laboratory, California Institute of Technology, under a contract with the National Aeronautics and Space Administration.

REFERENCES

[1] J.C. Aubele and E.N. Slyuta. Small domes on Venus: characteristics and origins. *Earth, Moon, and Planets*, 50/51:493–532, 1990.

[2] L. Breiman, J.H. Friedman, R.A. Olshen, and C.J. Stone. *Classification and Regression Trees*. Monterey, CA: Wadsworth and Brooks, 1984.

[3] S. Djorgovski, N. Weir, and U. M. Fayyad. Processing and analysis of the Palomar-STSCI digital sky survey using a novel software technology. In D. Crabtree, J. Barnes, and R. Hanisch, editors, *Astronomical Data Analysis Software and Systems III*, page 39. A.S.P. Conf. Ser. 52, 1994.

[4] R. O. Duda and P. E. Hart. *Pattern Classification and Scene Analysis*. New York, NY: John Wiley and Sons, 1973.

[5] J. E. Guest et al. Small volcanic edifices and volcanism in the plains of Venus. *Journal Geophys. Res.*, 97(E10):15949, 1992.

[6] J. W. Head et al. Venus volcanic centers and their environmental settings: Recent data from Magellan. *American Geophysical Union Spring meeting abstracts*, EOS 72:175, 1991.

[7] J. W. Head et al. Venus volcanism: classification of volcanic features and structures, associations, and global distribution from Magellan data. *Journal Geophysical Res.*, 97(E8):13153–13197, 1992.

[8] U.M. Fayyad. Branching on attribute values in decision tree generation. In *Proc. of the Twelfth National Conference on Artificial Intelligence AAAI-94*, pages 601–606, Cambridge, MA: The MIT Press, 1994.

[9] U.M. Fayyad and K.B. Irani. What should be minimized in a decision tree? In *Proc. of the Eighth National Conference on Artificial Intelligence AAAI-90*, pages 749–754, Cambridge, MA: The MIT Press, 1990.

[10] U.M. Fayyad and K.B. Irani. The attribute selection problem in decision tree generation. In *Proc. of the Tenth National Conference on Artificial Intelligence AAAI-92*, pages 104–110, Cambridge, MA: The MIT Press, 1992.

[11] U.M. Fayyad and K.B. Irani. Multi-interval discretization of continuous-valued attributes for classification learning. In *Proc. of the Thirteenth Inter. Joint Conf. on Artificial Intelligence*, pages 1022–1027, Chambery, France, 1993.

[12] U.M. Fayyad, N. Weir, and S. Djorgovski. SKICAT: A machine learning system for the automated cataloging of large-scale sky surveys. In *Proc. of the Tenth International Conference on Machine Learning*, pages 112–119, San Mateo, CA: Morgan Kaufmann, 1993.

[13] D. J. Finney, R. Latscha, B.M. Bennett, and P. Hsu. *Tables for Testing Significance in a 2x2 Contingency Table*. Cambridge University Press, Cambridge, 1963.

[14] K. Fukunaga. *Introduction to Statistical Pattern Recognition*. San Diego, CA: Academic Press, 1990.

[15] J. Jarvis and A. Tyson. Focas: Faint object classification and analysis system. *Astronomical Journal*, 86:476, 1979.

[16] N. Weir, S. Djorgovski, and U. M. Fayyad. Initial galaxy counts from digitized POSS-II. *The Astronomical Journal*, 110(1):1–20, 1995.

[17] G.H. Pettengill, P.G. Ford, W.T.K. Johnson, R.K. Raney, and L.A. Soderblom. Magellan: radar performance and data products. *Science*, 252:260–265, 1991.

[18] J. R. Quinlan. The induction of decision trees. *Machine Learning*, 1(1), 1986.

[19] J. R. Quinlan. Probabilistic decision trees. In *Machine Learning: An Artificial Intelligence Approach vol. III, Y. Kodratoff & R. Michalski (Eds.)*, San Mateo, CA: Morgan Kaufmann, 1990.

[20] P. Smyth. Learning with probabilistic supervision. In S. J. Hanson T. Petsche and J. W. Shavlik, editors, *Computational Learning Theory and Natural Learning Systems, Volume 3: Selecting Good Models*, pages 163–182, Cambridge, MA: The MIT Press, 1995.

[21] P. Smyth, M. C. Burl, U. M. Fayyad, P. Perona, and P. Baldi. Inferring ground truth from subjectively labeled images of Venus. In *Advances in Neural Information Processing Systems 7*, G. Tesauro, D. S. Touretzky, and T. K. Leen (eds.), pp.1085–1092, Cambridge, MA: The MIT Press, 1995.

[22] M. Turk and A. Pentland. Eigenfaces for recognition. *J. of Cognitive Neurosci.*, 3:71–86, 1991.

[23] U.M.Fayyad. *On the Induction of Decision Trees for Multiple Concept Learning*. PhD thesis, Department of Electrical Engineering & Computer Science, The University of Michigan, Ann Arbor, 1991.

[24] F. Valdes. The resolution classifier. In *Instrumentation in Astronomy IV*, volume 331:465, Bellingham, WA: SPIE, 1982.

[25] N. Weir. *Automated Analysis of the Digitized Second Palomar Sky Survey: System Design, Implementation, and Initial Results*. PhD thesis, California Institute of Technology, 1994.

[26] N. Weir, S. Djorgovski, and U. M. Fayyad. SKICAT: A system for the scientific analysis of the Palomar-STSCI digital sky survey. In *Proc. of Astronomy from Large Databases II*, page 509, Munich, Germany: European Southern Observatory, 1993.

[27] N. Weir, S. Djorgovski, U. M. Fayyad, J. D. Smith, and J. Roden. Cataloging the northern sky using a new generation of software technology. In H. MacGillivray, editor, *Astronomy From Wide-Field Imaging, Proceedings of the IAU Symp. #161*, Dordrecht: Kluwer, 1994.

[28] N. Weir, U.M. Fayyad, and S. Djorgovski. Automated star/galaxy classification for digitized POSS-II. *The Astronomical Journal*, 109(6):2401–2414, 1995.

[29] C.R. Wiles and M.R.B. Forshaw. Recognition of volcanoes on Venus using correlation methods. *Image and Vision Computing*, 11(4):188–196, 1993.

Genetic Algorithms for Adaptive Image Segmentation

Bir Bhanu and *Xing Wu*
University of California at Riverside

Sungkee Lee
Kyungpook National University

Abstract

Image segmentation is an extremely important and difficult low-level task. The difficulty arises when the segmentation performance needs to be adapted to the changes in image quality which is affected by variations in environmental conditions, imaging devices, time of day, etc. In this Chapter, we describe an adaptive image segmentation system that incorporates a feedback loop consisting of a machine learning subsystem, an image segmentation algorithm, and an evaluation component which determines segmentation quality. The machine learning component is based on genetic adaptation and uses separately a pure genetic algorithm and a combination of genetic algorithm and hill climbing. We present experimental results which demonstrate learning and scalability of the technique with the number of parameters to adapt the segmentation performance in outdoor color imagery.

1. Introduction

Image segmentation is an old and difficult problem. It refers to the grouping of parts of an image that have "similar" image characteristics. All subsequent interpretation tasks including object detection, feature extraction, object recognition, and classification rely heavily on the quality of the segmentation process. The difficulty arises when the segmentation performance needs to be adapted to the changes in image quality. Image quality is affected by variations in environmental conditions, imaging devices, time of day, etc. Despite the large number of segmentation techniques presently available [7, 13], no general methods have been found that perform adequately across a diverse set of imagery, i.e., no segmentation algorithm can automatically generate an "ideal" segmentation result in one pass (or in an open loop manner) over a range of scenarios encountered in practical applications. Any technique, no matter how "sophisticated" it may be, will eventually yield poor performance if it cannot adapt to the variations in real-world scenes. The following are the key characteristics of the image segmentation problem:

- When presented with a new image, selecting the appropriate set of algorithm parameters is the key to effectively segmenting the image. Most segmentation techniques contain numerous **control parameters** which must be adjusted to obtain optimal performance, i.e., they are to be *learned*. The size of the parameter search space in these approaches can be prohibitively large, unless it is traversed in a highly efficient manner.

- The parameters within most segmentation algorithms typically interact in a complex, non-linear fashion, which makes it difficult or impossible to model the parameters' behavior in an algorithmic or rule-based fashion.

- The variations between images cause changes in the segmentation results, the objective function that represents segmentation quality varies from image to image. The search technique used to optimize the objective function must be able to adapt to these variations.

- The definition of the objective function itself can be a subject of debate because there are no universally accepted measures of image segmentation quality.

Hence, a need exists to apply an adaptive technique that can efficiently search the complex space of plausible parameter combinations and locate the values which yield optimal results. The approach should not be dependent on the particular application domain nor should it have to rely on detailed knowledge pertinent to the selected segmentation algorithm. Genetic algorithms (GA), which are designed to efficiently locate an approximate global maximum in a search space, have the attributes described above and show great promise in solving the parameter selection problem encountered in the image segmentation task.

The next section of this Chapter argues about the genetic algorithms as the appropriate optimization technique for the segmentation problem. Section 3 describes the adaptive image segmentation algorithm. Section 4 presents the experimental results on a sequence of outdoor images. Section 5 presents the adaptive segmentation results when we scale the number of parameters in a scheme that uses genetic algorithms and hill climbing. Finally, Section 6 provides the conclusions of this Chapter.

2.   IMAGE SEGMENTATION AS AN OPTIMIZATION PROBLEM

Fig. 1 provides an example of an objective function that is typical for the image segmentation process. The figure depicts an application in which only two segmentation parameters (*maxmin* and *absscore*) are being varied, and the corresponding segmentation quality obtained for any pair of algorithm parameters.

Because the algorithm parameters interact in complex ways, the objective function is multimodal and presents problems for many commonly used optimization techniques. Further, since the surface is derived from an analysis of real-world imagery, it may be discontinuous, may contain significant amounts of noise, and cannot be described in closed form. The derivation of this surface will be described in Section 3, where we discuss the segmentation evaluation process.

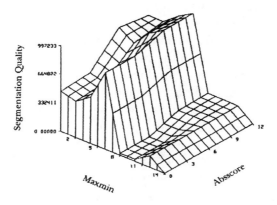

Figure 1: *Segmentation quality surface.*

The conclusion drawn from an analysis of many segmentation quality surfaces that we have examined is that we must utilize a highly effective search strategy which can withstand the breadth of performance requirements necessary for the image segmentation task.

Various commonly used search techniques for functional optimization exist. These include (a) exhaustive techniques (random walk, depth first, breadth first, enumerative), (b) calculus-based techniques (gradient methods, solving systems of equations), (c) partial knowledge techniques (hill climbing, beam search, best first, branch and bound, dynamic programming, A*), and (d) knowledge-based techniques (production rule systems, heuristic methods). The limitations of these methods are given in [3, 15, 24]. There are other search techniques such as genetic algorithms, simulated annealing and hybrid or integrated methods [3]. To address the characteristic of image segmentation problem as discussed earlier, we have selected genetic algorithms and hybrid methods for adaptive image segmentation.

2.1. GENETIC ALGORITHMS

Genetic algorithms were pioneered at the University of Michigan by John Holland and his associates [6, 10, 14]. The term genetic algorithm is derived from the fact that its operations are loosely based on the mechanics of genetic adaptation in biological systems. Genetic algorithms can be briefly characterized by three main concepts: a Darwinian notion of fitness or strength which determines an individual's likelihood of affecting future generations through reproduction; a reproduction operation which produces new individuals by combining selected members of the existing population; and genetic operators which create new offspring based on the structure of their parents.

A genetic algorithm maintains a constant-sized population of candidate solutions, known as individuals. The initial seed population from which the genetic process begins can be chosen randomly or on the basis of heuristics, if available for a given application. At each iteration, known as a generation, each individual is evaluated and recombined with others on the basis of its overall quality or fitness. The expected number of times an individual is selected for recombination is proportional to its fitness relative to the rest of the population. Intuitively, the high strength individuals selected for reproduction can be viewed as providers of "building blocks" from which new, higher strength offspring can be constructed. New individuals are created using two main genetic recombination operators known as crossover and mutation. Crossover operates by selecting a random location in the genetic string of the parents (crossover point) and concatenating the initial segment of one parent with the final segment of the second parent to create a new child. A second child is simultaneously generated using the remaining segments of the two parents. The string segments provided by each parent are the building blocks of the genetic algorithm. Mutation provides for occasional disturbances in the crossover operation by inverting one or more genetic elements during reproduction. This operation insures diversity in the genetic strings over long periods of time and prevents stagnation in the convergence of the optimization technique.

The individuals in the population are typically represented using a binary notation to promote efficiency and application independence of the genetic operations. Holland [14] provides evidence that a binary coding of the genetic information may be the optimal representation. Other characteristics of the genetic operators remain implementation dependent, such as whether both of the new structures obtained from crossover are retained, whether the parents themselves survive, and which other knowledge structures are replaced if the population size is to remain constant. In addition, issues such as the size of the population, crossover rate, mutation rate, generation gap, and selection strategy have been shown to affect the efficiency with which a genetic algorithm operates [12]

The inherent power of a genetic algorithm lies in its ability to exploit, in a highly efficient manner, information about a large number of individuals. By allocating more reproductive occurrences to above average individuals, the overall net affect is an upward shift in the population's average fitness. Since the overall average moves upward over time, the genetic algorithm is a "global force" which shifts attention to productive regions (groups of highly fit individuals) in the search space. However, since the population is distributed throughout the search space, genetic algorithms effectively minimize the problem of converging to local maxima.

To date, genetic algorithms have been applied to a wide diversity of problems.

They have been used in combinatorial optimization [16], gas pipeline operations [9, 11] and machine learning [15]. With regards to computer vision applications, Mandava et. al [18] have used genetic algorithms for image registration, Gillies [8], and Roth and Levine [22] for feature extraction, and Ravichandran [21] for object recognition.

3. GENETIC LEARNING FOR ADAPTIVE IMAGE SEGMENTATION

Genetic algorithms can be used in several different ways to provide an adaptive behavior within a computer vision system [3]. The simplest approach is to allow the genetic system to modify a set of control parameters that affect the output of an existing computer vision program. By monitoring the quality of the resulting program output, the genetic system can dynamically change the parameters to achieve the best performance. In this paper, we have adopted this strategy for adaptive image segmentation.

The block diagram of our approach is shown in Fig. 2. After acquiring an input image, the system analyzes the image characteristics and passes this information, in conjunction with the observed external variables, to the genetic learning component. Using this data, the genetic learning system selects an appropriate parameter combination, which is passed to the image segmentation process. After the image has been segmented, the results are evaluated. If the quality of segmentation ("fitness") is acceptable, an update to long-term population is made. If the quality is unacceptable, the process of new parameter selection, segmentation and evaluation continues until a segmentation result of acceptable quality is produced, or the termination criteria are satisfied.

3.1. IMAGE CHARACTERISTICS

A set of characteristics of the image is obtained by computing specific properties of the image itself as well as by observing the environmental conditions in which the image was acquired. Each type of information encapsulates knowledge that can be used to determine a set of appropriate starting points for the parameter adaptation process. For the experiments described here, we compute twelve first order properties for each color component (red, green, and blue) of the image. These features include mean, variance, skewness, kurtosis, energy, entropy, x intensity centroid, y intensity centroid, maximum peak height, maximum peak location, interval set score, and interval set size [17, 23]. The last two features measure histogram properties used directly by the *PHOENIX* segmentation algorithm used in this research and provide useful image similarity information. Since we use a gray scale image to compute edge information and object contrast during the evaluation process, we also compute the twelve features for the Y (luminance component) image as well. Combining the image characteristic data from these four components yields a list of 48 elements. In addition, we utilize two external variables, time of day and weather conditions to characterize each image. The

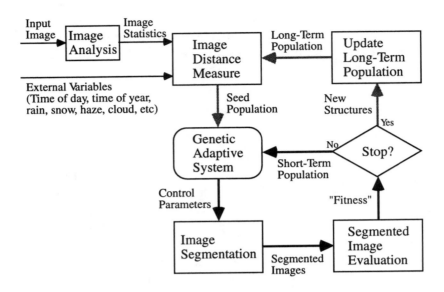

Figure 2: *Adaptive image segmentation system.*

external variables are represented symbolically in the list structure (e.g., time = 9am, 10am, etc. and weather conditions = sunny, cloudy, hazy, etc). The distances between these values are computed symbolically when measuring image similarity. The two external variables are added to the list to create an image characteristic list of 50 elements. The representation of an individual knowledge structure of the genetic population is shown in Fig. 3, where I is the number of image statistics, J is the number of external variables and N is the number of segmentation parameters.

3.2. GENETIC LEARNING SYSTEM

Once the image statistics and external variables have been obtained, the genetic learning component uses this information to select an initial set of segmentation algorithm parameters. A knowledge-based system is used to represent the image characteristics and the associated segmentation parameters. The image statistics and external variables shown in Fig. 3 form the condition portion of the knowledge structure, C_1 through C_{I+J}, while the segmentation parameters indicate the actions, A_1 through A_N, of the knowledge structure. The fitness, W, which ranges in value from 0.0 to 1.0, measures the quality of the segmentation parameter set. Note that only the fitness value and the action portion of the knowledge structure are subject to genetic adaptation; the conditions remain fixed for the life of the knowledge structure.

When a new image is provided to the genetic learning system, the process begins by comparing the image characteristics of the new image (Fig. 2) with

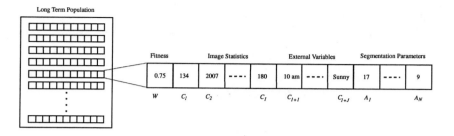

Figure 3: *Representation of a knowledge structure used by the genetic learning system. The image characteristics (image statistics and external variables), segmentation parameters, and the image quality or fitness of the parameter set are stored in each structure.*

the knowledge structures in the long-term population (also called global population, Fig. 3). The long-term population represents the accumulated knowledge of the adaptive system obtained through previous segmentation experience. The algorithm computes a ranked list of individuals in the population that have characteristics similar to the new image. Ranking is based on the normalized Euclidean distance between the image characteristic values as well as the fitness of the knowledge structure. The normalized distance between images A and B is computed using

$$dist_{AB} = \sum_{i=1}^{I+J} W_i \left| \frac{C_{iA} - C_{iMIN}}{C_{iMAX} - C_{iMIN}} - \frac{C_{iB} - C_{iMIN}}{C_{iMAX} - C_{iMIN}} \right|,$$

where C_{iMIN} is the minimum value of the ith numeric or symbolic feature in the global population, C_{iMAX} is the maximum value of the ith feature in the global population, and W_i is the weight attached to the ith feature. For the results presented in this paper, the ranges are normalized and the W_i values have been set to 1 so that each feature contributes equally to the distance calculation.

When the distance between an image and several members of the global population are the same (e.g., if a previous image contributed multiple individuals to the global population), fitness values are used to select the best individuals from the population. Temporary copies of the highest ranked individuals are used to create the initial or seed population for the new image.

Once the initial or seed population is available, the genetic adaptation cycle begins. (The seed population is the same as the initial population, when the genetic algorithm begins its search operation.) The segmentation parameter set in each member of the seed population is used to process the image. The quality of the segmented results for each parameter set is then evaluated. If the maximum segmentation quality for the current population is above a predefined threshold of acceptance or other stopping criteria are satisfied, the cycle terminates and the high quality members of the current image population are used to update the global population. Less fit members of the global population are discarded in favor of higher strength individuals obtained from processing the current image. In this manner, the system is able to extend the knowledge of the adaptive segmentation system by incorporating new experience into the knowledge database.

Alternatively, if after segmenting and evaluating the performance of the current or local (also called short-term) population, the system has not achieved acceptable segmentation quality and any other termination criteria are not satisfied, the genetic recombination operators are applied to the members of the current population. The crossover and mutation operators are applied to the high strength individuals in the population, creating a new set of offspring which will theoretically yield better performance [3, 14]. The new population is supplied back to the image segmentation process, where the cycle begins again. Each pass through the loop (segmentation-evaluation-recombination) is known as a generation. The cycle shown continues until the maximum fitness achieved at the end of a generation exceeds some threshold or other termination criteria are satisfied. The global population is updated and the system is then ready to process a new image.

3.3. SEGMENTATION ALGORITHM

Since we are working with color imagery in our experiments, we have selected the *PHOENIX* segmentation algorithm developed at Carnegie-Mellon University and SRI International [17, 19, 23]. The *PHOENIX* algorithm is a recursive region splitting technique. An input image typically has red, green, and blue image planes, although monochrome images, texture planes, and other pixel-oriented data may also be used. Each of the data planes is called a feature or feature plane. The algorithm recursively splits nonuniform regions in the image into smaller subregions on the basis of a peak/valley analysis of the histograms of the red, green, and blue image components simultaneously. Segmentation begins with the entire image, considered to be a single region, based on histogram and spatial analyses. If the initial segmentation fails, the program terminates; otherwise, the program fetches each of the new regions in turn and attempts to segment them. This process terminates when the recursive segmentation reaches a predefined depth, or when all the regions have been segmented as finely as various user-specified parameters permit.

PHOENIX contains seventeen different control parameters [17], fourteen of which are used to control the thresholds and termination conditions of the algorithm. There are about 10^{40} conceivable parameter combinations using these fourteen values. For the outdoor image sequence that we have used, these parameters can be divided into three groups according to their effect on segmentation results.

GROUP I: ESSENTIAL *PHOENIX* PARAMETERS.

Parameter (default)	Description	Range
Hsmooth (9)	The width of the averaging window used to smooth each feature histogram.	1 – 100
Maxmin (160)	The minimum acceptable ratio of apex height to higher shoulder.	$100 - 10^4$

GROUP II: IMPORTANT *PHOENIX* PARAMETERS.

Parameter (default)	Description	Range
Absscore (70)	The lowest interval set score that will be passed to the threshold phase.	0 – 1000
Splitmin (4)	Direct manipulation of the segmentation queue, for which fetched regions are to be segmented further	1 – 200
Noise (10)	The size of the largest area that is to be considered noise	$0 - 10^4$
Height (20)	The minimum acceptable apex height as a percentage of the second highest apex	0 – 100

GROUP III: LESS IMPORTANT *PHOENIX* PARAMETERS

The rest of the parameters have relatively much less influence on the segmentation result.

To minimize the problem complexity, four parameters have been selected for GA to search for the combination that gives best segmentation result using *PHOENIX*. Thirty two values are sampled for each of these four parameters. This results in a search space whose size is about one million. The parameters are shown in Table 1, together with the formula by which they are sampled, and the associated test range for each. In Section 4, we will present results using the first two parameters (*hsmooth* and *maxmin*). In Section 5, we show scaling results when we adapt all the four parameters.

3.4. SEGMENTATION EVALUATION

After the image segmentation process has been completed by the *PHOENIX* algorithm, we must measure the overall quality of the segmented image. There are a large number of segmentation quality measures [2] that have been developed in the past, although none has achieved widespread acceptance as a universal measure of segmentation quality. In order to overcome the drawbacks of using only a single quality measure, we have incorporated an evaluation technique that

Table 1: PHOENIX *parameters used for adaptive image segmentation.*

Parameter	Sampling Formula	Test Range
Hsmooth: $hsindex \in [0:31]$	$hsmooth = 1 + 2 \cdot hsindex$	$1 - 63$
Maxmin: $mmindex \in [0:31]$	$ep = \log(100) + 0.05 \cdot mmindex$ $maxmin = \exp(ep) + 0.5$	$100 - 471$
Splitmin: $smindex \in [0:31]$	$splitmin = 9 + 2 \cdot smindex$	$9 - 71$
Height: $htindex \in [0:31]$	$height = 4 + 2 \cdot htindex$	$4 - 66$

uses five different quality measures to determine the overall fitness for a particular parameter set. In the following, boundary pixels refer to the pixels along the borders of the segmented regions, while the edges obtained after applying an edge operator are called edge pixels. The five segmentation quality measures that we have selected are,

1. *Edge-Border Coincidence*: Measures the overlap of the region borders in the image acquired from the segmentation algorithm relative to the edges found using an edge operator. In this quality measure, we use the Sobel operator to compute the necessary edge information. The original, unthinned Sobel edge image is used to maximize overlap between the segmented image and the edge image. Edge-border coincidence is defined as follows (refer to Fig. 4(a)).

   Let E be the set of pixels extracted by the edge operator after thresholding and S be the set of pixels found on the region boundaries obtained from the segmentation algorithm:

$$E = \{p_1, p_2, \cdots, p_E\} = \{(x_{p1}, y_{p1}), (x_{p2}, y_{p2}), \cdots, (x_{pE}, y_{pE})\} \quad and$$
$$S = \{q_1, q_2, \cdots, q_S\} = \{(x_{q1}, y_{q1}), (x_{q2}, y_{q2}), \cdots, (x_{qS}, y_{qS}\}, \quad then$$

$$\text{Edge-border Coincidence} = \frac{n(E \cap S)}{n(E)}$$

$$E \cap S = \{(x_k, y_k), k = 1, \cdots, m, where (x_y, y_k) \in E \text{ and } S\}, \quad and$$
$$n(A) = \text{the number of elements in set A.}$$

2. *Boundary Consistency*: Similar to edge-border coincidence, except that region borders which do not exactly overlap edges can be matched with each

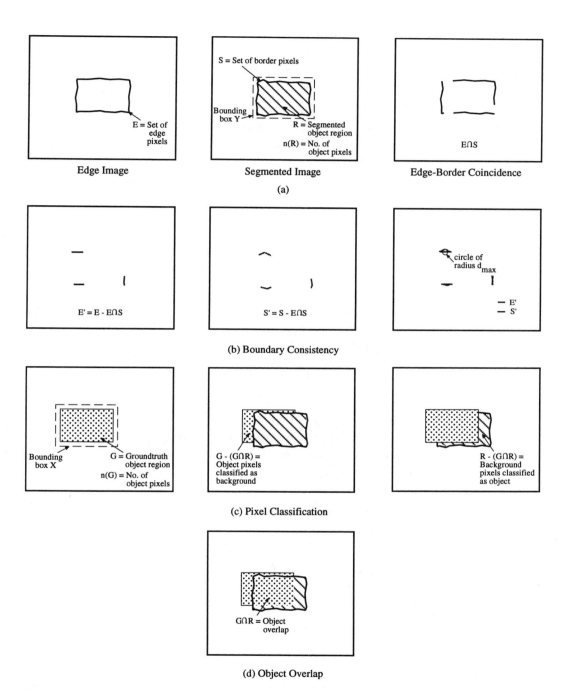

Figure 4: *Illustration for the quality measures used in the adaptive image segmentation system. (a)Edge-border coincidence, (b)Boundary consistency, (c)Pixel classification, (d)Object overlap. Object contrast is defined by using the symbols shown in the center figure in (a) and the left most figure in (c).*

other. In addition, region borders which do not match with any edges are used to penalize the segmentation quality. The Roberts edge operator is used to obtain the required edge information. As with the edge-border coincidence measure, the Roberts edge image is not thinned to maximize the overlap between images. Boundary consistency is computed in the following manner (see Fig. 4(b)).

The first step is to find neighboring pixel pairs in the region boundary and edge results. For each pixel in the segmented image region boundary results, S, a neighboring pixel in the edge image, E, that is within a distance of d_{max} is sought. A reward for locating a neighbor of the ith boundary pixel is computed using

$$R_i = \frac{d_{max} - d_i}{d_{max}},$$

where $d_{max} = 10$, and $d_i =$ the distance to the nearest edge pixel.

Thus, if the pixels had overlapped, $R_i = (10 - 0)/10 = 1$. Pixels that do not directly overlap contribute a reward value that is inversely related to their distance from each other. As matching pairs of pixels are identified, they are removed from the region boundary and edge images (S and E). The total reward for all matching pixel pairs is obtained using

$$R_{TOTAL} = \sum_i R_i$$

Once all neighboring pixel pairs have been removed from E and S, the remaining (i.e., non-overlapping and non-neighboring) pixels correspond to the difference between the two images. The average number of these pixels is used to compute a penalty

$$P = \frac{n(\text{all remaining pixels in } E \text{ and } S)}{2}.$$

Finally, since the value of boundary discrepancy must be positive, we define an intermediate value, M, as $M = (R_{TOTAL} - P)/n(E)$, then

Boundary Consistency $= M$,   if $M \geq 0$,   and zero otherwise.

3. *Pixel Classification*: This measure is based on the number of object pixels classified as background pixels and the number of background pixels classified as object pixels. Let G be the set of object pixels in the groundtruth image and R be the set of object pixels in the segmented image (see Fig. 4(c)). Formally, we have

$$G = \{p_1, p_2, \cdots, p_A\} = \{(x_{p1}, y_{p1}), (x_{p2}, y_{p2}), \cdots, (x_{pA}, y_{pA})\} \quad and$$
$$R = \{q_1, q_2, \cdots, q_B\} = \{(x_{q1}, y_{q1}), (x_{q2}, y_{q2}), \cdots, (x_{qB}, y_{qB}\}.$$

Since pixel classification must be positive, we define the intermediate value N as follows

$$N = 1 - \left[\frac{(n(G) - n(G \cap R)) + (n(R) - n(G \cap R))}{n(G)} \right]$$

where $G \cap R = \{(x_k, y_k), k = 1, \cdots, m, \quad \text{where } (x_k, y_k) \in G \text{ and } R\}$

Using the value of N, pixel classification can then be computed as

$$\text{Pixel Classification} = N, \quad \text{if } N \geq 0, \quad \text{and zero otherwise.}$$

4. *Object Overlap*: Measures the area of intersection between the object region in the groundtruth image and the segmented image, divided by the object region. As defined in the pixel classification quality measure, let G be the set of object pixels in the groundtruth image and R be the set of object pixels in the segmented image (Fig. 4(d)). Object overlap can be computed as

$$\text{Object Overlap} = \frac{n(G \cap R)}{n(G)}$$

where $G \cap R = \{(x_k, y_k), k = 1, \cdots, m, \quad \text{where } (x_k, y_k) \in G \text{ and } R\}$

5. *Object Contrast*: Measures the contrast between the object and the background in the segmented image, relative to the object contrast in the ground-truth image. Let G be the set of object pixels in the groundtruth image and R be the set of object pixels in the segmented image, as shown in Fig. 4(a). In addition, we define a bounding box (X and Y) for each object region in these images. These boxes are obtained by enlarging the size of the minimum bounding rectangle for each object (G and R) by 5 pixels on each side. The pixels in regions X and Y include all pixels inside these enlarged boxes with the exception of the pixels inside the G and R object regions. We compute the average intensity for each of the four regions (G, R, X, and Y) using the equation $I_L = \sum_{j=1}^{L_{max}} I(j)/L_{max}$, where $I(j)$ is the intensity of the jth pixel in some region L and L_{max} is the total number of pixels in region L. The contrast of the object in the groundtruth image, C_{GT}, and the contrast of the object in the segmented image, C_{SI}, can be computed using

$$C_{GT} = \left| \frac{I_G - I_X}{I_G} \right|, \quad C_{SI} = \left| \frac{I_R - I_Y}{I_R} \right|.$$

The object contrast quality measure is then computed as

$$\text{Object Contrast} = \frac{C_{SI}}{C_{GT}}, \quad \text{if } C_{GT} \geq C_{SI}$$

$$= \frac{C_{GT}}{C_{SI}}, \quad \text{if } C_{GT} < C_{SI}.$$

The maximum and minimum values for each of the five segmentation quality measures are 1.0 and 0.0, respectively. The first two quality measures are *global* measures since they evaluate the segmentation quality of the whole image with respect to edge information. Conversely, the last three quality measures are *local* measures since they only evaluate the segmentation quality for the object regions of interest in the image. When an object is broken up into smaller parts during the segmentation process, only the largest region which overlaps the actual object in the image is used in computing the local quality measures. In the experiments described in this chapter, we combine the five quality measures into a single, scalar measure of segmentation quality using a weighted sum approach. Each of the five measures is given equal weighting in the weighted sum. Elsewhere we have investigated a more complex vector evaluation approach that provides multidimensional feedback on segmentation quality [3, 4].

4. SEGMENTATION RESULTS

4.1. SEGMENTATION USING GENETIC ALGORITHM

The adaptive image segmentation consists of the following steps:

1.   Compute the image statistics.
2.   Generate an initial population.
3.   Segment the image using initial parameters.
4.   Compute the segmentation quality measures.
5.   WHILE not <*stopping conditions*> DO
5a.   select individuals using the reproduction operator
5b.   generate new population using the crossover
                  and mutation operators
5c.   segment the image using new parameters
5d.   compute the segmentation quality measures
             END
6.   Update the knowledge base using the new knowledge structures.

We have tested the performance of the adaptive image segmentation system on a time sequence of outdoor images. The outdoor image database consisted of twenty frames captured using a JVC GXF700U color video camera. The images were collected approximately every 15 minutes over a 4 hour period. A representative subset of these images is shown in Fig. 5. The original images were digitized to be 480×480 pixels in size but were subsequently subsampled (average of 4×4 pixel neighborhood) to produce 120×120 pixel images for the segmentation experiments. Weather conditions in our image database varied from bright sun to overcast skies. The changing environmental conditions caused by movement of the sun also created varying object highlights, moving shadows, and many subtle contrast changes between the objects in the image. Also, the colors of most objects in the image are subdued. The auto-iris mechanism in the camera was functioning, which causes a similar appearance of the background foliage throughout the image sequence. Even with the auto-iris capability built into the camera, there was still a wide variation in image characteristics across the image sequence. This variation required the use of an adaptive segmentation approach to compensate for these changes.

(a) Frame 1   (b) Frame 11

Figure 5: *Sample outdoor images used for adaptive segmentation experiments.*

The car in the image is the object of interest for the pixel classification, object overlap, and object contrast segmentation quality measures. The groundtruth image for the car was obtained by manual segmentation of Frame 1 only for the image sequence. The Sobel and Roberts edge operator results, which are used in the computation of the edge-border coincidence and boundary consistency measures respectively, are obtained from the gray scale image (Y component of the YIQ image set) for each frame [5]. For the results presented in this section, the *maxmin* and *hsmooth* parameters of the *PHOENIX* algorithm were used to control the segmentation quality and the segmentation quality surfaces were defined for preselected ranges of these two parameters as shown in Table 1. All the parameters that were not optimized were set at the default *PHOENIX* parameter values. These parameters remain fixed throughout all the experiments. By selecting 32 discrete values (5 bits of resolution) for each of these parameter ranges, the search space contained 1024 different parameter combinations. Fig. 6 presents the five individual segmentation quality surfaces and the combined surface for Frame 1 of the database. Notice that the surfaces are complex and hence, would pose significant problems to traditional optimization techniques.

The genetic component used a local or seed population size of 10, long-term population size of 100, a crossover rate of 0.8, and mutation rate of 0.01. A crossover rate of 0.8 indicates that, on average, 8 out of 10 members of the population will be selected for recombination during each generation. The mutation rate of 0.01 implies that on average, 1 out of 100 bits is mutated during the crossover operation to insure diversity in the local population. The stopping criterion for the genetic process contains three tests. First, since the global maximum for each segmentation quality surface was known *a priori* (the entire surface was precom-

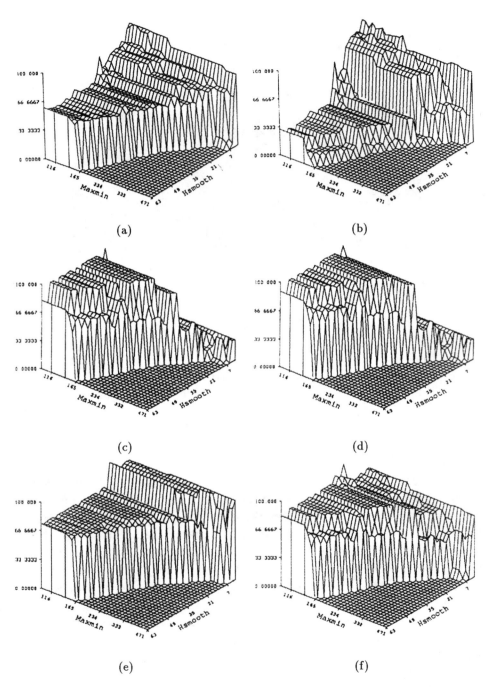

(a)   (b)

(c)   (d)

(e)   (f)

Figure 6: *Segmentation quality surfaces for Frame 1. (a)Edge-border Coincidence, (b)Boundary Consistency, (c)Pixel Classification, (d)Object Overlap, (e)Object Contrast, (f)Combined Segmentation Quality.*

puted to evaluate results), the first test is the location of a parameter combination that produces quality of 95% or higher. In experiments where the entire surface is not precomputed, this test would be discarded. Second, the process terminates if three consecutive generations produce a decrease in the average population fitness for the local population. Third, if five consecutive generations fail to produce a new maximum value for the average population fitness, the genetic process terminates. If any one of these three conditions is met, the processing of the current image is stopped and the maximum segmentation quality currently in the local population is reported.

Numerous experiments [3, 5] were performed for training and testing to measure the optimization capabilities of the genetic algorithm and to evaluate the reduction in effort achieved by utilizing previous segmentation experience. In the following we present some of these results.

4.2. PERFORMANCE COMPARISON WITH OTHER TECHNIQUES

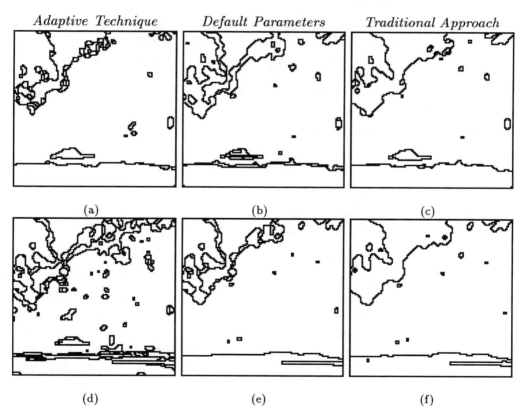

Figure 7: *Segmentation of Frame 1 (a–c) and Frame 11 (d–f) for the adaptive technique, default parameters, and the traditional approach.*

Since there are no other known adaptive segmentation techniques with a learning capability in both the computer vision and neural networks fields to compare our system with, we measured the performance of the adaptive image segmentation system relative to the set of default *PHOENIX* segmentation parameters [17, 23] and a traditional optimization approach. The default parameters have been suggested after extensive amounts of testing by researchers who developed the *PHOENIX* algorithm [17]. The parameters for the traditional approach are obtained by manually optimizing the segmentation algorithm on the first image in the database and then utilizing that parameter set for the remainder of the experiments. This approach to segmentation quality optimization is currently a standard practice in state-of-the-art computer vision systems. Fig. 7 illustrates the quality of the segmentation results for Frames 1 and 11 using the default parameters and the traditional approach and contrasts this performance with our adaptive segmentation technique. By comparing the extracted car region in each of these images, as well as the overall segmentation of the entire image, it is clear that the adaptive segmentation results are superior to the other methods. For the 20 frames the average segmentation quality for the adaptive segmentation technique is 95.8%. In contrast, the performance of the default parameters is only 55.6% while the traditional approach has a 63.2% accuracy. The size of the search space in these experiments is 1024, since each of the two *PHOENIX* parameters are represented using 5 bits. The price paid for achieving consistent higher quality of segmentation is the average number of times (2.5) one has to go through the genetic loop. Thus, only 2.4% of the search space is explored to achieve the global maximum. Many additional tests, including the comparison with random walk approach, are performed to demonstrate the effectiveness of the reproduction and crossover operators [3].

4.3. DEMONSTRATION OF LEARNING BEHAVIOR

The above experiments were conducted in a parallel fashion, i.e., all training and all testing was performed without the aid of previous segmentation experience. Although the testing experiments used the knowledge acquired during training, the tests were still performed in parallel. None of the segmentation experience obtained during testing was applied to subsequent testing images. The following multiple day experiment shows that experience can be used to improve the segmentation quality over time. The test simulates a four day scenario where the frequency of image acquisition decreases to approximately one hour. The order of the images in this test is 1, 5, 9, 12, 16, 20, 3, 7, 11, 14, 18, 2, 6, 10, 13, 17, 4, 8, 15, 19. Each group of images in the sequence of Frames (1, 5, 9, 12, 16, 20), (3, 7, 11, 14, 18), (2, 6, 10, 13, 17), or (4, 8, 15, 19) was designed to represent a collection of images acquired on a different day.

The genetic population of the first frame in the image sequence was randomly selected. Once the segmentation performance for that frame was optimized by the genetic algorithm, the final population from that image was used to create the initial global population. This global population was then used to select the seed population for subsequent frames in the image sequence. The global population size was set to 100 for these experiments to insure a diversity of segmentation experience in the population. While the size of the global population remained below 100 members (prior to processing 10 frames), the final populations for each image were merely added to the current global population. After the size of the global population reached 100 individuals, the final populations from each successive image had to compete with the current members of the global population. This competition was based on the fitness of the individuals; highly fit members of a new local population replaced less fit members of the global population, thus keeping the size of the global population constant. Fig. 8 presents the performance results achieved by the adaptive image segmentation system during each of the three sequential tests. The images in the first "day" (frames 1, 5, 9, 12, 16,

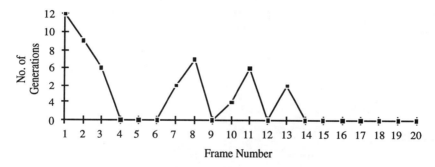

Figure 8: *Performance of the adaptive image segmentation system for a multiple day sequential test.*

20) show a continually decreasing level of computational effort. When the second sequence (frames 3, 7, 11, 14, 18) is encountered, the effort increases temporarily as the adaptive process fills in the knowledge gaps present as a result of the differences between the images in each sequence. The image sequence for the third "day" (frames 2, 6, 10, 13, 17) was handled with almost no effort by the genetic learning. Finally, the fourth image sequence (frames 4, 8, 15, 19) requires no effort by the genetic learning at all; each image is optimized by the information stored in the global population. Twelve of the twenty frames in this test were optimized using the global population.

5.   SCALING THE NUMBER OF PARAMETERS

For the results presented in Section 4, we selected only two (*hsmooth* and *maxmin*) parameters of the *PHOENIX* algorithm. In this section, we present details when we select four parameters (*hsmooth*, *maxmin*, *splitmin* and *height*) for adaptive image segmentation. In this case the size of the search space is about 1 million. Table 1 shows the parameter values. As the number of segmentation parameters for adaptation increases, the number of points to be visited on the surface will also increase. However, genetic algorithms offer a number of advantages over other search techniques. These include parallel search from a set of points with the *expectation* of achieving the global maximum. Unlike the Hough transform, which is essentially an exhaustive search technique commonly used in Computer Vision, it is expected that the genetic algorithm will visit only a small percentage of the search space to find an adequate solution that is sufficiently close to the global maximum.

5.1. SEARCH SPACE AND GA CONTROL MECHANISM

Visualization of the Search Space: Visualization of the search space allows one to understand its complexity—the number and distribution of local peaks and the location of global maximum. But this 5-dimensional space (four parameters plus the fitness or quality of image segmentation) is difficult to be visualized with traditional methods. So we project this 5-dimensional data into a 4-dimensional space by slicing it into 32 pieces along the *Height* axis. Fig. 9 shows the 3-D volume

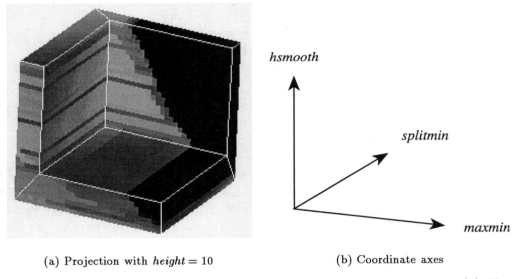

(a) Projection with *height* = 10   (b) Coordinate axes

Figure 9: *Volume representation of segmentation parameter search space. (a) The original 5-dimensional data (hsmooth, splitmin, maxmin, height, segmentation quality) is projected along height axis, where the color represents the fitness or segmentation quality value. (b) The coordinate system.*

representation of this 4-dimensional data using the brick and slice visualization technique, where the x, y, z axes are *maxmin, hsmooth*, and *splitmin* respectively, and the color associated with each point represents the combined segmentation quality for a given parameter set. Blue color represents segmentation quality of 0, while the red color represents 100% quality.

GA Control Mechanism: GA learning requires 3 operations: selection, crossover, and mutation. In our approach, a chromosome is formed by combining the 4 segmentation parameters together. Using our method of crossover point selection, the ordering of these parameters within the chromosome does not affect the search process. Tests are carried out to select the best control parameters for GA, which include the number of crossover points, crossover rate, method of selection, population size, and quality threshold. The results given below are averaged over 1000 independent tests.

Crossover Rate: Table 2 shows the number of segmentations that are needed for frame 1 for different crossover rates. The threshold for minimum acceptable segmentation quality is 95%, population size varies from 50 to 200. We can see that a lower crossover rate leads to smaller number of total segmentations.

Table 2: *Number of segmentations under varying population size and crossover rate. The threshold for minimum acceptable segmentation quality was set at 95%.*

Population	Crossover Rate	2-Point Crossover
50	80%	9439
	50%	6077
100	80%	5805
	50%	4675
200	80%	7548
	50%	5068

Population Size and Number of Crossover Points: Table 3 shows the number of segmentations required for different population sizes and crossover points. The threshold for acceptance of segmentation quality is 95% and the crossover rate is set at 80%. From the results we can see that using more crossover points and larger population size, the total number of required segmentations can be reduced. This experiment also showed that the total number of segmentations will not reduce further when population size is greater than 500. A complete scenario for crossover operation using four points is shown in Fig. 10.

Segmentation Quality Threshold: Table 4 shows how different thresholds for minimum acceptable segmentation quality affect the total number of required

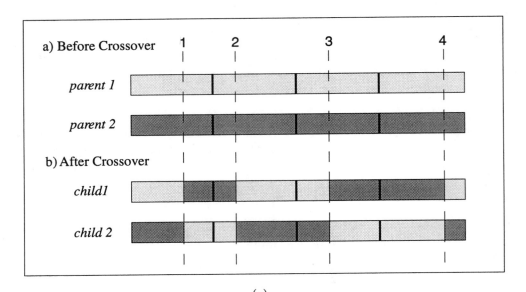

(a)

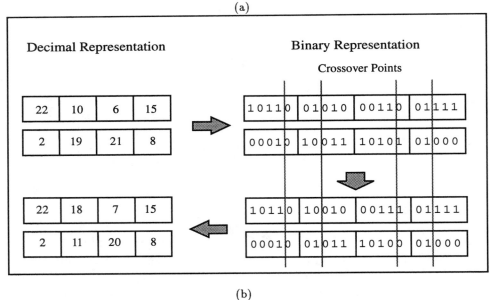

(b)

Figure 10: *Genetic algorithm crossover operation. (a) Scheme for doing 4-point crossover with each chromosome containing four parameters. (b) A complete scenario for one crossover operation.*

Table 3: *Number of segmentations under varying population size and crossover points (Segmentation quality threshold = 95% , Crossover rate = 80%).*

Population	1-Point Crossover	2-Point Crossover	4-Point Crossover
10	7102	6553	5941
100	4960	5805	5528
200	4131	3939	3900
500	3575	3332	2878

segmentations. The difference is not significant between 90% and 95% because these segmentation qualities are quite close.

Table 4: *Number of segmentations under varying threshold (Population = 500, Crossover rate = 80%).*

Threshold	1-Point Crossover	2-Point Crossover	4-Point Crossover
95%	3575	3332	2878
90%	2943	2788	2325

The results presented for Frame 1 in Tables 2-4 show that the number of points that are visited on the surface varies from 0.9% to 0.3% for 95% quality of segmentation. In the best case only 0.28% of the search space is visited to achieve 99.89% (threshold is 95%) quality of segmentation.

5.2. GENETIC ALGORITHMS AND HILL CLIMBING

Integrated search techniques have the potential for improved performance over single optimization techniques since these can exploit the strengths of the individual approaches in a cooperative manner [1, 4]. One such scheme which we describe in this section combines a global search technique (genetic algorithms) with a specialized local search technique (hill climbing). Hill climbing methods are not suitable for optimization of multimodal objective functions, such as the segmentation quality surfaces, since they only lead to local extrema. The integrated scheme provides performance improvements over the genetic algorithm alone by taking advantage of both the genetic algorithm's global search ability and the hill climbing's local convergence ability. In a sense, the genetic algorithm first finds the hills and the hill climber climbs them.

The search through a space of parameter values using hill climbing consists of the following steps: (1) Select a starting point; (2) Take a step in each of the fixed set of directions; (3) Move to the best alternative found; and (4) Repeat until a point is reached that is higher than all of its adjacent points. An algorithmic description of the hill climbing process is given below.

1a.   Select a point x_c at random.
1b.   Evaluate the criterion function, i.e., obtain $V(x_c)$.
2a.   Identify points $x_1, \cdots, x_n$ adjacent to x_c.
2b.   Evaluate the criterion function, i.e., obtain $V(x_1), \cdots, V(x_n)$.
3.   Let $V(x_m)$ be the maximum of $V(x_i)$ for $i = 1, \cdots, n$.
3a.   If $V(x_m) > V(x_c)$ then
                set $x_c = x_m, V(x_c) = V(x_m)$.
                goto Step 2.
3b.   Otherwise, stop.

In this algorithm, a set of points that are "adjacent" to a certain point can be defined in two ways. First, it can denote the set of points that are a Euclidean distance apart from the given point. Thus, the adjacent points are located in the neighborhood of the given point. Second, "adjacent" points can denote the set of points that are unit Hamming distance apart from the given point pair. Each point in this set differs by only one bit value from the given point in binary representation of points. It defines the set of points with varying step size from the given point. The set of Hamming adjacent points was used in this research. Hamming adjacent points have an advantage over Euclidean adjacent points in our implementation because all the segmentation parameter values are represented as binary strings when using the GA. The set of Hamming adjacent points also represents the set of points which can be generated by a genetic mutation operator from the given point.

A conventional hill climbing approach, as described above, finds the largest $V(x_m)$ from $V(x_i), i = 1, \cdots, n$, and the search moves to its corresponding point, x_m. For a space of n adjacent points, it requires n function evaluations to make each move. To reduce the cost of evaluating all the adjacent points before making each move, the approach is designed to try alternatives only until an uphill move is found. The first uphill move is undertaken without checking whether there are other (higher) possible moves. After the hill climbing process has examined all the adjacent points by flipping each bit in the binary representation of the current point, in turn, without finding an uphill move, the current point is taken as a local maximum. The algorithmic description of the hill climbing process used in the search scheme is as follows:

1.   Select a starting point x_c with fitness value $V(x_c)$ from the
         genetic population.

2.   Set $i = 0$.
3.   Set $j = i$.
4a.   Generate an adjacent point x_a by flipping the ith bit in x_c.
4b.   Obtain $V(x_a)$. Set $i = (i+1) \bmod n$.
5.   If $V(x_a) > V(x_c)$ then
                        set $x_c = x_a$.
                        goto Step 3.
            Else if $i < j$ then
                        goto Step 4.
            Otherwise, pass the control to the GA.

5.3. EXPERIMENTAL RESULTS

There are several possibilities in which genetic algorithms and hill climbing can be used. In one case the control moves back and forth between GA and hill climbing [3, 4]. In this approach when GA finds a new maximum, hill climbing is used to keep climbing until local maximum or termination condition is satisfied. If a local maximum is found then GA is again used to find a new maximum. For the experiments presented in this Chapter this approach is used for the first frame only. Specifically, the integrated technique used is given below:

1. Perform GA and hill climbing search for frame 1 using a population size of 10 (chosen from available hardware consideration) and 4 point crossover operation with a crossover rate of 0.8 (same as in Section 4). The goal here is to use small population size to achieve the desired segmentation quality with a minimum number of segmentations.

2. For frame 2 to frame 20 perform hill climbing with accumulated knowledge structures. The parameter set generated from previous frames is used to hill climb. The best result obtained for the current frame is kept as a new knowledge structure and added to the parameter set for hill climbing for the next frame.

After we are done with frame 20, a total of 29 knowledge structures are accumulated, with 19 of them generated by hill climbing.

The experimental results for frame 1 are shown in Table 5. The results show that for 95% threshold for image segmentation quality, the technique helps to reduce the required number of segmentations by almost half. For low segmentation quality threshold (90%), this effect is not dramatic.

Fig. 11 summarizes the performance of the technique for frames 1 to 20, and compares it with the performance of the default parameter set of the *PHOENIX* algorithm [17]. The performance corresponds to the parameter set in the population that has the highest fitness. The average performance improvement for the technique over the default parameter set is about 50%, performance improvement over the technique that uses the parameter set generated by GA plus hill

Table 5: *Performance comparison between pure GA and GA with hill climbing (crossover points = 4, crossover rate = 80%, mutation rate ≈ 1%).*

Population = 10	Genetic w/o hill climbing	Genetic with hill climbing
Threshold = 95%	5941	3340
Threshold = 90%	1720	1631

climbing learning for frame 1 only (no subsequent hill climbing) is also significant. This shows that learning from frame 1 does provide a good starting point for hill climbing for subsequent frames. The maximum improvement over the default parameter set shown in Fig. 11 is 107.8%.

Fig. 12 shows the sample segmentation results obtained by using the default parameter set and the parameter set generated by the technique. Using the default parameter set, it is seen that the car does not show up at all in the segmentation result of frame 16, but the corresponding result using GA and hill climbing is quite good. The overall results show that by combining genetic search and hill climbing techniques the performance improvement is significant when the search space is large.

6. CONCLUSIONS

The goal of this research was to perform adaptive image segmentation and evaluate the convergence properties of the closed-loop system using outdoor data. In this Chapter we have provided sample results. Using the outdoor data we have shown in [3, 4, 5] that the performance improvement provided by the adaptive system was consistently greater than 30% over the traditional approach or the default segmentation parameters [17, 23].

The adaptive image segmentation system can make use of any segmentation technique that can be controlled through parameter changes. The adaptive segmentation system is only as robust as the segmentation algorithm that is employed. It may be possible to keep multiple segmentation algorithms available and let the genetic process itself dynamically select the appropriate algorithm based on image characteristics. Further, it is possible to define various evaluation criteria which can be automatically selected and optimized in a complete vision system. In a complete computer vision system, the segmentation evaluation component can be replaced by the object recognition component(for example, see [20]). In our adaptive image segmentation system, the focus is the image segmentation component. Therefore, we supplied the manually generated groundtruth image to the segmentation evaluation component and used local and global measures.

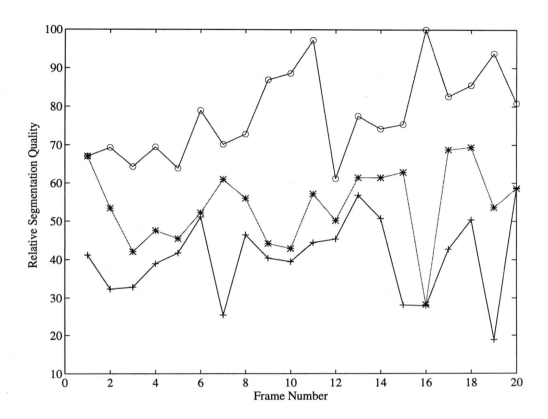

Figure 11: *Performance comparison for techniques based on (a) default parameters (+), (b) GA plus hill climbing to generate the best parameter set for frame 1 only (*), and (c) integrated technique, (parameter set generated for frame 1 in the same manner as in (b) and hill climbing for all subsequent frames (o)).*

Elsewhere, we have optimized both global and local measures in a multi-objective optimization framework [4]. In the future we plan to use a data set with dramatic environmental variations and we will utilize several segmentation algorithms. Ultimately, we will incorporate the adaptive segmentation component into a learning integrated object recognition system.

ACKNOWLEDGEMENTS

This material is based upon work supported by the ARPA/AFOSR under award no F49620-93-1-0624.

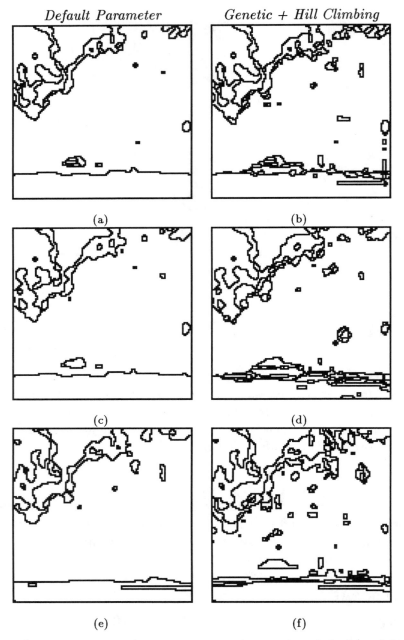

Figure 12: *Segmentation performance comparison using default and learned parameters. (a) and (b) Frame2, (c) and (d) Frame 3, (e) and (f) Frame 16.*

REFERENCES

[1] D. Ackley. Stochastic iterated genetic hill climbing. Technical Report CMU-CS-87-107, Carnegie Mellon University, Dept. of Comp. Sc., March 1987.

[2] B. Bhanu. Automatic target recognition: State-of-the art survey. *IEEE Trans. on Aerospace and Electronic Systems*, AES-22(4):364–379, July 1986.

[3] B. Bhanu and S. Lee. *Genetic Learning for Adaptive Image Segmentation*. Kluwer Academic Publishers, Boston, MA, Summer 1994.

[4] B. Bhanu, S. Lee, and S. Das. Adaptive image segmentation using genetic and hybrid search methods. *IEEE Trans. on Aerospace and Electronic Systems*, 31(4), Oct 1995.

[5] B. Bhanu, S. Lee, and J. Ming. Adaptive image segmentation using a genetic algorithm. *IEEE Trans. on Systems, Man and Cybernetics*, 25(12), December 1995.

[6] K. DeJong. Learning with genetic algorithms: An overview. *Machine Learning*, 3:121–138, 1988.

[7] K. S. Fu and J. K. Mui. A survey on image segmentation. *Pattern Recognition*, 13:3–16, 1981.

[8] A. M. Gillies. *Machine Learning Procedures for Generating Image Domain Feature Detectors*. PhD thesis, Dept. of Comp. Sc., Univ. of Michigan, Ann Arbor, MI, April 1985.

[9] D. Goldberg. *Computer-Aided Gas Pipeline Operation using Genetic Algorithms and Rule Learning*. PhD thesis, Dept. of Civil Engineering, University of Michigan, Ann Arbor, MI, 1983.

[10] D. Goldberg. *Genetic Algorithms in Search, Optimization, and Machine Learning*. Addison-Wesley, Reading, MA, 1989.

[11] D.E. Goldberg. Dynamic system control using rule learning and genetic algorithms. In *Proc. of Int. Joint Conf. on Artificial Intelligence*, pages 588–592, Los Angeles, CA, August 1985.

[12] J. Grefenstette. Optimization of control parameters for genetic algorithms. *IEEE Trans. Systems, Man, and Cybernetics*, 16(1):122–128, January 1986.

[13] R.M. Haralick and L.G. Shapiro. Image segmentation techniques. *Computer Vision, Graphics and Image Processing*, 29:100–132, 1985.

[14] J. Holland. *Adaptation in Natural and Artificial Systems*. Univ. of Michigan Press, Ann Arbor, MI, 1975.

[15] J. Holland. Escaping brittleness: The possibilities of general-purpose learning algorithms applied to parallel rule-based systems. In R. Michalski, J. Carbonell, and T. Mitchell, editors, *Machine Learning: An Artificial Intelligence Approach*, volume II, pages 593–623. Morgan Kaufman, Los Altos, CA, 1986.

[16] J.J.Grefenstette, R.Gopal, B.J.Rosmaita, and D.Van Gucht. Genetic algorithm for the traveling salesman problem. In *Proc. of Int. Conf. Genetic Algorithms and their Applications*, pages 160–168, July 1987.

[17] K.I. Laws. The Phoenix Image Segmentation System: Description and Evaluation. Technical Report 289, SRI International, Dec. 1982.

[18] V.R. Mandava, J.M.Fitzpatrick, and D.R. Pickens III. Adaptive search space scaling in digital image registration. *IEEE Trans. on Medical Imaging*, 8(3):251–262, 1989.

[19] R. Ohlander, K. Price, and D.R. Reddy. Picture segmentation using a recursive region splitting method. *Computer Graphics and Image Processing*, 8:313–333, 1978.

[20] J. Peng and B. Bhanu. Closed-loop object recognition using reinforcement learning. In *Proc. ARPA Image Understanding Workshop*, pages 777–780, Monterey, CA, November 1994.

[21] B. Ravichandran. 2D and 3D Model-Base Matching Using a Minimun Representation Criterion and Hybrid Genetic Algorithm. Technical Report 105, Center for Intelligent Robotic Systems for Space Exploration, Rensselaer Polytechnic Institute, 1993.

[22] G. Roth and M. D. Levine. Geometric primitive extraction using a genetic algorithm. In *Proc. IEEE Conf. on Computer Vision and Pattern Recognition*, pages 640–643, Champaign, IL, June 1992.

[23] S. Shafer and T. Kanade. Recursive region segmentation by analysis of histograms. In *Proc. of IEEE Int. Conf. on Acoustics, Speech, and Signal Processing*, pages 1166–1171, 1982.

[24] P.H. Winston. *Artificial Intelligence*. Reading, MA: Addison-Wesley, 1984.

12   NON-PARAMETRIC TEXTURE LEARNING

Hayit Greenspan
California Institute of Technology

ABSTRACT

Texture is one of the most informative visual cues that help us understand our environment. Texture analysis is an important step in many visual tasks, such as scene segmentation, object recognition, and shape and depth perception. In this chapter we consider the problem of texture recognition and provide an overview of our recent work on this topic ([21, 19, 18]). Our method is based on representing textures in frequency and orientation space, and using non-parametric learning schemes for classification. We present state-of-the-art recognition results on a 30 texture database and compare the performance of a rule-based network, the k-nearest neighbor and feedforward neural-network classifiers. An important extension to the system allows for rotation invariance. Experimental results are presented for large-database rotation-invariant natural texture recognition.

1. INTRODUCTION

Textures in an image are usually very apparent to a human observer (for example see Fig. 1), but no simple mathematical definition captures all aspects of the very diverse texture family. It is this lack of good models that makes automatic description and recognition of these patterns a complex and, as yet, an unsolved problem.

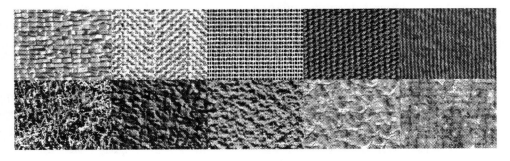

Figure 1: *Structured and unstructured textures (top and bottom, respectively).*

Although researchers approach texture differently, most would agree that the texture family can be categorized into two main categories — *structured* (or oriented) and *unstructured* (non-oriented) textures. We can loosely identify textures as structured when there are clearly defined microstructures with a specific repetitive ordering. The unstructured textures are more fractal-like or stochastic in their appearance. Much effort has been expended to automatically segment and recognize the different types of natural textures. We will briefly mention next some of the classical methods in the literature.

Methods that can handle the more structured textures use structural models which assume that textures are composed of texture primitives. The texture is produced by the placement of these primitives according to certain placement rules (e.g., [39, 28]). One needs to be able to define a priori a good set of primitives and placement rules (a tree grammar is commonly used) in order to characterize the textured input. This approach can handle regular patterns, such as those textures shown in the top row of Fig. 1.

One of the most well-known and widely used methods in texture analysis is the computation of gray-level co-occurrence matrices (GLCM). These matrices provide a full representation of the second-order gray-level statistics of textured images. Haralick [22] has proposed a number of useful texture features that can be computed from the co-occurrence matrices. These include properties such as *energy, entropy, correlation* and more. Many additional properties have since been introduced in the literature (for a review see [5, 23]). Some problems associated with the co-occurrence matrices are that they require a fair amount of computation, as many co-occurrence matrices need to be computed, for varying neighborhood sizes. In addition, a large number of features can be computed from the matrices, requiring an additional, usually ad-hoc, feature selection method to select the most relevant ones.

Stochastic models, such as the Markov Random Field (MRF) models, can be used to represent unstructured or stochastic textures. These models capture the local (spatial) contextual information in an image with the assumption that the intensity at each pixel depends on the intensities of only its neighboring pixels. The image is seen as an instance of a random process, defined by a set of model parameters (e.g., [7, 10]). The model parameters need to be estimated in order to adequately define the perceived qualities of the texture. The model-based techniques can capture certain textures very well (see bottom row of Fig. 1), but textures can be found which fall outside the model definition. In [36] it is summarized that the MRF's fail with the more regular textures as well as inhomogeneous ones.

The methods discussed above use the image pixels as their input space. Other methods exist in the literature which compute texture features by filtering the image, i.e. taking shift-invariant (linear) combinations of the pixels, and using these filtered characteristics in the classification or segmentation tasks. *Spatial domain filters* which include simple edge masks and more complicated masks which are based on spatial moments, can be used to filter images. The resulting filtered images are then used as texture features. Studies in physiology and psychophysics indicate that the human visual system analyzes images by decomposing the image into frequency and orientation components (e.g., [4, 13]). The concept of using multi-resolution processing (channels tuned to different frequencies) as well as localization in space and orientation selectivity, can be found in works which use the *Gabor and wavelet models*, and similar families of filters, such as derivatives or difference of Gaussians, quadrature-pair filters and more (e.g., [26, 29, 1, 15, 33]). An open issue here is the decision regarding the appropriate number of frequencies and orientations required (i.e. the number of filters required) for the representation of the input domain.

Further review of the texture analysis field, its applications and the different methods available in the literature, can be found in (e.g., [36, 23]). Although texture analysis has been a subject of intense study, it is still an open challenge to achieve a high percentage classification rate on the varied texture family within a single framework. Fulfilling this challenge is our ultimate goal.

1.1. WHAT DO WE MEAN BY LEARNING TEXTURES?

As discussed above, there are a variety of methods for handling textures. Learning schemes can be defined and utilized in these different domains.

For the more structured textures, geometrical models are frequently used to define primitives and the spatial arrangement between them. Learning can be utilized here to adapt the geometrical templates to the texture data, as well as to extract an informative set of rules for the discrimination task at hand.

For stochastic textures, statistical model-based methods are used. A model for the task is defined *a priori*, the parameters of which are to be estimated. Learning is used to estimate the model parameters, via an optimization process. Neural-network architectures have been utilized to parallelize the estimation (or energy-minimization) process (e.g., [30]).

When using filters for feature extraction, learning can be important in defining the shape and/or the number of filters necessary for the task at hand.

In this chapter we use *non-parametric* classification schemes (as opposed to parametric model-based schemes) for the texture recognition task. Here, learning from examples is used to identify the important characteristics of the input domain and to extract the relevant set of features for the task. In addition, we advocate filtering the textured image prior to the recognition process. Filtering the input image can allow us to preserve the information-content of the image (the number of filters required will be discussed in section 2), while providing for greater noise immunity relative to the original pixel representation (this will be shown in the experiments of section 3). In addition, filtering enables invariant characteristics in the classification task. The texture recognition system is presented in section 2. The performance of the system is demonstrated and compared to the texture literature in section 3. In section 4 we extend the scope of the recognition system to handle rotation invariance.

2.   MULTI-RESOLUTION REPRESENTATIONS AND LEARNING FOR TEXTURE RECOGNITION

The system we present is composed of a feature extraction stage followed by a learning stage (a diagram of the system, for the case of the rule-based classifier, is shown in top of Fig. 4). The two building blocks of the system are described next.

2.1.   THE FEATURE EXTRACTION STAGE

There is both biological and computational evidence supporting the use of a bank of orientation-selective bandpass filters, such as the Gabor filters, for the initial feature extraction phase of many image-processing tasks [21, 26, 37, 1]. Orientation and spatial frequency responses are extracted from local areas of the input image and the statistics of the coefficients characterizing the local areas (or 'windows') form representative feature vectors.

In its general form the 2-D Gabor function and its Fourier transform can be written as:

$$g(x, y; u_0, v_0) = e^{-(x^2/2\sigma_x^2 + y^2/2\sigma_y^2) + 2\pi i(u_0 x + v_0 y)} \; ; \; G(u, v) = e^{-2\pi^2(\sigma_x^2(u-u_0)^2 + \sigma_y^2(v-v_0)^2)}$$

$$(1)$$

where σ_x and σ_y define the widths of the Gaussian in the spatial domain and (u_0, v_0) is the frequency of the complex sinusoid. The above functions are schematically shown in Fig. 2 left. The biological motivation for these filters lies in their goodness of fit to the receptive-field profiles of simple cells in the striate cortex [11]. Computationally, the Gabor filters have received much attention as they achieve optimal joint resolution in both space and spatial frequency [11]. This is an important property for the texture recognition task. Filters with smaller bandwidths in the spatial-frequency domain are desirable in order to make finer distinctions among different textures, while filters that are localized in the spatial domain are of value in order to localize texture boundaries.

The feature extraction stage of the presented system consists of a computationally efficient Gabor wavelet decomposition scheme, to extract orientation and frequency responses from local areas of the input image. We use a computationally efficient filtering scheme, which is based on a pyramidal approach, reminiscent of the Laplacian Pyramid [3]. A pyramidal representation of the image is convolved with fixed spatial support (5×5) oriented Gabor filters (labeled as $O_{n\alpha}$, with n and α representing the scale and orientation components, respectively). Three scales are used with 4 orientations per scale (0, 90, 45, -45 degrees). A set of oriented-pyramid filters are displayed in Fig. 2, center. The interested reader can refer to [19] for more elaborate details on the specific implementation and characteristics of the oriented pyramid.

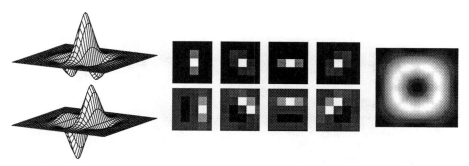

Figure 2: *Left: Real (top) and imaginary (bottom) components of the Gabor filters. Center: A set of oriented pyramid filters, $O_{n\alpha}$. Real and imaginary components are presented, top and bottom, respectively, for $n = 0$ and $\alpha = 1..4$. Right: Power spectra characteristics for the chosen filter set (plus conjugate counterparts).*

2.1.1. HOW MANY FILTERS DO WE NEED?

A large set of techniques can be found in the literature for the filtering stage; from close to two hundred filters acting in parallel and in a multi-level scheme [29] to the selection of one filter per texture based on its Fourier spectrum analysis [1]. We have recently introduced a systematic way to calculate the minimum number of filters needed to span the orientation (or frequency) space, up to a desired accuracy [19]. Singular-value decomposition is used for this task (following [32]).

In the case of the oriented pyramid, we find that a set of eight filters, i.e., an orientation bandwidth of 45°, is sufficient to span the 360° of orientation space with more than 99% accuracy. The four filters, O_{n1} through O_{n4}, and their conjugate counterpart, satisfy this requirement. The filters' combined power spectra thus covers the 360° orientation space, as can be seen in Fig. 2, right.

2.1.2. EXTRACTING FEATURES

It is the local statistics of the oriented pyramid's coefficients which characterize the image local-area response to the different orientations and frequencies. A measure of power or energy is associated next with each filtered map, as the nonlinear operation given below:

$$P_{n\alpha} = |O_{n\alpha}|, n = 0, 1, 2 \quad \alpha = 1, 2, 3, 4. \tag{2}$$

This non-linearity was found to be important in order to discriminate texture pairs with identical mean brightness and identical second-order statistics [29].

Feature-*vectors* are formed from the extracted power maps. These are 15 dimensional vectors which consist of a non-oriented component (L_n) as well as the 4 oriented components per scale ($P_{n\alpha}$). Each feature vector represents the response of an 8×8 window in the input image. An array of such vectors, viewed across the input image, is the output of the feature extraction stage.

To illustrate the feature-representation space, an example of power maps extracted for the French-canvas ("frcanv") texture is shown in Fig. 3, top right,

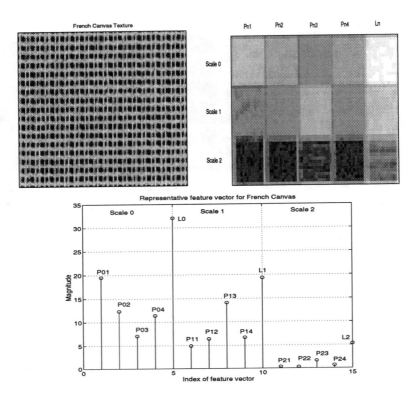

Figure 3: *Power maps (top right) for the French Canvas ("frcanv") texture (top left). Log of brightness level is displayed. Stronger power responses are brighter. A representative feature vector extracted from the power maps (bottom).*

followed by a display of a feature vector which was randomly extracted from the power maps, in Fig. 3, bottom. In the presented power maps stronger responses are indicated in brighter regions (the log of the power response is displayed). We first notice that most power is allocated to the highest resolution scale (scale 0). This corresponds to the high-resolution nature of the input texture. Looking across the oriented components, we see that in the highest resolution scale most of the power is detected in the vertical direction (P_{01}). In the lower resolution scale (scale 1) the power shifts to indicate a strong horizontal direction in the texture. These characteristics are reflected in the displayed feature vector. In general, in the database of textures which we are interested in for this work, we will find one dominant oriented component per scale for the more structured (oriented) textures. A more uniform distribution of power across the oriented components is a characteristic of the unstructured (non-oriented) textures.

2.2. THE LEARNING STAGE

Many techniques exist in the literature for learning classification functions. Each classification scheme has its own advantages and disadvantages, but on most problems one or more of these methods will prove successful in predicting the class output at a performance approaching the Bayes rate. Choosing a classifier is therefore determined by both its performance and its special characteristics. In this part of the system we utilize an information theoretic *rule-based* learning scheme, which provides for probabilistic classification, along with two more standard non-parametric classifiers: the k-nearest neighbor classifier and the multi-layered perceptron (MLP).

2.2.1. THE RULE-BASED NETWORK CLASSIFIER

The rule-based classifier is based on an information-theoretic rule induction algorithm (ITRULE) which searches across large databases for rules of greatest information content. The workings of the algorithm, as well as its application in a variety of domains (such as financial, medical, and so forth), have been reported in detail elsewhere [17]. The focus here is on its specific application to texture classification.

Two building blocks compose the rule-based classifier, as shown in Fig. 4 (top and center). These consist of an unsupervised clustering stage followed by supervised classification. The learning mechanism derives a subset of the input feature maps (or filters) which conveys sufficient information about the visual input for its differentiation and labeling. In addition, the most informative set of correlations (or rules), between the attributes and the texture classes, are learned.

The *unsupervised learning* stage can be viewed as a preprocessing stage for achieving a more compact representation of the filtered input. The goal is to quantize the continuous valued features which are the result of the initial filtering. The need for discretization becomes evident when trying to learn associations between attributes in a symbolic representation, such as rules. Moreover, in an extended framework, the dimensionality of the feature domain can be reduced.

We wish to detect characteristic behavior, across the 15-dimensional feature space, for the family of textures to be learned. In this work each dimension is individually clustered. All samples are thus projected onto each axis of the 15-dimensional space and one-dimensional clusters are found using the K-means clustering algorithm [14]. Each continuous-valued input sample gets mapped next to the discrete codeword representing its associated mean. The output of this preprocessing stage is a 15-dimensional *quantized* vector of attributes which is the result of concatenating the discrete-valued codewords of the individual dimensions. It is the goal of the following supervised stage to find the most informative dimensions for the desired task (with the higher discrimination capability) and to label the combined clustered domain.

In the *supervised learning* stage a rule-based information theoretic approach is

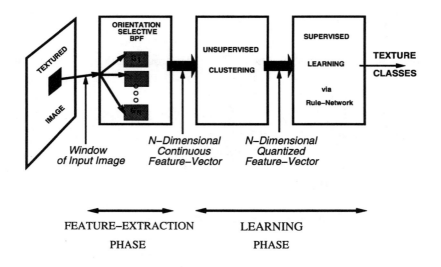

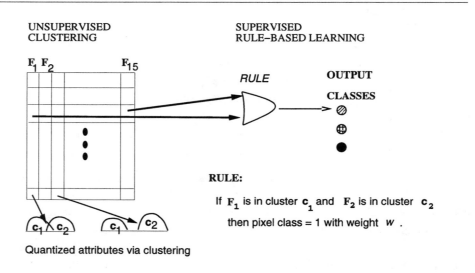

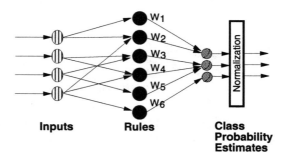

Figure 4: *Rule-based system. Top: System block diagram; Center: Outline of rule-based classifier; Bottom: Rule-based network.*

used to utilize the existing information in the feature maps for labeling and classification. Correlations between input features and output classes are defined as probabilistic rules of the form:

If $Y = y$ then $X = x$ with probability P.

Here, $Y = (Y_1, ..., Y_N)$ represents the input attribute vector ($N = 15$) and X is the set $(x_1, ..., x_m)$ of m possible output texture classes. Given an initial labeled training set of examples, where each example is of the form $(Y_1 = y_1, .., Y_N = y_n, X = x_i)$, our goal is to learn a classifier such that when presented with future test attribute vectors, it will estimate the posterior probability of each class.

The most informative links or rules between features and class labels are learned using an information-theoretic measure, the J measure, defined in [35] as:

$$J(\mathbf{X} = x_i; y) = p(y)\left(p(x_i|y)\log\left(\frac{p(x_i|y)}{p(x_i)}\right) + (1 - p(x_i|y))\log\left(\frac{(1 - p(x_i|y))}{(1 - p(x_i))}\right)\right). \tag{3}$$

Here, the information content of a rule is represented as the average amount of information that attribute values y give about the class X. The J measure is comprised of two main terms. The first is $p(Y = y)$, the probability that the particular set of attribute values will occur. The second term is a measure of the average change (in bits) necessary to specify X between the *a priori* distribution $p(X)$ and the *a posteriori* $p(X|y)$ distribution. This measure can be interpreted as a special case of the cross entropy of the two distributions and satisfies all the properties of an information measure (see [35]). The simplicity of the rule, or the conjunction y, corresponds directly to the number of attribute-value conjunctions, the so-termed rule *order*. Lower-order rules have fewer conditions and thus have a higher probability of occurring. Higher-order rules are more specialized and can therefore be better predictors. Maximizing the J measure results, therefore, in a tradeoff between accuracy and generality (higher-order and lower-order rules, respectively) in the prediction process.

The J-measure is used in a search algorithm to search the space of all possible rules relating the attributes to the class, X, and produce a ranked set of the most informative rules which classify X. For details about the rule-extraction algorithm, bounds on the search and pruning techniques, refer to [35].

The set of most informative rules, according to the J measure, is learned in a training stage. Once the rule set is constructed, the rules may be used in parallel to compute the *posterior probability* of each class. When presented with new input evidence, y, a set of rules can be considered to "fire." These are a subset of the learned correlations which match the input attribute vector. Using Bayes' rule, the classifier estimates the log posterior probability of each class given the rules that fire. Let F be the set of rules which fire and $s_1, ..., s_{|\mathcal{F}|}$ be the actual attribute-value conjunctions corresponding to the fired rules. We get (for a derivation see

[17]):

$$\log p(x_i | s_1, \ldots, s_{|\mathcal{F}|}) = \log p(x_i) + \sum_{j=1}^{|\mathcal{F}|} W_{ij}, \tag{4}$$

with

$$W_{ij} = \log\left(\frac{p(x_i | s_j)}{p(x_i)}\right),$$

where $p(x_i)$ is the prior probability of the class x_i, and W_{ij} represents the evidential support for the class as provided by rule j. In the absence of any rules firing, the estimate of each class is given by the bias value, namely the log of the prior probability of the class. Given a set of rules which fire, each rule contributes a weight to its corresponding output class. A positive weight implies that the class is true, while a negative weight implies it is false. The W_{ij}s provide the user with a direct explanation of how the classification decision was determined. Each class estimate can now be computed by accumulating the "weights of evidence" incident on it from the rules that fire. The largest estimate is chosen as the initial class label decision. The probability estimates for the output classes can be used for feedback purposes for spatial smoothing and further higher-level processing.

The rule-based classification system can be mapped into a three-layer feed-forward architecture as shown in Fig. 4, bottom. The input layer contains a node for each attribute. The hidden layer contains a node for each rule and the output layer contains a node for each class. Each rule (second layer node j) is connected to a class i via the multiplicative weight of evidence W_{ij}. This hybrid rule-based neural model combines the explicit knowledge representation in the form of rules with the parallel implementation of neural-network architectures.

In implementing the rule-based network the relevant parameters are:
- K: The number of clusters in the unsupervised clustering stage.
- N: The maximum number of rules allocated.
- O: The maximum order of the rules.
Unless otherwise noted, we use the following default values:
$K = 10$; $N = 10,000$; $O = 3$.
We allow for a large number of rules as our initial starting point. The actual number of rules allocated is not as important as the fact that there are rules present for each output class. It is usually the case that the lower order rules ($O = 1, 2, 3$) are the most informative ones. As an increase in the order substantially effects the rule-extraction search, we limit the maximum order to 3. We find that the sensitivity of the classification results to the parameter K is low, thus allowing for a fixed default value in the experiments presented (for example, we get a std. of 0.08% in classifying a 10 texture set, with K=5,7,10,15,20).

2.2.2. THE K-NEAREST NEIGHBOR CLASSIFIER

The nearest-neighbor classifier is one of the simplest learning methods. It is completely non-parametric, as nothing apriori is assumed about the population.

Geometrically, the nearest-neighbor method can produce any arbitrary complex surface to separate the classes based only on the configuration of the sample points and their metric.

Let $\mathbf{x}_1, ..., \mathbf{x}_n$ be a set of n labeled samples, and let $\mathbf{x}_m$ be the sample nearest to $\mathbf{x}$ (we will be using the Euclidean distance); i.e.,

$$||\mathbf{x}_m - \mathbf{x}|| = min_i||\mathbf{x}_i - \mathbf{x}||, i = 1, .., n. \tag{5}$$

Then the *nearest-neighbor rule* for classifying $\mathbf{x}$ is to assign it the label associated with $\mathbf{x}_m$. An immediate extension of the nearest-neighbor rule is the *k-nearest-neighbor rule*. This rule classifies $\mathbf{x}$ by assigning it the label *most frequently represented* among the k nearest samples. In other words, a decision is made by examining the labels on the k nearest neighbors and taking a vote.

In our experiments the variability of the classification results as a function of k is found to be low (we get a std. of 0.9% across the classification results, with $k = 1, 5, 10, 20, 50, 100$, for both a 10 and a 30 texture database). In the results presented (section 3.2) we choose to present the average over $k = 1, 5, 10$ and 50.

In its standard form, the nearest-neighbor method involves no data processing in *learning* from the samples. The tradeoff is the requirement that all of the samples be stored, as well as the computational load in predicting the classification of a new case. Each new input sample must be compared with every sample in the prestored sample space.

2.2.3. THE MULTI-LAYERED PERCEPTRON CLASSIFIER

The multi-layered perceptron (MLP) has been successfully used in a variety of application domains [34]. We are therefore motivated to evaluate its performance in the texture recognition task. We use a three-layer network with the first layer containing a single node for each attribute (in our case = 15), the third layer containing a node for each class and the center layer containing hidden units that connect between the input and output units. A known problem associated with neural-network techniques is the definition of the network architecture. If one chooses too few hidden units, the network may have a limited hypothesis space to learn the required concepts, while with too many it may overfit the training data. In the experiments of the following section we average over three runs. For the 15-dimensional input space that we have, we use 30, 60 and 90 hidden units. The std. in the classification results is very small across these 3 architectures (with 0.15% for a 10 texture dataset and 0.3% for a 30 texture set). The results presented (in section 3.2) are the average over these 3 cases. We use the conjugate gradient scheme with 500 training epochs and a threshold set at 10^{-6}. Each run is averaged over 5 different random seed values.

3. SYSTEM PERFORMANCE

3.1. INTRODUCTION

In order to test the capabilities of our system, we have attempted to build a large and heterogeneous texture database resembling a real-world scenario. It is composed of the 30 textures shown in Fig. 6. Most of the textures are taken from the standard Brodatz database of textures [2]; others have been scanned in from a variety of real-world texture sources (e.g., jeans, printed text, checkbook cover).

3.1.1. OUR EXPERIMENTAL SETUP

In most of the following experiments the input to the system is a 256×256 size texture patch. The original image of size 256×256 is input to the oriented pyramid, resulting in feature maps (power maps) of size 32×32. Feature vectors are extracted from the feature maps and are input to the classification system. For a classification resolution of 8×8 windows in the original image, we classify each pixel in the feature map independently. Boundary effects are eliminated by extracting a 30×30 patch from the feature maps (see Fig. 5, left). We thus have a set of 900 feature vectors for the classification task. We use 300 vectors for training and 100 different ones for testing. These are chosen from small disjoint patches (chosen to be as far away as possible). Different size windows in the feature maps are averaged to produce feature vectors corresponding to $16 \times 16, 32 \times 32$ and 64×64 windows of the original image. The training and testing set sizes for the variety of window sizes are listed in Fig. 5 right. In all of the above cases

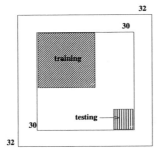

window size	# training vectors per class	# testing vectors per class
8×8	300	100
16×16	125	100
32×32	40	9
64×64	12	4

Figure 5: *Experimental setup (left). Training and testing sets for different classification windows (right).*

no overlap exists between and within the training and testing sets. In cases of limited data (such as the 32×32 and 64×64 cases) 4 different runs are made (interchanging the test vectors) and the average result is presented.

3.1.2. COMPARING TO THE LITERATURE

There is a large variability in the experimental setups presented in the literature, which makes a comparison very difficult. The variety one finds includes: the dataset size and complexity (with a database size of less than or equal to 10 textures being used for comparison for many years); a variety of preprocessing methods (such as histogram equalization techniques); varying classification window sizes, and more.

Due to the large variability in texture databases and in experimental setups, an exact comparison across reported results is difficult. In the following set of experiments we address some of these experimental issues directly and we point out relevant results for comparison as we go along.

3.2. RESULTS
3.2.1. CLASSIFICATION OF A 10 TEXTURE SET

We start by looking at a 10 texture discrimination task with an 8×8 classification resolution. Table 1 presents the class-confusion matrix for the 10 textures of Fig. 1, using the rule-based network classification scheme. The overall classification rate is 94.3%. Very high percentage classification rates are achieved for both the structured and the unstructured textures which compose the set. The classification results of the rule-based network, the k-nearest neighbor scheme and the multi-layered perceptron are summarized in the top row of Table 2. We note the comparable high-performance across the 3 classifiers. These results compare favorably with the literature (e.g., [7, 38, 8]).

	raffia	herr	frc.	cotc.	jeans	grass	cork	hmpaper	pig	cloth
raffia	**91**	0	0	0	0	0	0	0	9	0
herr	13	**85**	0	2	0	0	0	0	0	0
frcanv	0	0	**100**	0	0	0	0	0	0	0
cotcanv	0	0	0	**100**	0	0	0	0	0	
jeans	0	0	0	0	**100**	0	0	0	0	0
grass	0	0	0	0	0	**100**	0	0	0	0
cork	0	0	0	0	0	7	**93**	0	0	0
hmpaper	5	0	0	0	0	0	4	**91**	0	0
pig	4	0	0	0	2	0	0	0	**87**	7
cloth	1	0	0	0	0	0	0	0	2	**97**

Table 1: *Class confusion matrix (shown is percent correct) for a 10 texture case.*

The relative difficulty of the classification task can be indicated by the *number* of rules which are required to cover the training sample space. We preserve the n most informative rules per class, with n varying ($n = 1, 2, ...$), and check classification results on the *training* set. In a raffia-wood case, 10 rules per class suffice to cover the space of examples with 100% accuracy. In the case of a pig and cloth texture pair, which is a perceptually similarly-looking texture pair (see Fig. 6), 430 rules are needed per class, and these are only able to correctly label 546 out of 600 training set examples at 91% accuracy.

3.2.2. SYSTEM ANALYSIS
- *Sensitivity to window size*

Figure 6: *30 texture database. Labels: ROW 1: bark(D12), calf(D24), cloth(D19), cardboard, jeans.   ROW 2: grass(D9), pig(D92), raffia(D84), water(D38), wood(D68). ROW 3: backpack, bookbox, brownbag, check-book cover, cork(D32). ROW 4: cotton canvas(D77), furcanv(D20), fur(D93), handmade paper(D57), napkin. ROW 5: particle board, reptile(D3), straw(D15), text, towel. ROW 6: vinyl, herringbone (D16), sand(D29), wire(D6), strawmat(D55). Textures taken from the Brodatz book are labeled with the corresponding plate number. Others have been scanned in from real-world texture sources. Adapted from [20].*

Classification results are very much dependent on the classification window size. Larger windows produce a more homogeneous feature set (better SNR) and thus result in an easier classification task. Table 2 presents classification results on varying window sizes. The increase in classification performance for the larger windows is evident. The presented results compete with results

10 TEXTURE CASE						
window size	**k-nn**	hist. eq.	**MLP**	hist. eq.	**Rule network**	
8×8	87%	79%	94.5%	91.4%	94.3%	
16×16	93%		96%		95%	
32×32	99%		100%		97.8%	

Table 2: *Classification results on different window sizes.*

in the literature. Several of the results for comparison can be found in A.1

- *Sensitivity to the input image format*
  In the literature one finds a variety of preprocessing steps which are performed on the input image to compensate for illumination variations that are common in some applications. The most common preprocessing scheme is *histogram equalization*. In this scheme one tries to eliminate the influence of first-order statistics in the texture recognition task, by making the gray-level histogram match a *uniform* distribution.

  Using a set of histogram-equalized images is considered to be a more challenging task for a classification system. In [5] Carstensen starts with a set of 15 gray-level co-occurrence matrices (GLCM) features which can discriminate among 15 Brodatz textures with close to 100% accuracy. Using the same set of features on a set of 15 histogram equalized textures, an accuracy rating of 74.3% is achieved; a decrease of approximately 26%. Carstensen concludes that histogram matching of textures has a significant effect on the discriminatory performance of GLCM features.

  We wish to check the sensitivity of our system to the input image equalization. A few classification results on the 10 texture set, with histogram equalization, can be found in Table 2. Only a small decrease in performance of 3% is seen with the multi-layered perceptron. A larger decrease is evident with the k-nearest neighbor classifier. The range of 3% decrease in performance will reappear as we increase our testing to a 30 texture case. These results suggest that the feature-space representation of the system is only minimally sensitive to the 1st-order statistics of the image, and that the combination with the learning schemes preserves the strong classification results. We conclude that the results presented here (in the lab setup) are strongly indicative of our system's performance in real-world scenarios (such as outdoor scenery analysis) where illumination is not predictable.

- *Sensitivity to number of input textures - Scaling up to 30*
  An interesting and important test of a system's performance is the *scalability* of the system with increasing the number of inputs. We extend the results in the literature and check the scalability of the system's performance as we increase the input number to 30 textures. Classification results of the 30 texture database, with varying window sizes, is presented in Table 3. The effect of changing the input representation space via histogram equalization is shown as well.

30 TEXTURE CASE						
window-size	**k-nn**	hist. eq.	**MLP**	hist. eq.	**Rule-based network**	
8×8	82%		89.6%		80%	
16×16	88%	84%	93.4%	91.3%	84%	
32×32	96.6%	95%	98.2%	97.4%	94.4%	
64×64	**95%**		**97.25%**		**97.5%**	

Table 3: *Classification results for 30 textures with different window sizes.*

Several things can be noted from the presented results.
1. There is a decrease in performance from the 10 texture case to the larger set of 30 textures. The decrease is less substantial (less than 3%) as we increase the classification window size to 32×32 and further to 64×64.
2. The results across the three classifiers are similar, especially with the 32×32 and 64×64 size windows.
3. Looking at the histogram equalization results we note the small reduction of $1 - 4\%$. This reinforces our earlier observation in the 10 texture case.

We have highlighted the result for the 64×64 case which is the standard window size in the literature. Strong results are achieved across all three classifiers. As mentioned earlier, very few results can be found in the literature which deal with large databases. A few results for comparison can be found in A.2

3.2.3. SEGMENTATION VIA THE RECOGNITION PROCESS

One advantage of a high-resolution classification scheme (in our case using the 8×8 window resolution), is the ability to achieve *segmentation* of input scenes during the recognition process. This will be exemplified next using the rule-based network.

In the training stage, a set of 6 textures is presented to the system, comprised of grass, raffia, wood, sand, herringbone weave and wool. The training input consists of a 128×128 image patch per texture (256 feature vectors per texture). In the testing phase, a 256×256 image is input to the system, which is a mosaic of 5 of the above textures as shown in Fig. 7 top left. The mosaic is comprised of grass, raffia, herringbone weave, wood and wool (center square) textures. Note that the patches forming the mosaic are *different* from the training patches, with no pixel overlap. The input poses a very difficult task which is challenging even to humans.

The test mosaic is input to the pyramid and feature vectors are extracted, corresponding to 8×8 windows in it. These vectors are quantized and labeled in the classification stage of the system, to give an output label map. Note that the 8×8 classification windows are allowed to overlap boundaries of the input mosaic.

In Fig. 7 we see the input test image (top left) followed by the labeled output map (top right) and the corresponding probability maps for the prelearned library of six textures (bottom). Based on the probability maps (with white indicating probability closer to 1) the very satisfying result of the labeled output map is achieved. The five different regions have been identified and labeled correctly (in different shades of gray) with the boundaries between the regions very strongly evident. We have achieved a segmentation of the image into homogeneous areas via the recognition process.

In this example no smoothing was performed on the output maps. This is evident looking at the output label map with isolated errors found in the interior of the mosaic and most errors located on the segmentation boundaries. The isolated errors can easily be eliminated by incorporating the 2D nature of the problem as a smoothing operation on the extracted probability maps or the final output maps.

3.2.4. PATTERN DISCOVERY

We conclude this section with an additional result which demonstrates the capability of the rule-based learning system to generalize to the identification of an unknown class. In this task a presented pattern, which is not part of the prelearned library, is to be recognized as such and labeled as an unknown area of interest. This task is termed "pattern discovery" and its application is widespread, from identifying unexpected events to the selection of areas of interest in scene exploration studies. Learning the unknown is a difficult problem in which the probability estimates prove to be valuable. Our criterion for declaring an unknown class is when the sum of W_{ij}s (equation (4)) is negative for each class; i.e. there is negative evidence for each prelearned class. In the presented example, of Fig. 8, a three texture library was learned, consisting of the wood, raffia and grass textures. The input consists of wood, raffia and sand (top left). The output label map (top right) which is the result of the analysis of the respective probability maps (bottom) exhibits the accurate detection of the known raffia and wood textures, with the sand area labeled in black as an unknown class. This conclusion was based on the negative weights of evidence for each of the prelearned classes —

indicated as zero probability in the corresponding probability maps. We have thus successfully analyzed the scene based on the existing source of knowledge.

3.3. SUMMARY OF EXPERIMENTS

In this section comparative results between three different classification schemes were presented. Some of the interesting characteristics of the rule-based network classifier in particular, include the following: A minimal (most informative) feature set is learned. The extracted set of classification rules are available to the user. The system can thus enhance the user's knowledge of the input domain via its own extracted rule knowledge base. In addition, the *number* of rules required to cover the input sample space is indicative of the difficulty of the task. Finally, the extracted output probability maps give more information about the decision process than does a hard-decision output.

In the results presented, we have shown high-percentage classification rates for a wide variety of both structured and unstructured textures. The robustness of the system to changes in the input representation as well as the scalability of the system's performance as we increase the input space to a 30 texture database has been demonstrated. Finally, the generalization capability of the system, based on the probability maps, to the identification of an unknown class, so called "pattern discovery", has been exemplified. Overall, the classification results presented in this work are competitive in performance with other techniques widely used in the literature.

Have we solved the texture recognition task at this point? Many of the papers in the field consider this a good stopping point. We pursue our investigation one step further, to ask: What happens to our learned system once we start rotating the inputs?

4.   EXTENDING TO A ROTATION-INVARIANT TEXTURE RECOGNITION SYSTEM

In object recognition and inspection applications controlling the environment to ensure that the samples tested have the same orientation and scale as the training samples is either costly, difficult or altogether impossible. We propose that the next challenge in texture analysis is to achieve rotation- and scale-invariant classification. We concentrate here on the rotation invariance issue. Our defined goal is to recognize new test inputs as belonging to the set of prelearned classes, even if the new input is rotated relative to the original input. Furthermore, we wish to preserve the rotation information and state with high accuracy the *orientation* of the test input relative to the original one.

4.1. THE NEED FOR ROTATION-INVARIANT RECOGNITION

The need to accommodate rotation-invariance in a recognition system can be shown by the decline in performance of a recognition framework, which is not designed with rotation-invariance in mind (and which is not trained on rotated samples). Fig. 9 shows a mis-classification curve for the texture recognition system of section 2. The classification results are averaged over the entire 30 texture database. The degradation in performance with increasing the rotation angle of the test images, is evident and unacceptable beyond 20°. The degradation phenomenon is related to the textures' orientation characteristics: oriented textures are strongly affected by the rotation (and exhibit sharp degradation curves) while nonoriented (or unstructured) textures are only mildly affected by rotation (producing almost uniform curves).

4.2. Previous work in rotation-invariance

Most of the methods presented in the literature address the classification problem under the assumption that the test samples from a given texture possess the *same* orientation as the training samples. Unfortunately, virtually all the methods proposed do not generalize naturally to rotation-invariant recognition. Substantial redesign is necessary to address this issue. A related issue is the one of computing the orientation of a test patch with respect to a reference/training texture.

A number of works can be found in the literature which specifically address the problem of rotation-invariant texture recognition. In [12] averaging over directional co-occurence matrices (such as the four GLCM matrices computed for 0°, 45°, 90° and 135°) is suggested. In this case the orientation information is lost. A "circular autoregressive" random field model, whose parameters could be taken as rotation-invariant features for classification, is suggested in [25]. A more recent work that attempts to classify rotated and scaled textured images using Gaussian MRF models is [9]. In [25] a small database of textures is used (9,12 Brodatz textures), with a small set of samples per texture. In several of the experiments the training actually includes all the rotations of the test set. Finally, there is no immediate generalization to scale invariance. In [9] good classification results are presented on a small database of 9 Brodatz textures, with a single 64×64 image patch used for training and another single 64×64 image patch used in testing. The scalability of the system to a larger database is not shown. In addition, only 2 orientations (0° and 60°) and 3 scales are actually used.

A common feature in the works found in the neural-network literature which "learn" the invariances (e.g.,[40, 31, 16]) is that once a certain network is formulated, it is restricted to recognize rotated input patterns at a specific discrete set of orientations. In addition, the rotation-angle information of the input is lost.

In summary, a limitation of most of the above mentioned (and other) studies is that the invariance is achieved on a small discrete set of orientations, rather than on the $[0, 2\pi)$ continuum. An additional important point is that many of these schemes shift to an invariant representation domain in which orientation information is eliminated altogether in order to achieve the rotation-invariance goal.

4.3. LEARNING THE INVARIANCES

Rotation invariance can be achieved in one of two ways, either by extracting rotation-invariant features or by appropriate training of the classifier to make it 'learn' invariant properties.

Learning invariances from the raw (filtered) data is substantially influenced by the rotation angles which have been included in the system's training set. The more angles, the better the performance. This is exemplified by the solid curves in Fig. 10. In this experiment a test set is constructed by rotating each test window by 5° increments, between 5° and 185°. The initial training set consists of textures rotated by 5° (leftmost point). This is so that all members of the testing and training set have the same amount of error due to the rotation algorithm. We note the low classification results, of 47% for 8×8 windows, 63% for 32×32 windows. As we increase the training set size, with more examples of rotated inputs, the classification results increase substantially. The final result presented (rightmost point) is the case of training on *all* rotations present in the test set. We now achieve 77% in the 8×8 case, and 92% in the 32×32 case.

It is clear that the system has a very difficult time learning to be invariant without sufficient training data. In addition it seems that good results are strongly dependent on the training data including the exact rotation resolution desired for the classification task. The increase in the number of training examples results in a substantial increase in the training time (perceptron) or in the classification time (k-nearest neighbor).

4.4. DFT-ENCODING FOR ROTATION INVARIANCE

In the following we describe a mechanism to extract rotation-invariant features, *prior to* the learning phase, thus allowing for the invariance while preserving the rotation information. For a given input texture we can define a *feature curve* (per scale) across orientation space, $f_c(\theta)$, as the texture's response to any oriented filter in the 360° space (using symmetry considerations we will concentrate on the 180° space). The 4 oriented filter components per scale (of the feature vector) sample the texture's feature curve with 45° sampling period. As an input texture is rotated, its feature curve, $f_c(\theta)$, shifts across the orientation axis. Alternatively we can visualize the sample points cycling along the continuous curve. It is our goal to find a rotation-invariant representation for the sampled curve .

Theoretical analysis into the pyramid filters has been pursued in [19], to show that the 4 oriented filters (per scale) span the orientation space with more than 99% accuracy and form a *steerable* basis. The steerability property indicates that we can interpolate across the 4 filter outputs to reproduce the continuous feature curve. The fact that the 4 samples form a basis on the space enables us to shift to any other 4-dimensional representation of the space, in particular one which provides for rotation-invariance. We will next describe how a Discrete Fourier Transform (DFT) encoding can be used for this task ([19, 18]).

Let $f(n), n = 0..3$, denote the oriented components at a single scale in a given feature vector. A *companion* feature vector, $\hat{f}(k)$, is defined in [19] to be the Discrete Fourier Transform of $f(n)$ as follows [1]:

$$\hat{f}(k) = \sum_{n=0}^{3} f(n)e^{-i\pi nk/2} \qquad k = 0, 1, 2, 3. \tag{6}$$

Using the $\hat{f}(k)$ coefficients, we can represent the original feature curve, $f_c(\theta)$, as:

$$f_c(\theta) = A + B\cos(\theta + C) + \text{rotation-variant term} \tag{7}$$

with the coefficients given by

$$A = \hat{f}(0), B = |\hat{f}(1)|, C = \arg[\hat{f}(1)], \tag{8}$$
$$\text{Nyquist component} = \hat{f}(2).$$

We note that A and B do not change as a result of rotation, while $C/2$ is equal to the rotation angle of the input (The division by two is necessary since $f(n)$ goes through *two* complete cycles during a rotation of the input image by 360°). The value of B represents the strength along the orientation indicated by $C/2$. In this case we do not have a high-enough sampling rate to extract the phase component of the second harmonic. The Nyquist component, which varies with rotation of the input, provides no useful information.

Using the DFT encoding step, we can thus create an *invariant* feature vector which, at each scale, consists of the values of A and B (as above), while the value of $C/2$ may be inspected to determine the rotation angle on the input. The DFT-encoded feature vector is the input to the recognition system. The recognition system we now have is very much the same as the system we had presented and analyzed in section 2, with the DFT encoding step added as part of the feature-extraction phase of the system. In the classification stage we continue to use the rule-based learning algorithm together with the multi-layered perceptron and the k-nearest neighbor algorithms. The updated system block diagram is depicted in Fig. 11.

With DFT encoding the system is successfully invariant, as is demonstrated by the dashed curves in Fig. 10, with almost uniform curves of performance. We note that in this case, training on the original set of 5 degree rotated examples allows us to classify the test inputs at any arbitrary rotation (we associate the slight slope of the curves to the effect of increasing the training set size). We conclude in this case that image deformation invariances are better built into the system than learned. With the original dataset of 5°, the DFT-encoding scheme gives 71% for 8×8 windows (as compared to 47% with learning the invariances) and 91% for the 32×32 windows (as compared to 63%). Direct learning of the invariances can

---

[1] The complete feature vector includes the DFT components for each scale together with the non-oriented components of the Laplacian pyramid.

achieve comparable performance only at a much higher computational complexity (with the dataset size more than 4 times the original size).

We continue with a demonstration of the performance of the DFT-encoded system on the 30 texture database. Here, the test set is constructed by rotating each test window by 5° increments, between 5° and 50°; thus we have 40 test vectors per texture. In the recognition process the extracted filter maps are averaged to produce one representative feature vector, f, per 64×64 window. The extracted feature vector is DFT-encoded to generate the companion feature vector, $\hat{f}$. The magnitudes of the set of DFT-encoded feature-vectors are next presented to the classification system for recognition. To augment the testing results 4 different runs are made, each with a different set of 4 testing windows, and the classification results are averaged over these runs.

30 TEXTURE CLASSIFICATION - 4 cases					
	rot.	DFT	k-nn	MLP	Rule-based
case 1:	N	N	95%	97.25%	97.5%
case 2:	Y	N	80%	67.5%	77.4%
case 3:	N	Y	90%	83%	85.8%
case 4:	Y	Y	91.5%	84.7%	86.6%

Table 4: *Classification results for the 30 texture database of Fig. 6.*

We compare results for 4 different classification scenarios, as given in Table 4. In *case 1* the data is nonrotated and no DFT conversion is performed. High classification rates are achieved (results taken from Table 3). These rates indicate the strength of the recognition system on non-rotated inputs.

In *case 2* the test data is rotated and no DFT conversion is performed. Here the strong decline in performance is evident, as is expected for a non rotation-invariant system. The result presented is averaged over both the oriented and non-oriented textures in the database. Misclassification is almost complete for rotated oriented textures.

In *case 3* the test data is nonrotated but a DFT representation is used. Here we get high classification results, though somewhat reduced from case 1. This is the price paid for shifting to a rotation-invariant representation which makes fewer assumptions about what is known. In using the *magnitude* of the DFT-encoded vectors for the classification task, we ignore the phase information. Therefore we are left with only 2 invariant components out of 4 (we zero out the single phase component and we cannot rely on the Nyquist component). This loss of information results in the reduced performance.

Finally, in *case 4* we have a rotated test set analyzed by the rotation-invariant system. The increase in the results from case 2 are evident. As expected the results are similar to case 3. We are able to classify the varied database of 30 textures rotated at 5° resolution at an accuracy of close to 90%.

Comparable results are achieved across the three classification schemes utilized. The above results augment the state-of-the-art in the domain of large-database rotation-invariant natural texture recognition.

ORIENTATION ESTIMATION

In the context of the recognition stage, only the magnitude of the DFT-encoded feature vector is used. Upon identification, the *phase* of the DFT can be inspected to determine the amount of rotation of the input texture relative to a prestored sample of that texture class. In [18, 19] a thorough investigation is pursued into texture orientation characteristics, via the phase component. The texture family is categorized into non-oriented vs. oriented textures, and rotation angles are extracted for the oriented textures, to an accuracy of approximately 1°. !

5. CONCLUSION

We have presented a texture recognition system which combines a powerful input representation space with learning paradigms for classification. Several non-parametric learning schemes have been used successfully to classify the filtered (feature) space with very high success rates on the challenging 30 texture database. Moreover, rotation-invariant recognition, as well as accurate rotation detection, is accomplished. A similar analysis into scale-invariance is currently under development.

A well known debate is where one should spend more computational effort - in the preprocessing of the input data or in the learning process. In this chapter we advocate the combination of a powerful preprocessing stage, via filtering and encoding the input data, together with non-parametric learning schemes for its classification. We have demonstrated that this combination allows for robustness and invariance.

The texture recognition system is suitable for inclusion in a general vision system. There are a variety of application domains, such as remote sensing [20], automated inspection, medical image processing and large image-database handling in which learning textures can be a valuable component.

The challenges that lie ahead will arise as we try to apply texture recognition systems to real-world scenarios. How many textures do we need to learn in the real world? Will 30 textures suffice, or do we need larger databases? Or is the real need to identify only a few texture classes, but with more variability within each individual class (such as identifying all "wood" textures in the environment, as a single class)? Certainly, a major challenge is the transition to fully-invariant recognition systems. Finally, another area that is yet to be addressed is the need and the capability for real-time implementations.

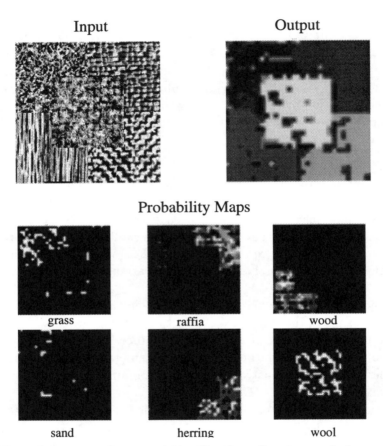

Input

Output

Probability Maps

grass   raffia   wood

sand   herring   wool

Figure 7: *Five class natural texture classification. Input mosaic is presented (top left), followed by the labeled output map (top right) and probability maps (bottom). White areas indicate high probability. In the label map the different grey levels correspond to the 5 classes identified. Adapted from [23].*

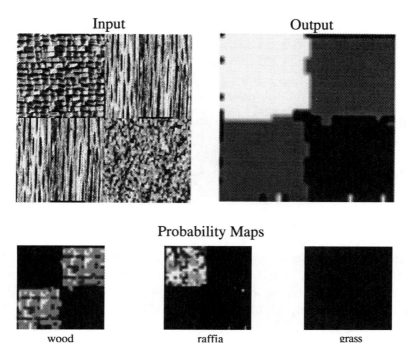

Figure 8: *Generalization to an unknown class. Adapted from [23].*

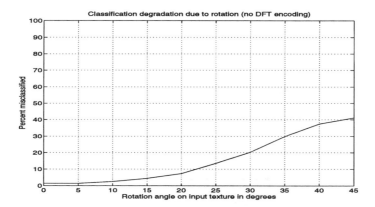

Figure 9: *Average degradation in the classification performance of a non rotation-invariant texture classifier with respect to rotation angle of the sample texture patch, 30 texture database.*

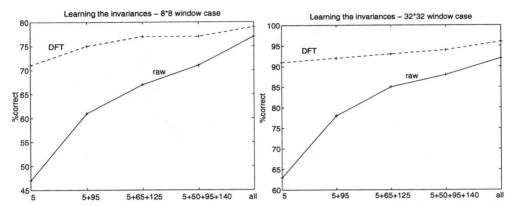

Figure 10: *Learning the invariances (solid) vs. DFT encoding (dashed — discussed in section 4.4). k-nearest neighbor classification is used on the 30 texture database. Test set includes 5° increments, between 5° and 185°. The 5 trials (x axis-left to right) include: training on 5°, training on 5°&95°, training on 5°, 65°&125°, training on 5°, 50°, 95°&140° degrees, and training on all test angles.*

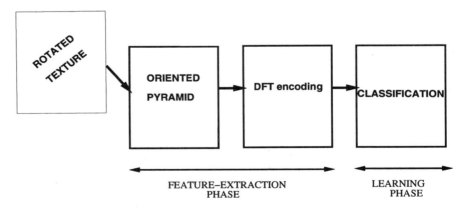

Figure 11: *System Block Diagram*

APPENDIX

A. COMPARISON WITH THE LITERATURE

A.1. 10 TEXTURE CASE

We will quote a few results from the computer vision literature for a set of 10 textures and varying classification window sizes. These results can be compared to the results in Table 2 of section 3. In [7] *GMRF models* are used on a set of 7 textures. Several features sets are used. Results presented are in the range of 93%–99% for 64×64 window sizes, with two cases of 82% and 93% given for the 32×32 window case. In [38] *sums and differences of histograms* are used and compared to *co-occurrence matrices* on a set of 12 textures. Results include (histogram results versus co-occurrence results): 88.2% versus 86.7% for 16×16 windows; 96.8% versus 93.23% for 32×32 windows; and 97.92% versus 95.83% for 64×64 windows. Finally, quoting one work which uses *Gabor filters* for the classification task we cite results from [8] in which a set of 8 textures are used with results of 98% for 64×64 windows reducing to 91% for 32×32 windows.

A.2. 30 TEXTURE CASE

A 25 texture case can be found in [24] in which information trees are used. The results quoted there vary from 70% on 20×20 window sizes to 87% on 40×40 size windows. The more recent results are related to the wavelet representation of textures. In [27] 25 textures are classified. Classification windows of size 128×128 are used with an overlap between the extracted windows. High classification results are achieved. Another recent wavelet work is [6] in which 30 textures are classified: 256×256 size windows are used in one experiment, 64×64 windows with strong overlap are used in another. Our results (see Table 3) compare favorably to the last two works mentioned. We have not found the 8×8 classification resolution quoted in the literature. In addition, the proposed wavelet schemes can not be generalized to be rotation invariant. This is a major feature of our system as presented in section 4.

ACKNOWLEDGEMENTS

I wish to thank my collaborators in the different stages of this work: Charles Anderson, Serge Belongie, Rama Chellappa, Rod Goodman and Pietro Perona. Thanks to Serge Belongie, Jeff Dickson, Rod Goodman, Bushan Gupta, Pietro Perona and Padhraic Smyth for reviewing this chapter and providing valuable comments. This work was supported in part by ARPA and ONR under grant no. N00014-92-J-1860. The author is supported in part by an Intel research grant.

REFERENCES

[1] M. Clark A. C. Bovik and W. S. Geisler. Multichannel texture analysis using

localized spatial filters. *IEEE Transactions on Pattern Analysis and Machine Intelligence*, 12:55–73, 1990.

[2] P. Brodatz. *Textures*. Dover, New York, 1966.

[3] P. J. Burt and E. A. Adelson. The Laplacian pyramid as a compact image code. *IEEE Transactions on Communications*, 31:532–540, 1983.

[4] F. W. Campbell and J. G. Robson. Application of Fourier analysis to the visibility of gratings. *Journal of Physiology*, 197:551–566, 1968.

[5] J. M. Carstensen. *Description and Simulation of Visual texture*. PhD thesis, The Technical University of Denmark, Lyngby, Denmark, 1992.

[6] T. Chang and C. C. J. Kuo. Texture analysis and classification with tree-structured wavelet transform. *IEEE Transactions on Image Processing*, 2(4):429–441, 1993.

[7] R. Chellappa and S. Chatterjee. Classification of textures using Gaussian Markov Random Fields. *IEEE Transactions on Acoustics, Speech and Signal Procesing*, 33(4):959–963, 1985.

[8] J. Coggins and A. Jain. A spatial filtering approach to texture analysis. *Pattern Recognition Letters*, pages 195–203, 1985.

[9] F. S. Cohen, Z. Fan, and M. A. Patel. Classification of rotated and scaled textured images using Gaussian Markov Random Field models. *IEEE Transactions on Pattern Analysis and Machine Intelligence*, 13(2):192–202, 1991.

[10] R. Cross and A. Jain. Markov random field texture models. *IEEE Transactions on Pattern Analysis and Machine Intelligence*, 5:25–39, 1983.

[11] J. G. Daugman. Uncertainty relation for resolution, spatial frequency, and orientation optimized by 2d visual cortical filters. *Journal of the Optical Society of America A*, 2:1160–1169, 1985.

[12] L. S. Davis, S. Johns, and J. K. Aggarwal. Texture analysis using generalized co-occurance matrices. *IEEE Transactions on Pattern Analysis and Machine Intelligence*, 1:251–259, 1979.

[13] R. L. Devalois, D. G. Albrecht, and L. G. Thorell. Spatial-frequency selectivity of cells in macaque visual cortex. *Vision Research*, 22:545–559, 1982.

[14] R. O. Duda and P. E. Hart. *Pattern Classification and Scene Analysis*. John Wiley and Sons Inc., 1973.

[15] D. H. Field. Relations between the statistics of natural images and the response properties of cortical cells. *Journal of the Optical Society of America A*, 4:2379–2394, 1987.

[16] M. Fukumi, S. Omatu, F. Takeda, and T. Kosaka. Rotation-invariant neural pattern recognition system with application to coin recognition. *IEEE Transactions on Neural Networks*, 3(2):272–279, 1992.

[17] R. M. Goodman, C. Higgins, J. Miller, and P. Smyth. Rule-based networks for classification and probability estimation. *Neural Computation*, 4:781–804, 1992.

[18] H. Greenspan, S. Belongie, P. Perona, and R. Goodman. Rotation invariant texture recognition using a steerable pyramid. In *Proceedings of the 12th International Conference on Pattern Recognition*, volume II, pages 162–167, 1994.

[19] H. Greenspan, S. Belongie, P. Perona, R. Goodman, S. Rakshit, and C. H. Anderson. Overcomplete steerable pyramid filters and rotation invariance. In *Proceedings of the IEEE Conference on Computer Vision and Pattern Recognition*, pages 222–228, June 1994.

[20] H. Greenspan and R. Goodman. Remote sensing image analysis via a texture classification neural network. In *Advances in Neural Information Processing Systems 5*, pages 425–432, San Mateo, CA, 1993. Morgan Kaufmann.

[21] H. Greenspan, R. Goodman, R. Chellappa, and C. Anderson. Learning texture discrimination rules in a multiresolution system. *IEEE Transactions on Pattern Analysis and Machine Intelligence*, 16(9):894–901, September 1994.

[22] R. Haralick. Statistical and structural approaches to texture. *Proceedings of the IEEE*, 67(5):610–621, 1979.

[23] R. M. Haralick and L. G. Shapiro. *Computer and Robot Vision*, volume I. Addison-Wesley Publishing Company, 1992.

[24] D. R. Hougen and S. M. Omohundro. Fast texture recognition using information trees. Technical Report UIUCDCS-R-88-1409, University of Urbana Champaign, 1988.

[25] R. L. Kashyap and A. Khotanzad. A model-based method for rotation invariant texture classification. *IEEE Transactions on Pattern Analysis and Machine Intelligence*, 8(4):472–481, 1986.

[26] H. E. Knutsson and G. H. Granlund. Texture analysis using two-dimensional quadrature filters. In *IEEE Workshop on Computer Architectures for Pattern Analysis and Image Database Management*, pages 206–213. IEEE Computer Society, 1983.

[27] A. Lain and J. Fan. Texture classification by wavelet packet signatures. *IEEE Transactions on Pattern Analysis and Machine Intelligence*, 15(11):1186–1191, 1993.

[28] S. Y. Lu and S. Fu. Stochastic tree grammar inference for texture synthesis and discrimination. *Computer Graphics and Image Processing*, 9:234–245, 1979.

[29] J. Malik and P. Perona. Preattentive texture discrimination with early vision mechanisms. *Journal of the Optical Society of America A*, 7:923–932, 1990.

[30] B. S. Manjunath, T. Simchony, and R. Chellappa. Stochastic and deterministic networks for texture segmentation. *IEEE Transactions on Acoustics, SPeech and SIgnal processing*, 38(6):1039–1049, 1990.

[31] S. J. Perantonis and P. J. G. Lisboa. Translation, rotation, and scale invariant pattern recognition by high-order neural networks and moment classifiers. *IEEE Transactions on Neural Networks*, 3(2):241–251, 1992.

[32] P. Perona. Deformable kernels for early vision. In *IEEE Conference on Computer Vision and Pattern Recognition*, pages 222–227, June 1991.

[33] M. Porat and Y. Y. Zeevi. The generalized gabor scheme of image representation in biological and machine vision. *IEEE Transactions on Pattern Analysis and Machine Intelligence*, 10:452–468, 1988.

[34] D. Rumelhart, G. Hinton, and R. Williams. Learning internal representations by error propagation. In D. Rumelhart and J. McClelland, editors, *Parallel Distributed Processing*, chapter 8. MIT Press, Cambridge MA, 1986.

[35] P. Smyth and R. Goodman. An information theoretic approach to rule induction from databases. *IEEE Transactions on Knowledge and Data Engineering*, 4(4):301–316, 1992.

[36] M. Tuceryan and A. K. Jain. *The Handbook of Pattern Recognition and Computer Vision*, chapter 11. World Scientific Publishing Company, 1992.

[37] M. R. Turner. Texture discrimination by gabor functions. *Biological Cybernetics*, 55:71–82, 1986.

[38] M. Unser. Sum and difference histograms for texture classification. *IEEE Transactions on Pattern Analysis and Machine Intelligence*, 8(1):118–125, 1986.

[39] F. M. Vilnrotter, R. Nevatia, and K. E. Price. Structural analysis of natural textures. *IEEE Transactions on Pattern Analysis and Machine Intelligence*, 8:76–89, 1986.

[40] B. Widrow, R. Winter, and R. Baxter. Layered neural nets for pattern recognition. *IEEE Transactions on Acoustics, Speech, and Signal Processing*, 36(7):1109–1118, 1988.

13   UNSUPERVISED VISUO-TACTILE LEARNING FOR CONTROL OF MANIPULATION

Marcos Salganicoff
University of Delaware

Michele Rucci
The Neurosciences Institute

Ruzena Bajcsy
University of Pennsylvania

ABSTRACT

Vision and touch are critical sources of sensory information for the control of manipulation. They provide consistent and shared information, in the sense that visual events can lead to predictable tactile events by means of motor interaction and vice-versa. By learning such correlations, the performance of manipulation tasks can be greatly improved.

We develop an artificial neural network learning method for the control of visual attention in manipulation. The system learns to react to visual and tactile stimuli, shifting the direction of gaze so as to foveate on them. An implementation of the approach by means of an articulated monocular camera head and a tactile sensitive arm is presented.

An active learning method for grasping objects based on visual input from a range scanner and tactile grasp assessment is then presented. A statistically–based exploration heuristic is used to decrease the amount of unnecessary training cost by smoothly combining exploration and exploitation. The active learning method allows the system to select its actions for more rapid performance improvement in a particular task. As a result, good performance is achieved in fewer trials than would be required by an equivalent passive learning system.

1.   INTRODUCTION AND OVERVIEW

One of the major efforts of robotics research is the development of systems that can autonomously operate in unknown and unstructured environments. An enormous number of applications, from the complete substitution of human operators in hazardous environments to assistive robotics for disabled users, require autonomy. Many basic problems related to perceptual and motor capabilities make the development of fully autonomous systems an elusive goal. Engineering vision and manipulation systems generally requires a large amount of *a priori* knowledge and assumptions about the system and environment of operation. Incorporating this information decreases the system's flexibility, since it is difficult to take into consideration all possible scenarios. Adding learning to a system endows it with an ability to adapt to new situations and changes in its own perceptual–motor apparatus, as well as enabling it to improve its performance in given tasks through practice.

1.1. Autonomous development of manipulatory capabilities

Thanks to recent technological advances, several models of robotic multi-fingered hands are now available [61, 27, 9] and they can be equipped with different kinds of tactile sensors [19, 25]. Also several control approaches have been proposed, based either on the kinematic and force modeling of the system [47, 34, 61, 19], 2-dimensional contour analysis [68], hierarchical voxel decompositions [6], or on the selection of stored hand configurations according to a variety of heuristic rules [8, 18]. However, many perceptual and motor subproblems must be considered in different tasks, and many of the basic problems have only been partially solved.

In this chapter we describe a general approach to manipulation based on attentive behavior and autonomous motor learning of sensorimotor coordination. In this approach, sensory inputs are associated with motor actions on the basis of sensory feedback and consistencies using unsupervised learning methods.

1.2. Learning multi-modal attention for manipulation

Sensory inputs to support manipulation consist primarily of vision, which returns shape and pose information, and touch (combined with proprioceptive inputs) which can return surface texture, information on the properties of the object material, and additional shape information. In general the role of visual and tactile perception in manipulation tasks is fairly complementary, and many properties of the explored objects can be acquired with only one of these sensory modalities. Events in one modality can prompt sensing actions for exploration and verification in the other modalities [2]. As a result, the study of manipulation implies the integration of attentive mechanisms belonging to different modalities.

Inter-modal attentive cues are crucial for successful manipulation in unstructured environments. Depending on the task and the current state of the system, different sensory stimuli require different motor responses, implying that at any time sensory inputs should have a different degree of conspicuousness. The capability of locating a new object to grasp or rapidly reacting to unexpected situations depends on attentive mechanisms. Selective attention has recently received the interest of researchers in the machine perception community, especially for controlling robotic head-eye systems [1]. However, most efforts have focused mainly on the case of vision, whereas other sensory modalities have not been considered.

This inter-modal attention problem is extremely challenging, since the separate perceptual processes express their output in vastly different coordinate systems which must be fused into a common coordinate system from which the correct action to control the attentive sensors may be computed. We derive the coordinate transformation using an on-line artificial neural network learning algorithm that obviates the need for a separate calibration phase and provides a common frame in which the different competing attentive perceptual cues may be combined and then selected.

1.3. ACTIVE LEARNING FOR VISION-BASED GRASPING

Grasping is probably the most studied manipulatory operation. From a mechanics standpoint, a successful grasp depends on a variety of parameters, such as the type of contact (e.g. point or soft), friction, shape, compliance, and mass distribution of the object. There has been much important progress in analytical approaches for designing grasps [47, 61, 19] and in heuristic approaches [26, 41, 18] for grasp selection. However, many of the analytical techniques employ simplifying assumptions which may or may not hold in all real cases, and both analytical and heuristic approaches require measurement of many object properties, such as shape and material properties, which are difficult to extract reliably. Instead of employing analytical techniques or fixed heuristic rules, we focus on learning grasp rules based on the results of the robot's attempts to grasp different objects, where the rules are expressed through an inductively generated decision tree over a real-valued feature space.

When a learning problem requires physical interaction during each attempt, each failure may be costly. For example, an expensive object may be dropped and damaged during grasping. Additionally, large costs in terms of time for sensory processing before and during the attempt may be incurred. Therefore each action should be carefully chosen to yield both the largest amount of new information in exploration and, if possible, to exploit the information gained during previous trials. *Active learning* refers to the selection of components of the learning set during the course of training so as to trade off exploration and exploitation. An active learning algorithm permits the selection of the input values of the input/output pairs in the learning set. By using active learning a system controls the course of its information gathering to improve learning speed and to begin exploitation as soon as possible.

1.4. CHAPTER OVERVIEW

The chapter is organized as follows: Section 2 focuses on the problem of attention control in manipulation tasks and describes a general attentional learning framework along with an implemented robot system which embodies the approach;

Section 3 describes the active learning algorithm, the associated grasping system and its performance; finally, we conclude with a discussion of the approach and future directions for research.

2.   AUTONOMOUS LEARNING OF SOMATOSENSORY SACCADES

Many recently proposed paradigms in the field of machine perception [4, 5] have demonstrated that selective attention can play a crucial role in overcoming some classical perceptual difficulties and help move towards real–time visual capabilities. Attentional mechanisms enable the system to select what is relevant from the flow of incoming data. When movement of the visual sensor is possible, attentive mechanisms are necessary to control the direction of gaze and the spatial orientations of the cameras. By using a set of sensorimotor transformations that convert the sensory locations of the stimuli into corresponding positions of the visual sensors, fixation on the selected stimuli is accomplished.

The majority of recent work in selective visual attention via control of eye movements has not investigated attentive mechanisms related to sensory modalities other than vision. In particular, tactile attentive mechanisms have so far received very limited interest, in spite of the fact that touch–driven attention is crucial for all systems that physically interact with the surrounding environment. *Somatosensory saccades*, defined as visual saccades triggered by tactile stimuli should be considered in basic interactive operations such as manipulation and navigation. By means of somatosensory saccades, visual processing can be focused on obstacles that have been unintentionally hit during a motor action and new motor control strategies can be planned. In general, touch–driven attention mechanisms are powerful tools for dealing with *a priori* unknown environments.

Humans can switch their attention toward cutaneous stimuli without conscious effort. Somatosensory saccades can occur whenever an unexpected tactile stimulus is sensed, such as when an insect moves on one's arm. However, the mechanisms involved in the process are not clear, and researchers in neurophysiology and psychophysics have only recently begun to investigate the point [22].

The system described in this section provides an example of an autonomous adaptive system with multi-sensory attentive capabilities. A general architecture for integrating attentive mechanisms belonging to different modalities depending on the task is described, and an implementation for vision and touch is illustrated. Learning capabilities are included in the system so as to build adaptive sensorimotor coordination whereby the system develops its own functional models and changes the way it interacts with the world depending on its goal.

2.1.   INTEGRATING MULTI-SENSORY ATTENTION PROCESSES

Deciding whether to attend to a specific sensory stimulus requires comparing the saliency of simultaneous attentive cues in the context of the task and the current state. This implies that cues should be represented in a common reference

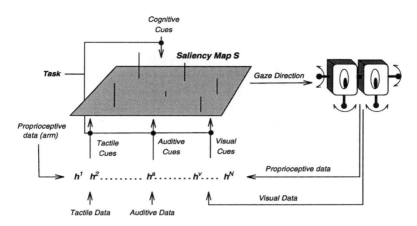

Figure 1: *The proposed architecture. Data belonging to different sensory modalities are separately processed by dedicated modules so as to activate corresponding locations of a common head-centered saliency map. The location with maximum value of activation indicates next gaze direction. Cues are weighted differently depending on the current task.*

frame, independent on the original sensory modalities. A series of *coordinate transformations* needs to be performed in order to transform input data expressed in specific sensory reference frames, such as activation of the receptors of cameras for vision or activation of specific tactile receptors for touch, into a reference frame suitable for the execution of visual saccades.

A general system architecture capable of integrating attention mechanisms operating in different sensory modalities in real–time, and also incorporating task constraints has been recently proposed in [17, 53]. The system is organized in a sensorimotor loop: the analysis of the incoming data produces a set of possible gaze directions. Within this set, the actual direction is selected on the basis of the absolute strength of the stimulus and of its importance in the context of the task. After gaze has been shifted, a new set of interesting directions is generated and is added to the previous one.

As illustrated in Figure 1, the logical center of the architecture is a modified saliency map S [36], whose location s_{ij} represents the saliency of a specific visual direction (ϕ_i, ψ_i) in an absolute head–centered reference frame. All possible visual directions are represented on the saliency map and a monotonic mapping exists between the saliency map and the motor of the cameras, so that, given a specific location of the map, corresponding positions of the cameras are determined. It is not necessary to specify which visual direction corresponds to a specific map location. The actual transformation is autonomously learned by the system so as to compensate for inaccuracies and alterations of the underlying mechanical and optical systems.

Let $D = \{d_1, \ldots, d_M\}$ be the input perceptual data to the system at time t and

P the current posture of the system $P = \{p_1, \ldots, p_L\}$. As illustrated in Figure 1, sensory data are analyzed by a set of continuous–time processes $\{\mathbf{h}^1, \ldots, \mathbf{h}^N\}$, for each of the outputs of processes which operate on sensory inputs. In general there can be more than one process for a single modality: for example, there might be a process which extracts points of high contrasts, while another selects regions with high brightness, and so forth. The resulting set of attentional processes are

$$\mathbf{h}^k(D^k, P^k) = \begin{pmatrix} l_{11}^k & \cdots & l_{1,N_s^\phi}^k \\ \vdots & \ddots & \vdots \\ l_{N_s^\psi,1}^k & \cdots & l_{N_s^\psi,N_s^\phi}^k \end{pmatrix} \tag{1}$$

$$l_{ij}^k \in [0,1]$$

where each process acts on a subset of the input data D^k typically belonging to a single sensory modality and gives the saliency l_{ij}^k for each location i, j on the saliency map. Here N_s^ψ and N_s^ϕ are the number of units in each dimension for the saliency map, which in the case of visual attention, code for the azimuth ψ and elevation ϕ of the sensor in head-centered coordinates. The l_{ij}^k values with nonzero saliency are the *attentive cues* generated by process $\mathbf{h}^k$ and are candidates for drawing attention.

In addition to the perceptual information, the function $\mathbf{h}^k$ is also dependent on the posture of some parts of the system, that is $\mathbf{h}^k = \mathbf{h}^k(D^k, P^k)$. For example, all the processes that operate on visual data provide cues located in the visual field, and the projection of the visual field on the saliency map changes with the position of the eyes with respect to the head. Each attentive process carries out the coordinate transformation necessary for activating the head–centered saliency map, starting from data expressed in a sensory reference frame. As illustrated in Figure 1, all the sensory processes contribute to activating the saliency map, so that the final value assumed by element s_{ij} is given by

$$S_{ij} = F_s(\sum_k w_T^k l_{ij}^k) \tag{2}$$

where F_s is a nonlinear monotonic function (in the experiments, a sigmoidal function has been applied) in $[0,1]$.

Due to system modularity, other cues can be easily included. For example, semantic cues produced from knowledge-based expectations can also contribute to the activation of the saliency map if the system incorporates a fragmentary representation of the objects to be recognized [54]. By means of such representation, the identification of a feature which characterizes a known object can stimulate the system to look in different directions in order to find other particular features that can contribute to better assessing object identity. A number of theories of visual recognition based on the sequence of gaze directions have been proposed [48, 44, 71]. In general, due to the organization of the system, no distinction is formally made between sensory and semantic cues, and both can contribute to attention control.

Several rules can be implemented for selecting the actual direction of gaze. In the experiments described, the direction with the maximum activation has been chosen.

The dependence on the task at hand is produced by the task weights w_T^k. As shown in Equation 2, the cues of each sensory process $\mathbf{h}^k$ are weighted in the saliency map by a set of time–varying values

$$\mathbf{w}_T = (w_T^1, w_T^2, \ldots, w_T^N)^T \qquad w_T^k \in [0, 1] \tag{3}$$

which are adjusted accordingly to the current task, and normalized so that

$$\sum_{k=1}^{N} w_T^k = 1 \tag{4}$$

In this way, on the basis of the task, a priority degree can be assigned to different sensory features. By properly arranging the weight values, it is possible to select a sensory stimulus with respect to others and/or to inhibit irrelevant cues. As a result, the attended task changes the way the system reacts to sensory stimuli and interacts with the external world.

2.2. A NEURAL NETWORK-BASED IMPLEMENTATION

The system is initially provided with basic motor reflexes which generate specific motor actions when input stimuli are detected. In particular, a shift of gaze direction is produced whenever a visual or a tactile stimulus is monitored. This is accomplished by means of the hard-wired connections existing between locations of the saliency map and positions of the visual system.

Two simultaneous learning processes are included in the system: *before* the execution of a saccade, the emerging coordinations can be refined on the basis of the inconsistencies among the representations of the same physical event in different sensory modalities. *After* the execution of the motor action, learning can occur by making use of the new sensory detections. Both the processes contribute to the final result and account for more robust behavior and shorter adaptation times.

In the first learning process, corrections occur on the basis of comparisons among the results of several processes. Usually, physical events can be detected by more than a single sensory modality, and the distances between the simultaneous cues give a measure of the current consistency of the process. A simple possibility is to assume one of the modalities is dominant and use it as a supervisor for the others. The association and consistency among separate modalities is a powerful tool for developing coherent behavior [39, 51]. Invariants in the multi-sensory stimuli patterns can be extracted and models of the world developed. Furthermore, if intrinsic sensory modalities such as proprioception, are considered, it is possible to develop dynamic models of the system's functional structure, that is, the system can discover its own organization while interacting with the environment [23, 42, 39].

In the second type of learning, sensorimotor coordination is modified on the basis of the retinotopic error recorded after the execution of a saccade. Sensory feedback-based learning has been applied to several problems, such as the autonomous development of invariant visual representations [38] and cutaneomotor coordination [55].

The considered system is derived from the general architecture described in the previous section, and it includes two attentive processes: a visual process $\mathbf{h}^v$ and a cutaneous one $\mathbf{h}^c$. In the initial stage of development, an *exploration task* is selected which gives priority to visual stimuli over tactile stimuli, that is the task weights for visual cues are larger. In this way, visuo-motor coordination can be developed faster than cutaneomotor coordination, and the visual sensory modality can be used as a reference in the consistency-based learning process. Processes $\mathbf{h}^c$ and $\mathbf{h}^v$ are implemented by means of neural networks techniques, as illustrated in Figure 2.

The input *sensory maps* C and R code the incoming tactile and visual stimuli in a somatotopic and retinotopic reference frame, respectively. That is, both maps show a topographic organization where units close to each other are sensitive to stimuli occurring in adjacent locations of the receptors layout. Two input *motor maps* M^v and M^c code the position of the system as detected by proprioceptive data (the data is provided by robot encoders). In particular, M^c represents the posture of the parts of the system which have tactile capabilities, and M^v codes the camera position. The units of all the input maps are characterized by coarse coded Gaussian receptive fields, so that the activation value of each unit is a Gaussian function of the distance between the input and a specific value for the unit.

As illustrated in Figure 2, in both sensory modalities the input sensory and motor maps activate the units of a three-layered sensory-topic columnar organization. In the visual sensory modality each column is composed of three units v_{ij}, v_{ij}^ϕ, v_{ij}^ψ located in the maps V, V^ϕ V^ψ respectively. Their activation is given by

$$
\begin{aligned}
V_{ij} &= d_{ij} R_{ij} \\
V_{ij}^\phi &= F_\tau(V_{ij}) \left(\textstyle\sum_{pq} w_{pq}^\phi M_{pq}^v + y_{ij}^\phi \right) \\
V_{ij}^\psi &= F_\tau(V_{ij}) \left(\textstyle\sum_{pq} w_{pq}^\psi M_{pq}^v + y_{ij}^\psi \right)
\end{aligned}
\tag{5}
$$

where F_τ is a step function with threshold τ, R_{ij} is the activation of unit r_{ij} in the retinotopic sensory map R, and M_{pq}^v is the activation of unit m_{pq}^v in the visual motor map M^v.

The units of the bottom map V are fully connected with the units of the saliency map S. However, the strength of the connections are weighted as a function of the activation of the other two units of the same column $< i, j >$, so

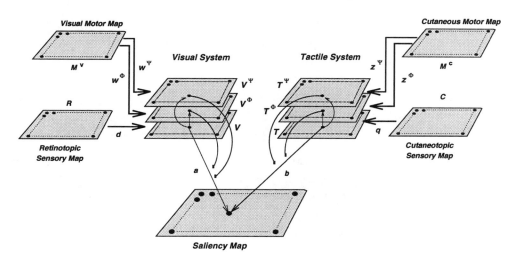

Figure 2: *In both sensory modalities, the activation of the motor–proprioceptive maps and the sensory maps are combined in a sensory-topic columnar organization which produces the corresponding cues for the saliency map.*

that a spatial inhibitory organization is present in the connection scheme. The connection weight between units v_{pq} and s_{ij} is given by

$$a_{pq}^{ij} = \begin{cases} 1 & \text{if } \|(V_{ij}^{\phi}, V_{ij}^{\psi}) - (i/N_s^{\phi}, j/N_s^{\psi})\| < \tau_v \\ 0 & \text{otherwise} \end{cases} \tag{6}$$

where τ_v is an *a priori* set threshold, and N_s^{ϕ} and N_s^{ψ} are the numbers of units along the two directions of the saliency map. This equation converts the activation of the units $v_{pq}^{\phi}, v_{pq}^{\psi}$ back into a topographic representation. In other words, the activations of v_{pq}^{ψ} and v_{pq}^{ϕ} determine where to project the retinotopic input on the saliency map.

Learning occurs by properly modifying the weights y_{ij} and w_{ij}. Weights are updated on the basis of the retinotopic error $\epsilon = (\epsilon_x, \epsilon_y)$ registered after the execution of a visuomotor saccade. System weights are modified as follows:

$$\begin{aligned} y_{ij}^{\phi}(t+1) &= y_{ij}^{\phi}(t) + k_y^{\phi} \epsilon_x V_{ij} \\ w_{ij}^{\phi}(t+1) &= w_{ij}^{\phi}(t) + k_m^{\phi} \epsilon_x M_{ij}^{v} \end{aligned} \tag{7}$$

$$\begin{aligned} y_{ij}^{\psi}(t+1) &= y_{ij}^{\psi}(t) + k_y^{\psi} \epsilon_y V_{ij} \\ w_{ij}^{\psi}(t+1) &= w_{ij}^{\psi}(t) + k_m^{\psi} \epsilon_y M_{ij}^{v} \end{aligned} \tag{8}$$

Here the k's represent the learning rate coefficients. In the visual case a linear model can be adopted by separately adding the visual and motor contributions, since they can always be considered independent for every position of the cameras and the stimuli. In the tactile system a similar linear separation is not feasible: foveation angles are a non-additive function of the position of the tactile stimulus in the cutaneotopic reference frame and all the angles defining arm position. Thus, in the columnar organization in Figure 2, the activation of the units t_{ij}, t_{ij}^{ϕ} and t_{ij}^{ψ} in the three layers $\mathcal{T}$, $\mathcal{T}^{\phi}$ and $\mathcal{T}^{\psi}$ is given by

$$
\begin{aligned}
T_{ij} &= q_{ij} C_{ij} \\
T_{ij}^{\phi} &= F_{\tau}(T_{ij}) \left(\sum_{pq} z_{pqij}^{\phi} M_{pq}^{c} \right) \\
T_{ij}^{\psi} &= F_{\tau}(T_{ij}) \left(\sum_{pq} z_{pqij}^{\psi} M_{pq}^{c} \right)
\end{aligned}
\tag{9}
$$

where C_{ij} is the activation of unit i, j in the cutaneotopic sensory map $\mathcal{C}$ and M_{pq}^{c} the activation of unit p, q in the tactile motor map $\mathcal{M}^{c}$. Also, in the tactile sub–system, the units of the bottom map $\mathcal{T}$ are fully connected with the units of the saliency map, and the connections are inhibited by the activation of the units of the other two layers. The connection weight between units t_{pq} and s_{ij} is given by

$$
b_{ij}^{pq} = \begin{cases} 1 & \text{if } \|(T_{ij}^{\phi}, T_{ij}^{\psi}) - (i/N_{s}^{\phi}, j/N_{s}^{\psi})\| < \tau_{c} \\ 0 & \text{otherwise} \end{cases}
\tag{10}
$$

In the tactile system adaptation is provided by changes in the weights $z_{pqij}^{\phi}, z_{pqij}^{\psi}$. In this case, both learning processes of Equation 8 contribute to updating the connection weights. If the tactile stimulus has a visual counterpart which happens to be in the visual field, then vision is the dominant sensory modality, and the difference between the visual and tactile cues on the saliency map is used as a target error for improving performance. If only a tactile stimulus is present, a somatosensory saccade is attempted on the basis of the current status of the system, and the resulting retinotopic error is then used in the learning equations. In both cases weights are updated as

$$
\begin{aligned}
z_{pqij}^{\phi}(t+1) &= b_{pqij}^{\phi}(t) + k_{b}^{\phi} \delta_{x} M_{pq}^{c} \\
z_{pqij}^{\psi}(t+1) &= b_{pqij}^{\psi}(t) + k_{b}^{\psi} \delta_{y} M_{pq}^{c}
\end{aligned}
\tag{11}
$$

where $\delta = (\delta_{x}, \delta_{y})$ can be the retinotopic or the angular error, depending on which learning process is applied. In the tactile subsystem it is worth noting that, even if the full connectivity of the adaptive layer may appear to necessitate a large number of connections, this is not necessarily the case. In general, highly accurate somatosensory saccades are not necessary; thus a smaller number of units in both the motor and sensory maps can be employed. Less accurate somatosensory saccades with respect to visuomotor saccades have also been found in humans [22].

2.3. EXPERIMENTAL RESULTS

In order to verify the approach and system performance both simulations and real robotic experiments have been carried out. The simulated system consists of the planar 1 d-o-f head-eye and 2 d-o-f arm illustrated in Figure 3.

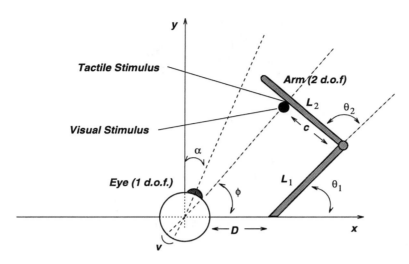

Figure 3: *The system used in the simulations. The position of a 1 d.o.f. eye with respect to a head–centered reference system is given by the angle $\alpha \in (-\pi/2, \pi/2)$, and the position of the 2 d.o.f. arm is specified by (θ_1, θ_2), both in the range $(0, 2\pi/3)$. Only tactile stimuli on the second joint were considered in the experiments $(c \in [0 - L_2])$.*

Random initial positions of the system (arm and head) and of the stimulus, which can be either in only one or both the sensory modalities, are selected. Visual stimuli are simulated as bright spots in the visual field, and tactile stimuli are assumed to always have a visual counterpart, as shown in the figure.

In this case, all the maps are mono-dimensional, except $\mathcal{M}^c$ which is bi-dimensional. The activation of the units in the cutaneotopic map code the position of the tactile stimulus c, whereas units in the retinotopic map code the position of the visual stimulus v on the mono-dimensional retina. The proprioceptive maps represent the position α of the eye and the posture (θ_1, θ_2) of the arm. Also, the saliency map is mono-dimensional and codes the saliency of the visual directions ϕ. Only two layers are present in the columnar organization since the saliency map codes a single visual direction in this case.

Figure 4 illustrates the accuracy of visuo-motor and somatosensory saccades at different developmental stages. After a few thousand iterations, typical performance values are around 1.5% of the visual field for visuo-motor saccades, and 10% of the manipulatory range for somatosensory saccades.

In the robotic experiments, two PUMA 560 robotic manipulators are used. One of the two PUMA manipulators is used as a head/eye visual system, with a monochrome camera mounted as an end–effector. Only the last two joints of the manipulator are allowed to move, so that the visual system is provided with two degrees of freedom ψ (pan) and ϕ (tilt). On the other PUMA a tactile sensitive probe was mounted as the end–effector. For this purpose, a Force/Torque sensor

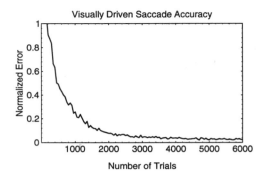 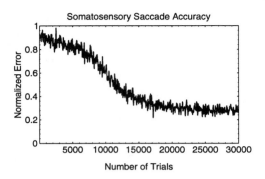

Figure 4: *Performance of the system with learning.* (Left) *Visual performance: average foveation error when visual stimuli are applied.* (Right) *Tactile performance: average foveation error when cutaneous stimuli are applied. Average errors are evaluated on a fixed number of tests. The system is implemented with 150 units in all the visual maps and 20 units in the tactile maps. All weights are updated with* $k = 0.05$

Foveation Error		
iteration	*mean*	σ^2
50	0.17	0.26
200	0.08	0.05
400	0.05	0.03
600	0.02	0.01

Table 1: *Accuracy of visuomotor saccades at different levels of learning*

is used, and the location of contact is derived by the monitored data values under the assumption that only a single contact occurs at any time. Also the manipulator holding the tactile probe is allowed 2 degrees of freedom, corresponding to movements along the first two joints.

Preprocessing is carried out in both the visual and tactile systems. Regarding tactile data, the activation of the input cutaneotopic map codes the position of the tactile event on the tool, evaluated as the distance z_f from the bottom of the tool. Preprocessing in the visual system allows the evaluation of the position of the contact between the tactile probe and external tool. This is achieved by thresholding the image and using suitably colored tools, both the end–effector and the tip of the tool used for providing stimulation were painted.

Figure 5 shows the execution of visuo-motor and somatosensory saccades. System performance at different levels of learning are shown in Tables 1 and 2. The values show that accuracy improves gradually with experience, and training times are not long. In both cases, good performance was achieved in less than two hours (600 stimuli).

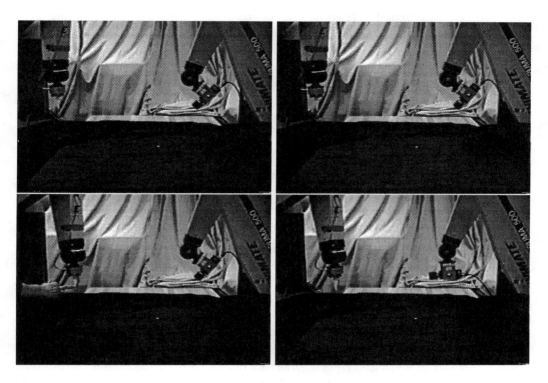

Figure 5: *Execution of a visuo-motor (top panels) and a somatosensory saccade (bottom panels). System attention is first drawn by a visual stimulus, then by a tactile stimulus.*

Foveation Error		
iteration	*mean*	σ^2
100	0.20	1.66
300	0.10	0.59
600	0.07	0.14

Table 2: *Accuracy of somatosensory saccades at different levels of learning.*

3. ACTIVE LEARNING FOR GRASP APPROACH SELECTION

The previous section describes a method for autonomously learning coordinate mappings so that visual attention can be controlled via different incoming perceptual modes. Once the attentional processes focus on the detected target object, higher resolution shape description information becomes available for manipulation purposes such as grasping. For the purpose of investigating the grasp selection approach described here, we achieve this richer level of shape description using a laser-range image of the detected object. Employing this representation, we describe an active learning solution for the grasp approach selection problem, which is to select the approach axis that maximizes the probability of successfully picking up the perceived target object.

Previous work in robotic grasping may be divided into two major approaches: analytical approaches based on detailed theoretical analysis of the mechanics of contacts and heuristic approaches inspired by research of neuropsychologists [29, 28] and orthopaedic medicine [62, 45].

Analytical approaches to grasping [47, 61, 19] have analyzed grasp selection based on mechanics, most often in terms of maximizing some objective function such as grasp stability, slip-resistance, or minimizing some objective function, such as internal forces (see [18] for a survey). If 2-D object contours can reliably be extracted from vision processing in a particular domain, then techniques employing analytical grasp point selection for optimal grasp on smooth closed 2-D contours can be used [68]. Alternative approaches such as Bard [7, 6] compute ellipsoidal decompositions of voxel description that rely on fusing multiple stereo vision views in a space occupancy grid of voxels. These approaches have given a great deal of theoretical insight into grasp planning, although they incorporate simplifying assumptions in order to be tractable and assume essentially perfect perception of relevant object properties such as shape and mass. Unfortunately, these *a-priori* assumptions may not be valid in all situations and may become less accurate as a system changes over time due to mechanical wear or other factors.

An alternative approach to selecting grasp approach and preshapes is to use a heuristic approach which employs domain-dependent rules based on objects and selections that are empirically observed. Heuristically-based grasp generators almost always include some equivalent of major grasp preshape types as categorized by Schlesinger [62] including the fingertip, hook, cylindrical, palmar lateral and spherical grasp types. These different categories were formed based on functional analysis of human grasping behavior where different characteristics classes of hand shapes were observed to be associated with the prehension of different object shapes and tasks combinations. A number of rule-based systems for grasp selection [26, 41, 18] were subsequently developed based on how skilled individuals chose grasps. Stansfield [65] describes a heuristic rule-based system for grasp selection that uses a symbolic multi-component representation of object views derived from a range scanning system. These systems incorporate production rules that capture how humans choose particular preshapes and grasp sites. These approaches share a significant limitation with the analytic systems discussed so far in that they treat grasp selection as a completely separate process from perception, assuming perfect perception of object shape and other object properties.

Unfortunately, retreating from a truly general purpose system by hand selecting reliable domain-dependent perceptual attributes (e.g. smooth object contours), feature extractors and special purpose grasping routines requires custom programming and engineering which can add significant cost to robot systems. This additional cost makes it difficult to justify the use of robots as a truly flexible task solution. One approach to avoiding the pitfalls of domain-dependent systems is to employ perceptual and/or motor learning techniques. Many researchers [37, 33, 20, 10, 32, 56, 57, 60] have taken the approach that it is preferable for robotic systems to learn a grasping strategy. The learning approach has the benefit that the system adapts to the characteristics of objects in its domain as well as to its perceptual and motor system, providing a system with higher autonomy. Robot learning systems can incorporate the true idiosyncrasies of their sensing and motor apparatus rather than rely on possibly inaccurate or outdated expectations of the system's designers. By taking a learning approach to vision-based robotic grasping (and robotic tasks in general), the noisiness and variability of both the perceptual, action systems and the environment can be incorporated into the robotic system to better ensure success, since many learning algorithms can handle noisy or missing inputs. Secondly, gradual drift or even catastrophic failure in sensor and motor systems and in the properties of the environment may be compensated for using learning without additional programming effort, leading to systems that are more robust and autonomous. If a sufficiently rich perceptual and motor representation is chosen, then the learning system can use these representations as needed over the many different environments where the robot might be placed.

3.1. THE ROLE OF EXPLORATION IN LEARNING

The advantages of a learning approach to vision-based grasping, such as increased autonomy, and self adaptation to limits in sensing, action and the particulars of a given domain, are, of course, not without tradeoffs. In robot learning, as in many other learning tasks, the costs of acquiring the learning set may be the single greatest barrier towards the application of learning in a task. The acquisition costs for each exemplar can be particularly expensive, since each sensing and/or motor action often takes a significant amount of time to execute, and has other concomitant risks as well. In fact, the computational complexity of invoking the learning algorithm may be small in comparison to the cost in time and material of gathering the learning set [67]. Therefore it is imperative to decrease learning set cost, and active learning provides an unsupervised way of doing so. Active learning systems allow the learner to control where in the input space their exemplars are drawn. They thus permit the learners to use strategies which balance the costs of gathering exemplars for learning (exploration) against the cost of misclassification during the execution of the task (exploitation).

Another way of looking at active learning is to view it as an optimization problem in which one is simultaneously building a model of a process and optimizing its performance. These problem has been studied by several different sets of researchers. In applied statistics, e.g. for the chemical process industries, evolutionary optimization (EVOP) has long been influential [12]. In EVOP, one fits a local linear or quadratic model to the available data, moves the process toward an optimum, fits the model again, moves again, etc.

A second line of research comes from statistical decision theory and multi-armed bandits, and uses methods such as the Sequential Probability Ratio Test (SPRT), which rigorously computes whether one should collect further data points (see [11], and Gittins indices [21]), which allow one to compare multiple arms (courses of actions) against a single reference arm, and thus avoid pairwise comparisons. As with all Bayesian methods, one must assume models of the distributions of the observations, including their correlation structures (if any) and one needs priors on the parameters in the models. The computations become exceedingly difficult for complex models of the probability distributions or costs.

A third line of research comes from the machine learning community, in particular workers in reinforcement learning and robot learning. Because of the unique demands of robot learning a number of active exploration approaches have been developed [69, 43, 63, 66, 3, 16] to accelerate learning in those domains. Reinforcement learning researchers have also developed a variety of active exploration heuristics [66, 31, 69] that tradeoff exploration and exploitation during adaptation. Active learning is well-suited to our grasping task since each grasping trial is lengthy (for example, approximately two minutes in the experiments to be described) and unnecessary experiments should be avoided.

Robots can invariably control some of their inputs (e.g. active perceptual systems) and outputs (actions) to facilitate learning and so are well-suited for active learning approaches. The general paradigm adopted in this work is to learn the mapping $\hat{f} : P \times A \to R$ where P is a perceptual vector which represents what the robot has perceived, A represents an action under consideration and R is a measure of reward or desirability of the outcome. In order for the system to perform well, we can attempt to pick A to maximize R. The system chooses the action which is expected to yield the maximum reward.

Given the common formulation of learning from examples, we have $f : X \to Y$ where $X = (P, A)$ and $Y = R$. The formal definition of active learning assumes that all of the components of X can be controlled by the learner, which is not feasible in most real robotic situations. In a robotic context such as grasping, only the action component of the input vector X can be selected by the learner. The perceptual vector P is uncontrollable to the robot, e.g. the geometrical characteristics of the object encountered by the grasping system. Consider the case of grasping: one cannot reasonably assume that the robot system would request that objects with desired dimensions and other properties be shown to it; we can, however, expect for the robot to actively select its actions once it has encountered the object.

3.2. THE IE/ID-3 ACTIVE LEARNING ALGORITHM FOR CONTINUOUS DOMAINS

The Interval Estimation (IE) algorithm [31] we utilize was originally intended for control of experimentation during learning where multiple *discrete* actions may succeed or fail depending on the state, and stemmed from some foundational work in learning automata and decision theory [46]. By keeping statistics on the number of times a given action has been executed and the number of times it has succeeded, the IE algorithm computes a confidence interval for the underlying probability of success for each of the actions. The action with the highest upper bound confidence interval is chosen. An action may have a higher upper bound for two reasons: either because the action is actually a good one to take or because very few trials of the action have been executed and more information needs to be gathered. A desirable feature of IE is that it rapidly stops executing actions which have a very low likelihood of success and focuses on sampling actions whose conditional probability of success cannot be ruled out as the best among alternatives.

Unfortunately, the requirement of IE that it have a finite number of discrete actions makes it unsuitable for continuous action spaces. We have addressed this limitation by combining IE with the ID-3 algorithm [49] so that ID-3 adaptively partitions the continuous action space, thus allowing IE's use in continuous valued perceptual and action spaces. ID-3 [49] automatically constructs decision trees by determining what questions (real-valued feature threshold values) give maximum information gain at each level of the tree. ID-3 and related methods such as CART [13] and C4.5 [50] are widely used and have been shown to be good at handling high-dimensional feature spaces, ignoring irrelevant features, and, when the trees are pruned to eliminate spurious branches, they are relatively insensitive to noise in the data. The resulting ID-3 decision tree induces a hard partition on the real-valued attribute space with its leaves. These leaves aggregate and generalize exemplars with similar outcomes.

IE and ID-3 are combined into the IE/ID-3 learning algorithm as follows. Let T be the current tree partitioning, based on binary outcome R, of the joint perception-action space $(P, A) = ((p_1, \ldots, p_l), (a_1, \ldots, a_m))$, where p_i and a_i are the individual perception and action attributes (see Figure 6). For example, P is the geometrical data from the major axes of a laser scan of an object, A is a description of the grasping approach angles, and R is the binary success or failure of a grasp. In other words T is a tree created by inducting on a learning set of $((P_i, A_i, R_i)$ for $i = 1, \ldots, N)$ where N is the current number of observations in the learning set.

To connect percepts to actions, we use an indirect indexing scheme [58, 56]. The system senses the current perception vector P and finds a feasible set of candidate actions F. Therefore, let F be the set of feasible leaves of the ID-3 tree

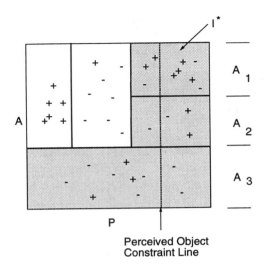

Figure 6: *A schematic of the exploration and action selection algorithm. The bold lines represent the ID-3 partitioning of the joint perception-action space (P, A). For the purposes of illustration assume a single degree-of freedom action A and a single sensed value P. When a new percept is sensed, this determines the discrete intervals for action values (the dotted line) and their associated statistics of task reward (+) and failure (-). The feasible set of leaves F is shaded. All feasible leaves are compared, and an action in the interval corresponding to the leaf with the highest upper bound l^* confidence value for probability of success is executed.*

that have perceptual interval values that contain the currently sensed attribute values of P. The set F represents a partitioning or binning of the attribute space by the current decision tree constrained by the perceived attributes P (see Figure 6). As we vary A over all possible values with P fixed, we move over all possible leaves which predict outcomes for different action parameters A based on the proportions of success and failure exemplars in each leaf. In Figure 6, A_1 has a higher probability of success than the leaves indexed by A_2 and A_3, and would be chosen. Since the leaves induce a partition on the space, we now have a finite and discrete number of action outcome bins given the observed P. Given this partitioning, the IE algorithm can now be applied. The statistics necessary for computing the confidence intervals (the number of successes and failures contained in a leaf partition) are already available because they are needed to form the tree using the ID-3 algorithm [50].

For each leaf l_i in F we compute the upper bound probability of success according to the binomial confidence interval formula [40]. To calculate a probability interval that contains the true probability value with confidence $(1 - \alpha)$ given x successes (rewarding outcomes) out of n exemplars in the leaf:

$$P_- \leq P_{success} \leq P_+ \tag{12}$$

where, P_- and P_+ are the lower and upper bounds of the probability interval estimate, respectively, one uses:

$$P_\pm = \frac{\frac{z_{\frac{\alpha}{2}}^2}{2n} + \frac{x}{n} \pm \frac{z_{\frac{\alpha}{2}}}{\sqrt{n}}\sqrt{\frac{z_{\frac{\alpha}{2}}^2}{4n} + \frac{x}{n^2}(1 - \frac{x}{n})}}{1 + \frac{z_{\frac{\alpha}{2}}^2}{n}} \qquad (13)$$

where $z_{\frac{\alpha}{2}}$ is the confidence interval coefficient.

The selected action leaf l^* is the leaf with highest upper bound P_+ of success probability. The next action is chosen as random within l^* using a uniform distribution bounded by the lower and upper action attribute intervals for l^*.

4. EXPERIMENTAL SYSTEM

The task of the system is to learn to pick up unknown objects based on perceptual measurements of the height, width and length of the object. The system must learn to select the azimuth θ and elevation ϕ values of the grasp approach axis for the gripper that is most likely to succeed given the recovered object description in h, w and l.

The robotic system used in the experiments consists of two PUMA 560 robots: the perceptual robot and the grasper. The key aspects of the system are summarized in Figure 7. The range image provided by the scanner is processed using a superquadric data reduction procedure [64] which fits a superquadric to the dense range data (see Figure 8). The superquadric fitting is a necessary data reduction step, as the range image contains thousands of depth points. It is selected as the representation since it yields a compact set of parameters that approximate the overall geometry of the object.

The fitting process yields the superquadric transformation and shape parameters in the image coordinates (see Figure 9). These values are then transformed into the scanner robot task frame by using the scanner-to-world transformation matrix. The resulting superquadric is put into canonical form, with $a_x \leq a_y \leq a_z$ and with the a_x, a_y and a_z values bound to h, w and l depending on the pose of the object to gravity. An object-centered action frame is chosen so that the θ and ϕ are relative to the direction of the w and h major axes, respectively.

The output reward R is binary: either the grasp succeeds or fails. The success or failure of a grasp is assessed by using the force-torque sensors on the gripper which measure the normal tactile forces when the object is held.

4.1. EXPERIMENTAL RESULTS

A total of six objects were chosen for grasping: a balsa block, whiteboard eraser, small flashlight, wire spool, screwdriver and a stapler (see Figure 10). Figure 11 shows the average success (or hit) rate over the thirty trials for the balsa block. The hit rate is the windowed proportion of successful grasps to attempts using a sliding window 10 attempts wide over the 30 instances in a learning run. It can

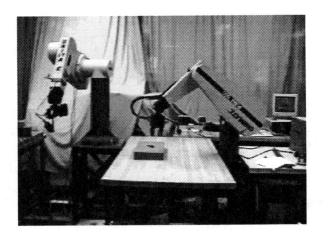

Figure 7: *The experimental system (a) consisting of the perceptual robot (left) and the grasping robot (right). The perceptual robot first scans the unknown object to yield a range image. A set of parameters is found which best fits the range data and this is used as a perception input to the learning system. The grasper then attempts to pick up the object based on the percept plus its acquired knowledge about the effectiveness of different grasp approach directions.*

(a)   (b)

Figure 8: *The vision system consists of a mobile laser range scanner mounted on the end of the perceptual robot which is swept over the object to be grasped (a). Compliant foam is placed under the object to prevent damage to the gripper or object in situations where the fingers would be stubbed and possibly damage the object or gripper (b).*

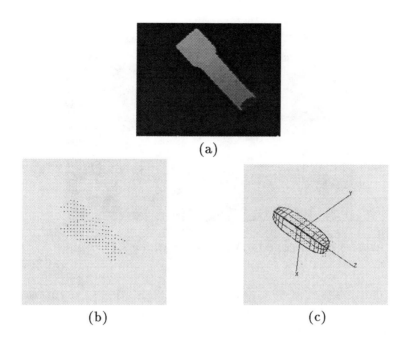

(a)

(b)   (c)

Figure 9: *Acquired three dimensional range points (a) for the stapler, the sub-sampled and eroded points (b) and the resulting superquadric fit to the range points (c).*

be seen that the robot rapidly converges on a strategy for selecting approaches that succeeds reliably (.9).

The scatter plot of Figure 11 also illustrates the effect of the exploration strategy. This figure shows the selected azimuth θ and elevation ϕ values for the balsa block trials in the range $0° < \theta < 90°$ and $0° < \phi < 60°$. Each point in the θ, ϕ space is marked by its outcome, 0 for failure or 1 for success. The action parameters are not uniformly distributed in the space, but concentrated in the region which has a small θ value (the constraint for gripper alignment) since the exploration algorithm focuses on the region of success.

In the case of the flashlight, the learning curve increases more slowly (see Figure 12) since the width of the screwdriver is quite close to the maximum width of the gripper and it takes more attempts to find a first successful grasp which can form the basis of a tree partition. Similar learning performance and action distributions were observed for the stapler (.83 cumulative hit rate with learning, .4 without), eraser (.83 with learning, .4 without), screwdriver (.8 with learning .4 without) and spool (.8 with learning, .27 without).

4.2. SIMULATION STUDIES

A simulation study was undertaken to explore scaling properties when larger numbers of objects are presented. In the simulation the gripper is modelled by taking

Figure 10: *The set of common objects for which learning was attempted.*

the coordinate transformations on the gripper consisting of a rotation (θ, z) followed by rotation (ϕ, x) and determining if the projection of the object in the two dimensional plane orthogonal to the approach direction is smaller than the maximum span of the fingers. If the gripper clears the object, it is graspable.

The objects for the simulation have dimensions that are selected from a uniform distribution of 35-90mm and the maximum gripper width is taken as 70mm. Additionally, to make the task more difficult, objects are generated so that only one of the object's aspects, w or l, clear the gripper. For the aspect that clears the gripper, a minimum of 5mm clearance is guaranteed. The allowable approach directions are in the range $0° < \theta < 90°$ and $0° < \phi < 90°$. The hit rate, in this case, is computed by dividing the total number of successful grasps at each trial by the total number of runs.

The learner attempts to grasp the object 10 times or until it succeeds 5 times in a row, whichever comes first, at which point a new simulated object is generated.

For comparison to the IE/ID-3, Open Loop (OL) alternating learning is performed in which each cycle first executes a random action to acquire the next point in the exploration set. ID-3 is then run on that exemplar plus any previously acquired exemplars and a test action is executed to form a trial for the performance curve. The test action is chosen by searching for the leaf with the highest raw probability of success given the current perceptual vector constraint P. Notice that the IE/ID-3 curve does not represent the classification rate on an independent test set, but the actual on-line performance of the system as it interacts with the simulation. As Figure 13 shows, the IE/ID-3 based learner (the black curve) performed almost twice as well the OL alternating strategy, which is the average alternating pure exploitation and exploration. OL is penalized since 50% of the grasp attempts are explorational and randomly chosen. Figure 14 illustrates the two components of the OL alternating curve: the performance curve (black) and exploration curve (light grey). IE/ID-3 learning performs much bet-

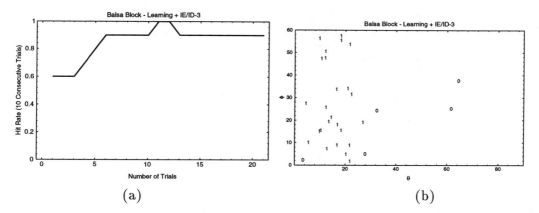

Figure 11: *The hit rate for the balsa block over the first 30 trials (b) and the corresponding scatter plot of chosen actions in the action space (b). The cumulative probability for successful grasping is .83 for the learning condition and .43 for the random approach.*

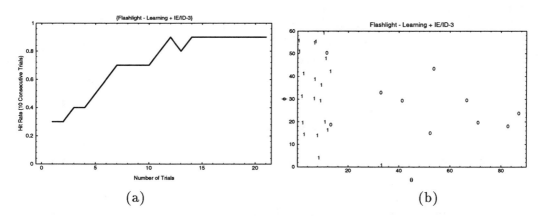

Figure 12: *The hit rate for the flashlight over the first 30 trials (a) and the distribution of actions in the action space (b). The cumulative probability for successful grasping is .67 for the learning condition and .23 for the random approach.*

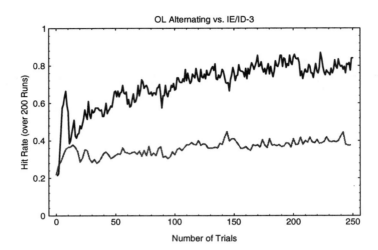

Figure 13: *Comparison of system performance over first 250 trials (averaged over 200 runs). The IE/ID-3 learner (black) exhibits much better performance than the open loop learner (grey) which suffers because it always alternates between the random training action mode and test.*

ter since it begins to exploit knowledge and abandons exploration as soon as it is judged possible based on statistical evidence.

We also investigated the effect of the focused experimentation on classification accuracy by running the OL strategy and measuring the probability of success only on the performance cases of each cycle and formed an equivalent test set for IE. Figure 15 shows that the IE/ID-3 test set success rate is slightly more accurate due to the selective data gathering. To summarize, OL can perform almost as well as IE/ID-3 from a classification standpoint, but from a *performance* standpoint IE/ID-3 has a much lower error rate during the earlier parts of the run.

5. DISCUSSION

Dexterous manipulation is one of the major issues of current robotics research. A number of highly sophisticated multi-fingered hands have been developed in recent years, but problems related to their control and to the proper combination of sensory inputs still have yet to be solved.

The systems we have presented in this chapter are part of a more general approach to manipulation that aims to avoid traditional limitations. It is based on (i) the capability of learning in real-time both the structural and functional organization of the system, and the sequences of motor interaction with the environment for the execution of a specific task, and (ii) on the cooperation of multi-sensory inputs mediated by selective attention mechanisms.

Particular care has been dedicated to the selection of suitable learning methods. In general, supervised learning techniques are not feasible for truly au-

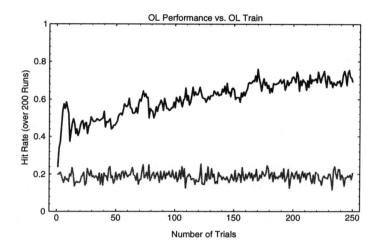

Figure 14: *The exploration (black) and exploitation (grey) performance of the open loop learner. Since these two strategies alternate, the combined performance is penalized for random exploitation.*

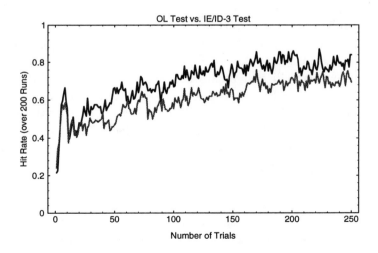

Figure 15: *Comparison of the hit rate for the IE/ID-3 (black) test vs OL test. (grey)*

tonomous systems, since they require the intervention of an external operator. In order to be effective, learning should occur throughout all the operative "life" of the system and as efficiently as possible for a given task. A learning algorithm should exploit the learned knowledge as soon as it is available, and both approaches exemplify this property.

There are some interesting parallels between active learning and active perception [4]. In active perception, by acting on information gathered by the sensors in previous sequential actions, task-directed sensing [24] may be achieved where sensors are controlled to be maximally informative with respect to the information extracted from the environment so far and the desired goal (e.g. recognition or reconstruction). Such a strategy prevents the execution of costly sensing actions that would yield little additional information about a perceptual task and allows the system to be efficient in terms of perceptual actions. Similarly, in active learning, the goal is to treat each action as an experiment that is efficient in yielding information about the task, based on what the results of previous actions in similar states have yielded.

Globally-directed active learning approaches attempt to improve generalization over the entire domain of a learner using an efficient sequence of actions. *Task-directed* approaches attempt to characterize only the sub-domain necessary for completing a given task or operating regime of a system. We chose to modify the IE algorithm (a task-directed technique) since we are most interested in minimizing the amount of trials to acceptable performance, rather than a global best solution. Almost all previous work in exploration control during learning has taken the globally-directed approach [70, 3, 16] ([70] also contains a good review.)

The ID-3 approach, which is memory-based, stores all of the exemplars it encounters and applies the tree induction algorithm repeatedly to the accumulated learning set. However if the environment changes due to sensor drift or mechanical wear of actuators, then older exemplars that are no longer representative of system performance will still be stored. Weight-based learning systems, such as artificial neural networks, correct for this phenomenon by re-adapting their weights, avoiding the problem of obsolete exemplars. Fortunately, it is possible to also make memory-based systems time adaptive. This can be done by the addition of forgetting algorithms [57] which retain the advantages of both weight-based and memory-based systems by removing exemplars from the learning set that are judged as obsolete

The exploration heuristic described can be applied to other learning formalisms. The key to the active learning approach is the combination of learning mappings from perception and action to reward with selecting actions which improve the expected reward over all future trials. In the IE/ID-3 algorithm we use ID-3 to build decision tree mappings and the IE algorithm to select actions. Other learning methods such as radial basis functions, nearest-neighbor approaches and hierarchically gated mixtures of Gaussians could equally well be used to build the mappings since they also can provide confidence intervals for the quantities they predict. Secondly, other optimal action selection methodologies taken from statistical decision theory, such as solutions to multi-armed bandit problems, can be utilized within this framework [21, 59]

Selective attention as proposed by several recent machine perception paradigms [4, 5] can be crucial for developing perceptual capabilities and achieving real–time performance. Furthermore, attention-based control methods can be effective in multi-sensory systems since they can determine what stimuli will be dynamically allocated computational resources. The capability to selectively attend and disregard a large amount of irrelevant data while still being able to react whenever a critical sensory event is detected is inherent in selective attention. As a result, researchers in the AI and robotics communities have begun to address the topic (for a review see [1]) on the basis of research in psychophysics and neurophysiology (see [30, 35] for reviews of attention processes in humans). Selective processing in computer vision has been mainly investigated in the context of pyramidal image representations [14] and space-variant sensing. More recently, with the development of fast moving head–eye systems, visual attention has been analyzed in the context of eye movements and selective fixations [15, 52]. However, the majority of work in the area has focused on the case of vision, due to the fact that machine vision applications are currently facing the bottleneck brought on by the need to process huge amounts of data.

Manipulation is a typical domain where attentive processes can be extremely useful. In general, visual, tactile and proprioceptive information should be analyzed in the context of operations that the system is executing for the production of motor actions. Depending on the task at hand, specific sensory information can have different degrees of relevance and may trigger different control procedures. This work represents the first effort to implement attention processes in manipulation systems and integrate multi-sensory attentive mechanisms which incorporate other types of sensing besides vision.

Although this work does not emphasize biological plausibility, the underlying philosophy has similarities to that of the work of Kuperstein [38] in terms of forming consistent projections between topographic maps of different senses, although the learning algorithm we use is different. We have also added third sensory modality, that of touch, to our system. This allows for associations between touch, proprioception and vision sensory frames. Furthermore, the architecture is expressly designed to deal with the simultaneous presence of multiple competing stimuli in different modalities, which is not accounted for in Kuperstein's architecture.

The systems that we have presented in this paper are clear examples of how interaction with the surrounding environment can benefit from real-time learning processes. The adaptability resulting from these processes substantially increases the robustness of the systems and broadens their range of operability. At present, both systems require partial constraints in the working environment. For example, the problem of visual segmentation in the execution of somatosensory saccades has been avoided by suitably structuring the scene. Analogously, during grasping, we have assumed that only a single object was present in the scene. However, even if partial structuring of the work space is necessary at this point in development, we believe that further work and extension to these learning approaches will be fruitful, and lead to superior real-world performance and more system autonomy.

Several directions for future research are possible. A logical next step is to apply the attentional learning approach to more sophisticated robotic systems and analyze more complex tasks with a large number of processes. For example, it would be interesting to apply the architecture to the implementation of touch-driven attention mechanisms in the context of manipulation with multi-fingered robotic hands. A number of theoretical issues can be further investigated, such as the autonomous selection of suitable task weights for performing specific tasks and the inclusion of other motor control procedures. The grasp selection system can be extended to include symbolic values, such as the grasp preshape (e.g. pinch, hook, cylindrical, spherical), along with real-valued parameters for grasp categories such as finger stiffness and extent of preshape.

6. CONCLUSION

The systems presented in this chapter provide examples of how learning can be applied to some aspects of vision-based manipulation. Using a saliency map representation and learning algorithm, we are able to combine inputs from vision and touch (as well as other possible input modalities) so that attention between different events is controlled. An active learning classification-tree approach is used to learn grasp selection. Both the foveation and grasping implementations are able to demonstrate significant performance increases over the period of one to two hours, making them competitive alternatives to explicit calibration of the visual and motor frames and hand coding of grasp selection strategies. Additionally, the resulting approaches are adaptive to changes in the actuators and sensors and to the presentation of new and unforseen objects, and thus well-suited for use in autonomous systems.

ACKNOWLEDGEMENTS

This work was supported by Arpa Grant N00014-92-J-1647, AFOSR Grants 88-0244, AFOSR 88-0296, Army Grant/DAAL 03-89-C-0031PRI, NSF Grants CISE/CDA 88-22719, IRI 89-06770, ASC 91 0813 and an NSF CISE Postdoctoral Associateship for Marcos Salganicoff (CDA-9211136). M. Rucci has been supported by a fellowship from the Italian National Research Council. Thanks to Lyle Ungar for many helpful discussions, Len Kunin for assisting in the implementation and experiments, and to Craig Reynolds for editorial assistance.

REFERENCES

[1] A.L. Abbott. A survey for selective fixation control for machine vision. *IEEE Journal of Control Systems*, August:25–31, 1992.

[2] P.K. Allen. Integrating vision and touch for object recognition tasks. *International Journal of Robotics Research*, pages 15–33, 1988.

[3] L. Atlas, D. Cohn, R. Ladner, M.A. El-Sharkawi, R.J. Marks II, M.E. Aggoune, and D.C Park. Training connectionist networks with queries and selective sampling. In *Advances in Neural Information Processing Systems 2*, pages 567–573. Morgan Kaufmann, December 1990.

[4] R. Bajcsy. Active perception. *Proceedings of the IEEE*, 76(8):996–1005, 1988.

[5] D.H. Ballard. Animate vision. *Artificial Intelligence*, 48:57–86, 1991.

[6] C. Bard, C. Laugier, C. Milesi, and J. Troccaz. Achieving dextrous grasping by integrating planning and vision based sensing. *The International Journal of Robotics Research*, 1995. in press.

[7] C. Bard, J. Troccaz, and G. Vercelli. Shape analysis and hand preshaping for grasping. In *IEEE/RSJ/GI International Conference on Intelligent Robots and Systems*, pages 64–69, 1991.

[8] G.A. Bekey, H. Liu, R. Tomovic, and W.J. Karplus. Knowledge-based control of grasping in robot hands using heuristics from human motor skills. *IEEE Journal of Robotics and Automation*, RA-9(6):157–165, 1993.

[9] G.A. Bekey, R. Tomovic, and I. Zeljkovic. Control architecture for the Belgrade/USC hand. In T. Venkataraman and T. Iberall, editors, *Dexterous Robot Hands*. Springer-Verlag, New York, 1990.

[10] S. Bennett. Planning to address uncertainty: An incremental approach employing learning through experience. In *Proceedings of the DARPA Workshop on Advanced Planning and Control Strategies*, pages 313–324, 1991.

[11] J.O. Berger. *Statistical decision theory and Bayesian analysis*. Springer-Verlag, NY, 1985.

[12] G.E.P. Box and N.R. Draper. *Evolutionary Operation: a Statistical Method for Process Improvement*. Wiley, 1969.

[13] L. Breiman, J. H. Friedman, R. A. Olshen, and C. J. Stone. *Classification and regression trees*. Wadsworth International, Belmont, CA, 1984.

[14] P.J. Burt. Smart sensing within a pyramid vision machine. *Proceedings of the IEEE*, 76(8):1006–1015, 1988.

[15] J.J. Clark and N.J. Ferrier. Attentive visual servoing. In A. Blake and A.Yuille, editors, *Active Vision*. MIT Press, Cambridge, MA, 1992.

[16] D.A. Cohn. Queries and exploration using optimal experiment design. In *Neural Information Processing Systems 6*, Denver, CO, 1994. Morgan-Kauffman.

[17] C. Colombo, M. Rucci, and P. Dario. Attentive behavior in an anthropomorphic robot vision system. *Journal of Robotics and Autonomous Systems*, 1994.

[18] M. R. Cutkosky. On grasp choice, grasp models and the design of hands for manufacturing tasks. *IEEE Journal of Robotics and Automation*, 5(3):269–279, 1989.

[19] M.R. Cutkosky. *Robot grasping and fine manipulation*. Kluwer Academic Publishers, Norwell, MA, 1995.

[20] G. B. Dunn and J. Segen. Automatic discovery of robotic grasp configuration. In *Proceedings, 1988 IEEE International Conference on Robotics and Automation*, pages 396–401, 1988.

[21] J.C. Gittins. *Multi-armed Bandit Allocation Indices*. John Wiley and Sons, Chichester, 1988.

[22] J. Groh. *Coordinate Transformations, Sensorimotor Integration and the Neural Basis of Saccades to Somatosensory Targets*. PhD thesis, University of Pennsylvania, Philadelphia, PA, USA, 1993.

[23] S. Grossberg. Nonlinear neural networks: Principles, mechanisms, and architectures. *Neural Networks*, 1:17–61, 1988.

[24] G. Hager. *Task-directed sensor fusion and planning: a computational approach*. Kluwer Academic Publishers, Norwell, MA, 1990.

[25] R.D. Howe and M.R. Cutkosky. Touch sensing for robotic manipulation and recognition. In O. Khatib, J.J. Craig, and J. Lozano-Perez, editors, *The Robotics Review 2*. MIT Press, Cambridge, MA, 1992.

[26] T. Iberall, J. Jackson, L. Labbe, and R. Zampano. Knowledge-based prehension: Capturing human dexterity. In *Proceedings, 1988 IEEE International Conference on Robotics and Automation*, pages 82–87, 1988.

[27] L.C. Jacobsen, E.K. Iversen, D.F. Knutti, R.T. Johnson, and K.B. Biggers. Design of the Utah/MIT dexterous hand. In *Proceedings, 1986 IEEE International Conference on Robotics and Automation*, pages 1520–1530, 1986.

[28] M. Jeannerod. *The neural and behavioural organization of goal-directed movements*. Clarendon Press, Oxford Science Publications, Oxford, 1988.

[29] M. Jeannerod and B. Biguer. *Advances in the analysis of visual behavior*, chapter Visuomotor mechanisms in reaching within extrapersonal space. MIT Press, Boston, 1981.

[30] W.A. Johnston and V.J. Dark. Selective attention. *Annual Review of Psychology*, 37:43–75, 1986.

[31] L.P. Kaelbling. *Learning in Embedded Systems*. PhD thesis, Stanford University, Stanford, CA, 1990. Dept. of Computer Science.

[32] I. Kamon, T. Flash, and S. Edelman. Learning to grasp using visual information. Technical Report, The Weizmann Institute of Science, Rehovot, Israel, 1994.

[33] S. Kang and K. Ikeuchi. Toward automatic robot instruction from perception-recognizing a grasp from observation. *IEEE Journal of Robotics and Automation*, 9(4):432–443, August 1993.

[34] J. Kerr and B. Roth. Analysis of multifingered hands. *International Journal of Robotics Research*, 4(4), 1986.

[35] R.A. Kinchla. Attention. *Annual Review of Psychology*, 43:711–742, 1992.

[36] C. Koch and S. Ullman. Shifts in selective visual attention: Toward the underlying neural circuitry. In L.M. Vaina, editor, *Matters of Intelligence*. D. Reidel Pub. Comp., 1987.

[37] T. Kuniyoshi, M. Inaba, and H. Inoue. Teaching by showing: Generating robot programs by visual observation of human performance. In *Proceedings of 20th Internation Syposium on industrial robotics*, pages 119–126, 1989.

[38] M. Kuperstein. An adaptive neural model for mapping invariant target position. *Behavioral Neuroscience*, 102(1):148–162, 1988.

[39] M. Kuperstein. Neural network model for adaptive hand–eye coordination for single postures. *Science*, 239:1308–13011, 1988.

[40] R. Larson and M. Marx. *An introduction to mathematical statistics*. Prentice Hall, Englewood Cliffs, NJ, 1986.

[41] H. Liu, T. Iberall, and G. A. Bekey. The multi-dimensional quality of tasks requirements of task requirements for dextrous hand control. In *IEEE International Conference on Robotics and Automation*, pages 452–457, 1989.

[42] B.W. Mel. *Connectionist Robot Motion Planning*. Academic Press Inc., San Diego, CA, 1990.

[43] A. W. Moore. Acquisition of dynamic control knowledge for a robotic manipulator. In *Proceedings of the seventh international conference on machine learning*, 1990.

[44] K. Nakayama. The iconic bottleneck and the tenuous link between early visual processing and perception. In C. Blakemore, editor, *Vision: Coding and Efficiency*. University Press, 1991.

[45] J. R. Napier. The prehensile movements of the human hand. *Journal of Bone and Joint Surgery*, 38b(4):902–904, 1956.

[46] K. S. Narendra and M. A. L. Thathacar. Learning automata: A survey. *IEEE Transactions on Systems, Man and Cybernetics*, SMC-4(4):323–334, 1974.

[47] V.D. Nguyen. Constructing force-closure grasps. *International Journal of Robotics Research*, 7(3), 1988.

[48] D. Noton and L. Stark. Eye movements and visual perception. *Scientific American*, 224(6):34–43, 1971.

[49] J. R. Quinlan. *Learning efficient classification procedures and their application to chess end-games*, pages 463–481. Morgan-Kauffman, Los Altos, CA, 1986.

[50] R. Quinlan. *C4.5: Programs for Machine Learning*. Morgan-Kaufmann, Los Altos, CA, 1992.

[51] G.N Reeke, O. Sporns, and G.M. Edelman. Synthetic neural modeling: The "Darwin" series of recognition automata. *Proceedings of the IEEE*, 78(9):1498–1530, 1990.

[52] R.D. Rimey and C.M. Brown. Control of selective perception using Bayes nets and decision theory. *Int. J. Computer Vision*, 12(2):173–207, 1994.

[53] M. Rucci and R. Bajcsy. Implementing selective attention in machines: The case of touch-driven saccades. Technical Report, University of Pennsylvania, Dept. of Computer and Information Science, Philadelphia, PA , 1994.

[54] M. Rucci and P. Dario. Selective attention mechanisms in a vision system based on neural networks. In *Proceedings of IEEE/RSJ International Conference on Intelligent Robots and Systems*, Yokohama, Japan, 1993.

[55] M. Rucci and P. Dario. Development of cutaneo–motor coordination in an autonomous robotic system. *Autonomous Robots*, 1(1):93–106, 1994.

[56] M. Salganicoff. *Learning and Forgetting for Perception-Action: A Projection-Pursuit and Density-Adaptive Approach*. PhD thesis, University of Pennsylvania, Philadelphia, PA, 1992. Dept. of Computer and Information Science.

[57] M. Salganicoff. Density-adaptive learning and forgetting. In *Proceedings of the Tenth International Conference on Machine Learning*. Morgan-Kauffman, June 1993.

[58] M. Salganicoff and R. Bajcsy. Robot sensorimotor learning in continuous domains. In *Proceedings, 1992 IEEE International Conference on Robotics and Automation*, Nice, France, May 1992.

[59] M. Salganicoff and L.H. Ungar. Active exploration and learning in real-valued spaces using multi-armed bandit allocation indices. In *Twelfth International Machine Learning Conference*, 1995.

[60] M. Salganicoff, L.H. Ungar, and R. Bajcsy. Active learning for vision-based robot grasping. *Machine Learning Journal*, 1995. To appear.

[61] J.K. Salisbury. *Robot hands and the mechanics of manipulation*, chapter Kinematic and force analysis of articulated hands. MIT Press, Cambridge, MA, 1985.

[62] G. Schlesinger. *Der Mechanische Aufbau der Kunstlichen Glieder*. Springer, Berlin, 1916.

[63] J. Schneider. Open loop motor skill learning. In *AAAI Fall Symposium Series: Machine Learning in Vision: What Why and How?*, Raleigh, N.C., 1993.

[64] F. Solina and R. Bajcsy. Recovery of parametric models from range images: The case for superquadrics with global deformations. *IEEE Transactions on Pattern Analysis and Machine Intelligence*, 12(2):131–147, February 1990.

[65] S. Stansfield. Knowledge-based robotic grasping. In *Proceedings, 1990 IEEE International Conference on Robotics and Automation*, pages 1270–1275, 1990.

[66] R. S. Sutton. Integrated architectures for learning planning and reacting based on approximating dynamic programming. In *Proceedings of the Seventh International Conference on Machine Learning*. Morgan-Kauffman, 1990.

[67] M. Tan. Cost-sensitive learning of classification knowledge and its applications in robotics. *Machine Learning*, 13(1):7–33, October 1993.

[68] M. Taylor, A. Blake, and A. Cox. Visually guided grasping in 3D. In *Proceedings, 1994 IEEE International Conference on Robotics and Automation*, pages 761–766, 1994.

[69] S. Thrun and K. Moller. Active exploration in dynamic environments. In *Neural Information Processing Systems 4*, pages 531–538. Morgan-Kauffman, 1992.

[70] S.B. Thrun. The role of exploration in learning control with neural networks. In *Handbook of Intelligent Control: Neural, Fuzzy and Adaptive Approaches.* Van Nostrand Rheinhold, Florence KY, 1992.

[71] A.L. Yarbus. *Eye movements and vision.* Plenum Press, 1967.

INDEX